Ex Umbris In Veritatem

THIS BOOK
WAS GIVEN TO
NEWMAN
COLLEGE

BY
DOREEN CODLING
Lecturer in Education
(Sept. 1st 1970 - Aug. 8th 1975)

THE SCIENTIFIC STUDY OF
PERSONALITY

THE SCIENTIFIC STUDY
OF PERSONALITY

by

H. J. EYSENCK
Ph.D., London

ROUTLEDGE & KEGAN PAUL LTD
Broadway House 68–74 Carter Lane
London

First published 1952
by Routledge & Kegan Paul Ltd
Broadway House, 68-74 Carter Lane
London, E.C.4
Printed in Great Britain by
Lowe & Brydone (Printers) Ltd., London

Second impression 1958
Third impression 1962
Fourth impression 1968

SBN 7100 1352 3

TO SYBIL

If we take in our hand any volume, let us ask, Does it contain any abstract reasoning concerning quantity or number? No. Does it contain any experimental reasoning concerning matter of fact and existence? No. Commit it then to the flames; for it can contain nothing but sophistry and illusion.—HUME.

FOREWORD

IN psychology, as in other sciences, knowledge has been advanced by new techniques and new instruments, as well as by new modes of thought, for 'the bare hand and the understanding left to itself have but little power; results are produced by instruments and helps'. Whether the methods so cogently set out in this book will have great potency in the study of human personality is yet uncertain: the subject is elusive and the past failures, as the author points out, many. But Dr. Eysenck's enterprise has now come a long way, in a rather short time, and even those who distrust statistical procedures and statisticians' reasoning, or who find some of Dr. Eysenck's conclusions at odds with their experience, will concede his two major claims: he has used methods of observation and analysis which are well defined and easily reproduced by other investigators, who can thus test the correctness of his findings; and there is immense gain to be had from a taxonomy which permits the cardinal attributes of each type to be measured, whether the types are of mental disease, of personality, or of general constitution. The more accurate the measurement and the more distinct the type, the greater the security which such a classification affords for further scientific inquiry. There are perhaps other advantages. If the types discerned show any constant relation with the course and pathology of disease, then they will be speedily enthroned, because of their value in clinical practice. But it is not on this ground that Dr. Eysenck takes his stand; he emphasizes rather the scientific and heuristic value of his research. He takes no obvious steps in his book to reconcile any complacent psychiatrists to what might seem a root and branch attack upon their beliefs and methods. Psychiatrists, however, are not complacent unless they are stupid; and Dr. Eysenck is by no means blind to the worth of clinical knowledge: clinical categories provide the indispensable starting-point for his investigation. His argument for an oscillating use, turn and turn about, of criterion and factor, clinical assessment and distillate of test-results, com-

FOREWORD

mends itself to the psychiatrist, well aware that current methods of diagnosis and appraisal, though less shaky than Dr. Eysenck believes, have signal weaknesses; they are the weaknesses to which Jaspers drew critical attention thirty years ago and which were openly reckoned with in the last edition of Kraepelin's great textbook.

The debt of psychiatry to the psychologist is now great and growing. Fortunately the indebtedness seems mutual, and the association between the two fields of study most profitably intimate. From these rigorous inquiries, sustained and resourcefully developed over years, psychiatry stands to gain an impetus and accuracy in some essential matters which will advance it and reinforce the free play of clinical skill and insight.

AUBREY LEWIS

Professor of Psychiatry
University of London

CONTENTS

LIST OF ILLUSTRATIONS

(16pp section between pages 128 & 129)

xi

LIST OF ILLUSTRATIONS

ACKNOWLEDGMENTS

Acknowledgments are due to the following for permission to quote:

Methuen & Co. Ltd., publishers of *A Modern Introduction to Logic*, by L. S. Stebbing.

Cambridge University Press, publishers of *History of the Planetary Systems*, by J. L. E. Dreyer.

Allen & Unwin Ltd., publishers of *Human Knowledge—Its Scope and Limits*, by B. Russell.

H.M.S.O., publishers of *Pilot Error—Some Laboratory Experiments*, by D. R. Davis.

Princeton University Press, publishers of *Studies in Social Psychology in World War II*, (4 vols.), by S. A. Stouffer *et al.*

American Psychological Ass., publishers of *Studies of Autonomic Balance*, by M. S. Wenger.

Figures 10, 11, 14, 15, 20, and 38 are taken, with the permission of the author, from:

Rao, C. R., & Slater, P. (1949).

Stouffer, S. A., *et al.* (1949*a*, 1949*b*, 1950).

Wexler, M. (1947).

Coville, W. J. (1947).

Rees, L. (1950).

Dorn, J. E. (1948).

The permission is also acknowledged of the publishers of the *Journal of Mental Science*, the *Journal of Personality*, the *Journal of Consulting Psychology*, and the *Psychological Review*, to quote at some length papers of my own published there.

INTRODUCTION

THIS book is a sequel to *Dimensions of Personality*, and reports the results of experiments carried out at the Institute of Psychiatry (Maudsley and Bethlem Royal Hospitals) in the University of London. Where the other book dealt almost exclusively with adult neurotics, we have now extended our scope, and the present report deals with normal and psychotic adults, as well as with neurotics, and with children as well as with adults. The aim has remained the same, namely 'to discover the main dimensions of personality, and to define them operationally, i.e. by means of strictly experimental, quantitative procedures'. An attempt has been made to advance more rigorous proofs for the heuristic hypotheses outlined in the previous work, and to make deductions, and test these hypotheses, in settings other than a mental hospital—among factory workers, nurses, students, teachers, and other normal groups. An attempt has also been made to indicate the practical usefulness of the methods outlined by employing them in studies of the effectiveness of occupational selection, both in the normal and the abnormal field, of the effectiveness of surgical operations in the alleviation of mental illness, and of the factors determining vocational adjustment. Throughout the book methods of statistical analysis and proof have been used which follow the time-honoured hypothetico-deductive method ; this has occasionally necessitated the introduction of novel techniques, such as the method of criterion analysis. At all times, an attempt has been made to imbricate closely the psychological theory which underlies this work and the experimental procedures adopted. Finally, I have tried to eschew that meretricious sesquipedalianism which threatens to turn psychology from a scientific discipline into a stamping-ground for experts in semantics and verbal magic.

Much of the material here reported was originally delivered in the form of a series of open lectures at the University of Pennsylvania during my tenure there of a Visiting Professorship. Other parts of the book were delivered as lectures at the E.T.S. Invitational Conference in New York, at the 1950 Psychiatric Congress in Copenhagen, at a Conference on 'Current Trends in Psychology' in Pittsburgh, at the International Congress of Anthropology in Paris, at the 1949 A.P.A. meeting in Denver, at the International Psychological Congresses in Edinburgh and Stockholm, at various meetings of the B.P.S., and at a number of American Universities from Canada to the South, and from California to New England, all of whom kindly gave me facilities to put before their students certain aspects of the methods used and the results achieved. The response of these very varied audiences, ranging from lay through undergraduate to graduate and professional levels, and having orientations ranging from the clinical and psychiatric to the mathematical and statistical, has taught me a great deal about possible lines of criticism and areas of difficulty. But above all they have taught me that an essential part of a book of this kind must be a clear statement of the aim and purpose which has motivated the investigator. It soon became clear to me that many who on the whole were sympathetic to the general tenor of the work were a little puzzled as to its main import. This difficulty of 'placing' was so universal that I have ventured to include an opening chapter in which I have tried to relate the accepted principles of scientific methodology to the experimental study of personality, and to indicate why in my opinion the areas investigated are important, and why the method used was thought superior to others more familiar. This was considered all the more vital in view of the wide divergence of aims which is so characteristic of the many different types of professional workers who are interested in human personality.

Several convictions which I held before work was started on the research reported here were strongly reinforced during its progress. The first is that in the field of personality study, close co-operation between psychologists and psychiatrists is not only desirable but may be considered essential. The psychologist may rightly consider much of what the psychiatrist says subjective and intuitive rather than exact and objective; that does not necessarily mean that it is wrong. He would be foolish to throw away the accumulated experience of centuries in the vain hope of starting with a *tabula rasa*. Regarded as a source of fruitful hypotheses, rather than as a store-house of revealed truth, psychiatric knowledge may save the psychologist much fruitless burrowing and searching, and lead him quickly to those areas most germane to his objective. The psychiatrist may rightly consider much of what the psychologist does as arid and unrevealing; to condemn it all may be a short-sighted attitude. In science, coming events do not always cast their shadows before them, and the growth of a genuinely scientific discipline of personality study may be the outcome of much that appears at first sight unpromising and irrelevant. Both sides have much to learn from each other, and our knowledge of human nature will advance more securely and more quickly by a pooling of knowledge, experience, and methodology.

The second conviction, which lay already at the basis of the work reported in *Dimensions of Personality*, is that research in this area, in order to be fruitful, has to be what Marquis (1948) has called 'programme research'. In other words, research has to be planned for a whole department around a common objective, it has to be continued over a period of years, and the research activities of students and teachers alike have to be integrated into it. Only in this way can one hope to avoid the inconclusive outcome which all too often characterizes the individual short-term research.

Individual students, of course, must be free to choose whether they want to take part in the departmental research, or whether they want to strike out for themselves; it is our experience that the majority welcome the opportunity of making an active contribution to the development of a programme which shows promise of furthering our knowledge of human nature. Such training will also prepare the student for the type of team research which is becoming more and more prevalent in the social field, where specialists in many disciplines must collaborate in order to solve a problem common to them all.

The third conviction, elaborated in various places throughout this book, relates to the use of different types of personality test. While questionnaires and so-called 'projective' tests constitute almost the only types of test used by clinical psychologists and research workers, the investigations described in *Dimensions of Personality* and here have more and more confirmed my belief that progress in the scientific study of personality is intimately bound up with what may be called 'objective behaviour tests' (Eysenck, 1950a). These appear to tap more fundamental layers of personality than do other types of test. If we deduce personality from behaviour (as surely we must if we want to stay on solid ground) then the argument from one item of behaviour to another seems more cogent than the argument from what a person says about his behaviour, or the inference from what he says about a picture or an ink blot, to what he actually does. This belief, of course, is subject to empirical verification; it is given here as an heuristic hypothesis, not as a statement of fact.

My last conviction relates to the importance of taxonomic work, of finding the dimensions along which we want to measure before we proceed to carry out any measurement. At the present moment, psychology and psychiatry are still in the pre-classificatory stage—although some optimists appear to think that both disciplines have already 'outgrown' this stage. Attendance at psychiatric case conferences inevitably calls to mind *Punch's* comment on the new freight charge system introduced by British railways around the middle of the last century, particularly in its application to livestock. An old lady is shown, carrying a tortoise in a case, whilst a porter, scratching his head to fit this exotic animal into the system of classification laid down by the Company, mumbles to himself: 'Cats is dawgs and pigs is dawgs, but this 'ere hanimal is a bloomin' hinsect.' I may be unduly sceptical about the systems of classification now in use, but they seem to me practically of little value, theoretically indefensible, and internally contradictory. Yet, for reasons to be explained in some detail later in the book, I cannot agree with those who would do away with any kind of taxonomic system either. As has been said of Christianity, a proper system of diagnosis has not been tried and found wanting; it has been found difficult to construct and therefore never tried. Surely our task should be that of patiently constructing such a system by using the well-known principles of scientific method; cut away ruthlessly those existing concepts and procedures which lack reliability and validity, and treasure those which stand up to the rigours of the hypothetic-deductive method. It is as a report on the first stages of such an endeavour that these pages should be read. If the results are less than startling, they are at least based on experiment and deduction; if the methods are less than sound, they are at least subject to disproof and discussion; if the conceptual framework is less than adequate, at least it is capable of growth and change. If this book has no other effect than to spur on others to devise better methods, achieve results of greater value, and arrive at more widely relevant concepts, I shall be amply repaid for my labour in writing it.

One of the pleasures attending the completion of a communal effort such as the work reported in this book, is the opportunity of expressing one's thanks to those whose help contributed so largely towards whatever success it may be deemed to have achieved. This group includes present and former colleagues, research assistants, students, and members of the clerical and computing staffs, as well as numerous friends here and in the United States whose criticism and advice helped me greatly in formulating problems and research designs more clearly. Special mention should be made of the work done by A. Petrie on the after-effects of leucotomy and on selection problems; by H. T. Himmelweit and A. Petrie on student selection and the measurement of neuroticism in children; by N. O'Connor and J. Tizard on the employability of mental defectives; by F. Goldmann-Eisler on the ætiology of the 'oral' type; by F. Loos on the relation of 'sense of humour' to neuroticism; by G. Granger on the applicability of atomistic and gestalt laws to preference judgments; by A. Clark and A. Gravely (now Mrs. Clark) on perceptual and motor tests as measures of personality; by S. Crown on after-effects of leucotomy, and on the Word Connection List as a measure of personality; by D. Prell on the inheritance of neuroticism; by M. Israel and D. Vinson on the subjective versus the objective method of Rorschach interpretation; by A. Heron on the objective measurement of personality in unskilled workers, as related to work adjustment and productivity; by A. Meadows on the reliability of the Rorschach test; by S. Cox on the validity of the Rorschach test; by A. Lubin on the application of discriminant function techniques to psychological problems; by J. May on the assumptions underlying Holzinger's h^2 statistic; by F. Freeman on the Character Interpretation Test, and by G. Yukviss and M. Malloy who carried out the testing for various researches.

Computations were carried out by the statistical section of the Psychological Department, under the direction of A. Lubin, J. May, and, for about one year, A. Jonckheere. The computors who carried the main burden were D. Burgess, I. Wiltshire, and J. Singleton; the latter also bore the main responsibility for the Hollerith work.

D. Furneaux contributed greatly by his advice on apparatus, and thanks are due to him and to J. Westhenry and W. Whithers, workshop technicians, on whom fell the burden of constructing and maintaining apparatus. J. Standen was also helpful in this connection.

S. Francis, now Mrs. McIntosh, typed the manuscript, checked the proofs, and assumed responsibility for the bibliography; her quick and accurate work considerably lightened the load of authorship. D. Webb drew the figures with skill and competence. F. Loos and S. Jeff took the photographs, which were posed by various members of the Psychological Department.

Professor P. E. Vernon read the manuscript and saved the reader from a good measure of repetition and obscurity; the writer can hardly refrain from accepting full responsibility for what has remained of these twin faults.

Professor Aubrey Lewis gave constant support to the research programme of the Department, and it is no exaggeration to say that without him this work could not have been completed. Many other colleagues and friends at the Bethlem and Maudsley Hospitals contributed of their time and advice, and lent their support to our plans; they are too numerous to name here.

My wife contributed directly to this research by her great skill in testing difficult and sometimes hostile patients; this, however, is not the only reason why this book is most fittingly dedicated to her.

H. J. EYSENCK

Institute of Psychiatry
Maudsley and Bethlem Royal Hospitals
University of London

Chapter One

SCIENCE AND PERSONALITY

THE word 'science' has great prestige value in our society. Like other words having great prestige value it is used in many contexts where one may legitimately doubt whether those who use it mean by it what philosophers, logicians, and scientists themselves have agreed upon as the correct usage. 'Scientific palmistry', 'Christian science', 'scientific marriage counselling', and 'principles of scientific Marxism' are catchwords which use an honoured term as a bait; their relation to science is at best tangential and usually non-existent. In the examples given, the deception will be obvious to most readers; in other cases we may not be so sure, and some kind of criterion may be required to judge accurately. If we look at the flood of articles dealing with 'personality', 'clinical psychology', 'counselling', 'psychoanalysis', 'diagnostic testing', 'projective techniques', and similar inter-related concepts, and attempt to judge their value from the point of view of science, we may be permitted at least a doubt as to whether all these contributions can be called genuinely 'scientific' —indeed, in a more jaundiced mood we may wonder if any of them deserve this title.

Much argument on this point has suffered from a lack of definition of the term 'scientific', both parties to the argument using this word in different senses. Finding their contributions unacceptable as scientific in the orthodox sense, many workers in the field of personality have surreptitiously altered the meaning of 'scientific' in such a way that it still retains its prestige value, but is now emptied of precisely those elements which originally gave rise to this esteem. This procedure of changing the meaning of words is familiar in the political field, where words such as 'democracy', which have relatively clear meaning and content, are used by some who wish to retain the prestige value of the term for régimes which clearly do not fall under this heading, to mean almost precisely the opposite to what the word has hitherto stood for. Semantic manœuvres of this type create much confusion and

7

necessitate a careful analysis of the meaning of the words used. They are illustrative of the Alice-in-Wonderland atmosphere which pervades so much of this field. 'When I use a word', said Humpty-Dumpty, 'it means just what I choose it to mean— neither more nor less.' 'The question is,' said Alice, 'whether you can make words mean different things.' 'The question is,' said Humpty-Dumpty, 'which is to be Master—that's all.'

There are clearly two kinds of psychology, just as there are two kinds of physics. Eddington (1928) has contrasted these two types of physics by writing about his two writing tables—the sensible table, as perceived by him, and as accepted by common sense, solid and impenetrable—and the table as modern physics sees it, being constituted mainly of empty space, with a very large number of very small electrons, protons, neutrons and other bodies and electric charges moving in this space. Absurd as this second conception of the table may sound to the naïve observer, we are willing to accept it because by accepting it, and all the concepts and laws which are involved in it, we are able to bring order into the great mass of facts which the world presents to us, and because predictions made on this basis have a habit of being borne out when we apply an empirical check. Physics started from the actual table as presented to sense experience, but it has left it a very long way behind. In doing so, it has also lost a good deal of the feeling of certainty which attaches to common-sense observation, replacing it by an attitude of tentative belief in the relative accuracy of current hypotheses.[1]

In a similar way, psychology starts out with the observations of common sense. In certain limited fields, it has succeeded in

[1] This opposition between science and common sense is well brought out by Galileo in his famous *Dialogues* (1661):

'I cannot sufficiently admire the eminence of those men's wits, that have received and held it to be true, and with the sprightliness of their judgments offered such violence to their own senses, as that they have been able to prefer that which their reason dictated to them, to that which sensible experience represented most manifestly to the contrary. I cannot find any bounds for my admiration, how that reason was able in Aristarchus and Copernicus, to commit such a rape on their senses, as in despite thereof to make herself mistress of their credulity.'

Einstein recently emphasized a similar point:

'Advances in scientific knowledge must bring about the result that an increase in formal simplicity can only be won at the cost of an increased distance or gap between the fundamental hypotheses of the theory on the one hand, and the directly observed facts on the other.'

getting beyond common sense, and in elaborating concepts and laws which bring order into a relatively small field and which enable us to make moderately accurate predictions. In other fields, it is still painfully close to common sense and has failed signally to elaborate concepts and laws of its own. In most fields, it shows a stubborn tendency to cling to feelings of certainty and to refuse to hold tentative beliefs, and to regard current hypotheses as at best very rough-and-ready approximations to those likely in the long run to be found most useful.

In contrasting common-sense observation and scientific theory, we do not mean to imply that common sense is invariably wrong and science invariably right. The difference lies essentially in the method by means of which one's opinion is arrived at. If this method follows the dictates of science, the result may be wrong, but it will be a wrongness that is self-correcting. If the method is not that of science the result may be right, but we have no way of knowing that it is right. If it is wrong, we have no way of correcting it. Many firmly held beliefs of common sense are wrong, although they may superficially have much to recommend them. Others may be right or wrong; we have no evidence to decide.

The two kinds of psychology which we have distinguished—that of common sense and that of science—do not differ only from the point of view of method; they also seem to differ from the point of view of aim. Common-sense psychology seeks to *understand*. If another person acts in the same way that I would act, then in some way I may say that I understand his actions. If he acts in a way different to the way in which I would act, but nevertheless familiar to me because I have seen many others behave in this fashion, I still feel that I understand him. If his action is unfamiliar to me, I may try to understand it by reducing it to familiar motives experienced in unusual circumstances. Much of psychiatry consists in such an attempt at understanding, and it is often stated that the good psychiatrist or psychologist must possess 'empathy' which enables him to 'feel himself into' his patient.

The aim of science is quite different, and rather more austere. Mach (1942), Ostwald (1911), Pearson (1911), and many other scientists have maintained that the only real world is a sensible world, and that scientific theories are merely descriptions of the sensible world. In other words, *science aims at description*. This dictum is easily misunderstood. 'A complete description of natural phenomena is impossible, and if it were not impossible it would be useless, for the aim of science is to make the primary data intelligible by exhibiting their mode of connection. Without abstraction this would be impossible but a complete description would not permit of abstraction' (Stebbing, 1930). Obviously, then, description may be understood in two senses. We may refer to description at an elementary level, as when we describe minutely the characteristics of a given table, or a blade of grass, or a whale. Or we may refer to description at a higher level, as when we describe the movements of the planets in terms of parabolas, or the behaviour of electric particles in terms of field theory. This latter type of description is often called 'explanation', because by referring the more elementary, individual phenomena observed at the low level of description to the laws which are abstracted from these elementary facts, and which constitute the higher level of description, we often feel that we have 'explained' the observed facts. All we have done, of course, is to give the individual fact a place in a unified, consistent system of description; more than this science does not attempt to do. If it is clearly understood that the term 'explanation' does not carry any overtones of intuitive or empathic understanding, no anthropomorphic 'feeling oneself into' things, but stands merely for the more abstract level of description, there is probably no great danger in using that term, and it will be so used in the remainder of this chapter.

Science, then, tries to describe and to explain. In doing so it follows certain rules which experience has shown to be indispensable to the development of descriptions so comprehensive as to deserve the name 'explanation'. Let us start with an example contrasting non-scientific and scientific explanation, using planetary motion as the problem to be explained. 'The ancient Egyptians, starting from the assumption that the universe is like a large box of which the earth forms the bottom and the sky the top, supposed the stars to be lamps either carried by gods or suspended by cords from the top of the box. The sun was supposed to be a god, Ra, carried daily in a boat along a river of which the Nile was a branch. He was born every morning, grew in strength until noon, when he turned into another boat. Finally, he was carried in another boat during the night back to the east. The eclipse of the sun was accounted for by the supposition that a huge serpent sometimes attacked the boat. A similar supposition accounted for lunar eclipses and the phases of the moon. Like the sun, the moon had its enemies. A sow attacks it on the fifteenth day of each month and after a fortnight's agony and increasing pallor, the moon dies and is born again. Sometimes the sow manages to swallow it altogether for a time, causing a lunar eclipse.

'Although these suppositions do not involve flagrant contradiction of the facts upon which they are based and although they are the outcome of a desire to explain these facts, nevertheless, this Egyptian doctrine is in no sense scientific. Its failure to be scientific is not due to the fact that it rests upon unproved assumptions. Every scientific theory rests ultimately on such assumptions. It fails because these assumptions were of such a kind that there could be no further evidence in support of them. They were essentially unverifiable; they were not susceptible of development; they did not suggest the deduction of observable data. . . . The Egyptian theory, therefore, could neither be developed nor tested. But a theory is scientific only if it admits of testing and development' (Dreyer, 1906).

As an example of scientific explanation, we may take Newton's law of gravitation. Included in his descriptive scheme are all the facts which enter into Ptolemy's mathematical description, into Copernicus' heliocentric scheme, and into Kepler's three laws of planetary motion. All these facts were not merely fitted into Newton's system; they could be deduced from it. And once the law had been enunciated, such apparently independent and disconnected facts as the phenomenon of the tides, planetary motions, the precession of the equinoxes, the phenomenon of weight, the motions of cyclones, and the orbit of the comet could all be explained in terms of the inverse square law of universal attraction.

'Such deductive power is a mark of constructive description. . . . By its comprehensiveness, by its deliberateness in leading to new discoveries, in suggesting fresh experiences, and in connecting what was hitherto disconnected, it achieves the aim of science in making the multiplicity of facts intelligible. Such a theory may be said to explain the sensible facts that constitute its data since it is not only based upon them but leads deductively back to them. Further . . . it leads on to other sensible facts which were not known and thus do not form part of the original data' (Stebbing, 1930).

The greater the degree of co-ordination achieved by a theory, the more it is liable to be upset by a small discrepancy. A constructive description, such as Newton's theory, possesses a high degree of co-ordination; it is coherent with respect to a comprehensive range of facts. A single fact which is in contradiction to the hypothesis may necessitate its rejection. Occasionally the theory may be salvaged through the use of an *ad hoc* hypothesis which accounts for the discrepant fact, and which can later on be verified. Thus, for instance, an irregularity in the orbit of the planet Uranus was accounted for by the *ad hoc* hypothesis that another, hitherto unknown planet, was responsible for these aberrations. This planet had to have certain qualities which could be specified precisely in accordance with Newton's laws, and when its position had been calculated on the basis of the theory, Neptune was actually discovered in the precise place required according to theory. Another irregularity in planetary motion, namely, that in the orbit of Mercury, was also explained by le Verrier on the basis of a similar *ad hoc* hypothesis, involving an interior planet which he called Vulcan. Careful observation failed to reveal any such planet, and the hypothesis was discredited.

'A multiplication of *ad hoc* hypotheses is contrary to the aim of science which seeks the greatest possible co-ordination of facts. Every additional *ad hoc* hypothesis marks a breakdown of the co-ordination. . . . An *ad hoc* hypothesis necessarily explains a given discrepant fact since it has been introduced solely for that purpose. If we can appeal to an *ad hoc* hypothesis whenever there is a discrepancy between theory and fact, then we can explain everything and foretell nothing. It is only permissible to introduce an *ad hoc* hypothesis when consequences can be deduced from it which are later verified. Otherwise an alternative method for dealing with a fact discrepant with a theory has to be resorted to, namely, the rejection of the fundamental assumptions upon which the theory is based' (Stebbing, 1930).

This is the course followed by Einstein in his attempts to account for the negative result of the Michelson-Morley experiment to detect the earth's velocity relative to the ether. The experiment showed that contrary to Newton's laws the motion of the earth has no influence upon the propagation of light over the earth's surface. While this discrepancy is minute, it nevertheless entails either a multiplication of *ad hoc* hypotheses, or a rejection of fundamental assumptions. In spite of the success and immense prestige of Newton's constructive description it had to be rejected under the pressure of experimental fact unless it were saved by the introduction of *ad hoc* hypotheses. When, as in the case of the Neptune hypothesis, the *ad hoc* hypothesis is verifiable, and suggests an explanation of the discrepancy which is of a kind already familiar, then the hypothesis is not objectionable. It does not conflict with the aim of science. When, however, it is essentially unverifiable since it suggests what transcends observation, or appeals to effects which neutralize each other (as was the case with the Lorentz-Fitzgerald contraction suggested to account for the Michelson-Morley experiment), then it is not admissible.

It is an interesting aspect of many modern theories of personality (particularly the analytic and so-called dynamic ones) that they capitalize precisely on these two inadmissible and unverifiable types of *ad hoc* hypotheses. The concept of reaction-formation, for instance, implies that cause A may result in behaviour-pattern X as easily as in non-X—and presumably anything in between. One dynamic may cancel out another. Prediction is thus impossible, and indeed hardly ever attempted. 'Verification' consists not in stating an hypothesis, making deductions, and then seeking evidence regarding these deductions; it consists in first obtaining the evidence and then seeking an explanation, which is invariably found through the invocation of unverifiable *ad hoc* hypotheses. It can hardly be argued that this type of procedure is in line with the precepts of science, as ordinarily understood.

To quote but one example from the research literature to illustrate this tendency, we may take Symonds' book on *Adolescent Fantasy* (1949). In it he gives a set of correlations between teachers' ratings of forty children studied in great detail, and their 'fantasy themes' as determined from the Thematic Apperception test. One hundred and seventy-five such correlations are given on page 368 of the book; they have been plotted in Figure 1 below. It will be seen that they cluster around zero, and that in view of the high sampling errors involved in the calculation of correlations from small numbers of cases these figures do not in any way deviate from a kind of distribution expected on the basis of the null hypothesis, i.e. on the basis of the hypothesis that there is no correlation whatever between rating and T.A.T. score. This is the only conclusion which can legitimately be drawn from these data, and in view of the far-reaching claims which have been made for this 'test', it is one which is of great interest and significance.

It is impossible to give an accurate estimate of the divergence of the empirical figures from chance expectation. The S.E. when $r = 0$ is ·16 for forty cases, so that one would expect 68 per cent of all observed correlations to lie within the limits of + ·16 and

— ·16. Actually the number of these effectively zero correlations is slightly larger than this, so that if anything the ratings and the T.A.T. scores are correlated to an even slighter extent than would be expected on a purely chance basis. However, the correlations are not independent from each other, so that no exact test can be made; such tests apply only to correlations which are themselves uncorrelated. This lack of independence also invalidates Symonds'

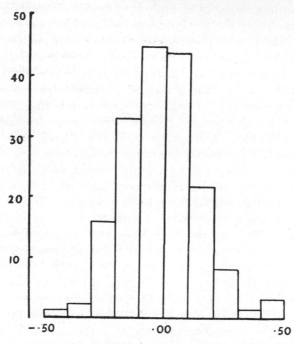

Figure 1.—Distribution of correlations between Thematic Appreciation Test scores and teachers' ratings

argument that 'there is a certain consistency in these relationships . . . that makes one believe that they have a higher degree of validity than the statistical probability of departing from chance would permit one to assume. Variables of opposite meaning will have relationships on opposite sides of the correlation zero point.' Such consistency is in no way proof of the extra-chance character of sets of correlations; it can be deduced from the laws of probability directly.

This brings us to the last argument advanced by Symonds. 'These consistencies and regularities . . . fit in too well with the meaning of the data to attribute them entirely to chance.' They are 'verified by their dynamic significance'. As an example Symonds quotes the fact that ratings of 'good adjustment' correlate positively with fantasies of anxiety. This is interpreted as meaning that 'the good adjustment was a reaction formation which kept the individual from recognizing his anxiety and gave him a way of defending himself against it'. Those with poor adjustment, it is claimed, 'did not show anxiety in their stories, because the anxiety expressed itself symptomatically in their poor adjustment to life'.

Here we have the full flavour of the type of argument characterized as unscientific in our preceding discussion. A correlation is found between 'good adjustment' and 'fantasies of anxiety' which is only just larger than its own standard error. If this correlation had been in the opposite direction, it might have been possible to argue that it was in the expected direction, and that there is nothing inherently absurd about maladjusted children having fantasies of anxiety. The fact that the correlation is in the wrong direction, however, does not worry the 'dynamic' psychologist; indeed, it is expressly cited because it is 'verified' by its 'dynamic significance'. All this is accomplished through that ready handmaiden, 'reaction formation'. The author is not concerned about the fact that in other projection tests, such as the Sentence Completion Test, there is a significant and negative correlation between adjustment and fantasies of anxiety; his 'explanation' is a purely *ad hoc* one which can of course be relied upon to 'explain' the facts which it was constructed specifically to account for. Nor is the author worried by the fact that he is forced to make assumptions of such magnitude as would make less 'dynamic' writers wince— assumptions, for instance, that good adjustment is a defence against anxiety! When it is realized that all this elaborate apparatus is set in motion, and all these tremendous theories and assumptions put forward, to explain a correlation which is completely insignificant, it will be apparent why such procedures are considered antagonistic to the spirit of science, and unlikely to advance our knowledge of human behaviour.

When we try to apply these precepts to the study of personality, we find that this discipline has charted for itself a dangerous course, threatened by the Scylla of nebulous Freudian generalizing, and by the Charybdis of pointlessly amassing unrelated 'facts'. Thus we have two great groups of workers whose efforts bring extraordinarily little return for the labour expended: On the one hand the Neo-Freudian, Crypto-Jungian group of 'intuition-ists', who scorn the pedestrian methods of scientific verification, who base their conclusions on very small biased samples, and whose alleged 'facts' are themselves only interpretations according to very dubious canons of evidence; on the other, the mole-like calculators of innumerable correlations between measures taken without any theory or hypothesis capable of proof or disproof, who mistake the collection of a thousand unrelated 'facts' for science, who seek to atone for the scientific barrenness of their results by stressing the mathematical beauty and purity of the methods used, and who seem incapable of seeing the wood for the trees. In other words, there appears to be a definite schizophrenic interlude in the development of a scientific psychology of personality; the building up of hypotheses and theories is divorced from the patient collec-tion of facts. 'Dynamic' psychology is almost entirely devoted to an exploitation of *ad hoc* hypotheses which are either unverifiable or appeal to effects which neutralize each other; 'actuarial' psycho-logy is almost entirely devoted to statistical analysis without benefit of theory or hypothesis. It is small wonder that neither separately nor conjointly do these two 'schools' succeed in con-structing a firm, scientific foundation on which to build. What is needed in psychology, as in any other science, is greater under-standing of, and more intensive use of, the hypothetic-deductive method, in which a clear, unambiguous hypothesis is stated, deductions, preferably of a quantitative kind, are made, and experiments performed to verify or disprove the hypothesis.

We may summarize our discussion so far by quoting Stebbing (1930):

'Scientific thinking is controlled and directed thinking; it is essentially methodical. Controlled thinking, in so far as it is successful, issues in the organization of facts originally appre-hended as fragmentary, disconnected, or it may be discordant. Organization is achieved by the discovery of connections whereby one fact is related to another. The isolated facts, given as discon-nected, are fitted together into an orderly arrangement which yields what relatively to the starting point may be regarded as a whole, or system.

'We may say that a set of elements exhibits order and there-fore becomes a system when, given the properties of some of the members of the set, the properties of other members of the set, or at least of some of them, are thereby determined. This determination is due to the *relation* that orders the set; it is not a property of the elements regarded as a class.

'The relevance of the subject of order to systematic inquiry may be regarded as evident. Scientific thinking essentially consists in the organization, or co-ordination, of the facts with which it deals. A collection of disconnected facts does not constitute a science any more than a mob of men constitutes a college, or a heap of bricks a building. The sciences are concerned not with facts as such but with ordered facts. One main difference between the earlier and the later stages of science is to be found in the growing prominence of order. What is ultimately important for science is the type of order rather than the elements that are ordered. It is for this reason that the most highly developed science, theoretical physics, appears to be concerned with something far removed from what the plain man would regard as a fact. Science has its origin in the attempt to co-ordinate the facts of sensible experience but in the discovery of the appropriate type of order it passes to the consideration of a different order of facts.

'Ultimately, the explanation of facts is to be found in their organization into a system. Thus, a mere collection of observable facts does not suffice to constitute a science. There is required in addition a certain kind of attitude to the facts and a certain kind of predominantly logical method. The requirements of this method determine whether a given observable fact is a possible datum for science. The scientists, that is to say, select those facts that can be treated in accordance with this method. We have then, two characteristics that belong to science; the selection of a certain kind of facts and the use of a certain kind of method. The scientist is concerned with the correlations of sets of properties. Hence, a scientific proposition is ultimately of the form: Whatever has the property X has the property Y. A scientist reaches such a proposition from propositions of the form: This A, this B, this C, etc., has the properties X and Y. That is to say, he generalizes from particular cases. The instrument by which the generalizations are obtained is scientific method. The scientist, then, considers particular facts only in order to obtain generalizations of increasing abstractness. All observation involves abstraction, that is, selection from something that is also there to be observed.

'The method of science sometimes called the inductive method has four essential stages. The first of these is constituted by the awareness of a familiar complex situation in which some one fact is apprehended as peculiar, and where the need is felt to account for this fact by connecting it with the total situation in which its occurrence would not be unexpected.

'The second stage is the formation of an hypothesis which would connect the unexpected fact with other facts.

'Third comes the deductive development of the hypothesis, and fourth comes the testing of the consequences deduced from the hypothesis by appealing to observable facts.

'With regard to such an investigation we may be said to explain a fact when we have shown that it is connected in an orderly manner with other facts that do not have to be explained.'

This general point of view is opposed by those who hold what is often called the *idiographic* as contrasted with the *nomothetic* point of view. These terms, coined by Windelband (1921) and introduced into Anglo-Saxon psychology by Allport (1937), refer to attempts to 'understand some particular event in nature or society' as opposed to the seeking of 'general laws and employing only those procedures admitted by the exact sciences'. The main battle-cry of the idiographically minded psychologist is that of 'uniqueness of the individual'. 'One may say (with penetrating accuracy) that each personality is a law unto himself, meaning that each single life, if fully understood, would reveal its own orderly and necessary process of growth. The course of each life is a lawful event, even though it is unlike all other of its class' (Allport, 1937).

The idiographic view has a certain appeal to most psychologists who have to deal with people because its main proposition is so obviously true. It is quite undeniably true that Professor Windelband is absolutely unique. So is my old shoe. Indeed, any existing object is unique in the sense that it is unlike any other object. This is true as much in the physical sciences as it is in the biological, sociological, and psychological sciences. So much, then, is agreed. Two points arise.

The first point relates to the meaning of this uniqueness. To Allport, it appears to be some mystical quality, something *sui generis*, something 'afar from the sphere of our sorrow'. *To the scientist, the unique individual is simply the point of intersection of a number of quantitative variables.* There are some 340,000 discriminable colour experiences, each of which is absolutely unique and distinguishable from any other. From the point of view of descriptive science, they can all be considered as points of intersection of three quantitative variables, hue, tint, and chroma. A combination of perfectly general, descriptive variables is sufficient to allow any individual to be differentiated from any other, by specifying his position on each of these variables in a quantitative form. Many writers 'seem unable to see that one individual can differ quantitatively from another in many variables, common variables though they may be, and still have a unique personality' (Guilford, 1936). Quite on the contrary, the very notion of 'being different from' implies at the same time the idea of direction and the idea of amount—in other words, the unique individuals cannot meaningfully be said to be different from each other unless they are being compared along some quantitative variable. Uniqueness, therefore, is not in any sense a concept antagonistic to science; it follows from the methods used in science to describe individual events in terms of common variables.

The second point relates to the importance attributed to the unique. 'Science is not interested in the unique event; the unique belongs to history, not to science.' Yet clearly applied science must deal with the unique, with the individual. We cannot build bridges in general, but only a particular bridge; we cannot cure patients as such, but only a particular patient. In dealing with the individual case, we must make use of such general laws as may be known to apply; our success in dealing with the individual case will be determined by how much is known by science regarding the laws governing this case. It is for this reason that bridges are built with greater success than has hitherto attended our efforts at curing patients by psychotherapy; it is not that patients are 'unique' and 'individual', and bridges not—a bridge is as unique and individual as a patient—but because the laws governing the behaviour of bridges are very much better understood than the laws governing the behaviour of patients. Here indeed we have the best possible defence of current psychiatry against charges that its procedures are unscientific: as long as psychology fails to discover general laws applicable to the psychiatrist's practical problems, the psychiatrist must use whatever methods common sense, practical experience, intuition and theory dictate. He cannot tell his patients to wait until the glorious sun of science comes forth to illuminate the scene; he has to deal with them here and now. As long as the psychiatrist does not claim to have solved the scientific problems of personality, the psychologist certainly has no right to blame him for making use of any and every possible weapon he can lay his hands on, or for making up his own conceptual schemata. Nothing that could be called a science of personality exists at the moment, and psychiatrists can hardly be blamed for refusing to base their procedures on the mere hope of the future. Pragmatism is therefore currently the only method open to psychiatry and clinical psychology; it is perhaps unfortunate that so many practitioners, instead of keeping an open mind in the very undeveloped state of the subject at the moment, have instead fallen prey to a 'premature crystallization of spurious orthodoxies'.

Another shibboleth, second only to that of 'uniqueness', is that of the 'total personality'. In a sense, again, what those who use this phrase mean is so obviously true that no one would dissent from their stress on studying personality *in toto*, as it were, and not hack it up into arbitrary, unconnected parts. It would not be true, however, to imagine that science holds a point of view opposed to such insistence. Even in physics, relativity theory lays great emphasis precisely on this 'interconnectedness' of all the phenomena which go to make up its field of study, and in psychology attacks on 'atomists' are largely attacks on men of straw, not on points of view held by any responsible psychologist. It is in the negative connotations of this phrase, rather than in the positive ones, that one may discern certain specious arguments. Thus believers in the 'wholeness' of personality often decry any type of analysis, and declare that analysis destroys what it seeks to study. Instead, they advocate methods and techniques which are said to 'study personality as a whole'.

It is difficult to attach any more meaning to this phrase than to a claim to study 'the universe as a whole'. Nor does an investigation of the methods actually used by those who employ these phrases show anything very different from the ordinary procedures used for many years—unless it be a lack of reliability, disregard of validity, and a contempt for the patient work needed for verifying theories and hypotheses. When we look into a manual of the Rorschach Test (Klopfer & Kelly, 1942), for instance, the preferred technique of the holistically-minded, we find there the claim that from the Rorschach record can be deduced: '(1) The degree and mode of control with which the subject tries to regulate his experiences and actions. (2) The responsiveness of his emotional energies to stimulation from outside and promptings from within. (3) His mental approach to given problems and situations. (4) His creative or imaginative capacities, and the use he makes of them. (5) A general estimate of his intellectual level and the major qualitative features of his thinking. (6) A general estimate of the degree of security or anxiety, of balance in general, and specific unbalances. (7) The relative degree of maturity in the total personality development.' The author is careful to point out that this is not all that the Rorschach can tell us. He goes on to say that 'this list does not represent a complete account of the personality aspects revealed by the Rorschach method'. Apparently the test is also 'remarkably effective in estimating the intellectual status of an individual; in revealing the richness or poverty of his psychic experience; in making known his present mood; and in showing the extent of his intuitive ability as well as in disclosing special talents and aptitudes'. Furthermore, 'it detects anxieties, phobias, and sex disturbances, as well as more severe disorders, and serves as a guide for appropriate treatment'.

According to this widely-accepted text, then, we are not dealing with the whole personality at all; we are dealing with creative and imaginative capacities, with intellectual level and status, with security, anxiety, balance and unbalance, with moods and intuitive abilities, with phobias, sex disorders, and other disturbances. It is not easy to see, then, how this treatment differs from the traditional analysis of personality into cognitive, conative, and affective areas, into abilities, temperament, character, intelligence, traits, and so forth. Obviously the total personality has to be analysed into smaller units before we can study it at all; we are thrown back to the question of what is the best method of analysis, and how we can determine its validity. There is no book on personality, and no test or technique, which deals with the unique, total personality; these words are merely used as camouflage to screen the absence of acceptable validity and reliability.

What has been said here of the Rorschach test applies with equal force to the psychoanalytic technique. Here also we do not encounter a unique, total personality; we find Oedipus complexes and super egos, regressions and transferences, cathexes and libidos, fixations, symbolisms, compensations, catharses, Narcissisms, and many other strange entities jostling each other; all of them attempts to analyse what is elsewhere declared to be 'unanalysable'.

Surely this whole argument rests on a misunderstanding. What we are dealing with, in psychology as well as in physics, are certain entities, parts, 'sub-wholes', or whatever they may be called, which stand in certain relations to each other. It is vitally important to identify the correct parts or sub-wholes; it is equally vital to discover the relations obtaining between them. It is absurd to call one of these tasks more important than the other; they are mutually interdependent, and progress in science is impossible without paying due regard to both. To say that orthodox psychology is 'atomistic', and is interested only in the parts, to the neglect of the relations between them, is manifestly untrue; techniques of curvilinear regression, of curve-fitting, and of trend analysis show clearly the concern statistical psychologists feel about the exact form of the relation obtaining between the various entities dealt with. What is important is not whether one party or the other to this dispute is right; the main consideration must be that each side should put its point of view in such a way that an empirical test, a crucial experiment, becomes possible. The question of the relation between the variables found useful in psychology must be an experimental problem; it cannot be solved on the philosophical level.

Sometimes this argument is put in a rather different form. It is said that the human mind is able to seize upon, and to coordinate, large numbers of small impressions ('petites perceptions', if the historical parallel be permitted), while the calculating machine cannot as fruitfully deal with such large numbers of determinants, all of them influencing each other in complex ways. Such an argument in favour of interviewing, of intuitive interpretation of projective productions, and similar subjective procedures, is not on the face of it unreasonable, although it may not appeal to the tough-minded scientist. It would appear to be a perfectly genuine hypothesis with much *prima facie* validity; unfortunately this common-sense appeal of the hypothesis has blinded many practitioners to the fact that there is little evidence in favour, and much against, this belief in the integrating power of the mind. I shall leave out of account the mathematical proof that given a number of facts (however large) and their interconnections and relations with a criterion (however complex), it can be shown that there is one best combination of these facts which gives the highest possible predictive accuracy, and that this best combination can be reached by orthodox statistical methods of multiple correlation; the intuitive brain being at best able to equal, but not to excel this prediction. I shall instead mention briefly three experimental studies which may cause the believer in subjective methods at least to suspend judgment until he can quote equally impressive evidence in his favour.

First we may quote the conclusion arrived at by the Bureau of Naval Personnel, in their large-scale studies of prediction of success at training schools (Stuit, 1947). 'The improvement in predicting school success by having in addition to test scores an interviewer's evaluation of experience, interest, and personality, is relatively small and may well be negative.' The actual figures quoted show that in many cases the addition of the interview to the straightforward prediction based on test scores alone lowers predictive accuracy; in no case is there a striking improvement. In view of the very large numbers involved, 37,862 trainees having been studied altogether, this conclusion and the data on which it is based deserve most careful study.

Another study giving similar results, although in a different sphere, is the experiment on student selection conducted by Himmelweit (1950, 1951). One of her aims was the comparison of existing methods of selection with objective test techniques. (A more detailed report of her results with objective tests of personality will be found in a later chapter.) One of the traditional techniques much valued by the University was the interview. 'The main object of the interview is to assess the candidate's suitability to pursue a course of study, special consideration being given to the following factors: (*a*) general intelligence. (*b*) Previous education, training and experience. (*c*) Interests and motivation. (*d*) Personality and character.' None of the tests of intelligence and temperament which proved to be successful predictors of student success correlated significantly with the interview; indeed, there was a tendency for low negative correlation coefficients to predominate. When correlated with success at University the interview again failed to show a significant correlation; its predictive accuracy was indicated by a correlation coefficient of ·067! In view of the relatively high correlations achieved by objective tests, we find again that belief in the integrating faculties of the human mind is not supported by experimental findings.

Probably the most impressive, as well as the most conclusive, study, however, is the experiment carried out by Kelly (1949) on the selection of clinical psychology students. Using a plethora of different methods—interviews, ratings, objective tests, projective tests, intelligence tests, sociometric techniques, interest and attitude schedules and questionnaires, and following the students up over several years, he concluded that 'the most valid individual clinical judgments tend to be those based on relatively incomplete data regarding the assessee. In general, clinicians seem to make their best predictions on the basis of materials contained in the credential file and an objective test profile. Subsequent predictions based on increasing amounts of data, e.g. the addition of the autobiography, the projective tests, the interview, and the situation tests seem to have resulted in successive decrements in validity, as each additional type of data was added to the picture. This finding appears all the more significant when it is remembered that assessment staffs have uniformly been of the opinion that the interview contributed relatively most to their understanding of the case.'

While the report from which this summary is quoted is only a preliminary one, its conclusion shows a striking agreement with one of the most interesting results of the O.S.S. assessment programme (1948). Using in the main two selection stations for recruits, S and W, of which the former devoted roughly three times as much time to each recruit as did the latter, with all the increase in information, testing, interviewing, and conferences that that implies, the authors of the report found that 'the job ratings given after the one-day assessment at Station W were generally more valid than those given after the three-day assessment at Station S'. The respective figures, giving correlations between rating and criterion, are ·37 and ·53, using the criterion which the writers themselves regarded as the most valid. The explanation that perhaps the candidates at these two stations differed in such a way as to account for the result will not hold; 'it is not possible to say that the candidates who went to W were any easier to assess'. The writers conclude: 'It would be profitable, in the long run, for us to assume that the additional information obtained by stretching the screening process from one to three days had diminished the validity of the final decision.'

The evidence from all these different writers, with their varying biases and divergent outlooks, appears to agree that the human brain is not a very good instrument for assessing, weighting, and combining many items of information in such a way as to make valid predictions; on the contrary, it is easily confused when presented with more than a very few such items, and added information tends to lower, rather than to raise, its forecasting efficiency. The evidence is perhaps not conclusive, but it is remarkably unanimous.

The history of science thus gives us guidance as to the methodology to be employed in scientific work; does it also help us in deciding which of the many pressing problems to attack first? There appears to be one type of problem which is fundamental to all progress in the study of personality, and which must find at least a preliminary answer before we can hope to advance in any direction at all. This problem is that of taxonomy or classification, and it can best be introduced by using a simple example of how other problems tend to lead back to it.

It is believed nearly unanimously by psychiatrists, psychoanalysts, clinical psychologists, counsellors, and the lay public that psychotherapy has the effect of alleviating, partly or wholly, the illnesses of the neurotic. A look at the evidence for this belief will show that it is a common-sense belief, not one which could be considered scientific. This does not mean that the belief is wrong; it merely means that no scientific evidence has been produced to justify it. All we have are statements of subjective feelings by psychotherapists regarding the outcome of their labours; it must be obvious that these statements cannot be taken as scientific evidence, in view of the long list of mistaken beliefs of this kind which history gives us.

It may be of interest to look at such evidence as there is, and to discuss possible methods of investigating the truth of the general belief. In the only previous attempt to carry out such an evaluation that has come to hand, Landis (1938) has pointed out that 'before any sort of measurement can be made, it is necessary to establish a base line and a common unit of measure. The only unit of measure available is the report made by the physician stating that the patient has recovered, is much improved, is improved or unimproved. This unit is probably as satisfactory as any type of human subjective judgment, partaking of both the good and bad points of such judgments.' For a base line Landis suggests 'that of expressing therapeutic results in terms of the number of patients recovered or improved per 100 cases admitted to the hospital'. As an alternative, he suggests 'the statement of therapeutic outcome for some given group of patients during some stated interval of time'.

Landis realized quite clearly that in order to evaluate the effectiveness of any form of therapy, data from a control group of non-treated patients would be required in order to compare the effects of therapy with the spontaneous remission rate. In the absence of anything better, he used the amelioration rate in state mental hospitals for patients diagnosed under the heading of 'neuroses'. As he points out, 'there are several objections to the use of the consolidated amelioration rate . . . of the . . . state hospitals . . . as a base rate for spontaneous recovery. The fact that psychoneurotic cases are not usually committed to state hospitals unless in a very bad condition; the relatively small number of voluntary patients in the group; the fact that such patients do get some degree of psychotherapy especially in the reception hospitals; and the probably quite different economic, educational, and social status of the State Hospital group compared to the patients reported from each of the other hospitals—all argue against the acceptance of (this) figure . . . as a truly satisfactory base line, but in the absence of any other better figure this must serve.'

Actually the various figures quoted by Landis agree very well. The percentage of neurotic patients discharged annually as recovered or improved from New York state hospitals is 70 (figure for the years 1925–34); for the United States as a whole it is 68 (figure for the years 1926–33). The percentage of neurotics discharged as recovered or improved within one year of admission is 66 for the United States (1933) and 68 for New York (1914). The consolidated amelioration rate of New York state hospitals, 1917–34, is 72 per cent; as this is the figure chosen by Landis we may accept it in preference to the other, very similar ones, quoted. By and large, we may thus say that of severe neurotics receiving in the main custodial care, and very little if any psychotherapy, over two-thirds recovered or improved to a considerable extent. 'Although this is not, strictly speaking, a basic figure for "spontaneous" recovery, still any therapeutic method must show an appreciably greater size than this to be seriously considered.'

Another estimate of the required 'base line' is provided by Denker (1946). 'Five hundred consecutive disability claims due to psychoneurosis, treated by general practitioners throughout the country, and not by accredited specialists or sanatoria, were reviewed. All types of neurosis were included, and no attempt made to differentiate the neurasthenic, anxiety, compulsive, hysteric, or other states, but the greatest care was taken to eliminate the true psychotic or organic lesions which in the early state of illness so often simulate neurosis. These cases were taken consecutively from the files of the Equitable Life Assurance Society of the United States, were from all parts of the country, and all had been ill of a neurosis for at least three months before claims were submitted. They, therefore, could be fairly called "severe", since they had been totally disabled for at least three months' period, and rendered unable to carry on with any "occupation for remuneration or profit" for at least that time.' These patients were regularly seen and treated by their own physicians with sedatives, tonics, suggestion, and reassurance, but in no case was any attempt made at anything but this most superficial type of 'psychotherapy', which has always been the stock in trade of the general practitioner. Repeated statements, every three months or so by their physicians, as well as independent investigations by the insurance company, confirmed the fact that these people actually were not engaged in productive work during the period of their illness. During their disablement, these cases received disability benefits; as Denker points out, 'it is appreciated that this fact of disability income may have actually prolonged the total period of disability and acted as a barrier to incentive for recovery. One would, therefore, not expect the therapeutic results in such a group of cases to be as favourable as in other groups where the economic factor might act as an important spur in helping the sick patient adjust to his neurotic conflict and illness.'

The cases were all followed up for at least a five-year period, and often as long as ten years after the period of disability had begun. The criterion of 'recovery' used by Denker is characterized by the following data: (1) Return to work, and ability to carry on well in economic adjustments for at least a five-year period. (2) Complaint of no further or very slight difficulties. (3) Making of successful social adjustments. Using these criteria, which are very similar to those usually used by psychiatrists, Denker found that 45 per cent of the patients recovered after 1 year, another 27 per cent after two years, making 72 per cent in all. Another 10, 5, and 4 per cent recovered during the third, fourth, and fifth years respectively making a total of 90 per cent recoveries after five years.[1]

This sample contrasts in many ways with that used by Landis. The cases on which Denker reports were probably not as severe as those summarized by Landis; they were all voluntary, non-hospitalized patients, and from a much higher socio-economic stratum. (The majority of Denker's patients were clerical workers,

[1] These percentages are plotted in Figure 1 to illustrate the process of recovery graphically.

executives, teachers, and professional men.) In spite of these differences, the recovery figures for the two samples are almost identical.
The most suitable figure to choose from those given by Denker is
probably that for the two-year recovery rate, as follow-up studies
seldom go beyond two years, and the higher figures for three-,
four-, and five-year follow-ups would overestimate the efficiency
of this 'base line' procedure. Using therefore the two-year recovery
figure of 72 per cent, we find that Denker's figure agrees exactly

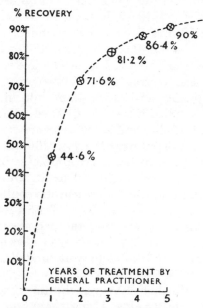

Figure 2.—Percentage of recoveries of 500 neurotic patients
not receiving psychotherapy

with that given by Landis. We may therefore conclude with some
confidence that our estimate of some two-thirds of severe neurotics
showing recovery or considerable improvement without the benefit of systematic psychotherapy properly so-called is not likely to be
very far out.

We may now turn to the effects of psychotherapeutic treatment.
The results of nineteen studies reported in the literature, covering
almost eight thousand cases, and dealing with both psychoanalytic and eclectic types of treatment, are quoted in detail on
page 30. An attempt has been made to report results under the
four headings: (1) Cured, or much improved. (2) Improved.

(3) Slightly improved. (4) Not improved, died, discontinued treatment, etc. It was usually easy to reduce additional categories given by some writers to these basic four; some writers only give two or three categories, and in those cases it was of course impossible to subdivide further, and the figures for combined categories are given. A slight degree of subjectivity inevitably enters into this procedure, but it is doubtful if this has caused much distortion. A somewhat greater degree of subjectivity is probably implied in the writer's judgment as to which disorders and diagnoses should be considered to fall under the heading of 'neuroses'. Schizophrenic, manic-depressive, and paranoid states have been excluded; organ neuroses, psychopathic states, and character disturbances have been included. The number of cases where there was genuine doubt is probably too small to make much change in the final figures, regardless of how they are allocated.[1]

Certain difficulties have arisen from the inability of some writers to make their column figures agree with their totals, or to calculate percentages accurately. Again, I have exercised my judgment as to which figures to accept. In certain cases, writers have given figures of cases where there was a recurrence of the disorder after apparent cure or improvement, without indicating how many patients were affected in these two groups respectively. I have subtracted all recurrencies of this kind from the 'cured' and 'improved' totals, taking half from each. The total number of cases involved in all these adjustments is quite small. Another investigator making all decisions exactly in the opposite direction to mine would hardly alter the final percentage figures by more than one or two per cent.

We may now turn to the figures as presented. Patients treated by means of psychoanalysis improve to the extent of 44 per cent;

[1] A number of studies have been excluded because of such factors as excessive inadequacy of follow-up, part duplication of cases with others included in our table, failure to indicate type of treatment used, and other reasons which made the results useless from our point of view. Papers thus rejected are those by Thorley & Craske (1950), Bennett & Semrad (1936), H. I. Harris (1939), Hardcastle (1934), A. Harris (1938), Jacobson & Wright (1942), Friess & Nelson (1942), Comroe (1936), Wenger (1934), Eitington (1922), Orbison (1925), Coon & Raymond (1940), Denker (1937), and Bond & Braceland (1937). Their inclusion would not have altered our conclusions to any considerable degree, although as Miles et al. (1951) point out: 'When the various studies are compared in terms of thoroughness, careful planning, strictness of criteria and objectivity, there is often an inverse correlation between these factors and the percentage of successful results reported.'

EFFECTS OF PSYCHOTHERAPY

Type of Therapy	No.	Cured, much Improved	Improved	Slightly Improved	Not Improved, Died, Left Treatment	Cured, much Improved, Percentage Improved
(A) Psychoanalysis						
1. Fenichel, O. (1930)	484	104	84	99	197	39
2. Kessel, W., & Hyman, H. T. (1933)	34	16	5	4	9	62
3. Jones, E. (1936)	59	20	8	28	3	47
4. Alexander, F. (1937)	141	28	42	23	48	50
5. Knight, R. P. (1941)	42	8	20	7	7	67
	760	335 }		425 }		44
(B) Eclectic						
1. Huddleson, J. H. (1927)	200	19	74	80	27	46
2. Matz, P. B. (1929)	775	10	310	310	145 }	41
3. Maudsley Hospital Report (1931)	1721	288	900	533 }		69
4. Maudsley Hospital Report (1935)	1711	371	765	575 }		64
5. Neustatter, W. L. (1935)	46	9	14	8	15	50
6. Luff, M. C., & Garrod, M. (1935)	500	140	135	26	199	55
7. Luff, M. C., & Garrod, M. (1935)	210	38	84	54	34	68
8. Ross, T. A. (1936)	1089	547	306	236 }		77
9. Yaskin, T. C. (1936)	100	29	29	42		58
10. Curran, D. (1937)	83		51 }	32		61
11. Masserman, T. H., & Carmichael, H. T. (1938)	50	7	20	5	18	54
12. Carmichael, H. T., & Masserman, T. H. (1939)	77	16	25	14	22	53
13. Schilder, P. (1939)	35	11	11	6	7	63
14. Hamilton, D. M., et al. (1942)	100	32	34	17	17	66
15. Hamilton, D. M., et al. (1942)	100	46	5	17	32 }	51
16. Landis, C. (1942)	119	40	47			73
17. Institute Med. Psychol. (quoted Neustatter)	270	58	132	55	32	70
18. Wilder, J. (1945)	54	3	24	16	25	50
19. Miles, H. H. W., et al. (1951)	53	13	18	13	9	58
	7293	4661 }		2632 }		64

patients treated eclectically improve to the extent of 64 per cent; patients treated only custodially or by G.P.s, it will be remembered, improve to the extent of 72 per cent. There thus appears to be an inverse correlation between recovery and psychotherapy; the more psychotherapy, the smaller the recovery rate! This conclusion requires certain qualifications.

In our tabulation of psychoanalytic results, we have classed those who stopped treatment together with those not improved. This appears to be reasonable; a patient who fails to finish his treatment, and is not improved, is surely a therapeutic failure. The same rule has been followed with the data summarized under 'eclectic' treatment, except when the patient who did not finish treatment was definitely classified as 'improved' by the therapist. However, in view of the peculiarities of Freudian procedures it may appear to some readers to be more just to class these cases separately, and deal only with the percentage of completed treatments which are successful. Approximately one-third of the psychoanalytic patients listed broke off treatment, so that the percentage of successful treatments of patients who finished their course must be put at approximately 66 per cent. It would appear, then, that when we discount the risk the patient runs of stopping treatment altogether, his chances of improvement under psychoanalysis are almost equal to his chances of improvement under eclectic treatment, and slightly worse than his chances under G.P. or custodial treatment.

Two further points require clarification. (1) Are patients in our 'control' groups (Landis & Denker) as seriously ill as those in our 'experimental' groups? (2) Are standards of recovery less stringent in our 'control' than in our 'experimental' groups? It is difficult to answer these questions definitively, in view of the great divergencies of opinion between psychiatrists. From a close scrutiny of the literature I should say that the 'control' patients were probably at least as seriously ill as the 'experimental' patients, and possibly more so. As regards standards of recovery, I should think that those in Denker's study are as stringent as most of those used by psychoanalysts and eclectic psychiatrists, but that those used by the State Hospitals whose figures Landis quotes are very probably more lenient. In the absence of agreed standards of severity of illness, or of extent of recovery, it is not possible to go further.

In general, certain conclusions are possible from these data. They fail to prove that psychotherapy, Freudian or otherwise, facilitates the recovery of neurotic patients. They show that roughly two-thirds of a group of neurotic patients will recover or improve to a marked extent within about two years of the onset of their illness, whether they are treated by means of psychotherapy or not. This figure appears to be remarkably stable from one investigation to another, regardless of type of patient treated, standard of recovery employed, or method of therapy used. From the point of view of the neurotic, these figures are encouraging; from the point of view of the psychotherapist, they can hardly be called very favourable to his claims.

In saying this, I do not mean to imply that the figures quoted necessarily disprove the possibility of therapeutic effectiveness. There are obvious shortcomings in any actuarial comparison, and these shortcomings are particularly serious when there is so little agreement among psychiatrists relating even to the most fundamental concepts and definitions. Definite proof would require a special investigation, carefully planned and methodologically more adequate than these *ad hoc* comparisons. But even the much more modest conclusion that the figures fail to show any favourable effects of psychotherapy should give pause. We are left in the position where any belief in psychotherapy depends on faith, not on scientifically demonstrated fact. This faith may be justified or not; until its truth is demonstrated, however, it clearly cannot form part of science. That such a demonstration would be difficult cannot be denied; that it is essential for the future progress of therapy will be obvious.

It may be asked what would be required in order to achieve a satisfactory proof. The basic requirements would appear to be: (1) A valid and reliable method of assigning patients to classes (neurotic, psychotic, organic, etc.) and subclasses (hysteric, anxiety state, depressive, schizophrenic, etc.). This assignment would of course have to be based on a satisfactory taxonomic or nosological system of classification. (2) A valid and reliable method of assessing degrees of disorder, so that a lesser degree of disorder could be correlated with the course of psychotherapy. (3) A control group of patients not treated at all during the period of the experiment, so that a base line could be obtained against which to compare the effects of therapy. Given these requirements, the problem appears a simple and straightforward one; if any one of the requirements is not forthcoming, the problem is insoluble at the scientific level.

The third condition is difficult to fulfil because of social and ethical objections; there is no systematic difficulty there that could not be overcome. It is conditions 1 and 2 which raise insuperable difficulties at present. Psychiatry has elaborated a system of classification (or indeed a series of such systems) which appears to have little support in empirical studies, but is almost entirely based on clinical insight and unsupported speculation. In many cases, different systems contradict each other; thus the Freudians assume that normality, neurosis, and psychosis form one continuum of regression, while orthodox psychiatry appears to support the view that neurotic and psychotic disorders are as it were qualitatively different diseases which are independent of each other. Several other views are held by various groups, and there are many facts in contradiction to any hypothesis so far advanced. This problem is recognized by most psychiatrists, who put very little faith in diagnostic systems, and often shrugged off as being of little importance. Yet unless it is solved, it is difficult to see how such questions as the one regarding the effects of psychotherapy can be answered. The importance of taxonomy is often underrated by those interested in the dynamics (so-called) of human behaviour, yet without an adequate taxonomy progress is difficult if not impossible in these more nebulous and even less easily accessible regions.

Even if there were agreement on the main psychiatric groupings, yet the reliability of assigning patients to these classes would not be regarded as sufficient by most psychologists. The work of Ash (1949), Doering (1934), Elkin (1947), and many others has shown how much disagreement there is among psychiatrists even when questions of major classification (neurotic, psychotic, normal, mental defective) are at issue; anyone familiar with case conferences will know the frequency of almost total disagreement with respect to major classification between equally competent psychiatrists. Of particular interest in this connection are some figures reported by the Research Branch of the Information and Education Discussion in the U.S. War Department, showing the almost incredible differences in diagnosis between psychiatrists working in different establishments (Stouffer, 1950). (A detailed discussion of these figures is given in Chapter III.)

If we may then regard it as agreed that psychiatric diagnosis is of doubtful validity and low reliability, we may turn with interest to the clinical psychologists, in the hope that he may have used his scientific training in a fruitful attempt to arrive at a useful, reliable, and valid taxonomy. Perusal of research contributions will soon

dispel such optimistic thoughts. Far from improving on the somewhat arbitrary criteria used by the psychiatrist, the psychologist
has by and large succeeded merely in elaborating devices which
will give rather low correlations with these psychiatric classifications; in other words, he is content to take over the conceptualiza-
tions of the psychiatrist, and tag behind in a fruitless endeavour to
do rather less well what the psychiatrist could do without his aid!
If this be indeed the function of psychology in its diagnostic aspect,
then it is small wonder that so many psychologists have eschewed
the Kraepelinian straight-jacket in order to indulge in Freudian
manic spells which give them at least the illusion of usefulness.

This example is intended to illustrate a very important generalization, namely, that taxonomy, nosology, or classification lies
at the very root of scientific progress, and that until taxonomic
problems are solved in at least a preliminary way, scientific progress towards answering more complex problems is barred. The
history of science illustrates this again and again. Without the
work of Ray and Linnæus biology could not have advanced as it
did; Mendeleeff and his periodic table of the elements prepared
the way for the fundamental advances in physics which culminated
in the splitting of the atom. The importance of taxonomic concepts
in the physical sciences is often neglected because they sometimes
seem self-evident, and because their discovery frequently precedes
recorded history; this hardly affects the argument, however.
Measurement is essential to science, but before we can measure we
must know what it is we want to measure. Qualitative or taxonomic
discovery must precede quantitative measurement.

Unfortunately, psychology has tried to abort this stage of
development; it has attempted to run before it could walk. In its
desire to be 'dynamic', it has forgotten that before it is possible to
study movement, one must know at least to a limited extent what
it is that moves. Where this was realized, taxonomic concepts were
invented *ad hoc* to suit the argument, rather than allowed to grow
organically from the accumulated mass of facts. Freud's Thanatos
and Eros, for example, so similar in essence to the ancient Chinese
principles of *yang* and *yin*, can hardly be said to be the result of
scientific observation. Rather, they appear superimposed on observation at the dictate of philosophical doctrine. Such subservience
of fact to fiction has often appeared in science. Ancient Indian
anatomy, for instance, taught that the body contained ten systems
of ducts bearing the ten fluid products of the body to all portions

of it. Ducts and fluid products were actually observed; ten was considered to be the perfect number. Anatomists consequently sought for, and believed they had found, structures which agreed with the philosophers' notions of perfection. This type of taxonomy can hardly be considered scientifically useful.

The rest of this book, then, is concerned with the problem of taxonomy in psychology; the question of classifying and isolating traits and types, and of measuring them objectively. In particular, our interest has centred around the following questions. (1) It is customary among psychologists and psychiatrists to study neurotics and psychotics because of the light these abnormal states are believed to throw on the functioning of normal personality. The assumption is made that in mental disorder we observe ordinary human behaviour 'writ large', as it were; the disease process is believed to serve as a kind of magnifying glass or microscope which enlarges what is normally invisible to the naked eye. This assumption may be well founded, but it has certain implications which are closely related to problems of taxonomy. If the main types of neurosis (hysteria and psychasthenia) are the prototypes of a classification of normal human beings into extraverts and introverts, as Jung maintains; or if the main psychotic division into schizophrenics and manic depressives should be used for grouping normal human beings into types, as Kretschmer believes—then it must follow that neurosis and psychosis are not disorders qualitatively different from the ordinary run of personality differences found in the general population, but simply extremes on a continuum which includes everyone. This assumption is made explicitly by Kretschmer and at least implicitly by Jung; many psychiatrists would hold an opposite view at least with respect to the psychotic states. Geneticists like Kallman, who believe they have isolated the genes responsible for the transmission of psychotic insanity, must inevitably hold the qualitative view, of course, and thus be added to the majority of orthodox psychiatrists. This question of quantitative continuum or qualitative difference is too important to be decided by subjective impression or majority vote, however, and experiment must decide which of these conflicting views presents us with a more accurate model of reality. It will be shown later that our experiments strongly support the quantitative continuum hypothesis, both in the case of neurotic and of psychotic disorders.

(2) If we have, then, a continuum from normal to neurotic, and also from normal to psychotic, the question arises whether we

are dealing with two continua, as many psychiatrists would have us believe, or only with one continuum of 'psycho-sexual regression', as Freud and his followers assert. As is well known, to Freud the neurotic has partly regressed from the adult psychosexual adjustment, while the psychotic has regressed to a considerably greater extent; thus we would on his hypothesis be dealing with a continuum going from the normal, well adjusted person at the one end, through the partly regressed, poorly adjusted neurotic, to the completely regressed psychotic at the other end. In terms of dimensional analysis, the question may be reworded in this form:—If we take three groups (normals, neurotics, psychotics), can these be represented as occupying one dimension only, or are two dimensions required? It will be shown later that the Freudian theory has to be rejected, and that two dimensions are required to represent these three groups adequately.

(3) We have so far discussed 'neurotics' and 'psychotics' as if these were homogeneous groups. Yet it is well known that subgroups can be distinguished within the major groupings—hysterics, anxiety states, obsessionals, neurasthenics, and so forth within the neurotic complex, paranoids, manic depressives, schizophrenics, involutionals and so forth within the psychotic complex. It is with respect to these sub-groupings that typologies such as the Jungian or the Kretschmerian arise; clearly our dimensional analysis must deal with the questions raised by these sub-groups, as well as with problems of allocation of such groups as psychopaths and epileptics, whose precise provenance is much in doubt among psychiatrists, and whose position with respect to the major factors of neurosis and psychosis cannot be predicted with any certainty. Our experiments have dealt more with points one and two than with the present problem, but certain results reported in later chapters are relevant, and may serve as an introductory orientation.

Experiments and statistical models cannot exist *in vacuo*; they must be based on observational data. For our purposes, the obvious and indeed the only type of data lending themselves to analysis of the kind required were those collected through the use of psychological tests. Choice of tests, therefore, became an important part of our experimental design. The following considerations will serve to make explicit our basis of choice, and the reasons why we rejected certain types of test which have gained wide currency, such as the so-called projective techniques, and have concentrated on tests which have been much neglected lately, namely those types of test which I have called 'objective behaviour tests' (1950a).

It will be agreed by most psychologists that the subject-matter of a science of personality must be human behaviour. We may require intervening variables, hypothetical constructs, and theoretical concepts such as instincts, drives, reflexes, complexes, attitudes, or fixations in order to bring some kind of order into the confused mass of facts which observation offers us, but nevertheless our starting point must be actually observed behaviour—provided we are careful to include all aspects of verbal, autonomic, and involuntary behaviour. Most psychologists would also agree, perhaps, with Wolfle's (1949) 'fundamental principle of personality measurement': 'An individual reveals his own personality through any change he makes upon any type of material.' Rephrased, this might read: An individual reveals his own personality through any observable item of behaviour. This would equate 'personality' with 'sum-total of behaviour', and with the reservation that some items of behaviour are more important than others—in the sense that they show a greater range of intercorrelation and of 'belongingness', and are more widely predictive than others—this definition would probably not be objected to too vehemently.

Personality study therefore starts with behaviour, and attempts to find general laws which will explain this behaviour; it must test these laws, and their predictive efficiency, against behaviour in situations relevant to the generalization embodied in the law in question. Measurement of a particular sector of behaviour is usually undertaken by means of a test. Such tests are often classified as being either 'projective' or 'psychometric', but this division is hardly adequate to denote a given test. There are a number of principles of classification which together denote a given test with sufficient accuracy.

(1) *Classification according to Type of Stimulus*

Test material may vary according to the degree of *organization* or *structure* present in it. In highly structured material, the correct response is uniquely determined by the relations existing between the different parts of the test; in less well structured material, the discrimination of the parts, and their interpretation, often form the major task of the subject. This classification clearly does not imply a dichotomy; there are different degrees of organization or structure from the typical intelligence test at the one extreme, through

38 SCIENCE AND PERSONALITY

the relatively well-structured Thematic Apperception Test, the less well-structured M.A.P.S. or Rorschach Tests, to the almost entirely unstructured Stern Cloud-Pictures or the Buck H-T-P test at the other. In general, we may say that the more firmly structured the test material or the test-situation are, the more restricted will be the variety of ways in which the subject can react to the test.

(2) *Classification according to Type of Reaction*

The two main ways in which the subject can react to the stimulus situation are the *verbal* and the *non-verbal*. These can themselves again be classified, the verbal mode of reaction into *written* and *spoken*, and the non-verbal into *autonomic* and *motor* response.

(3) *Classification according to Mode of Response*

The two main modes of response are the *creative* and the *selective*. In the creative type of response, the subject is required to supply the solution to the problem quite unaided and entirely from within himself, while in the selective type of response he is merely asked to choose one of several predetermined solutions. While the selective response method is used more frequently in connection with intelligence tests, and the creative response method in connection with tests of temperament and character, this correlation is far from perfect, and interesting advances have been made recently by using selective responses in connection with such tests as the Rorschach, the Word Association, and the Sentence Completion.

(4) *Classification according to Method of Scoring*

Scoring may be objective or subjective. Scoring is objective when only one symbol, numerical or otherwise, can be assigned to any particular reaction and when all observers would assign the same symbol to that reaction. Scoring is subjective when either there is considerable disagreement between different competent observers regarding the symbol to be assigned or when no attempt is made to assign a symbol at all, but only a general impressionistic interpretation is given of the subject's performance.

(5) *Classification according to Interpretation of Score*

The final product of the subject's reaction to the stimulus, whether it be verbal or non-verbal, creative or selective, may be classified as being either *symbolic* or *non-symbolic*. Tests of fluency, of persistence, of suggestibility, of perseveration, or of level of aspiration give scores which are interpreted directly; others, such as the Frank Sexual Symbol test, the Dream Interpretation technique, or most drawing, painting, and play tests and techniques make use of symbolic interpretation of the products. Both methods of interpretation may of course be combined in dealing with the results of any one test.

(6) *Classification according to Mental Mechanism used*

Tests can be classified on the rather theoretical basis of the mental mechanisms believed to be employed in them. Thus, some tests are thought to call forth responses based on the principle of *projection* (such as the Thematic Apperception Test, for instance); others are based on the hypothesis that responses are determined by the principle of *identification* (the Szondi test); others still make use of *reaction-formation*, *regression*, and various other Freudian mechanisms. Clearly, little agreement can be expected on allocation of tests according to this principle, particularly as experimental evidence for the very existence of the mental mechanisms in question is almost completely lacking.

It is interesting to note in this connection that the one mental mechanism which 'projective' tests do not usually employ, in the opinion of experts in this field, is the mechanism of *projection*. Sargent (1945), in her review of 'projective' tests, makes a rather disingenuous defence of this confusing practice, as does Bell (1948) in his book on *Projective Techniques*. Semantic oddities of this kind, however, have not prevented the widespread use of this term.[1]

[1] A word should be said here about the term 'test'. A test is defined by Warren (1934) as 'a routine examination administered to individuals belonging to the same group in order to determine the relative position of a given individual in the group with respect to one or more mental traits, motor abilities, etc., or in order to compare one group with another in these characteristics'. It will be seen that, if we accept this definition, a projection test becomes a contradiction in terms, as the 'projective hypothesis' seems to deny the very existence of these mental traits which are presupposed in the definition of the term 'test'. By and large, then, it would appear that the term 'projection test' has an unfortunate resemblance to the term 'Holy Roman Empire', which was not, strictly speaking, an Empire, not entirely Roman, and very far from holy; projection tests are not tests as the term is usually understood and they do not even claim to make use of the mechanisms of projection as defined by Freud and his adherents. The term is a bad one and should be dropped from psychology.

(7) Classification according to Method of Administration

Tests may be administered in the form of *individual* or *group* tests; it is doubtful if this differentiation is of any fundamental importance. It is included here for the sake of completeness.

The seven principles of classification briefly discussed above are relatively independent of each other; all possible combinations of type of stimulus, type of reaction, method of response, method of scoring, interpretation of score, and mental mechanism hypothesized may be found. Frequently the same test may be used in different ways by different investigators, changing its classification under some of these headings.

Two techniques are used almost exclusively in current practice of personality testing. They are the questionnaire—well structured, with verbal reactions, selective response, objectively scored, and not symbolically interpreted—and the so-called projective tests— little structured, with verbal reactions, creative response, subjectively scored, and often symbolically interpreted. It will be noted that both procedures duplicate psychiatric methods, and may under special circumstances be substituted for them. The questionnaire duplicates the psychiatric interview; the 'projective' test duplicates the interpretation of dreams and symptoms by the psychiatrist. Both are essentially verbal in nature.

While in our research we have not neglected these procedures, we have laid most stress on what might be called 'objective behaviour tests'. These tests are highly structured, call for non-verbal reactions—either autonomic or motor, are objectively scored, and require no interpretation. This type of test has appeared to us to be in the tradition of behaviouristic psychology. It seems premature for clinical psychologists to throw over what is most distinctive in their intellectual heritage, in order to don with unseemly haste the Emperor's New Clothes. It is our belief—and some support for it will be found in the pages that follow—that objective behaviour tests tap fundamental, constitutional depths of personality organization which questionnaires and 'projective tests' do not reach, while conversely these psychiatric types of tests are highly reflective of passing moods, sentiments, feelings, and so forth. As we are concerned more with the underlying dimensions of personality than with the small ripples on the surface, our choice may perhaps be intelligible.

In one other respect will our work be found to deviate from

that of many others in this field. Students of personality have often used personality ratings, made by psychiatrists, teachers, supervisors, or laymen as an aid in the classification of human traits. Outstanding examples here are, for instance, Burt (1937), Cattell (1946), and Moore (1930). In our opinion the value of ratings cannot compare with that of tests; tests are measured items of performance, while ratings imply judgments formed on the basis of personal impression of performances inaccurately perceived, sampled under biased conditions, and evaluated according to unknown standards. Quite frequently, the very traits rated are selected according to criteria which would encounter severe criticism; Burt's work, for example, is based on the rating of the strength of McDougallian 'instincts' in children by teachers. The choice of a system of classification some thirty years out of date, and discredited in contemporary psychology for many valid reasons, makes this work interesting more as a statistical exercise than as a genuine contribution to the study of personality. Cattell's work is not subject to this criticism, and it must be admitted that he has seen quite clearly that the value of syndromes and factors derived from ratings is dependent on verification through the use of other methods. Nevertheless, until such verification is forthcoming—and it will be noted that some of the results reported in this volume agree well with Cattell's analysis—conclusions based on ratings must at best be regarded as suggestive only, and as possibly telling us more about the rater than about the ratee.

It might be retorted that in our own work ratings have played an important part also. This is true, but it should be pointed out that our use of ratings and diagnoses has been fundamentally different from that of the above-mentioned authors. We have used ratings as a kind of scaffolding, to aid in the construction of a solid edifice based on objective measures of behaviour; once this edifice is constructed the scaffolding may be taken down. It plays its part merely as a transitional aid; it is not intended to replace the finished building. Just how this method works is described in detail in the following chapter.

Chapter Two

THE DIMENSIONAL APPROACH

IF our main task is to provide at least a provisional solution to the taxonomic problem in personality research, then we are involved automatically in the problem of finding appropriate *dimensions of personality*. And for a method to aid in the solution we must turn to factor analysis, because in spite of the acknowledged difficulties and weaknesses of this method there does not exist, at the present stage of our knowledge, any other method which could aid us in our quest (Eysenck, 1949). This chapter will be devoted to a discussion of the relation between factor analysis and dimensional research, as well as to an investigation of certain criticisms often made of the factorial method. It will also contain an elementary introduction to the method of *criterion analysis* which has been introduced to overcome some of these criticisms, and to bring factor analysis into closer touch with the hypothetico-deductive method (Eysenck, 1950).[1]

All through this book, then, we are concerned with problems of psychological dimensions. These problems are absolutely fundamental in science. If science depends on measurement, we must know what to measure. Thus we cannot make direct comparisons of magnitude between things which are qualitatively unlike, i.e. which do not lie along one dimension. We cannot form a dimensionally inhomogeneous equation, such as '23 hours + 14 horses = 20 sacks of potatoes + 17 miles' without violating common sense as well as physical propriety. Yet similarly dimensionally inhomogeneous equations are formed constantly by psychologists and psychiatrists because of our fundamental lack of knowledge regarding 'dimensional homogeneity'.

The reader may object that choice of dimensions in psychology,

---

[1] The first part of this chapter has on purpose been written at a very simplified level in order that the rest of the book might be intelligible to readers without a background in factor analysis. It should be omitted by readers already fully familiar with factorial techniques and their logical basis.

particularly if such choice is dependent on statistical procedures such as factor analysis, is arbitrary, thus setting psychology off from the remainder of science. This implies a profound misunderstanding of the procedures of physical science. In a very real sense, we may say that in physics 'the choice of dimensions is arbitrary' (Scott-Blair, 1950). 'If we are moving towards or away from a source of light or sound, the colour or pitch appears to change. It is easy to calculate our speed from the ratio of change in wavelength to normal wave-length, which is, of course, a dimensionless number . . . we should be quite justified in *defining* velocity by this number instead of as a length divided by a time.' 'There is nothing absolute about dimensions . . . they may be anything consistent with a set of definitions which agree with the experimental facts' (Bridgman, 1931).

If, then, dimensions are in a sense arbitrary in physics, it seems unreasonable to expect factor analysis or any other statistical procedure to give us psychological dimensions which are not up to a point arbitrary. All possible systems of dimensions to describe a given set of facts must be convertible into each other, as they all must agree with the experimental facts; if two systems of dimensions disagree an empirical test becomes possible to decide which of the two leads to deductions verifiable by experiment. Whenever two factor analysts disagree in their analysis of a given table of intercorrelations, it is possible either (1) to convert one set of factors into the other through a set of intermediate equations, thus showing that these are merely alternative dimensional systems equally adequate to represent the facts, or else it is possible (2) to show that one solution is statistically unsound, or leads to deductions which can be disproved. The argument between Spearman (1927) and Thurstone (1935) was of the latter kind, leading to a disproof of Spearman's original position; most arguments in the literature, however, are of the former kind.

To acknowledge that one's choice of dimensions is arbitrary does not mean, of course, that *any* set of dimensions may be chosen. In practice, the restriction imposed by the requirement that dimensions 'may be anything consistent with a set of definitions which *agree with the experimental facts*' rules out all but a very few alternative sets of dimensions, and as facts accumulate choice becomes very restricted indeed. Even to find one single set of dimensions to embrace all the known facts of personality research may appear a tall order; to find several such sets would tax the imagination of most psychologists unduly. The undoubted existence of several sets of dimensions, proposed by the various schools, is accountable in the main by the very simple procedure of unmercifully rejecting all facts not fitting into a given scheme. If psychologists followed the example of physicists and rejected any model which was clearly in opposition to experimentally verified facts, the ground would be cleared of much rubbish the main effect of which is to hinder the advance of psychological knowledge.

Science, as we have seen, attempts to describe the multiform world of experience through the formulation of abstract laws and the creation of abstract categories. This process of abstraction is absolutely fundamental to science; without abstraction there can be nothing but observation of particular occurrences. As Whitehead (1929) puts it, 'the paradox is now fully established that the utmost abstractions are the true weapon with which to control our thought of concrete fact. To be abstract is to transcend particular concrete occasions of actual happenings. The construction with which the scientist ends has the neatness and orderliness that is quite unlike the varied and multiform world of common sense, yet, since science grows out of and returns to the world of common sense, there must be a precise connection between the neat, trim, tidy, exact world, which is the goal of science, and the untidy fragmentary world of common sense.'

There is of course an abundance of abstractions in psychology —instincts, Œdipus and other complexes, reflexes and conditioned reflexes, maternal overprotection, transference, need and press, ergs and metanergs, abilities and propensities, sensory thresholds and acuities, colour blindness, hereditary predisposition—all these concepts are to varying degrees abstracted from observed happenings. Criticism of concepts such as these must rest, not on the fact that they are abstractions, but rather on the fact that they fail to show the 'precise connection' with the observed happenings; that they fail to account for all the observations made; and that they fail to forecast accurately future observations not yet made. Similarly, 'factors' and other statistical conceptions should not be criticized for being abstract concepts; valid criticism can come only from a demonstration that they fail to show a precise connection between observation and hypothesis. Questions regarding the 'actual existence' of factors, or criticisms of factors as being 'statistical artefacts', show a complete misunderstanding of the use of concepts in science; a physicist would regard as meaningless questions regarding the 'real existence' of the ether, or criticisms of the concept of the electron as being a 'statistical artefact'. Concepts are useful in science in so far as they help in introducing order into a confused field; they cease to be useful when they fail to account for all the relevant phenomena, or when they cease to give rise to accurate predictions regarding new and hitherto unobserved phenomena.[1]

Let us start our discussion of factor analysis with a simple and straightforward example, in which we shall as always pay attention to the scientific logic of the method rather than its mathematical foundations. Let us assume, as Spearman did in his revolutionary article in 1904, that underlying all cognitive tasks there is one general ability, which we may call 'g' or 'intelligence'. Let us also assume that different people possess this ability to varying degree, and that different tasks call for this ability in varying degree. Let us make one further assumption, namely, that there is no other ability required in order to succeed in these tasks except 'g' and something which is specific to each particular task—a specific ability which we may call s_1 for task 1, s_2 for task 2, and so on to s_n for task n.

Now if by some magic we could obtain an accurate measure of the 'intelligence' of a random sample of people, it would be possible to correlate this measure—which we may denote by a capital 'G'—with each of our tests. Let us suppose that we have four tests—A, B, C, and D—and that the correlations of these tests with 'G' are ·9, ·8, ·7, and ·6 respectively. It can be shown that, given our assumptions, the correlation between any two tests is given by the product of their respective correlations with 'G'. In other words, tests A and B will correlate ·9 × ·8 = ·72, tests C and D will

---

[1] We may in this connection draw attention to the procedure used by Einstein in constructing his theory of relativity. In the first edition of his *General and Special Theory of Relativity*, Einstein based his physical interpretation of the universe on Minkovsky's and Riemann's geometrical premises. Thus, he established for all space-time momenta, including their electro-magnetic behaviour, a hypothetical, geometrical system of parameters: X_1, X_2, X_3, X_4. *It is neither essential for these parameters to have actual existence in this universe nor for them to correspond to our sensory perception.* They are assumed in a purely mathematical sense as tools that enable us to explain what we know as the physical universe. During the year 1933 Einstein adopted the five parameter system (X_1, X_2, X_3, X_4, X_5) because the previous system failed to explain certain physical momenta, thus requiring the introduction of a new parameter. No physicist would take seriously the question: 'Have X_1, X_2 etc. any real existence?'

correlate ·7 × ·6 = ·42, and so forth. This may best be shown in the form of a table (Table I):

TABLE I

Correlations with 'G'	Test A ·9	Test B ·8	Test C ·7	Test D ·6
·9	(·81)	·72	·63	·54
·8	·72	(·64)	·56	·48
·7	·63	·56	(·49)	·42
·6	·54	·48	·42	(·36)

The two-digit values in the central part of the table form what is known as a matrix, that is to say a rectangular array of figures. It will be seen that the diagonal values are put in brackets; this is done because it is impossible to correlate a test with itself. We can of course correlate parallel forms of a test, or repeat the administration of a test, or use split halves. None of these methods, however, would give us values dependent only on 'g'; they would all be influenced by the specific ability required by the test in question, by memory, practice, and all sorts of other factors.   Consequently they are estimated by analogy with the other values in the matrix, i.e. they are formed by multiplying the 'G' correlation of a test with itself, i.e. by squaring it. In this way, ·9 × ·9 = ·81 for test A, and so forth. These values are not, as are the other values in the table, subject to empirical check. They form part of the general hypothesis we are investigating.

Let us look at this table a little more closely. All the values in column D will be seen to be proportional to those in column C; ·63/·54 = ·56/·48 = ·49/·42 = ·42/·36 = 1·167. Similarly, any other pair of columns is proportional. This fact can be put in many different ways. Let us take the intercorrelations of two tests—say A and D—with two other tests—say B and C. These correlations are:

$$·72 \quad ·63$$
$$·48 \quad ·42$$

By the proportionality rule, ·72/·48 = ·63/·42. This can also be expressed in the form: ·72 × ·42 = ·48 × ·63, which is identical with (·72 × ·42) − (·48 × ·63) = 0. This last expression is known as the tetrad criterion; it expresses the general rule that if in a given set of tests the assumptions made above are borne out in fact, then any tetrad (set of four correlations) formed in this manner must come to zero within the limits of the sampling error.

We can now dispense with the idea that by some magic we had managed to obtain an accurate measure of the 'intelligence' of the persons in our sample, a measure which enabled us to calculate the correlations of 'G' with tests A, B, C, and D. We start out, as in fact we always must do, with the matrix of intercorrelations, as actually observed on a sample of the population. We also start out with an hypothesis—the hypothesis that these intercorrelations are due to one factor ('g') only, and that there is nothing in common between any two tests that cannot be accounted for in full by this factor. We can then deduce, in the manner shown above, that if our hypothesis is indeed correct, then it would follow that the observed intercorrelations should show a certain pattern of pro-portionality—in other words, that all the possible tetrads should come to zero. Having verified this deduction, we may wish to know how closely each of our four tests correlates with this hypothetical factor 'g'. This can be calculated very easily in a number of ways. Quite obviously, if we knew the diagonal values, we could immediately calculate the required correlations by taking in each cast the square root of the diagonal value; $\sqrt{\cdot81} = \cdot9$, $\sqrt{\cdot64} = \cdot8$, and so forth. Unfortunately, the diagonal values are not given to us. But we may deduce them from a knowledge of the proportional arrangement of the whole table. We can form a tetrad in which one of the values is the sought-for diagonal value, which as it is unknown we may denote by an X. We then get equations of the kind:

$$(X \times \cdot48) - (\cdot72 \times \cdot54) = 0$$

from which we can then calculate that $X = \cdot81$, and that conse-quently the correlation between 'G' and A is equal to $\cdot9$. This correlation is customarily referred to as the 'saturation' of test A with factor 'g', or more simply test A's factor saturation. The factor saturations of the other tests can be calculated in a similar manner.

So far, we have been dealing with a purely hypothetical example. To lend an air of verisimilitude to the proceedings, let us look at the actual correlations observed between four 'tests' of neuroticism (Table II). Each of these 'tests' is a questionnaire, carefully designed to measure a different area of this general field. Test A measures psychosomatic complaints, test B measures childhood symptoms, test C measures acceptance of soldier role, and test D measures sociability. Each of these tests had been shown previously to be a scale or a quasi-scale in Guttman's (1947) sense of the term; the sample consisted of some four thousand normal and neurotic soldiers.[1] Here are the correlations, together with the diagonal values and the 'saturations' of each test with the hypothetical factor of 'neuroticism'.

TABLE II

Correlation with Neuroticism	Test A ·83	Test B ·67	Test C ·56	Test D ·46
·83	(·69)	·55	·50	·38
·67	·55	(·45)	·36	·34
·56	·50	·36	(·32)	·25
·46	·38	·34	·25	(·21)

As these correlations are observed correlations, they are of course subject to sampling errors, and the products of the factor saturations will not reproduce the observed correlations exactly. A matrix showing the products of the factor saturations is called a product matrix, and can be compared with the original matrix of observed correlations, to show how closely the hypothetical factor accounts for the actual test intercorrelations. Below (Table III) is given the product matrix for comparison with Table II.

TABLE III

	·83	·67	·56	·46
·83	(·69)	·56	·46	·38
·67	·56	(·45)	·38	·31
·56	·46	·38	(·32)	·26
·46	·38	·31	·26	(·21)

It will be seen that observed and hypothetical correlations agree fairly well. Where the observed correlation is ·55, the hypothetical one is ·56, and so forth; the average deviation, regardless of sign and omitting the diagonal values, is less than ·02. We may conclude that our hypothesis gives a fairly good picture of the 'untidy, fragmentary world of common sense'.

If we subtract the (hypothetical) 'product' correlations, as

[1] These figures are taken from Stouffer et al. (1950).

shown in Table III from the observed correlations, as shown in Table II, we get what are known as 'residual' correlations, i.e. correlations between the tests after the influence of the hypothetical factor has been removed. These residual correlations, in the present case, are all insignificant and due only to sampling and other chance errors, but that is not always so, and it will be clear that in principle it is possible to analyse a matrix of residual correlations in exactly the same way as it was possible to analyse the original matrix of observed correlations. Computations are actually performed in a rather different manner, but this does not invalidate the point made.

It is often said that while the argument from the original hypotheses to the necessity of finding proportionality and zero tetrad differences is rigorous, the finding of such zero tetrad differences can by no means be taken as a proof that the hypotheses are justified. That of course is true; no hypothesis can ever be *proved* to be right. All we can do is to make deductions from our hypotheses and attempt to show that within the limits of sampling errors and errors of observation these deductions are verified. If deductions are not verified, the hypothesis is disproved; if deductions are verified, the hypothesis is confirmed. There is, however, no way of assuring that if further deductions are made, these will also be confirmed; in that sense proof is forever impossible. Newton's hypothesis continued to be confirmed for three hundred years in the wide variety of deductions made from it; yet finally some deductions were shown to be contrary to observed fact (motion of Mercury; bending of light rays). Here, as in so many other respects, factorial theory should not be singled out for criticism which, if justified, applies to all scientific methodology. The hypothesis of a single factor can be put forward, deductions can be made from it, and these deductions can be verified or refuted. If the deduction of tetrad differences amounting to zero is verified, this does not *prove* the correctness of the hypothesis, but it does provide striking support for it.

We may now turn to two questions which are of the greatest importance in factorial analysis, and which we are in a position to discuss even on the basis of the very simple statistical model we have constructed so far. The first of these questions is: 'Having found a factor in this manner, how can we interpret it?' The second question is: 'If our interpretation of a factor involves, as it often does, an external criterion, why factor analyse at all—why not work through multiple regression and other orthodox procedures in order to get maximum correlation between tests and criterion?'

Let us take an example. In the matrix of correlations below (Table IV) let A stand for a conventional test of intelligence, and B, C, and D for ratings made by three teachers of the intellectual ability of a group of children known to them, all of whom have been given the test. From these intercorrelations we can show that the hypothesis of a single factor as being responsible for all the observed values is tenable, and we can proceed to calculate the factor saturations of test and teachers' ratings alike. These are shown at the top and at the left side of the matrix of intercorrelations.

TABLE IV

	A ·9	B ·7	C ·6	D ·5
·9	(·81)	·63	·54	·35
·7	·63	(·49)	·42	35
·6	·54	·42	(·36)	·30
·5	·45	·35	·30	(·25)

If we correlate the average of our three teachers' ratings with our test, we find a value of ·71. We might therefore say that as far as orthodox statistics carries us we end up with a moderate correlation between our test and what we may regard provisionally as our criterion. We cannot tell why this correlation is not higher—possibly the test is at fault, possibly the criterion is imperfect.

The factor analysis shows us that teachers' ratings and test are measuring one and the same trait; it also shows us that there is nothing in common to the three teachers' ratings that is not also in common to the test. In other words, test and ratings alike are giving an estimate of the same underlying, hypothetical trait of intelligence. That being so, we can see that the test is successful to the extent indicated by its factor saturation (·9), while the teachers' ratings are rather less successful (·7, ·6, and ·5). Even if we average the teachers' ratings, the correlation of the combined rating with the factor would only amount to ·79. Factor analysis, therefore, has enabled us to supersede the original criterion and to show that our test is a better measure of intelligence than was the criterion we started out with. We may now dismiss the original criterion and rely exclusively on our test, as giving us a better estimate of a child's intelligence than do the ratings. (In practice, of course, many more tests, teachers, and children would have to be used before such a conclusion could be accepted. We are only interested here in the logic of the argument, not in its practical aspects.)

Another method of looking at the question of the criterion suggests itself. In Table II we gave the intercorrelations of four tests of neuroticism, and calculated their saturations for this factor. It is possible to analyse the differences in score on each of these four tests for a normal and a neurotic group, and to compare the success with which each test accomplishes the task of segregation with its factor saturation. If the factor we have isolated is really identified correctly as one of neuroticism, then we should expect the ability of a test to discriminate between normals and neurotics to be proportional to its saturation for the factor; the test with the highest factor saturation should give the best discrimination, the test with the second highest saturation the second best discrimination, and so forth. Table V shows percentage of normals and neurotics having 'neurotic' scores on each of the tests, difference between the two percentages, biserial correlation of each test with the 'normal versus neurotic' dichotomy, and the factor saturations previously given.

TABLE V

	Normals	Neurotics	Difference	Biserial Correlations	Factor Saturations
	%	%			
Psychosomatic complaints	29	89	60	·66	·83
Childhood symptoms	20	53	33	·38	·67
Acceptance of soldier role	31	59	28	·35	·56
Sociability	16	45	29	·33	·46

It will be seen that the column giving the factor saturations is directly proportional to the column giving the biserial correlations of each test with the dichotomy 'normal versus neurotic', as required by our hypothesis. As this column of correlations between tests and criterion will play a considerable part in our argument later, we may perhaps give it a special name and call it the 'Criterion Column'. At the moment, let us merely note the fact that this proportionality is unlikely to have arisen by chance; that it is in line with our prediction based on a certain interpretation of our factor; and that our faith in the accuracy and correctness of our interpretation is therefore considerably strengthened. We have not *proved* that our hypothesis is correct; we have merely shown that a relatively large number of facts can without distortion be subsumed under one consistent set of concepts.

In doing so, however, we have made an assumption which is not supported by the data so far given. We have assumed that 'neuroticism' is a trait which forms a continuum from the 'normal' to the 'neurotic' end, and that our groups of normals and neurotics are merely random samples chosen from different points of this continuum. We may present this assumption diagrammatically, as in Figure 3, letting the ordinate represent the hypothetical

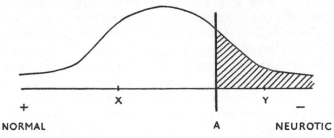

NORMAL   A   NEUROTIC

Figure 3.—Hypothetical 'Neuroticism' Continum

continuum, and plotting the number of people falling at each point along the abscissa. We may assume a normal distribution for the sake of the argument; in actual fact the particular form of distribution is not of any importance. Points near the plus end of our hypothetical continuum represent well integrated, emotionally stable, non-neurotic personalities; points towards the minus end of the hypothetical continuum represent poorly integrated, emotionally unstable, neurotic personalities. At point A we have drawn a line to indicate that people located to the right of this point are particularly liable in our society to be referred to psychiatrists, to be labelled 'neurotic', and to be treated by means of a variety of medical and psychological methods. Chance errors will ensure that some people to the right of this point will not in fact be so diagnosed and treated, although strictly speaking they ought to be, while some people to the left of point A, particularly those in its close proximity, will be diagnosed as neurotics, although they deserve this label less than others who manage to avoid it. But by and large such chance errors will only attenuate the accuracy of this division into two classes; they will not invalidate it.

This hypothesis should be contrasted with another hypothesis which is not contradicted by any of the data we have so far considered. It may be maintained, and in fact it is often maintained both by popular opinion and by some psychiatrists, that 'neurotics' are *qualitatively* different from 'normals'. This view would recognize no intervening stages; a person is either a neurotic, or he is not. In some cases this clear qualitative difference is obscured, to all appearances, by other factors overlaying this fundamental dichotomy, but when these are cleared away a person is found to fall quite definitely into one or the other of these two categories. Such categorical or qualitative thinking has always characterized early stages of scientific progress; usually it is shown later that what was considered qualitatively different at one time is really reducible to quantitative variation along some kind of continuum. What is required is an *experimentum crucis*, i.e. an experiment in which deductions are made from the two contrasting hypotheses which are mutually contradictory, so that one set of deductions can definitely be shown to be false. Again, this does not prove that the other hypothesis is correct; it merely adduces evidence in its support.

On the basis of the qualitative hypothesis, we would assume that with respect to whatever it was that differentiated normals from neurotics, both populations would be homogeneous; in other words, there would be no gradations of 'normality' or 'neuroticism'. This in turn would imply that tests which differentiated between normals and neurotics would not show any particular pattern of intercorrelations within the normal group only, or within the neurotic group only. On the average, these intercorrelations should amount to zero.

On the basis of the quantitative hypothesis, our prediction would be quite different. We may approach this matter in the following way. Let us consider two tests, A and B, both of which are known to discriminate significantly between normals and neurotics. Now let us take our group of normal subjects only. If our quantitative hypothesis is correct, it follows that this normal group may be subdivided into two parts at some arbitrary point X. Those to the left of X are relatively more stable, better integrated people than those to the right of X. It would follow that they should do better on both tests A and B than those on the right. But if there is a tendency for some people to do well on both tests, and for others to do poorly, then quite clearly these two tests would be found to be correlated. On the basis of our quantitative hypothesis, therefore, we would expect A and B to be positively correlated. Generalizing this to n tests, we may say that any group of tests which discriminate between normals and neurotics should show positive intercorrelations when only the normal group is considered. The same considerations, of course, apply to the neurotic group. This group also may arbitrarily be divided into two at an arbitrary point Y, and again it can be shown that on the basis of our quantitative hypothesis positive intercorrelations would be expected.

We go one step further. Not only should the intercorrelations (within either the normal or the neurotic group) be positive; they should be proportional to the ability of the respective tests to discriminate between normals and neurotics. If a test discriminates well between normals and neurotics, then it should intercorrelate highly with other tests; if it discriminates poorly, then it should show low intercorrelations. In other words, if we take our matrix of intercorrelations for the normal group and factor analyse it, then our factor saturations should be proportional to the correlations of the tests with the normal versus neurotic criterion. Similarly, if we take our matrix of intercorrelations for the neurotic group and factor analyse it, then our factor saturations should be proportional to the correlations of the tests with the normal versus neurotic criterion. As a corollary, it follows that the factor saturations derived from the two matrices (the normal and the neurotic) should be proportional to each other.

An example may make this argument clearer. In Table II we have given the intercorrelations and the factor analysis of four tests of neuroticism, for a mixed normal and neurotic population. Below are given the matrices of intercorrelations for normal and neurotic subjects separately. Results of a factor analysis are also given in each case.

In Table VIII are given the factor saturations for the four tests for the normal and the neurotic groups separately and the Criterion Column (i.e. the column of biserial correlations between tests and the dichotomy normal versus neurotic). It will be obvious to the casual observer that the three columns show a distinct proportionality.

TABLE VI

NORMAL GROUP

	·80	·52	·50	·28
·80	(·64)	·41	·46	·19
·52	·41	(·27)	·20	·16
·50	·46	·20	(·25)	·15
·28	·19	·16	·15	(·08)

TABLE VII

NEUROTIC GROUP

	·65	·68	·42	·42
·65	(·42)	·44	·28	·28
·68	·44	(·46)	·30	·31
·42	·28	·30	(·18)	·18
·42	·28	·31	·18	(·18)

TABLE VIII

Criterion Column	Factor Saturations: Normal Group	Factor Saturations: Neurotic Group
·66	·80	·65
·38	·52	·68
·35	·50	·42
·33	·28	·42

In practice, of course, no conclusions should be based on results from four tests, and on simple casual observation of degree of proportionality. We may therefore broaden the scope of our example and present data from a rather larger sample of tests. Our example was originally taken from an investigation employing fifteen tests altogether (Stouffer, 1950). We have calculated, from correlations given in the original report, factor saturations for the normal group and factor saturations for the neurotic group, and compared these with the criterion column. The full results are set out in Table IX. Again, it will be seen that the factor saturations are proportional to each other, and to the Criterion Column. This proportionality can best be expressed in the form of a correlation coefficient. The two columns of factor saturations correlate together ·82; the Criterion Column correlates with the factor saturations for the normal group ·88, and with the factor saturations for the neurotic group ·81. All three values are highly significant, and are clearly different from the zero values to be expected on the basis of the qualitative hypothesis. We may therefore conclude that our data lend support to the quantitative hypothesis, and refute the qualitative hypothesis.

TABLE IX

Title of Scale	Criterion Column	Factor Saturations: Normal Group	Factor Saturations: Neurotic Group
1. Psychosomatic complaints	·66	·69 (·15)	·56 (·16)
2. Childhood neurotic symptoms	·38	·49 (·09)	·58 (− ·01)
3. Personal adjustment (−)	·42	·67 (·09)	·68 (·05)
4. Over-sensitivity	·33	·48 (·45)	·56 (·50)
5. Childhood fears	·33	·42 (·16)	·52 (·02)
6. Acceptance of soldier role (−)	·35	·58 (− ·15)	·48 (− ·29)
7. Worrying	·27	·59 (·02)	·56 (·09)
8. Sociability (−)	·33	·33 (·03)	·56 (·08)
9. Participation in sports (−)	·28	·28 (− ·14)	·34 (− ·26)
10. Identification with war (−)	·12	·40 (− ·02)	·31 (− ·00)
11. Childhood fighting behaviour (−)	·18	·30 (− ·32)	·17 (− ·59)
12. Childhood school adjustment (−)	·11	·15 (·09)	·19 (·06)
13. Relations with parents	·12	·10 (·06)	·20 (·20)
14. Emancipation from parents (−)	·08	·20 (− ·34)	·18 (− ·24)
15. Mobility	·09	− ·04 (·31)	·05 (·24)

Figures in brackets are referred to on page 58 and should be omitted at first reading. Tests whose scores have been multiplied by − 1 in order to make coefficients in the Criterion Column positive are marked thus: (−).

So far, we have been concerned with patterns of intercorrelations which show the particular hierarchical or proportional features which are summed up in saying that the tetrad differences vanish. As it happens, however, matrices showing this particular pattern are quite rare, and in the majority of cases the hypothesis that only one factor is responsible for the intercorrelations can be shown to be false. When that happens we move over into rather more difficult territory, and begin to deal with multiple factor analysis, i.e. we attempt to account for our observed correlations in terms of several independent factors.

Let us again begin with an example. Below (Table X) are given the intercorrelations of four tests (questionnaires) dealing with lack of personal adjustment, oversensitivity, lack of emanci-

pation from parents, and mobility. No factor analysis was carried
out, and no diagonal values are therefore given.

TABLE X

	A	B	C	D
A	—	·49	·11	·04
B	·49	—	·05	·12
C	·11	·05	—	−·28
D	·04	·12	−·28	—

It will be seen that the negative correlation between tests C and
D completely upsets any attempt to account for the correlations in
this table in terms of one factor common to all the tests. Except
for it, all the other tests correlate together positively, showing that
they all measure something in common—presumably the same
factor of 'neuroticism' we found before. Then how can we account
for the presence of this negative correlation?

Perhaps the nature of the tests will give us a clue. 'Emancipation from parents' is defined by the authors of the test as involving
both actual physical emancipation involved in leaving home, and
the psychic emancipation implied by the establishment of satisfactory heterosexual relationships. 'Mobility' denotes unstable employment record and much geographical moving around. Both
the 'mobile' and the 'non-emancipated' tend to be more neurotic;
yet the correlation between the two tendencies is negative. Clearly
another factor is at work over and above 'neuroticism', and it may
be surmised that there are two kinds of neurotic: the type that is
caught up in mother's apron strings, is shy, sensitive, worrying,
'dysthymic', anxious, and depressed; and the more hysterical type
that has no difficulty in breaking emotional bonds (perhaps because they are never very firmly established?), that has never
settled down, has little persistence and seldom sticks long at anything once the initial enthusiasm has worn off. In other words,
we may here be dealing with a manifestation of the introvert-
extravert dichotomy as popularized by Jung (1923), which
stemmed from just such a clinical differentiation, made originally
by Janet (1909), of the main neurotic syndrome.

This hypothesis was suggested by our small matrix of intercorrelations; clearly it requires some proof before it can be taken
very seriously. If it were correct, what other tests would we expect

to correlate with this hypothetical introvert-extravert continuum? The introverted, non-emancipated child would presumably not have done as much childhood fighting as the extravert; he would not have participated in sports to the same extent; he would have greater difficulties in assuming the soldier role. The extravert might be expected to show, in addition to greater mobility, a tendency to have less close relations with his parents, and to be easily offended and resentful of criticism (grouped together by the authors of the test of 'oversensitivity'—perhaps a somewhat misleading term).

Let us return to Table IX. We have extracted a general factor of 'neuroticism' from the intercorrelations of fifteen tests for normal and neurotic groups separately. Perhaps we have left something unaccounted for in the original tables of correlations. Let us therefore form our product matrices and subtract them from our original matrices of observed correlations. These new residual matrices, i.e. matrices consisting of correlations left over after the first factor has been extracted, may be factor analysed in a similar way to that used on our original matrix. When we do that, we obtain the results given in Table IX, in brackets. It will be noticed that the new factors (one from the normal, the other from the neurotic group) are bipolar, that is to say, they have both negative and positive saturations. This is an inevitable feature of the method of extraction to which we shall return again; here let us just note that very roughly our anticipation is borne out. We find that 'emancipation' is at the opposite end of the scale to 'mobility', and that roughly at least the other tests are grouped as predicted. This second, bipolar, factor is not likely to be a mere chance phenomenon, because it appears in a very similar form in two entirely independent factor analyses—the one for the normal, the other for the neurotic group; the correlation between the two factors is ·91.

This example is not presented as proof of the existence of an introversion-extraversion factor; quite clearly there are too many steps missing in the argument, and too much subjectivity in the reasoning, to allow us to reach any such far-reaching conclusions. What we can conclude, however, without much doubt attaching to our argument, is that more than one factor is required to account for the observed correlations. Does this requirement affect in any way the methodological considerations discussed in connection with the case of the 'single factor' hypothesis? Unfortunately the breakdown of the simple model necessitates a somewhat complex rethinking of the logic underlying factor analysis, and to this we must next turn. Before doing so, however, we must introduce a simplified, diagrammatic method of presenting the results of factorial analyses which will be indispensable for our argument if we wish to avoid complex mathematical expressions.

Let us go back to Table IX, in which were given two factors extracted from each of the two matrices of intercorrelations observed, i.e. that derived from the normal and that derived from the neurotic population. Consider only the values obtained from the normals. Casual observation shows, and it can be proved by actual calculation, that the two factors we extracted from this matrix are independent of each other, i.e. they are not correlated. The fact that a test has a high saturation on one factor does not enable us in the slightest to predict whether its saturation on the other factor will be high, low, or negative. This notion of independence can be shown to correspond to the concept of orthogonality (being at right angles to each other) in geometry. We may therefore plot our two factors at right angles to each other, as in Figure 4. Each line represents a factor, the horizontal line the first factor, the vertical line the second factor. Both are equal in length, and degrees of saturation are marked off on each, going from + 1·00 through ·00 to − 1·00. A circle is drawn around this structure to delimit what is called the 'two-factor space'. It is of course easy to add other factors to this structure; thus a third factor might be added, at right angles to the other two, which would stick out from the intersection of factors one and two (the origin) at right angles to the plane of the paper. Factors beyond three cannot be represented visually, but can easily be treated mathematically according to the rules of n-dimensional geometry; factors are then considered to lie in hyper-space.

So far we have only drawn the framework within which our observed factors can be plotted. Test 1 has saturations of ·69 and ·15 on the two factors; consequently we plot it in Figure 4 in the corresponding position. Tests 4 (with saturations of ·48 and ·45), 6 (with saturations of ·58 and − ·15), and 14 (with saturations of ·20 and − ·34) have also been plotted in the diagram. The other tests are not plotted because they would obscure certain important relations which are vital to an understanding of the implications of this graphic method of representation.

Let us connect the points marking the positions of tests 4 and 14 to the origin by means of straight lines. It can be shown by simple

trigonometric calculation that if we multiply the cosine of the
angle separating these two lines (angle α) by the product of the
lengths of these two lines, we obtain the correlation between the

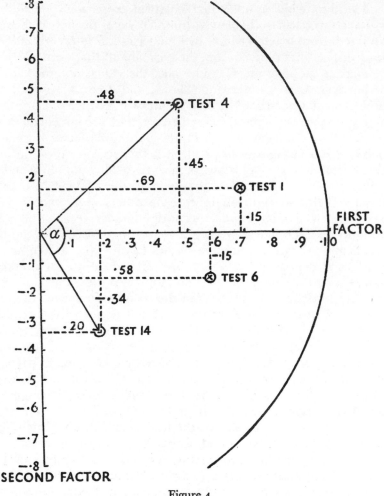

Figure 4

two tests in question. It can be seen from the diagram that the
angle α is about 90 degrees. The cosine of an angle of 90 degrees
is of course zero, so that the total product must be close to zero.
(The actual correlation in fact is ·02.)

Similar lines can be drawn between the origin and the points representing tests 1 and 6. In each case, the correlation between any two tests is represented by the product of the length of the lines connecting them with the origin, multiplied by the cosine of the angle between the two lines.

The lines which we drew between the origin and the points representing tests 4 and 14 are technically called vectors. (A vector is a line having a given length and direction.) It will be seen that

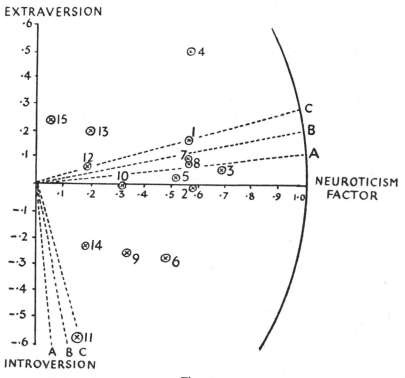

Figure 5

each test is represented by a vector, and that these vectors form a system which gives a diagrammatic representation of the relations obtaining between the tests, just as the matrix of intercorrelations gave an arithmetical representation of these relations. In either case we are dealing with a pattern which we are seeking to describe in the simplest possible way.

Let us next plot in two factors space all 15 tests, using the neurotic sample values from Table IX. Figure 5 shows the results. The reader may care to plot the values from the normal sample himself for comparison; they are very similar to, though not exactly identical with, those shown in Figure 5.

It will be noted that the upper and the lower halves of this diagram are rather nicely balanced. There are more points in the upper half, but those in the lower half have higher saturations on the second factor. In fact, it would appear as if the first factor axis passed exactly through the centre of the whole swarm of points. This is indeed the case; the method of extraction of a factor ensures that it will as it were be a multidimensional average (a 'centroid') of all the vectors involved. This feature of factor analysis is at the same time a strength and a weakness; just as an average may be meaningful or meaningless, dependent upon precisely what is being averaged, so the factors extracted from a matrix may be meaningful or not dependent upon what precisely is being intercorrelated. Factor analysis is often considered as a kind of sausage machine—correlations are put in and out comes the psychologically meaningful and scientifically valuable result. This view is not shared by any responsible investigator; like all other statistical methods, factor analysis is far from fool-proof, and where psychological insight, careful planning, and an understanding of the hypothetico-deductive nature of scientific methodology are lacking, no mathematical brilliance can suffice to salvage the results of misapplied ingenuity. To admit that factor analysis has occasionally been misapplied, and that results reported by some of its overenthusiastic users have often been absurd, does not amount to an admission that critics are justified in quoting such examples in condemnation of factor analysis as a scientific method; almost any scientific tool can be misused by the uninitiated, regardless of its general value and importance. Criticism must be based, not on occasional absurdities, but on the best available examples of the methods properly used and correctly interpreted according to its own rules. Any other evaluation is merely semantic shadow-boxing.

The admission that our factors are nothing but averages is a very damaging one; indeed, criticism of factor analysis which is not merely based on misunderstanding centres largely on this point. The 'g' we extract from a matrix obeying the rules of the tetrad criterion is not an average in this sense; we can add or subtract tests from our battery at will, and as long as each obeys the tetrad criterion, we can be sure that we are always measuring the same, identical 'g'. But the moment that we are dealing with a matrix which does not obey the tetrad criterion, and which requires therefore more than one factor, we leave objectivity dangerously far behind, and are forced to enter into many circuitous byways before emerging once more into the main stream of scientific methodology.

A factor, in order to be useful in ordering our descriptions of the multiform facts of psychology, must have two characteristics. It must be *unique*, and it must be *invariant*. By unique we mean that from a given matrix one and only one solution should be possible if the rules of extraction are followed. By invariant we mean that however much the battery of tests may be altered by adding other tests, or subtracting tests already included in it, nevertheless the factor saturations of those tests which are retained in the battery should not change. It may be said that rules can be laid down which ensure the uniqueness of the factors extracted by any of the current methods; it is with respect to invariance that our troubles start.

Let us look again at Figure 5. Factor 1 is balanced carefully between the positive and the negative sides of the bipolar second factor, in such a way that the factor saturations of the tests having positive saturations on the second factors balance out almost exactly the factor saturations of the tests having negative saturations. What would happen if we omitted test 11 from our calculations? The relations between all the other tests (as indicated by their positions in the two-factor space) would remain quite unaffected, because they represent the correlations of these tests, which are of course not changed in any way by dropping any particular test. But the position of our two axes would be changed. The first one would pass through the new average (centroid) of our cluster of fourteen tests, and would therefore lie approximately as shown in Figure 5 as position A. The second factor axis, in order to remain at right angles to the first factor axis, would of course shift through a similar angle to position A'. Take out another test now, say test 6, and again the position of the axes will shift, this time to B and B'. Take out tests 9 and 14 too, and now our axes would assume positions C and C'. Clearly, these axes are in no way invariant, but shift about depending entirely on the make up of the battery of tests. In other words, they are almost useless in their present form for our purpose.

One way out of this difficulty has been suggested by Thurstone (1935), and has given worthwhile results in the field of mental abilities. He lays down certain mathematical rules which, in a suitable matrix, will give a rotation which is at once unique and invariant. This final position he calls 'simple structure', and he defines it by saying that in simple structure as many of the axes as possible should be at right angles to as many of the original test vectors as possible. As we have seen, 'being at right angles to' means simply 'having zero correlations with', and this demand therefore means that as many of the tests should have zero saturations for as many of the factors as possible. More particularly, he requires that every factor axis should be at right angles to at least as many test vectors as there are factors, and that every test should be at right angles to at least one factor. In practice, these demands amount to this: (1) Each test should have at least one zero saturation. (2) Each factor should have at least as many zero saturations as there are factors. (3) There should be at least as many XO or OX entries in each pair of factors as there are factors. (An XO or OX entry means simply a zero saturation in one factor accompanied by a non-zero saturation in another.)

Experience has shown that these requirements are met by matrices of observed correlations too rarely to be of much significance as long as the orthogonal pattern of factor axes is retained. Thurstone therefore permits his factors to be correlated with each other, so that his factor axes are no longer at right angles to each other. Figure 6 shows the kind of pattern which is frequently found in a Thurstone-type analysis. I and II are the centroid factors as determined from the original matrix; I' and II' are the rotated factors showing 'simple structure' and a correlation given by the cosine of the angle α. Thus once the factors in a matrix have been found and rotated, we can write another matrix of intercorrelations giving the correlations between factors. This in turn can be analysed, and in the case of tests of ability, seems to obey the tetrad criterion, thus giving rise to one second-order or superfactor which corresponds very closely to Spearman's 'g'. We thus seem to be able to recover the impressive simplicity and orderliness of Spearman's original picture, without leaving out of account the additional 'group factors' which made his simple model inapplicable.

The advantage of this method of analysis which gives us, first of all, unique and invariant primary factors, and then a 'g' based on the intercorrelations of these primary factors, is obvious. Our 'g' will not change with addition or omission of new tests, but will

remain uniquely and invariantly defined. This would not be so if
we were to extract '*g*' from our original battery of tests, without
first fitting them into a 'simple structure' pattern. Such at least
would be the claim of those who follow Thurstone in his method.
To a considerable degree these claims appear to be justified.

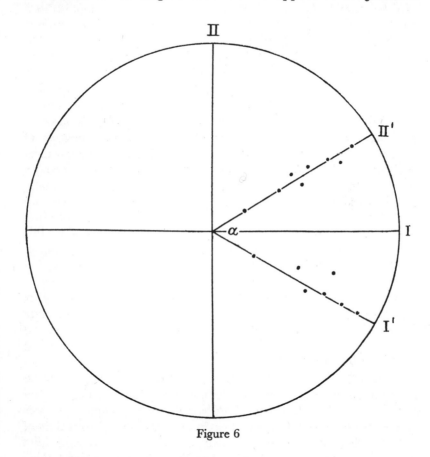

Figure 6

Experimental results do appear to efforts in patterns of intercorrelations which allow the research worker to use the methods of
'simple structure', and factors thus discovered do seem to correlate
in a hierarchical pattern which obeys the tetrad criterion. It may
be objected that angles of rotation are not really uniquely determined, in view of the difficulties caused by sampling errors, and
that the invariance of the resulting factors has not been demon-

strated experimentally under stringent conditions of univariate and multivariate selection. These objections do not attack the principle which Thurstone is attempting to establish, and there is good prospect that in time the mathematical problems may be solved, and the experimental evidence be supplied. At the very least, we would appear to have here a method which holds out a hope that through its use we may be able to solve the taxonomic difficulties in the cognitive field.

Let us look at the general picture given of the organization of mental abilities by factor analysis. We discern four main levels. At the lowest level we are dealing with single observations of behaviour which may be regarded as falling into the general domain with which we are concerned. Many thousands of such observations are made by all of us every day, with varying degrees of objectivity, reliability, and validity. We attain a much higher level when we can measure the consistency of this behaviour, through reliability coefficients or other statistical means. This will usually be possible only with test or examination behaviour, although teachers' or other persons' ratings, social achievement, or repeated success at some intellectual task might be considered here. At this level we would be dealing with mental tests of known reliability, dealing with a very restricted universe of content—a test of speed in simple addition might be quoted as an example, or a test of ability in completing letter series of a given level of difficulty. A third level is reached when we find that these tests in turn correlate to produce primary mental abilities, such as the verbal, numerical memory, or visuospatial factors. The fourth and highest level of all is reached when these primary mental abilities in turn are found to correlate and give rise to a second-order factor corresponding to '*g*' or general mental ability or intelligence. A diagrammatic representation of these levels is given in Figure 7. Factor analysis enables us to give fairly exact estimates of the contribution of each of these levels to the total variance of a given test, and quite generally to give a reasonably accurate picture of the interrelations of all the thousands of separate facts represented even in such a simple diagram as the one presented here.

What we are doing in factor analysis is simply the breaking up of the total variance (the total variability on a test shown by the sample of people tested; the variance is equal to the square of the standard deviation) into various component parts. Thus we may let the total variance equal 100 per cent, or unity in order to keep

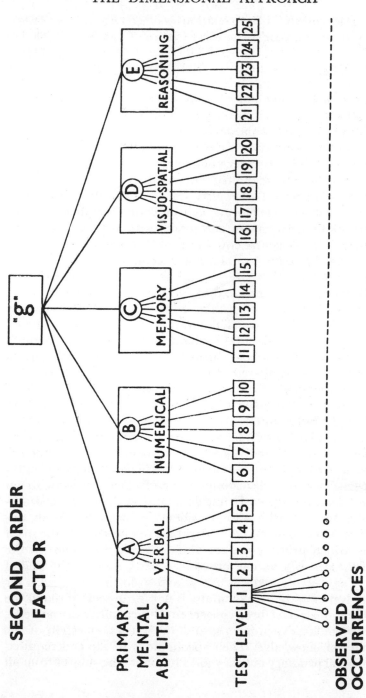

Figure 7

to the order of size of correlation coefficients, and write an equation to account for all of the variance of test A:

$$\sigma_A{}^2 = a_1{}^2 + a_2{}^2 + a_3{}^2 + \ldots + a_n{}^2 + a_s{}^2 + a_e{}^2 = 1$$

In other words, the total variance of test A ($\sigma_A{}^2$) is accounted for by the squares of the saturations of this test on factors 1, 2, 3, to n, plus the squares of the specific factor saturation (s) plus the error variance (e^2). The various parts of this equation have separate names. The variance contributed by the factors from 1 to n is known as the 'communality', because they constitute what the test has in common with other tests; it is usually written h^2. Specific and error variance together are known as the 'uniqueness' of the test, because these factors are not shared with any other test. The uniqueness (u^2) is of course equal to $1 - h^2$, because u^2 and h^2 add up to 1. The reliability (r_{aa}) of a test (its empirical test reliability) is given by the formula $r_{aa} = 1 - a_e{}^2$, from which we can deduce that if the reliability is known, the error variance can be calculated by the formula $a_e{}^2 = 1 - r_{aa}$. These various relations allow us to calculate the contribution of the various factors—communality, specificity, error—to the total variance of any test in the battery. These various relations hold for orthogonal factors; with certain changes they can be altered to fit the oblique pattern also.

Can this method of multiple factor analysis with rotation to 'simple structure' be taken over into the field of temperament, character, attitudes, interests, and so forth? There are a number of reasons why such a transfer would be of doubtful value. In the first place, the factor analysts who worked in the field of mental abilities had concepts and tests available which had already undergone a long period of development. The faculty psychologists on the one hand, and the early test designers on the other, had outlined the general field with considerable ingenuity. Even untutored common sense might be expected to give clues to the main areas in which primary mental abilities could be found: in the field of *test material*—verbal, numerical, perceptual; in the field of *method of approach*—speed, accuracy, and so forth. The reason for this relatively happy state of affairs is not far to seek; through the ages philosophers have been concerned with cognitive phenomena, with epistemological problems, and the general question of the possibility of knowledge. Their speculations in the end required much factual pruning, but they did illuminate the subject from all sides, and created a background of sophistication against which more recent workers could proceed.

Not so in the non-cognitive field. This has always been the step-child of philosophy, psychology, and medicine, and the investigator will not find ready to hand a large number of objective tests which he may use, or a set of reasonable hypotheses which he may investigate. Instead, he will find a subject still apparently enjoying its birth trauma without giving any signs of growing up, but filled instead with return-to-the-womb phantasies; a subject in which the most remarkable theories are bandied about with careless abandon, and in which not even the notion that some sort of proof is required before hypotheses can be accepted is widely known or shared. Instead of objective tests, he will find the field dominated by ratings (in spite of their known unreliability), questionnaires (in spite of their known lack of validity), and so-called projective techniques which multiply in a horrifying Malthusian fashion before his very eyes (in spite of the almost complete absence of proof that they measure anything whatever).[1] Under these circumstances he cannot begin—as could the student of ability—by taking a number of tests and intercorrelating them in an effort to bring order out of chaos; the very tests which he may wish to use are not yet in existence, and indeed, it is not at all clear which mental functions he should attempt to measure even if he were ready to construct new tests.

In the second place, even if the intrepid investigator were to succeed in locating a few objective (or even not-so-objective) tests which in his opinion measured temperament, he would find their intercorrelations woefully low, and obstinately determined not to fall into a pattern even remotely resembling simple structure. His troubles would be increased by the fact that the notion of the 'positive manifold' (that all saturations should be zero or positive) makes sense in the field of abilities, where negative correlations are hardly ever found, but does not apply in the field of affection and conation. And while the notion of the 'positive manifold' is not absolutely essential to 'simple structure', there is no experience to guide the research worker to find simple structure in the absence of a positive manifold.

In the third place, there are certain practical difficulties which militate against wholesale testing in the field of temperament. It

---

[1] Gresham's law would appear to apply in the field of psychological tests no less than in that of economic theory!

is easy to devise group tests for mental abilities, and to test many thousands of school children, students, and adults with them; to repeat these tests, or alternate versions of them, in order to obtain reliability coefficients; and to carry out all these procedures in the class-room, the factory, or any convenient large hall. Not so for the type of test which might be used for the measurement of temperament. Group testing is nearly always impossible (except for the egregious and not very useful questionnaire); special apparatus is required, such as the P.G.R., the Luria, or the C.F.C. machine; each test takes a great deal of time—sometimes up to two or three hours—and can only be carried out in the laboratory, or the hospital, with consequent loss of time to the subject who has to journey thither on many separate occasions. Add to all this the fact that intelligence testing is 'respectable', and encounters little opposition nowadays, while tests of temperament are almost by definition emotion-rousing, and frequently frightening or unpleasant, as well as relating to thought content not considered 'nice' by many people, and it will be appreciated why methods which can be used in the cognitive field may not be easily transferred to the non-cognitive field.

Do we have an alternative to the method suggested by Thurstone in our attempt to find a set of factors which corresponds to a set of psychologically real influences? Cattell (1946) has pointed out that there are two ways of arriving at such an objective. The investigator, he writes, 'may (1) devise possible ways of over-determining the analysis of the given correlation matrix so that only one set of true factors will emerge, or (2) start from the opposite shore and propound, on psychological grounds alone, a hypothesis about what source traits are operative in the variables. Then he will see if these factors correspond to any of the possible mathematical factors found in the matrix.' The first of these methods is that adopted by Thurstone. The second of these methods, which is clearly the hypothetico-deductive method which has shown itself to be so fruitful in science generally, is rejected by Cattell on two grounds. '. . . in the first place, personality study has so few other reliable avenues for arriving at, or even suspecting, the basis source traits, that hypotheses are likely to be erratic. In the second place, the mathematical solutions to any set of correlations are so numerous and varied that unless the hypothesis can be stated in very precise quantitative terms the "proof" of it is easy— so easy as to be worthless.' Cattell repeats his position in slightly different terms: '. . . we have rejected one of the two major approaches normally approved by scientific method—namely, that of inventing a hypothesis about the particular factors expected and attempting to discover a factorization to match it—because in this field almost any hypothesis could be so "confirmed". Instead, we seek general guiding principles for the mathematical analysis itself which will lead to a unique solution.'

While I appreciate the great contribution which Thurstone has made to the analysis of mental abilities, and while I am fully conscious of the difficulties Cattell has pointed out in arriving at a hypothetico-deductive method of analysis which shall be capable of being refuted (i.e. one where the 'proof' would not be so easy as to be worthless), I nevertheless believe that progress in the non-cognitive field depends on the discovery of such a method. Accordingly we turn next to an attempt to define the principles underlying such a combination of factor analysis and hypothetico-deductive method; the general name given to this procedure is that of 'Criterion Analysis' (Eysenck, 1950). The rest of this chapter will be devoted to an exposition of this method; the rest of this book to an application of this method to a variety of theoretical and practical problems.

For a clue to the procedure which might be adopted here, we may return to an example given earlier in this chapter. It will be remembered that several (questionnaire) tests of 'neuroticism' were given to groups of normal and neurotic soldiers, the intercorrelations for the normals and the neurotics separately calculated, and factor analyses on the two matrices carried out. As shown in Table IX, two factors emerged from each of the matrices which were very provisionally identified as 'neuroticism' and as 'extraversion-introversion'. Let us concentrate on the first factor only for the time being; the arguments which apply to it will be shown to apply to subsequent factors also. Let us deal only with the factor emerging from the intercorrelations matrix of the neurotic group as plotted in diagram form on page 61 ; this is so similar to the normal group factor pattern that what is said of the one is also applicable to the other.

Right from the beginning we seem to be involved in a contradiction. We have 'identified' the first factor as extracted with 'neuroticism'; yet we have used the diagram on which we have plotted this factor (Figure 5) to show that the factor axis has no fixed position, but changes with the addition or subtraction of tests in the matrix. If the factor found is meaningless (as is implied in the notion that it fails to be invariant), how can it be interpreted at all? The answer lies in the fact, emphasized before, that a factor is an average; an average may be meaningful or meaningless according to what it is that is being averaged. If we throw together tests of intelligence, neuroticism, and introversion, the resulting average intercorrelation will be a meaningless jumble impossible to interpret. If we throw together a lot of tests of neuroticism, the resulting average will have at least a rough-and-ready resemblance to meaningfulness, because what is being averaged is all measuring much the same underlying dimension. While therefore the axis is not permanently fixed, and is certainly not invariant, it will point roughly in the right direction—with an error of some 10 or 20 degrees either way. Consequently, the interpretation of such a factor, unrotated as it is, is possible, although one's confidence in this interpretation is purely subjective.

TABLE XI

List of Tests

A. Maudsley Medical Inventory—40 item neuroticism questionnaire. Score = number of questions answered 'No' (non-neurotic).
B. Dark Adaptation—U.S. Navy Radium Plaque Adaptometer. Score = goodness of dark vision.
C. Non-Suggestibility—body-sway test. Ability to resist suggestion to sway forward.
D. Motor Control—absence of static ataxia; given as preliminary test to C.
E. Goal Discrepancy Score—*smallness* of level of aspiration scores on O'Connor tweezers test.
F. Judgment Discrepancy Scores—*smallness* of judgment discrepancies on O'Connor tweezers test.
G. Index of Flexibility—number of shifts in aspiration scores on O'Connor tweezers test, irrespective of size or direction.
H. Manual Dexterity—best score of nine trials on tweezers test.
I. Personal Tempo—speed of writing 2, 3, 4, repeatedly for two trials of 15 seconds each.
J. Fluency—number of *round things* and of *things to eat* mentioned during 30-second periods.
K. Speed Test (1)—speed of tracing when instructed to be both quick and accurate. (Choice conditions.)
L. Speed Test (2)—speed of tracing prescribed path on track tracer under instruction to be quick.
M. Persistence Test I—length of time during which leg is held in uncomfortable and fatiguing position.
N. Persistence Test B—holding breath as long as possible, without inhaling or exhaling.
O. Stress Test—ability of S to recover previous scoring rate on pursuitmeter type of test after special stress period.
P. Non-Perseveration—extremes of perseveration (SZ test), either very high or very low, are scored low, while scores nearer the average are scored high.

However, it will be remembered that we did go a little further than this and provided a criterion to indicate that this interpretation was at least partly justified. We calculated the 'criterion column', i.e. the column of correlations of each test with the normal-neurotic dichotomy, and showed that our factor saturations correlated to the extent of ·81 with this 'criterion column'. This is objective evidence in favour of our hypothesis, and represents a genuine application of the hypothetico-deductive method, because we had shown previously that on the basis of our main hypothesis regarding the existence of a neuroticism continuum, and on the basis of subsidiary hypotheses regarding the differential success of the various tests used in measuring this continuum, such a correlation could be predicted. This still leaves our factor rather 'wobbly' and far from invariant, but it does suggest a further step which will tie it down completely to a position which is both unique and invariant. That position is one in which the correlation between the column of factor saturations and the criterion column is a maximum. In other words, the factor axis is to be rotated in such a way that factor saturations correlate as highly as possible with the criterion column.

Let us give an example of this procedure by reference to an experiment using objective tests rather than questionnaires. The tests enumerated in Table XI were given to 93 normals and 105 neurotic subjects, and the correlations calculated between each test and the normal-neurotic dichotomy. These correlations are given in Table XII under the heading C_N (Criterion Column—Neuroticism). Product moment intercorrelations were worked out between the tests for 64 of the normal subjects who had carried out all of the tests, and the matrix of intercorrelations factor analysed. Two factors were extracted, and are given in Table XII under the heading F_1 and F_2; the heading h^2 indicates in each case what portion of the total variance of each test is accounted for by these two factors. Rotation of the two factor axes through an angle of five degrees makes the correlation between first factor saturations and criterion column a maximum ($r = ·574$), and gives us the values for the rotated first factor given in column D. A graphic demonstration of the results is given in Figure 8; axes I and II are the centroid axes as found; D is the rotated first factor axis. To show what would happen if an attempt were made to approach simple structure, axes I' and II' have been drawn in; they will be seen to be almost completely uninterpretable.

TABLE XII

	C_N	F_1	F_2	h^2	$\hat{D}$	$\hat{D}_1$
A	·23	·143	·211	·065	·080	·127
B	·27	·392	− ·220	·202	·256	·407
C	·51	·620	− ·416	·557	·409	·650
D	·54	·644	− ·438	·607	·425	·675
E	·06	·100	·089	·018	·059	·094
F	·10	·497	− ·455	·454	·333	·529
G	·05	·275	− ·397	·233	·191	·303
H	·57	·405	− ·078	·170	·258	·410
I	·30	·438	·175	·222	·267	·424
J	·03	·300	·018	·090	·188	·299
K	·27	·523	·100	·284	·324	·515
L	·17	·565	·461	·532	·333	·529
M	·46	·607	·384	·516	·363	·576
N	·26	·632	·430	·584	·377	·599
O	·24	·294	− ·103	·097	·189	·300
P	·21	·207	·241	·101	·119	·189
		·203	·093	·296		

Explanation of Column Headings:

C_N = Criterion Column, i.e. correlation of each test with normal-neurotic dichotomy.

F_1 and F_2 = First and second unrotated factors from analysis of intercorrelations of normal group only.

h^2 = Communality.

$\hat{D}$ = F_1 rotated into maximum correlation with criterion column.

$\hat{D}_1$ = $\hat{D}$ with vector extended to unity

$$r_{C_N \hat{D}_1} = \cdot574$$

$$\rho_{C_N \hat{D}_1} = \cdot587$$

Several points should be noted in this example. The angle required to get maximum correlation between F_1 and C_N is very small; as all the tests were chosen as measures of neuroticism, their average (the first centroid factor) is therefore meaningful and close to the optimum position. This optimum position is unique and invariant; the addition of new tests, or the subtraction of old ones, would not alter the position of $\hat{D}$. The relatively high, positive correlation between C_N and F_1 is in line with our hypothesis that the factor is one of neuroticism and supports the view that neuroticism is a continuum. The grouping of the tests on the second factor is in conformity with what in previous investigations had

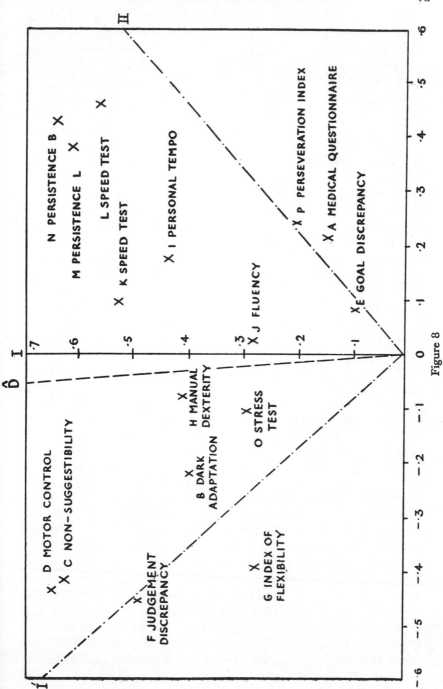

Figure 8

been shown to be characteristic of the introvert-extravert dichotomy. Thus introverts have been shown to be more persistent, and extraverts to show less judgment discrepancy, and somewhat less suggestibility, as well as better dark-adaptation. None of these points will be stressed here as the study mentioned was only a preliminary one, using too few subjects to be convincing, and employing a selection of tests which was much improved in later work. It is given here only for the purpose of illustrating the method under discussion.

At this point the critical reader may feel that we have jumped from the frying-pan into the fire. We have managed to get rid of the subjective element involved in locating our factor axes, only to link up this rotation with the even more subjective criterion of psychiatric diagnosis. If our final aim were merely to obtain maximum correlation with the criterion, i.e. with the diagnosis 'normal' or 'neurotic', then some form of multiple correlation or discriminant function analysis would be indicated. Clearly, a further step is required.

Let us look more closely at our criterion. 'Neurotics' are people who have been thus diagnosed by a qualified psychiatrist, after full consideration of their past work history, illness record, sexual behaviour, phantasy life, and social adaptation, as well as their current symptomatology. 'Normals' are the undifferentiated mass of people who have not at any time of their lives been so diagnosed, and who at the time of the investigation are leading relatively normal lives and are not experiencing symptoms severe enough to lead them to seek help from a psychiatrist. The 'neurotic' group itself is of course not entirely homogeneous, but subdivided in various ways. Some are bright, others are dull; some are extraverted (hysterics), others are introverted (dysthymics); some show additional psychotic symptoms, others do not. There is much agreement among experts that certain groups fall into the general field of 'neurosis', e.g. hysterics, anxiety states, reactive depressions; there is no agreement at all regarding other groups, such as the psychopathic states, or the obsessional and compulsive groups. Some people would argue that 'psychotics' cannot be differentiated from 'neurotics', and should therefore form part of the criterion group; others would claim that psychotics and neurotics are entirely different disease forms, in no way resembling each other. Clearly, our criterion is in a very doubtful state, and itself in need of clarification. This can be applied by an inverse application of our principle of maximizing the correlation between factor (F_1) and criterion (C_N), which leads us to a *double maximization principle*. It is well known that the correlation between a test and a criterion can be increased in two ways: by improving the test, and by improving the criterion. Similarly, we can increase the correlation between factor and criterion column in two ways: by improving our factor measurements, and by improving our criterion. So far, we have considered examples in which the criterion group consisted of neurotics suffering from those disorders and symptoms most commonly agreed to define neurosis: hysterical conversion symptoms; somatic correlates of anxiety; feelings of depression, worry, and fears unreasonably severe in relation to their causes; amnesias and other disorders of memory not caused by any obvious physical agent or injury. This criterion may be only a relatively rough approach to a correct and perfect criterion, and this lack of perfection in the criterion may be reflected in the failure of the correlation between F_1 and C_N to reach perfection. If that be so, then clearly any improvement in the criterion would result in an increase in the correlation between F_1 (always rotated into a position of maximum correlation with C_N) and C_N, determined now by the new criterion chosen.

As an example, let us suppose that the large group of psychopaths belongs functionally into the neurotic field, as is maintained by many psychiatrists. Then if we changed our group of neurotics, as used in the experiment summarized in Table XI, to include a large percentage of psychopaths, we would presumably obtain different scores on all our tests for this new, enlarged 'neurotic' group, and consequently a changed column of correlations between tests and normal-neurotic dichotomy (C'_N). If the hypothesis that psychopaths did belong to the neurotic group were correct, we would expect the correlation between F'_1 (rotated into maximum correlation with the new C'_N) and the new C'_N to be as large or larger than the correlation of F_1 had been with the old C_N. A drop in this correlation would indicate very clearly that our criterion had not improved, but had become attenuated by the inclusion of this 'foreign body', and that consequently 'psychopathy' did not form a part of the neurotic criterion. The same procedure could of course be gone through with other groups—obsessionals, epileptics, and so forth, in an attempt to obtain the maximum possible correlation between criterion and factor. Given that the proper criterion could be approached in this manner, a correlation of near unity should be capable of achievement—as will be shown later, correlations of ·90 and ·95 have already been reached between factor saturations and criterion columns.

The essential points in 'criterion analysis' will now have become clear. We start with a given criterion for some hypothetical continuum which we suspect, on purely psychological grounds, to be of general interest and importance. This criterion will in all probability be very impure, attenuated, and inaccurate. We create measuring instruments which can be shown to give some rough measure of correspondence with the criterion; we then study the interrelations of these measuring instruments by means of factor analysis, to obtain evidence of the existence of our hypothetical continuum, and to discover whether it is related in some rough way to our criterion. As has been shown early in this chapter, we may in this way actually transcend our criterion (the example of the teachers' ratings of intelligence as opposed to the intelligence test will be remembered). We may therefore now use our factor to improve our criterion, until we reach a position of exact equivalence. When this is done, we may assume that our original hypothesis was justified. This process may appear like arguing in a circle, but in reality this method of argument corresponds precisely to the method used by physical science to define even such elementary concepts as 'length'. We may with advantage quote Bertrand Russell's (1948) discussion of physical measurement at this point.

'Measurement, even of the distance to remove nebulæ, is built up from measurements of distances on the surface of the earth, and terrestrial measurements start with the assumption that certain bodies may be regarded as approximately rigid. If you measure your room, you assume that your foot-rule is not growing appreciably longer or shorter during the process. The ordnance survey of England determines most distances by triangulation, but this process demands that there shall be at least one distance which is measured directly. In fact, a base line on Salisbury Plain was chosen, and was measured carefully in the elementary way in which we measure the size of our room: a chain, which we may take as by definition of unit length, was repeatedly applied to the surface of the earth along a line as nearly straight as possible. This one length having been determined directly, the rest proceeds by the measurement of angles and by calculation; the diameter of the earth, the distance of the sun and moon, and even the distances of the nearer fixed stars, can be determined without any further measurement of lengths.

'But when this process is scrutinized it is found to be full of difficulties. The assumption that a body is "rigid" has no clear meaning until we have already established a metric enabling us to compare lengths and angles at one time with lengths and angles at another, for a "rigid" body is one which does not alter its shape or size. Then again we need a definition of a "straight line", for all our results will be wrong if the base line on Salisbury Plain and the lines used in triangulation are not straight. It seems, therefore, that measurement presupposes geometry (to enable us to define "straight lines") and enough physics to give grounds for regarding some bodies as approximately rigid, and for comparing distances at one time with distances at another. The difficulties involved are formidable, but are concealed by assumptions taken over from common sense. . . . Common sense assumes, roughly speaking, that a body *is* rigid if it *looks* rigid. Eels do not look rigid, but steel bars do. . . . Common sense, in so thinking, is Newtonian: it is convinced that at each moment a body intrinsically has a certain shape and size, which either are or are not the same as its shape and size at another moment. Given absolute space, this conviction has meaning, but without absolute space it is *prima facie* meaningless. . . .

'As in the case of the measurement of time, three factors enter in: first, an assumption liable to correction; second, physical laws which, on this assumption, are found to be approximately true; third, a modification of the assumption to make the physical laws more nearly exact. If you assume that a certain steel rod, which looks and feels rigid, preserves its length unchanged, you will find that the distance from London to Edinburgh, the diameter of the earth, and the distance from Sirius, are all nearly constant, but are slightly less in warm weather than in cold. It will then occur to you that it will be simpler to say that your steel rod expands with heat, particularly when you find that this enables you to regard the above distances as almost exactly constant, and, further, that you can see the mercury in the thermometer taking up more space in warm weather. You therefore assume that apparently rigid bodies expand with heat, and you do this in order to simplify the statement of physical laws.

'Let us get clear as to what is conventional and what is physical fact in this process. It is a physical fact that if two steel rods, neither of which feels either hot or cold, look as if they were of the same length, and if, then, you heat one by the fire and put the other in snow, when you first compare them again the one that has been by the fire looks slightly longer than the one that has been in the snow, but when both have again reached the temperature of your room this difference will have vanished. I am here assuming pre-scientific methods of estimating temperature: a hot body is one that feels hot, and a cold body is one that feels cold. As a result of such rough prescientific observations we decide that the thermometer gives an exact measure of something which is measured approximately by our feelings of heat and cold; we can, then, as physicists, ignore these feelings and concentrate on the thermometer. It is then a tautology that *my* thermometer rises with an increase of temperature, but it is a substantial fact that all other thermometers likewise do so. This fact states a similarity between the behaviour of my thermometer and that of other bodies.

'But the element of convention is not quite as I have just stated it. I do not assume that my thermometer is right by definition; on the contrary, it is universally agreed that every actual thermometer is more or less inaccurate. The ideal thermometer, to which actual thermometers only approximate, is one which, if taken as accurate, makes the general law of the expansion of bodies with rising temperature as exactly true as possible. It is an empirical fact that, by observing certain rules in making thermometers, we can make them approximate more and more closely to the ideal thermometer, and it is this fact which justifies the conception of temperature as a quantity having, for a given body at a given time, some exact value which is likely to be slightly different from that shown by any actual thermometer.

'This process is the same in all physical measurements. Rough measurements lead to an approximate law; changes in the measuring instruments (subject to the rule that all instruments for measuring the same quantity must give as nearly as possible the same results) are found capable of making the law more nearly exact. The best instrument is held to be the one that makes the law most nearly exact, and it is assumed that an ideal instrument would make the law quite exact.

'This statement, though it may seem complicated, is still not complicated enough. There is seldom only one law involved, and very often the law itself is only approximate. Measurements of different quantities are interdependent, as we have just seen in the case of length and temperature, so that a change in the way of measuring one quantity may alter the measure of another. Laws, conventions, and observations are almost inextricably intertwined in the actual procedure of science. The result of an observation is usually stated in a form which assumes certain laws and certain conventions; if the results contradict the network of laws and conventions hitherto assumed, there may be considerable liberty of choice as to which should be modified.'

The close similarity between this mutual interplay of rough-and-ready, common-sense observation, measurement based upon such observation, and modification to give more precise inter-relations of measurements, with the procedure of 'criterion analysis' will be obvious. Criterion analysis attempts to do in a formal manner in psychology what has always been done in the physical sciences. Our original hypotheses about temperature are derived from 'clinical' observation of our own feelings of hot and cold; this forms our original criterion. There is no doubt that this criterion is inaccurate, fallible, unreliable, and impure. One person's judgments of 'hot' and 'cold' are not necessarily identical with another's, and may deviate considerably; external factors such as humidity play an important part in our judgment, as do internal factors such as our state of nutrition, or the amount of exercise we have taken. But roughly these feelings of 'hot' and 'cold' can be shown to correspond with certain physical phenomena, such as the contraction and expansion of metals, the pressure of gases, or the emission of electrons from a heated surface. As these physical phenomena constitute an interconnected system of observations which in turn fits in well with other observations (rigidity of bodies, measurement of distances) the criterion is revised to obtain the best possible fit (the highest possible correlation) between all these sets of phenomena.[1]

[1] It should not be imagined that physical measurement of even such simple and well-understood variables as heat and length is without difficulties and pitfalls analogous with those we experience in psychology. Thus in psychological testing we often encounter the phenomenon of 'threshold' and 'ceiling' effects, i.e. of tests which measure effectively over a certain range, but either fail to measure the variable in question at all outside this range, or else give biassed or meaningless results. In physics, we encounter the same difficulty. Thus temperature is defined in terms of the resistance of a platinum wire from − 183° C. to 660° C.; from 660° C. to 1063° C. it is defined and measured by the electro-magnetic force of a standard thermocouple. At even higher temperatures, definition and measurement are in terms of the intensity of radiation of a

In the same way, 'clinical' observations of certain types of behaviour gives us our original hypothesis regarding the existence of a continuum of 'neuroticism'; these observations, regularized and formalized in legal and psychiatric practice, form our original criterion. There is no doubt that this criterion is inaccurate, fallible, unreliable, and impure. One person's judgments of 'neurotic' and 'normal' are not necessarily identical with another's, and may deviate considerably; external factors such as intelligence, or beauty, play an important part in our judgment, as do internal factors such as the state of our liver, or our general attitudes. But roughly these assessments of 'neurotic' and 'normal' can be shown to correspond with certain objective tests, such as body-sway suggestibility, or persistence. As these objective tests constitute an interconnected system of observations which in turn fits in well with other observations (employability of mental defectives, effects of prefrontal leucotomy, selection of nurses and students, monozygotic and dyzygotic twin differences) the criterion is revised to obtain the best possible fit (the maximum correlation) between all these sets of phenomena. Empirical evidence for these statements will be given in later chapters; here we are concerned merely with the general theory underlying scientific methodology.

The method of criterion analysis will become clearer as its various applications are studied as they occur throughout this book. In essence, it is nothing but the application to the special taxonomic problems of human behaviour in its non-cognitive aspects of the general principles of scientific method, more particularly of the hypothetico-deductive method. It requires a main hypothesis regarding the existence of a quantitative continuum underlying a given area of human behaviour; it also requires subsidiary hypotheses regarding the nature of this continuum, which will determine the tests to be used, and the linearity or otherwise of the relations anticipated. . . . Deductions made from such a set of hypotheses can be disproved (an example of this will be given

defined wave-length from a 'black body'. As Scott-Blair points out, 'particular interest lies in the fact that these conventions result in serious ambiguity, since it so happens that pure aluminium freezes ("becomes solid") at just over 660° C. using the resistance thermometer, thus falling within the official range of the thermocouple, whereas when the thermocouple is used, the freezing temperature is just below 660°, implying that the resistance thermometer is required! Until a suitable adjustment was made, it was therefore impossible to quote an accurate freezing point for aluminium' (Scott-Blair, 1950).

later in the book), or they can be supported with varying degrees of evidence by the results of specially planned experiments. We must now turn to the empirical evidence, to test the value of our procedures by application to a variety of hypotheses.

Chapter Three

THE NEUROTIC DIMENSION: OPERATIONAL DEFINITION

IN this chapter we will begin to discuss the formal proof for our hypothesis of the existence of a general factor of neuroticism or stability. These terms, which are intended to denote the extreme points of what is conceived of as a continuum, will be used interchangeably according to the particular direction implied in any particular case, just as one speaks of intelligence and mental deficiency depending on which of the two extreme points of the cognitive continuum one may be concerned with. A diagrammatic statement of the hypothesis is given on page 52; it suggests immediately the necessity for a formal disproof of what we may call the null hypothesis, i.e. the hypothesis that our two extreme groups (normals and neurotics) are not in fact objectively discriminated at all, but are merely chance and random selections from a homogeneous population. To many readers, disproof of the null hypothesis will appear merely pedantic and completely unnecessary, because this hypothesis goes so much counter to common sense and current psychiatric teaching; however, as we noted in our discussion of the evidence available with respect to the effects of psychiatric treatment, current beliefs are not always accurate guides to scientific knowledge, and a rigid proof must not be built on the shifting sands of hearsay and assumption.

In citing evidence against the null hypothesis, we have grouped the studies quoted into four main divisions: Studies dealing with psychiatric ratings, studies dealing with questionnaires and inventories, studies dealing with objective behaviour tests, and studies dealing with constitutional differences. In reviewing this evidence, we will at the same time have an opportunity of discussing hypotheses regarding the traits which may be said to correlate with the neuroticism continuum, and to characterize the neurotic, unstable end as opposed to the normal, stable end. We will also be able to review some of the evidence which suggests that neither ratings nor self-ratings can be relied on to give us the reliable,

84

valid, and objective type of evidence which we are looking for. No attempt has been made to give a complete survey of the literature. We have attempted rather to pick out important landmarks relevant to our main hypothesis, and characterized by proper research design, adequacy of statistical treatment, and use of a sufficiently large number of cases. The principle of selection was that one convincing demonstration is superior to a discussion of a hundred papers all of them deficient from one point of view or another; in cases of doubt, preference has been given to material otherwise not easily accessible.

(1) *Ratings and Psychiatric Diagnoses*

The first of the studies chosen to illustrate this section was carried out by Reyburn and Raath (1950), and involved the rating by 83 observers of two subjects each. The total experimental population consisted of 160 ratees, evenly balanced with respect to sex and University education. Inter-rater reliability on a few subjects who were rated by two observers was ·806. Ratings were on a five-point scale, covering 45 well-defined personality traits; the actual ratings were gone over in each case with the rater by one of the experimenters to ensure proper understanding of the categories used.

The table of intercorrelations was subjected to several methods of analysis; of particular interest here is the oblique solution which resulted in six factors which were not independent of each other, and the correlations between which clearly gave rise to higher-order factors. These were not derived by the writers, but were calculated from their Table V for inclusion in this book. Thirteen iterations were required before the communalities began to converge. The results are very clear-cut, and are set out in Table XIII below. It will be seen that the first factor, which was rotated to

TABLE XIII

FACTOR SATURATIONS FOR ORIGINAL AND ROTATED SOLUTIONS

	I	II	I′	II″	h^2
1. Spontaneity	− ·230	·575	− ·461	·414	·387
2. Stability	·872	− ·428	·972	·000	·945
3. Persistence	·554	− ·215	·592	·050	·353
4. Assertiveness	·621	·789	·210	·978	1·001
5. Sensitivity	− ·401	− ·044	− ·340	− ·218	·163
6. Inferiority	− ·472	− ·384	− ·256	− ·554	·372

pass through 'stability', has a saturation of ·972 for that item; this identifies it as the opposite end of the 'neuroticism' factor with which we are concerned. It is reasonable to find that persistence is closely associated with stability, and that assertiveness also has a positive projection on this factor. Inferiority feeling and sensitivity are understandably loaded negatively with stability, as is also the factor 'spontaneity'.

The second factor opposes 'assertiveness' and 'spontaneity' to 'inferiority' and 'sensitivity'; this falls in with our conception of introversion and extraversion respectively. We thus get a very interesting confirmation here for our view of 'neuroticism' and 'introversion-extraversion' as second-order factors in the orectic sphere, corresponding to Thurstone's intellectual second-order factor in the cognitive sphere. Figure 9 gives a diagrammatic representation of the results.

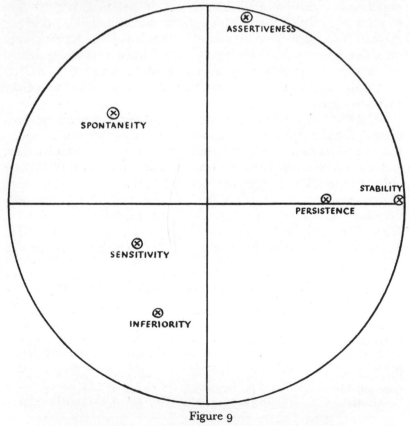

Figure 9

The other main research to be discussed under this heading is one reported in three papers by Mayer-Gross *et al.* (1949), Slater (1947), and Rao *et al.* (1949). A total of 201 neurotic and 55 normal officers were rated by a psychiatrist on thirteen main behaviour 'pointers', which are defined at some length in the original publication. Ratings were confined to noting either the presence or the absence of the particular trait to be rated. A brief statement of the traits used is given in Table XIV, together with the proportion of cases showing any of the traits in either the normal or the neurotic group. All the differences observed were

TABLE XIV

Personality 'pointer' rated	Percentage Incidence		D	Factor * Loadings
	Neurotics	Normals		
1. Heredity	·41	·13	76	2·13
2. Physical ill-health	·27	·00	54	2·11
3. Neurotic traits in childhood	·45	·16	82	4·62
4. Former psychiatric illness	·37	·05	71	3·45
5. Shy, solitary, etc. in childhood	·40	·11	74	3·96
6. Difficulty in making social contacts	·33	·07	62	3·28
7. Emotional instability	·73	·09	141	4·42
8. Obsessional features	·37	·13	67	1·74
9. Apprehensiveness	·59	·02	117	5·25
10. Dependence	·53	·04	105	4·61
11. Unstable work record	·23	·07	43	2·00
12. Marriage or sexual difficulties	·34	·05	65	2·81
13. Alcoholism	·21	·00	42	·57

* Values of p' $i\sqrt{n}$ obtained directly from a matrix of 2 × 2 tables on the assumption of a general factor and two group factors.

shown to be significant by means of a chi squared analysis. Also given is a column headed 'D', showing the absolute differences in occurrence of each 'pointer' between the normal and the neurotic groups; this column will be referred to as the 'difference column'.

A table showing the frequency of concomitance of pairs of items was prepared, and factor analysed directly, i.e. without conversion into correlations first, as would be the more usual procedure. This analysis resulted in one prominent general factor, and two relatively unimportant subsidiary factors. The general factor saturations correlated + ·79 with the 'difference column', thus leaving little doubt about the identification of this factor as one of 'neuroticism', or 'constitutional adequacy', as the writers prefer to call it. The other factors are identified as 'episodic instability' and 'shyness' respectively. Scores for these three factors were derived very simply by noting the number of pointers of each class for each individual, thus obtaining three scores (A, B, and C) for each individual. These three variables can be considered as defining a space of three dimensions so that any particular individual can be represented by a point in such a space. Groups of individuals, as for instance the clinically-diagnosed syndromes of obsession, hysteria, anxiety state, or post-traumatic personality change, can then be represented by a cluster of points around the mean value of that cluster.

As the neurotic members of the sample used by the investigators had been diagnosed in these various categories, it was possible to test the hypothesis that the mean values of the groups in question were collinear in the three-dimensional test space; in other words, that differences between these syndromes could be accounted for entirely by differences in severity of neurosis, without any other principle of differentiation. The appropriate tests of significance indeed show that this is the case. However, it appeared of some interest to calculate the first two canonical variates, and plot the position of the various groups in the two-dimensional space thus generated. The resulting picture is shown in Figure 10 and the figures are given in Table XV. Much the greater part of the variation occurring is obviously taken up by the 'severity of neurosis' component, λ_1, ranking the groups in order from normal to obsessional and psychopathic. However, the second dimension, λ_2, although not significant, suggests a grouping closely in accord with the hypothesis outlined in *Dimensions of Personality*, namely, that additional to the dimension of neuroticism, and orthogonal to it, we have another dimension, that of extraversion-introversion, which finds its prototype in the neurotic population in the hysteric-psychopathic (extraverted) and the anxious-obsessional (intro-verted) type of personality. It will be seen that the main division suggested by the λ_2 variable is precisely between the hysteric-psychopathic group on the one hand, and the anxious-obsessional group on the other. The lack of significance is perhaps explicable in terms of the small number of cases involved—there were only 17 cases in the obsessional group, for instance, and only 5 in the 'personality change' group. Alternatively, the suggestion may be advanced that through condensation of the original 13 scores into 3 only, too much information was lost to allow existing differences to appear clearly. Or again, the original choice of variables, made in order to maximize normal-neurotic differences, may not have been adequate for bringing out differences within the neurotic group itself. That one of these explanations is likely to be true is indicated by our success in differentiating between introverted and extraverted neurotic groups by means of psychological tests.

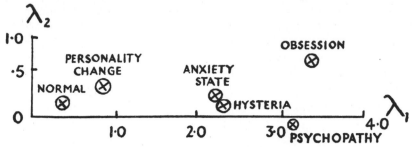

Figure 10.—Configuration of Diagnostic Groups

TABLE XV

MEAN VALUES OF FIRST TWO CANONICAL VARIATES

Group	λ_1	λ_2
Normal	·39	·16
Personality Change	·79	·36
Anxiety State	2·22	·21
Hysteria	12·32	·11
Psychopathy	3·13	−·11
Obsessional	3·36	·62

These ratings were made *post hoc*, as it were, and dealt with subjects who had already broken down; consequently they can hardly escape the criticism that they do not furnish us with evidence of predictive validity. Unless a rating can be made *before breakdown* which will identify the potential neurotic the value of the method must remain in doubt. Evidence on this point is given by two important studies by W. A. Hunt *et al.* (1949), using what they call the 'historico-experimental' method. Their experiment was designed to test the hypothesis that Naval neuro-psychiatric screening was efficacious in lowering the subsequent rate of neuro-psychiatric attrition during service, and was based on the premiss that 'the more neuropsychiatrically unfit individuals who are removed from a sample of recruits during the recruit training period, the smaller should be the number of medical surveys for neuropsychiatric reasons among that sample during their later military service . . . if neuropsychiatric screening performed its assumed function, an inverse relation should exist between the recruit screening rate at the Naval Training Station level, and the subsequent rate of neuropsychiatric attrition during service'.

Three training stations were selected in such a way that recruit populations and professional psychiatric competence of interviewing staff were roughly comparable; the major difference between the stations lay in the differential discharge rate for neuropsychiatric reasons, based on different attitudes towards psychiatry held by the Commanding Officers of these stations. The results of this study are clearly shown in Table XVI; it will be seen that in the stations which tended to act upon the psychiatrist's recom-

TABLE XVI

Training Station	N	Percentage Discharged during Training	Percentage Discharged Subsequently	Percentage Discharged Subsequently by Years		
				1943	1944	1945
Great Lakes	1525	4·5	1·5	·3	·5	·7
Newport	1173	.2·6	1·8	·5	·4	·9
Sampson	2823	·7	3·0	·6	1·0	1·5
Total:	5521	2·2	2·4	·5	·7	1·1

mendation, subsequent attrition rate for neuropsychiatric reasons was only about half of that shown by the station which tended to reject psychiatric advice. It will also be seen from the figures that there appears some evidence of a law of diminishing returns in neuropsychiatric screening; the subsequent attrition rates of 'Great Lakes' and 'Newport' stations are very similar, although in one of them only half as many recruits were discharged during training as in the other, due to the fact that the Commanding Officer attempted to set some upper limit to the number of screening discharges. These results were confirmed in another paper by the same authors, using further large groups of recruits, and since the sample involved in these studies is now over 17,000 cases, and since the controls are probably as satisfactory as can be hoped for with such large scale research carried out in wartime conditions, 'the authors feel that the use of neuropsychiatric screening by the Navy in World War II has been validated, and that the rational argument for neuropsychiatric screening has been confirmed by experimental findings'. With this statement the present writer is in full agreement; the importance of these studies in proving the possibility of identifying the potential neurotic before he is exposed to the stress that leads to later breakdown can hardly be exaggerated.

However, while it can thus be shown that psychiatric rating procedures have a certain amount of validity, complacency is hardly in order when we look at certain results published by the Information and Education Division in the U.S. War Department (Stouffer, 1949). These results have a bearing on the question of reliability rather than on the question of validity, except that validity, in the long run, cannot outstrip reliability; as far as they go, however, they show a picture of unreliability which must cause one to pause before accepting ratings as conclusive evidence in relation to the type of problem we are discussing here. A brief discussion of some of the data on which this judgment is based will now be given.

During August, 1945, 42·3 per cent of all literate preinduction examinees were rejected, 14 per cent for psychiatric reasons: 5·6 per cent were rejected with the diagnosis of 'psychoneurotic', 3·9 per cent with the diagnosis of 'psychopathic', ·3 per cent with the diagnosis of 'psychotic', and 4·2 per cent for other psychiatric reasons. When rejections are analysed by induction station (there were fifty-five of these) the percentage of psychiatric rejections is found to be very unstable, ranging from ·5 and 3·8 per cent at the one end to 50·6 per cent at the other! In other words, for every one inductee rejected for psychiatric reasons in one centre, there are over one hundred rejected in another. The plausible argument that perhaps the figures represent a faithful picture of the actual incidence among the populations drawn into these various induction stations is rejected by the writers of the report, who give convincing reasons why this is most unlikely. We are left with the unreliability of psychiatric assessment as the most probable cause.

Among rejects, there are equally large differences between stations with respect to the different diagnoses. With an average of 39·9 per cent being diagnosed as psychoneurotic among all the rejects, the percentage varies from 2·7 to 90·2 per cent for different stations! Percentage of psychotic diagnoses varies from 26·8 to ·0 per cent. Percentage of psychopathic diagnoses varies from 70·9 to 2·0 per cent. Such differences again must be put down to unreliability of psychiatric classification, and while it is true that the psychiatrist was not given much time in these stations for arriving at a diagnosis, this handicap should not affect the relative incidence of different forms of disorder.[1]

It might be objected that in the study just quoted, psychiatrists were working under a disadvantage, due to being under heavy pressure and not having sufficient time to arrive at an accurate diagnosis, as well as to being forced to use diagnoses which might not be in line with their special training or with their theoretical outlook. We may therefore quote briefly a study of psychiatric reliability in which the dice were, as it were, loaded in favour of the psychiatrist (Air Ministry, 1947). A number of air crew who had been referred for examination by a psychiatrist, had in actual fact been seen by two psychiatrists at intervals of a few weeks; both psychiatrists made a report on the case which included a three-point rating on his neuroticism ('predisposition to neurosis'). Unfortunately, the two opinions were not independent; the second psychiatrist had available to him some part of the opinion of the first psychiatrist to study the case, thus possibly increasing the probability of agreement. Also, the variance of the trait under consideration (neuroticism) is likely to have been much larger in this sample than in an unselected group—some 25 per cent were rated as having had severe predisposition, a rating very much less frequently encountered in unselected populations. This extension of range again would tend to increase the inter-observer reliability. Thirdly, judgment here is *ex post facto*; the psychiatrist is not asked to make a forecast as to what a person may do under unspecified conditions (as is the case in the American work quoted above). He is asked to rate the person in the light of his knowledge of that person's behaviour in a specified situation or set of situations, manifestly a much easier task. On the other hand, presumably these 541 people were seen twice because they presented certain difficulties in diagnosis, a fact which would tend to lower the inter-observer reliability. On the whole, probably these various considerations almost balance out, making the final figure for the reliability of psychiatric ratings a slight overestimate.

Yet the overall results, in spite of these relatively favourable

[1] It should not be supposed that medical diagnoses in fields other than the psychiatric are invariably characterized by a high degree of reliability; the papers by Franzen & Brimhall (1942a, 1942b) should be consulted in this connection.

conditions, are rather disappointing. Total misclassification (disagreements of one observer with the other) is 31 per cent. The coefficient of contingency is ·459; when this is corrected for the small number of categories in order to make it comparable with a product moment correlation, the value only rises to ·534. This value is far below anything that would be considered acceptable in connection with a psychological test, and when in other parts of this book correlations are run between psychological tests and psychiatric criteria, it must be borne in mind that even under favourable conditions this criterion has a reliability of only ·534, and that consequently even a perfect test of neuroticism could not correlate higher than $\sqrt{\cdot534} = \cdot731$ with this criterion.[1]

While it might be objected that a diagnosis is not the same thing as a rating, it is in fact difficult to draw a line between the two; a rating of 'emotional instability' is often *de facto* equivalent to a diagnosis of 'neurotic' in certain situations. On the whole, these large-scale data bear out the widely-accepted and well-documented view that valid and reliable evidence of the personality of the person rated is difficult to obtain by means of ratings, and should never be accepted without empirical verification (Vernon, 1938). Ratings may give suggestive results, as for instance in the important attempts of Cattell (1946) to isolate the fundamental source traits in the 'personality sphere', but as Cattell himself would be the first to agree, it is not until we go from the sphere of ratings into the field of testing congruence of ratings with objective measures that our findings are worthy of general acceptance. Ratings, fundamentally, are the product of an interaction between two personalities—rater and ratee—and as long as the former cannot be regarded as forming a constant part of the total situation, so long will the final rating be partly an indication of the

[1] This is of course a maximum figure assuming a perfectly reliable and perfectly valid test, and assuming that psychiatrists' judgments are perfectly valid apart from their unreliability. In practice we can only approach this condition by using, not a single test, but a whole battery of tests, and extracting from the intercorrelations of these tests a factor of neuroticism which is, within the limits of sampling errors, a valid and reliable estimate of a person's 'true' neuroticism. It is interesting, in this connection, to note that in a previous study along factorial lines the reliability of the psychiatrist's judgment was computed, using the inverse of the above equation for the maximum validity of a psychiatrist's rating, i.e. using the psychiatric rating's known validity in terms of its factor saturation to find the psychiatrist's reliability (Eysenck, 1947). The validity was ·71, the reliability was $\cdot71^2 = \cdot50$, which agrees admirably with the figure found empirically in the R.A.F. study under discussion.

rater's personality as well as reflecting to an unknown degree the personality of the subject who is being rated.

(2) *Pencil and Paper Tests*

(a) *Questionnaires.*—The evidence in this field shows quite clearly that *under suitable conditions* questionnaire responses can be relied on to give excellent discrimination between normals and neurotics. One example has already been given on page 56, where it was shown that fifteen separate questionnaire-type scales gave positive correlations of varying size with the normal-neurotic criterion; it was also shown that the intercorrelations of these scales followed a pattern which could be shown by means of criterion analysis to support the general hypothesis of a general factor of neuroticism or stability advanced here. The actual discrimination obtained by the use of a questionnaire based on the first of the fifteen scales described is shown in Figure 11; it will be seen that when a cutting

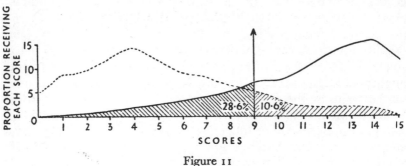

Figure 11

score of 9 is used, only 10·6 per cent of neurotics are misclassified as normals, and 28·6 per cent of normals misclassified as neurotics. The use of weighted scores gives a slight improvement, but the gain would not be sufficient to compensate for the complexity of the procedure.

Similar results may be quoted from many different sources. Typical of questionnaires used in this connection is the Maudsley Medical Questionnaire, which is reproduced below (Table XVII). In Table XVIII are given the scores (number of 'Yes' answers) of 1,000 normal and 1,000 neurotic (discharged) members of H.M. Forces; these figures are shown in diagrammatical form in Figure 12. A more detailed comparison of answers to individual items is given in Figure 13, which shows percentage endorsements of normals and neurotics respectively for the sixteen most discriminating items of the scale.

TABLE XVII

THE MAUDSLEY MEDICAL QUESTIONNAIRE

NAME.....................................ARMY NO. ....
Read through these questions and underline the correct answer, either 'Yes' or 'No'. Do not omit any item.
It is important that you should be quite frank.

(1) Do you have dizzy turns?	Yes	No
(2) Do you get palpitations or thumping in your heart?	Yes	No
(3) Did you ever have a nervous breakdown?	Yes	No
(4) Have you ever been off work through sickness a good deal?	Yes	No
(5) Did you often use to get 'stage fright' in your life?	Yes	No
(6) Do you find it difficult to get into conversation with strangers?	Yes	No
(7) Have you ever been troubled by a stammer or stutter?	Yes	No
(8) Have you ever been made unconscious for two hours or more by an accident or blow?	Yes	No
(9) Do you worry too long over humiliating experiences?	Yes	No
(10) Do you consider yourself rather a nervous person?	Yes	No
(11) Are your feelings easily hurt?	Yes	No
(12) Do you usually keep in the background on social occasions?	Yes	No
(13) Are you subject to attacks of shaking or trembling?	Yes	No
(14) Are you an irritable person?	Yes	No
(15) Do ideas run through your head so that you cannot sleep?	Yes	No
(16) Do you worry over possible misfortunes?	Yes	No
(17) Are you rather shy?	Yes	No
(18) Do you sometimes feel happy, sometimes depressed, without any apparent reason?	Yes	No
(19) Do you daydream a lot?	Yes	No
(20) Do you seem to have less life about you than others?	Yes	No
(21) Do you sometimes get a pain over your heart?	Yes	No
(22) Do you have nightmares?	Yes	No
(23) Do you worry about your health?	Yes	No
(24) Have you sometimes walked in your sleep?	Yes	No
(25) Do you sweat a great deal without exercise?	Yes	No
(26) Do you find it difficult to make friends?	Yes	No
(27) Does your mind often wander badly, so that you lose track of what you are doing?	Yes	No
(28) Are you touchy on various subjects?	Yes	No
(29) Do you often feel disgruntled?	Yes	No
(30) Do you often feel just miserable?	Yes	No
(31) Do you often feel self-conscious in the presence of superiors?	Yes	No
(32) Do you suffer from sleeplessness ?	Yes	No
(33) Did you ever get short of breath without having done heavy work?	Yes	No
(34) Do you ever suffer from severe headaches?	Yes	No
(35) Do you suffer from 'nerves'?	Yes	No
(36) Are you troubled by aches and pains?	Yes	No
(37) Do you get nervous in places such as lifts, trains or tunnels?	Yes	No
(38) Do you suffer from attacks of diarrhœa?	Yes	No
(39) Do you lack self-confidence?	Yes	No
(40) Are you troubled with feelings of inferiority?	Yes	No

TABLE XVIII

Score	Normal	Neurotic
0–2	118	55
3–5	171	34
6–8	187	52
9–11	165	66
12–14	120	80
15–17	101	81
18–20	65	96
21–23	42	123
24–26	21	124
27–29	12	144
30+	1	145
Average:	9·98	20·01

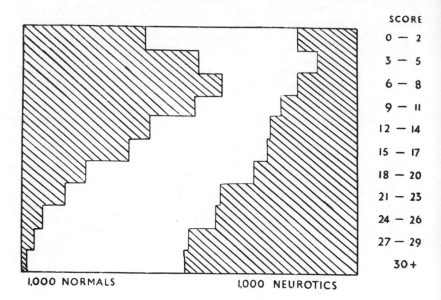

SCORE

0 — 2

3 — 5

6 — 8

9 — 11

12 — 14

15 — 17

18 — 20

21 — 23

24 — 26

27 — 29

30+

1,000 NORMALS   1,000 NEUROTICS

Figure 12.—Distribution of Scores

Comparable results to those quoted above are available from the selection and screening work of the U.S. Navy, an example of the results of which is given in Figure 14. The differentiation between well-adjusted, doubtful, and discharged sailors is quite clear and springs to the eye (Stuit, 1947). The War Shipping

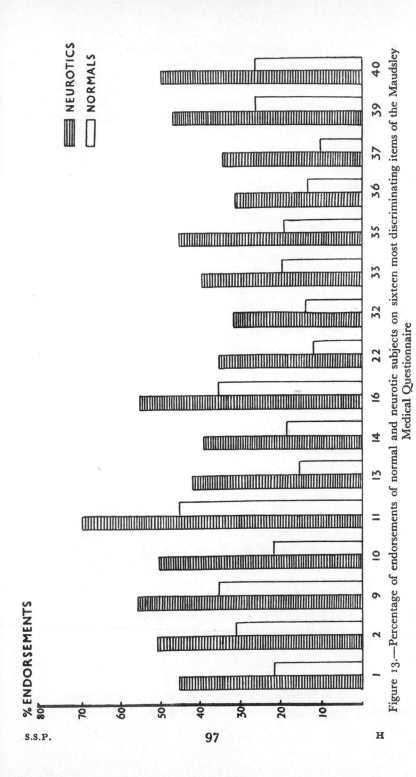

Figure 13.—Percentage of endorsements of normal and neurotic subjects on sixteen most discriminating items of the Maudsley Medical Questionnaire

Administration has also published some of the results achieved through the use of neuroticism questionnaires; Figure 15 shows a typical picture of the differentiation achieved between normal and neurotic merchant seamen (Killinger, 1947). There is little advantage in multiplying instances; it is hardly possible to deny that unselected subjects make scores markedly different from those made by subjects diagnosed as 'neurotic' by psychiatrists, and separated from the service.

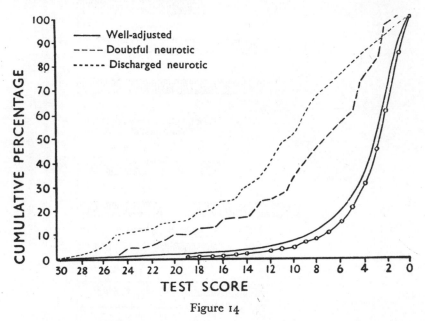

Figure 14

It might be maintained that these results are artefacts due to the selection process, in the sense that it is only after their breakdown and separation from the service that neurotics give answers differing from those of normals; if that were so it would not be possible to use questionnaires in attempts to predict breakdown, and in screening out those recruits most prone to neurotic disability. Three studies tend to invalidate this common objection.

In the first place, questionnaires tend to show high correlations with psychiatric opinion. Thus in one experiment in which over 500 subjects were given the Maudsley Medical Questionnaire, and interviewed by a psychiatrist, a correlation of + ·70 was obtained, although the psychiatrist was of course quite ignorant of the

questionnaire results (Eysenck, 1947*b*). But as we have shown in
the preceding section, the validity of psychiatric ratings for future
breakdown has been established; it would seem to follow that
methods correlating highly with psychiatric assessment would also
show a certain degree of validity.

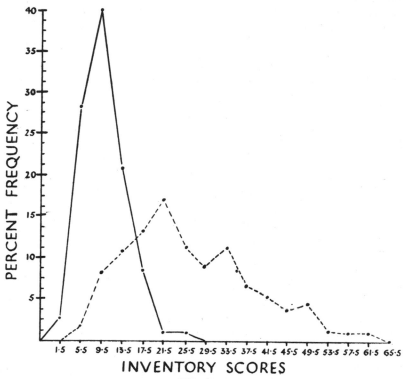

Figure 15

In the second place, questionnaire results within an unselected
population can be shown to be related to independent variables
such as age and education in precisely the same way in which
these variables are related to the incidence of neurosis. 'If we
examine the age-education distributions of the cross section of
white enlisted men . . . and the hospitalized psychoneurotics
from among their number . . . it is at once apparent that there is
an excess of psychoneurotics in exactly those classes in which the
Anxiety Symptoms Index (the questionnaire used in these studies)
was shown to select relatively higher proportions—among older

men and among the less well educated men' (Stouffer, 1949). This striking agreement argues strongly in favour of the general validity of the questionnaire results.

In the third place, we have in addition to such indirect evidence as has been presented above, direct evidence regarding the forecasting efficiency of questionnaire items, and followed up over a period of six months. A sample of 73 men who had had a neurotic breakdown subsequent to their test was compared with a sample of 730 men who had had no such breakdown subsequent to their test, and who were matched with the 'breakdown' group for age, education, and marital status. The results of this experiment (Stouffer, 1949) show very clearly marked differences in questionnaire responses between the experimental and the control group. This result is all the more interesting as typical neuroticism questions were intermingled with questions dealing with various aspects of morale; the former (e.g. 'In general, how would you say you feel most of the time, in good spirits or low spirits?' or 'What kind of physical condition are you in?') were far superior in differentiating the two groups than were the latter (e.g. 'In general how well do you think the Army is run?' or, 'In general what sort of time do you have in the Army?'). It seems clear, then, both from our discussion of the indirect evidence and from the direct evidence just quoted, that questionnaire responses do not only differentiate between acknowledged neurotics and normals, but also that such responses can be used to single out the prospective neurotic from a group of unselected recruits.

This general conclusion is in agreement with Vernon's (1938) appraisal of questionnaire studies: 'We are probably justified in concluding that they do measure psychologically significant variables when the testees are adequately motivated to give candid responses.' In a similar vein, Ellis (1946, 1948) concludes his review of some four hundred validation studies by saying: 'Military applications of personality inventories have yielded enough favourable results to command attention. In contrast, personality inventories in civilian practice have generally proved disappointing.' Regarding the use of questionnaires in civilian practice, he holds that 'the older, more conventional, and more widely used forms of these tests seem to be, for practical diagnostic purposes, hardly worth the paper on which they are printed.' In support of this statement he presents a summary table showing that validation studies in non-military groups very frequently show 'negative validity', which appears to be his somewhat surprising way of saying that validity coefficients are below + ·40. While his use of descriptive epithets is unusual—a validity coefficient of + ·69 would be called by him 'questionable positive'—here is little doubt that he has succeeded in showing that questionnaires in civilian work are less valid than in military research.

This diversity of results obtained with questionnaires underlines the dependence of results on the motivation of the subjects, and the general conditions under which the testing is carried out. As long as neither motivation nor conditions can be adequately controlled, so long will it be impossible to regard questionnaires and inventories as anything more than supplementary evidence, to be regarded with suspicion unless shown to be valid in the particular set of circumstances which happens to be under investigation. Under favourable conditions, as the figures quoted above show, questionnaires can be of very great utility and scientific value; under less favourable conditions, validity coefficients may approach zero, or even be negative. As in the case of ratings, it is difficult to see how a scientific analysis of human personality can proceed on such an unreliable, shifting basis.

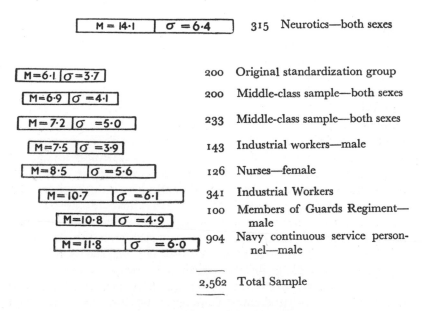

Figure 16.—Description of Sample

(b) *Word Connection List.*—This test, which is essentially an 'alternative choice' version of the word association test, is reproduced in Table XIX. Of the two responses offered for each stimulus word, one is more frequently chosen by neurotics, the other by normals (Crown, 1948). Total score is the number of neurotic responses underlined. The validity and reliability of this test has been established on large numbers of different populations, and representative means and standard deviations are given in Figure 16 to illustrate typical results. These values, which are taken from Crown's (1951) paper summarizing work on this test, show a marked difference between the neurotic and the normal groups. Further results will be quoted later on to substantiate the claims made for this test.

(c) *Annoyances, Interests, Worries, etc.*—Many pencil and paper tests make use of lists of items which might be considered annoying, worrying, interesting, or in some other way related to the emotional life of the subject; the number of items underlined or crossed out is then taken as the score. This type of test, pioneered by Pressey in his X–O test, is less direct than a questionnaire, but more direct than the word connection list; consequently its usefulness would appear to lie between these two other methods of eliciting information through pencil and paper responses. The experimental study to be described was carried out by Bennett (1945) and Slater (1945) on 80 normal and 80 neurotic subjects. The following tests were used:

(1) A neurotic inventory divided into three sections dealing with questions related to the clinical syndromes of anxiety, hysteria, and depression. (2) An annoyances test, listing sixty possibly annoying stimuli or situations of four kinds, fifteen of each, the whole in random order. These four types of stimuli or situation are: (a) frustration of self-assertion, (b) personal inadequacy, (c) dirt or untidiness, (d) noise. (3) Three sections of the Pressey X–O test, modified from the original, and dealing with: (a) activities for which an individual should be blamed, (b) things about which he has ever felt worried, nervous or anxious, (c) items which he likes or in which he is interested. Scores on these ten sub-tests were obtained, and intercorrelations established for the two groups separately, as well as for the combined group of normals and neurotics. Biserial correlations were calculated between the normal-neurotic dichotomy and each of the ten tests; these are reproduced under 'D' in Table XX. Also given are first-factor saturations for

TABLE XIX

WORD CONNECTION LIST

SURNAME.................Christian Names.......................
Below you will find a list of familiar words printed in capital letters, each
followed by two words in small letters. Look at the word SINK in the example
below. Now glance at the two other words. Does the word SINK make you
think more of 'wash' or of 'drown'? Draw a line under whichever word is more
connected in your mind with SINK.

EXAMPLE: SINK wash drown

Some people connect 'wash' with SINK and so they underline 'wash' as
follows: SINK wash drown. Other people connect 'drown' with SINK and
therefore they underline 'drown' as follows: SINK wash drown. There are
no right or wrong answers because one word connection is just as good as
another. Just look at the two words that follow the word in capital letters and
underline the one that *you* feel is more connected in your mind with that word.
WORK FAST. Don't stop to think long about any one word. Be sure not to
leave any words out.

SCISSORS nurse cut
HANDS feet moist
LOUD yell soft
WOMAN girl trouble
LION eat tiger
LIGHT dark sentence
BLUE sad sky
STOMACH food ache
LEFT home right
THOUGHTS ideas strange
SLOW beware fast
BOY girl mischief
SHORT little tall
CONTENTED happy discontented
FAIRY shameful wand
UNHAPPY no yes
THIRSTY dry drink
EATING drinking fasting
FEEL useless good
HEAVY weight heart
TROUBLE lawyer sorrow
DEEP ocean hurt
FRIEND double-crossed close
FOOT hand tingle
MAN work woman

WEIGHT scale losing
DIGNIFIED snobbish poised
TALKED spoke about
SLEEP nightmares bed
RIVER lake danger
BABY foundling little
LOSE find mind
SALMON dislike like
HUNGRY thirsty heart
MAN hard boy
MUTTON eat flesh
SWIFT hurricane slow
BRING take disaster
SWEET affected bitter
FOOD stomach poisoned
RAW deal meat
PARTY crowd myself
BITTER medicine sweet
GRAVE serious funeral
WOMAN excitement man
SOUR lemon stomach
CAN'T concentrate fly
PINT quart whiskey
NEEDLE drug sharp
WOUND bandages feelings

Remember: There are no right or wrong answers. Go as fast as you can.

the normal, the neurotic, and the combined groups. Statistical
tests showed the feasibility of combining the two groups, by comparing the hypothetical matrix derived from the combined analysis
with the correlation tables for the separate groups ($p = \cdot 10$ in each
case).

TABLE XX

	First Factor			'D'
	Neurotics	Normals	Combined	
Inventory: Anxiety	·77	·70	·77	·72
Hysteria	·49	·55	·53	·43
Depression	·78	·75	·70	·72
Annoyances: a	·18	·03	·13	·25
b	·46	·50	·47	·49
c	·12	·21	·13	·10
d	·63	·48	·54	·72
Pressey X–O: a	·06	− ·02	− ·08	·19
b	·43	·55	·49	·65
c	·29	− ·23	− ·18	·56

It will be seen that there is a high correlation between the
criterion column ('D') and the first factor saturations of the groups,
whether separate or combined ($r = \cdot 64$ for the combined values).
This fact may be taken as another indication of the correctness of
the hypothesis of a general factor of 'neuroticism', as can also the
fact that the two matrices derived from the normal and the neurotic
subjects show patterns of intercorrelations substantially identical.

Standard deviations of summed weighted standardized scores
were estimated separately for neurotics and normals, giving values
of $2 \cdot 17$ and $1 \cdot 74$, an insignificant difference statistically. As Slater
comments, 'this is an interesting finding. If neurotic personality
were a unitary characteristic persons selected for the possession of
it would have more homogeneous scores of tests which measure it
than unselected persons; instead they are found slightly, though
not significantly, more heterogeneous.' Here we have an argument
independent of criterion analysis which essentially leads to the
same conclusion of the quantitative nature of neuroticism, as
opposed to the qualitative concept.

(d) *Food Aversions.*—The common psychiatric observation that
neurotics tend to have special emotional attitudes to food has been
quantified by Wallen (1945) in the form of a food aversion list. A
list of twenty foods is read out to the subjects, and aversions, as
well as the reasons for dislikes, are recorded. Alternatively, printed

questionnaires may be used; there appears to be little to choose between the two methods. Wallen has shown that neurotics report on the average a significantly larger number of food aversions than do normal recruits.

Gough (1946) applied this list to 79 neurotic and 254 normal soldiers, and found mean number of aversions of 5·14 for neurotics and 1·23 for normals, a very significant difference statistically. Less than 5 per cent of the normals disliked more than three foods, while about 70 per cent of the neurotics did so. Table XXI gives the actual food names used, the percentages of normals and neurotics disliking each, and the CR of each difference. The most interesting feature in this table from our point of view lies in the fact that the dislikes of normals and neurotics are highly correlated (*rho* = ·82); in other words, foods disliked by neurotics are also disliked by normals, but not to the same extent, and similarly, foods liked by normals are also liked by neurotics, but not to the same extent. Here, then, we have again support for the quantitative view of the difference between normals and neurotics.

TABLE XXI

PERCENTAGE OF AVERSIONS FOR NEUROTICS AND NORMALS
ON EACH OF TWENTY FOODS

Food	Percentage of Neurotics Disliking	Percentage of Normals Disliking	Critical Ratio
Tea	29·1	9·0	4·5
Grapefruit juice	38·0	4·3	8·0
Bean soup	34·2	5·5	6·8
Potato soup	45·6	5·1	8·9
Salmon	31·6	8·7	5·1
Beefsteak	1·3	·0	1·8
Veal chops	20·3	2·4	5·6
Chicken	8·9	1·2	3·5
Fried eggs	16·4	1·2	5·5
Cottage cheese	51·9	14·6	6·8
Swiss Cheese	36·7	8·7	6·0
Lime beans (broad beans)	24·0	6·7	4·3
Cabbage	35·4	12·2	4·7
Corn	12·7	1·6	4·3
Mushrooms	53·2	25·2	4·3
Radishes	26·6	9·8	3·8
Tomatoes	11·4	2·4	3·4
Cantaloupe	13·9	3·5	3·4
Cherries	13·9	·0	6·0
Pears	8·9	·8	3·9

(3) *Objective Behaviour Tests*

In a sense, the major part of this book deals with objective behaviour tests of one kind or another, and it may seem superfluous to add a special section dealing with them here. However, as this type of test is still relatively unknown to many psychiatrists and clinical psychologists, and neglected almost completely in the practical work of the clinic, the hospital, and the workshop, it seemed worth while to present briefly some of the main developments this type of test has received by psychologists like Luria and Davis in the field of motor control, Hull in the field of suggestibility, Ryans and others in the field of persistence, and various members of the writer's department in several other fields. No attempt will be made to duplicate the summaries given in Dimensions of Personality of these various areas; only one major research will be quoted in each case to establish landmarks, as it were, to guide later interpretations of factorial studies.

(a) *Suggestibility.*—It has been shown elsewhere (Eysenck, 1947) that the most convenient, most reliable, short test of this personality trait, established in two factorial studies, was Hull's Body Sway test. In this test the subject, standing with his eyes closed, his hands hanging down by his side, and his feet together, is made to listen to a gramophone record which repeats the words: 'You are falling, you are falling forward, you are falling forward all the time. You are falling, you are falling, you are falling now. . . .' His maximum forward or backward sway in response to this suggestion during the $2\frac{1}{2}$ minutes' duration of the test is his score, and it has been shown in several distinct researches that the amount of sway, and the frequency of complete falls, increases with an increase in the degree of neuroticism.[1] As an example we quote below results from 960 male and 390 female subjects; 60 subjects in each group were normal, the others were neurotics rated by psychiatrists on a six-point scale as to severity of disorder, I being the mildest, VI the most severe grade (Figure 17). The amount of body sway in inches is shown for each of these groups; the number of cases in each group is given in brackets underneath each column. It will be seen that there is a completely regular progression in amount of sway from the normal group through the intermediate neurotic groups to the most neurotic group, both for the men and for the women. Where a sway of 1 inch is about the normal average, the most

[1] This test is illustrated in photographs 5, 6, 7, 8.

severe neurotic groups swayed 5·55 and 6·72 inches respectively for the two sexes. This study is but one of several showing a strong correlation between neuroticism and suggestibility. In none of the studies, incidentally, were any marked differences noted between hysterics and other types of neurotics.

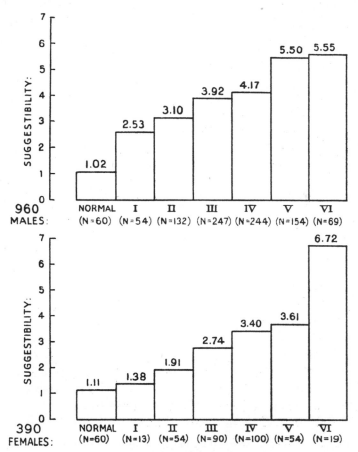

Figure 17.—Average suggestibility of Normals and Neurotics, showing increase in suggestibility correlated with increase in 'Neuroticism'

(b) *Manual Dexterity.*—While tests of this type have usually been regarded as tests of ability pure and simple, it has been shown that very large and significant differences can be observed between normals and neurotics with respect to various tests in this group, such as the O'Connor Tweezers test (Eysenck, 1950), for instance, or the U.S.E.S. tests (Lubin, 1951).[1] Correlations with the neurotic-normal dichotomy are in the neighbourhood of + ·60. Psychotics also appear to be deficient in these tests, but their pattern of disability is very different from that of the neurotics, as will be shown later.

(c) *Level of Aspiration.*—The general technique of level of aspiration tests requires the repeated performance of a task (usually a mechanical one) which can be carried out with varying degrees of speed, accuracy, or goodness; it is essential that the variable chosen should be expressible in numerical terms (number of seconds, number of errors, etc.), and that the subject should not be able from his performance to estimate with great precision his actual score.[2] The subject is made acquainted with the task; he is then asked to give an estimate of how well he expects to do on his next performance. (This estimate must be made in quantitative terms, of course.) This estimate is called his 'aspiration score'. He then performs the task, and is asked to give an estimate, again in numerical terms, of how well he has done; this estimate is called his 'judgment score'. He is then told what his actual score on the performance was (his 'performance score'), and asked to estimate how well he will do next time. This procedure is repeated a number of times—usually from five to ten repetitions are required to get reliable data. Two main scores are derived from these data: (1) Mean goal discrepancy score. This is based on the difference between actual performance on trial X and aspiration for trial (X + 1); it is positive if the aspiration is higher than the preceding performance, and negative if it is lower. Discrepancy scores are averaged for all trials. (2) Mean judgment discrepancy score. This is based on the difference between actual performance score and judgment score on trial X; underestimation of past performance gives a negative score, overestimation a positive one.

The relation of these scores to neurosis appears to be curvi-

---

[1] These and several other tests used at various times are illustrated in photographs 19, 20, 23, 25, 26.

[2] The most frequently used task in our work has been the Triple Tester, illustrated in photograph no. 10. The subject is required to manipulate the handwheel so as to move the stylus which plays on the drum; the connection between wheel and stylus is through an integrating disc. Object is to touch with the stylus as many holes in the ivorine cover of the drum as possible; hits are scored automatically on an electric counter (Eysenck, 1947). This instrument was developed by the Cambridge Psychological Department for quite different purposes, but proved to be particularly useful for work on level of aspiration.

linear rather than linear. We find that when the neurotic sample is broken up into the introverted (dysthymic) and extraverted (hysteric) groups, these groups show large differences. Introverts have high levels of aspiration (high positive goal discrepancy score) and severely underestimate their past performance (high negative judgment discrepancy scores). Extraverts have low levels of aspiration (low positive or even negative goal discrepancy scores) and show no tendency to underestimate their past performance—indeed, they may overestimate it (low negative or even positive judgment scores). Normals in either case are intermediate between these two extremes, having medium high positive goal discrepancy scores and medium high negative judgment discrepancy scores (Eysenck, 1947; Himmelweit, 1946; Miller, 1951). Figure 18 gives a schematic drawing of these relations. It follows from what has been said that differences between a normal group and a neurotic group would depend on the proportion of hysterics and dysthymics

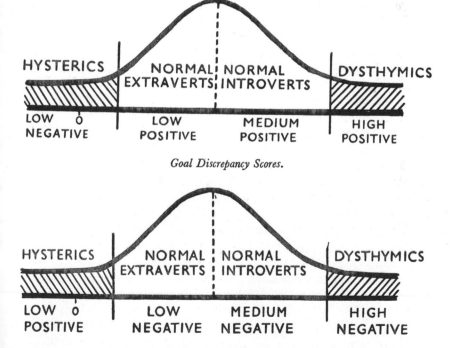

Goal Discrepancy Scores.

Judgment Discrepancy Scores.

Figure 18

in the neurotic group; unless this is controlled it is difficult to make any prediction.

Not only do normals and neurotics differ with respect to actual scores; they also differ with respect to the pattern of scoring. When goal and judgment discrepancies are correlated, these correlations tend to be positive for normal and negative for neurotic groups. As an example, we may take the following correlations, based on male and female groups respectively: $+ \cdot 59$ and $+ \cdot 39$ for normals, and $- \cdot 68$ and $- \cdot 39$ for neurotics. These differences are presumably due to the peculiar curvilinear relation between neuroticism and the discrepancy scores.

(d) *Motor Response Disorganization.*—The view that under emotional stress there is a disorganization of motor processes, and that this disorganization will be more noticeable in neurotics than in normals, is not a novel one, and may be traced in its experimental development to the early work of Nunberg at the time of the First World War, who combined the Word Association test with measurement of hand movements of an involuntary kind (1918).

These early and technically somewhat unsatisfactory studies were taken up by Luria (1932), in a series of researches too well known to be detailed here. Although others, such as Olson and Jones (1931), Crosland (1931), Huston *et al.* (1934), Barnacle *et al.* (1935), Houtchens (1935), Runkel (1936), Burtt (1936), Krause (1937), Gardner (1937), Shuey (1937), Speer (1937), Sharp (1938), Reymert (1938), Morgan and Ojeman (1942), Albino (1948), and particularly Clarke (1950), have shown the essential correctness of the general thesis through use of the Luria technique, the example given here is taken from the methodologically somewhat different work of Davis (1948).

This writer carried out a series of investigations into the causes of pilot error. These experiments were carried out in a simulated Cockpit, which is similar to the Link trainer, except that it does not itself move; instruments on the panel respond realistically to movements of the controls. The effects of control movements were less complex than those of an aircraft, but the test was apparently accepted by the subjects as an exercise in instrument flying. This exercise consisted of a series of four manœuvres, together occupying ten minutes, repeated between intervals of straight and level flying. Only the periods of manœuvre were scored; instructions and recording were so arranged that a perfect performance was recorded as a straight line, any deviation indicating an error. Other detailed records of performance which were necessary were also made.

Two types of error were observed; *errors of overaction* and *errors of inertia*. Subjects exhibiting overactivity 'obtained large scores on control movements. Their errors in instrument reading were small and of short duration. . . . Responses to instrument deviations were excessive, the extent and gradient of the movements being greatly increased and over-correcting frequent, with the result that secondary responses were required. Numerous restless movements were observed. . . . Subjects felt excited and under strain, tense and irritable and sometimes frankly anxious. They felt that correction was urgent and made it impatiently. . . . Although . . . subjects were dissatisfied with their performance, they were not discouraged, but keen to improve and continued to try to do the test well. . . . Several pilots reported preoccupation by the test for some time after it was finished. Some returned later in the day and asked for a further opportunity of doing the test.'

Subjects exhibiting the inertia reaction made 'errors which were large and of long duration, whereas activity, represented by scores of control movements, was relatively little. . . . The individual responses were less hurried and less disturbed by restless movements than were those of the pilots showing the overactivity reaction, but they were often more extensive than at the beginning of the test, due probably to the larger size of the instrument deviations and the tendency to make responses proportionate to the size of the deviations. . . . Subjects reported that their interest had flagged and that their concentration had failed. A feeling of strain had now given way to one of mild boredom, tedium or tiredness. . . . In contrast to the restless striving of the overactive class, the pilots in the inert class gave the impression that they had lowered their standards of performance to a level well within their powers. . . . Subjects' judgment of the degree of accuracy to which they had attained was usually faulty, and they were unaware of the degree to which they had failed to correct deviations of the instruments. . . . There was . . . an emotional indifference as far as the test itself was concerned.'

These results are closely in accord with Nunberg's observation in his original work, which led him to posit the existence of two types of individual, the one showing inhibition under affect (the inertia reaction), the other exhibiting increased excitability (the overaction response). They also link up remarkably well with experimental work on the extravert-introvert dimension reported in *Dimensions of Personality* (Eysenck, 1947) showing that introverts (like the overactive response type) tend to show anxiety, to be irritable, to have a high level of aspiration, and to be dissatisfied with their performance. Extraverts (like the inertive response type) tended to show emotional indifference, to have low levels of aspiration, adjusted to actual performance, and to be satisfied with their performance, however poor.

These experiments thus give rise to two main hypotheses which admit of proof or disproof: (1) Pilots who are neurotic should show a larger proportion of abnormal (overactive or inert) reactions than pilots who are not diagnosed as neurotic, and (2) pilots who are diagnosed as suffering from dysthymic disorders (anxiety state) should show the introverted, overactive behaviour pattern, while pilots suffering from hysteric disorders should show the extraverted, inert behaviour pattern. Both these hypotheses were tested by Davis on 355 normal and 39 neurotic pilots. Taking the comparison between normal and neurotic pilots first, it will be seen from Table XXII that both predictions are verified: 75 per cent of

TABLE XXII

TEST RESULTS OF NORMAL AND NEUROTIC PILOTS

	Reactions						Total N
	Normal		Overactive		Inert		
	No.	%	No.	%	No.	%	
Normal Pilots	268	75	59	17	28	8	355
Neurotic Pilots	13	33	11	28	15	38	39
Acute Anxiety State	6	43	7	20	1	7	14
Hysteria	1	12·5	1	12·5	6	75	8
Other	6	35	3	18	8	47	17

the normals show normal reactions, but only 33 per cent of the neurotics do so. 7 per cent of anxiety states show inert reactions, while 75 per cent of hysterics do so. These conclusions are statistically significant. The number of neurotics is so small that any subdivision would appear unlikely to contain sufficient large numbers of subjects to make conclusions very impressive. Repetition of the experiment, using a modified and much simpler type of apparatus, gave results which show again, at an acceptable level of statistical significance, that the acutely anxious (introvert) type of patient tends to make more extensive responses than did the normal subject, while the hysteric (extravert) patient tends to make less extensive ones. This apparatus is illustrated in photographs 13 and 14. The task consists of aligning the central pointer with the line at the right or at the left, according to the brightness of two lights flashed on at both sides. Movement of the pointer is mediated through an integrating disc, and is produced by turning the hand-wheel. Provision is made for automatic recording of movements, time sequences, etc. (Cf. Davis (1948).)

Our hypothesis of a normal-neurotic continuum would also require that within the normal group there should appear a correlation between neurotic predisposition and percentage of abnormal responses. The percentage of abnormal responses made by the 355 normal pilots is given in Table XXIII after they had been divided in three groups according to psychiatrically assessed degree of neurotic predisposition; it will be seen that there is an increase in abnormal responses from 16 per cent in the group showing least predisposition, through 27 per cent to 46 per cent in the group showing the greatest amount of predisposition. Thus this third hypothesis is also confirmed by Davis's results at a reasonable level of statistical significance. We may take it as established, therefore, that under emotional stress there is a disorganization of motor processes, a disorganization which is closely correlated with neuroticism or lack of emotional stability.

TABLE XXIII

ASSOCIATION OF NEUROTICISM AND TEST SCORE

Predisposition to Neurosis	Normal	Overactive	Inert	Percentage Abnormal
Nil	130	13	12	16
Slight	113	32	9	27
Moderate	25	14	7	46

(e) Body Control.—Several experiments on static ataxia, the Heath rail walking test,[1] and other tests of body control have shown that neurotics are notably inferior in this respect. Results shown below in Figure 19 give data on a simple static ataxia test with 120 normal and 1,230 neurotics, in which instructions were

[1] Illustrated in photograph 18.

simply to stand still and relaxed, with the eyes closed and the hands hanging down the side, feet together. The test lasted for 30 seconds only, and maximum sway either forward or backward was the score of the subject who was being tested.

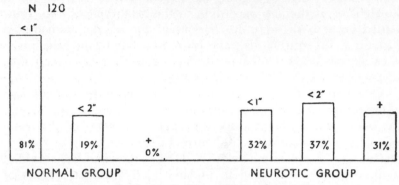

Figure 19.—Static Ataxia Test of Body Controls N= 1,230

(*f*) *Rorschach Test.*—It is possible to treat the Rorschach test in exactly the same manner as any other objective test, by transforming responses into 'scores', and dealing with these scores statistically. Several examples will be given in later chapters; here we will quote one investigation to illustrate the procedure adopted. The example chosen is a factorial analysis of Rorschach responses by A. Sen (1949). The importance of this study lies in two main points. In the first place, the subjects were Indian students (60 men and 40 women, aged for the most part between twenty and twenty-five); thus we have evidence from a racial group differing radically from those on whom our original evidence of neuroticism was based. While this group was 'westernized' to a greater extent than one would ideally have desired, nevertheless these students had spent by far the greater part of their lives in India, and had only recently come into contact with European modes of living.

In the second place, this study enables us to form an opinion on an important theoretical point raised by Burt (1915). In his analysis of personality, he places much emphasis on a trait of 'general emotionality', which in the orectic field assumes an importance reserved in the cognitive field for the general factor of intelligence. This factor was first reported in 1915, in a paper submitted to the Psychological Subsection of the British Association. 'The analyses, based on data from 172 normal children and 157 normal adults, led to the hypothesis of a common factor underlying all the primary emotions, which was termed "general emotionality" (by analogy with "general intelligence").' In a recent paper Burt (1950) has taken this notion up again, and has contrasted the factor of 'emotionality' with the factor of 'neuroticism'. 'A number of investigators who have carried out factorial studies on neurotic cases have found a similar general factor. Many have inferred that, since this factor is common to all the traits assessed for such groups, it can therefore be designated a "general factor of neuroticism". . . . But a general factor for neuroticism would be a factor that is found among neurotic cases only or among traits peculiar to neurotics; and to prove such a conclusion it would be essential to examine a control group of normal persons, and demonstrate that the factor in question is not found among the normal.'

This argument is rather curious, as the general factor of neuroticism has always been presented as constituting a continuum ranging from the most extreme instability to the most marked stability on the other side; to imagine that it should appear only among the neurotic would be equivalent to saying that a general factor of intelligence should appear only among the intelligent, and that to prove such a conclusion it would be essential to examine a control group of dull persons, and demonstrate that the factor in question is not found among the dull! However, arguments in science are not usually as convincing as experimental demonstrations, and Sen's experiment does enable us to reach a conclusion, if only a provisional one, regarding the nature of this factor.

Her subjects were given an individual Rorschach test, a verbal and a non-verbal group test of intelligence, and Cattell's test of fluency. In addition, each subject was rated independently by two judges for the following traits: Intelligence, verbal ability, imagination, perception of relations, general emotionality, extraversion-introversion, assertion-submission, cheerfulness-depression, sociability, anxiety, neurotic tendencies, and extent of vocational and cultural interests. Ratings were on a fifteen-point scale, inter-rater reliabilities ranging from ·51 to ·79, with an average of ·71. Scoring of the Rorschach was carried out, using Beck's procedure with two minor changes. A slight modification of his 'Z-score' was introduced, and Klopfer's 'form level' score was used in addition.

Correlations between scoring categories and the mean intelligence test score are relatively slight, only four being above the 5 per cent level of significance for both men and women. These

four categories are: Good form (·46 and ·44 respectively), movement response (·41 and ·42), modified Beck 'Z score' (·41 and ·42),
and 'form level' score (·50 and ·59). To obtain evidence on correlations with non-cognitive ratings, a factor analysis was performed
on tetrachoric intercorrelations between 36 Rorschach scoring
categories. Three main factors were extracted, contributing 29, 19,
and 7 per cent to the total variance. Approximate factor measurements were calculated for these three factors by reducing the
original scores to standard measure, and then weighting them with
the saturations for the three factors. As a last step, in order to
interpret the factors, these factor measurements were correlated
with the tests and ratings, which thus form an outside criterion.

The first factor is one of associative fluency. This is shown by
the fact that its highest saturation is for total number of responses
(·96), and by the fact that its only significant correlations are with
the fluency test (·48) and with the rating for imagination (·53) and,
very much lower, with the rating for general emotionality. The
second factor is clearly one of intelligence, having correlations of
·51 and ·46 with the two intelligence tests, and a correlation of ·50
with the rating for intelligence. There is also a very small negative
correlation of — ·21 with the rating for neurotic tendencies, which
is well in line with the frequently observed tendency of neuroticism
to show a slight negative correlation with intelligence.

The third factor is identified more clearly even than the other
two. Its only significant correlation is with the rating for neurotic
tendencies (·68), but this is the highest of all the correlations
reported between factors and external criteria. The correlation of
this factor with general emotionality is only ·11, which is quite
insignificant statistically. When it is borne in mind that the reliability of the ratings was itself below ·8, it will be seen that the
third-factor scores provide a remarkably good measure of neuroticism, a conclusion well in line with Cox's (1951) study of normal
and neurotic children, and one which supports the general view
taken throughout this chapter. There is no support at all in favour
of the view that general emotionality has any claim to be regarded
as a strongly-marked and important trait of personality. If relevant
at all, it would appear to be slightly related to the fluency factor,
and through it with extraversion-introversion, as suggested tentatively in *Dimensions of Personality*. But the correlation between
fluency and emotionality (·25) is too low to be of any systematic
importance, and no other significant correlations are reported for

general emotionality. Consequently we may conclude that this experiment has failed to bring forward any evidence in favour of Burt's claims, and that instead the results fit in extremely well with the general scheme of personality description developed here.

(4) Constitutional Differences

The type of study reviewed here deals with tests and measures which are related not so much to behaviour, but rather to qualities of the organism which underlie such behaviour. In the literature, this type of work is frequently listed under the general heading of 'physiological psychology', because constitutional factors are obviously closely related to the physiological make-up of the person. It is primarily on the European continent that constitutional research has flourished, and it may be worth-while to emphasize the main difference between the physiological and the constitutional approaches. In the writer's view, this difference is one of emphasis. To the physiological psychologist, reactions are segmental, and to be studied as far as possible by excluding any facets of the personality not immediately relevant to the ostensible problem. To the constitutional psychologist, reactions are not segmental, but always integrated with the whole personality, and therefore useful in throwing some light on the person who is reacting, as well as on the particular neural or muscular mechanism which is being studied. To the physiological psychologist, dark vision is a segmental phenomenon, to be studied in terms of physiological variables, vitamin A deficiency, and the like; to the constitutional psychologist, its interest lies primarily in its high correlation with emotional instability and behaviour disorders—a correlation to be discussed below. These two approaches are not antithetical, but complementary; the phenomena studied have more than one aspect and need to be studied from many different points of view.

(a) *Body Build (physique)*.—In *Dimensions of Personality* it was shown that a correlation existed between body build and neuroticism. Factor analysis was used in establishing two main factors in body build: (1) A general factor of body growth or body size, and (2) a type factor distinguishing between growth in length and growth in breadth. An index of body build was based on this second factor,

$$\text{I.B.} = \frac{\text{Stature} \times 100}{\text{Transverse Chest Diameter} \times 6}$$

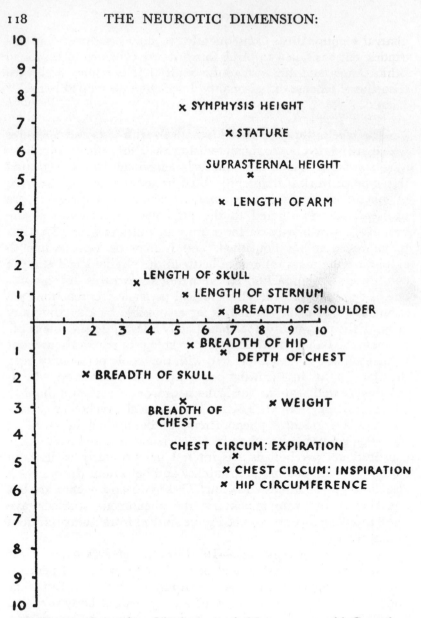

Figure 20.—Saturation of Anthropometric Measurements with General
and Type Factors—Women

which discriminated very significantly between normal and neurotic
soldiers, the neurotics having higher index values, and therefore
being more prone to the lean type of body build (leptomorph)

than the normals who showed a larger number of mesomorphs (index of body build within one ± S.D. of 100) and eurymorphs (thick-set, broad body build, more than one S.D. below 100.) It was also shown that hysterics tended to be significantly more eurymorph than dysthymics, who were markedly leptomorph in body build.

These results were taken from work on men only. Since then, further work has been carried out on women by Rees (1950), showing that intercorrelations of body measures among them also give rise to two factors; diagrammatic representation of these two factors—body size and body type—is given in Figure 20. (An index of body type for women was derived from the saturations of the various measures for the type factor, giving $I.B._w = \cdot 59$ Stature $+ \cdot 47$ symphysis height $- \cdot 31$ chest circumference $- \cdot 64$ hip circumference.) Again, hysterics were found to be more frequently characterized by eurymorph body build, dysthymics by leptomorph body build. And again, the more leptomorph subjects tended to be more severely neurotic. It may therefore be regarded as established that body build is related to the general neuroticism factor, both in men and in women.

(*b*) *Dark Vision.*—Neurotics have poorer dark vision than normals, as has been demonstrated in several independent studies. Figure 21 shows the result on the Livingstone Hexagon test of the

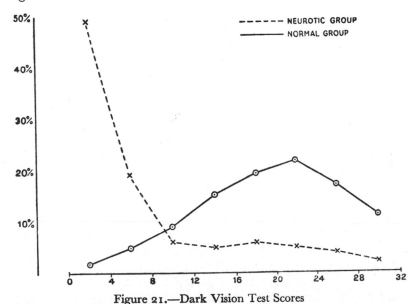

Figure 21.—Dark Vision Test Scores

scores of some 6,000 R.A.F. personnel and 96 neurotics; a score of 0 denotes complete failure in the test situation, while a score of 32 denotes maximum success. The marked difference between the normals and the neurotics springs to the eye (Eysenck, 1947).

(c) *Autonomic Imbalance.*—The hypothesis that neurotics are characterized by imbalance of the autonomic nervous system finds its strongest support in a monograph by Wenger (1948), following up his earlier work with children. Abstracting only a few of his many important findings, we reproduce in Table XXIV C.R.s for autonomic tests used by him on 488 normal and 225 subjects

TABLE XXIV

Item	I CR, Normal v. Operational Fatigue	II Factor Saturations, Normal Group	III Factor Saturations, Operational Fatigue Group	IV CR, Normal v. Neurotics
10. Salivary Output	2·86	·25	—	8·13
12. Salivary pH	2·50	—	·48	4·23
13. Dermographic Latency	1·00	·17	—	·38
14. Dermographic Persistence	·93	·11	—·01	·61
15. Palmar Conductance	4·84	·19	·45	·47
17. Log Conductance Change	1·06	·31	·23	3·36
19. Volar Conductance	1·43	·19	·14	·00
21. Systolic Blood Pressure	6·52	—	·37	4·46
23. Diastolic Blood Pressure	8·60	·30	—	4·60
28. Heart Period	7·82	·60	·36	6·65
30. Sublingual Temperature	2·50	·47	·45	2·00
32. Finger Temperature	3·08	·03	—·02	3·81
44. Tidal Air Mean	5·92	—	·00	2·47
46. Tidal Air Sigma	·42	·15	—	1·58
48. Oxygen Consumption	·80	·13	·35	3·43
52. Pupillary Diameter	·00	—	·00	·00

suffering from operational fatigue. Also given in this table are factor saturations obtained by him from intercorrelations of the normal group only. Only his factor two is considered here, which in his view 'may be defined as representing the autonomic nervous system'. A third column of the table is made up from the factor saturations obtained by him from intercorrelations of the operational fatigue group only (factor 4, page 85). These factors were obtained by Wenger following Thurstone's method of rotation; it will be seen that the factor loadings of the tests are roughly proportional to the discriminatory ability of the tests as shown by their

C.R.s. The correlations between columns 1 and 2 in the table, and between columns 1 and 3, are ·55 and ·29 respectively. Both values rise somewhat when subjected to criterion analysis, but even without this refinement it is clear that the factors existing within each group are essentially similar to, and identical with, the autonomic imbalance factor which causes normals to differ from operational fatigue cases, who from our point of view may be regarded as falling towards the 'unstable' end of the neuroticism factor.

The fourth column of Table XXIV gives C.R.s for a comparison on the same set of tests between a normal group of 488 subjects, and a group of 98 neurotics. This set of C.R.s is proportional to the one given in column 1, and also to the factor saturations in columns 2 and 3; the correlations are respectively ·51, ·42, and ·38. These values are sufficiently high to support the general hypothesis that autonomic imbalance, operationally defined through this set of tests, acts in a unitary manner and distinguishes between normals and neurotics.

We have now shown that when we take large groups of persons diagnosed as 'neurotic' by competent psychiatrists, and compare them with large unselected groups of persons who have never come under psychiatric supervision, and whom we may for convenience label 'normal', large differences appear along each of the four main types of approach we have outlined. In ratings based on interviews, large differences are observed with respect to heredity, neurotic traits in childhood, shyness and difficulty in making social contacts, emotional instability, apprehensiveness, dependence, marriage and other sexual difficulties, physical ill health, unstable work record, and former psychiatric illnesses. In self-ratings obtained from questionnaires, large differences are apparent with respect to items referring to dizzy turns, palpitations, worrying, nervousness, easily hurt feelings, shaking and trembling, irritability, nightmares, sleeplessness, shortness of breath, lack of self-confidence and feelings of inferiority. On objective behaviour tests, differences are marked on suggestibility, manual dexterity, level of aspiration, motor response disorganization, and body control. In the field of constitutional differences, body build (physique), autonomic imbalance, and defective dark vision were noted as effective differentiating tests. This survey of the literature is far from complete, but it does depict a mutually consistent pattern of personality traits which may be regarded as an approach to the operational definition of the personality of the neurotic. It also disproves, at a very high level of confidence, the null hypothesis; there is very little doubt that the group of 'neurotics' is differentiated from the group of 'normals' on a basis distinctly different from chance.

We have also been forced to postulate that the 'neurotic' group shows a lack of homogeneity which cannot be attributed to the general factor of neuroticism, and our hypothesis has been that we are dealing with a second factor, orthogonal to the neuroticism one, which resembles in many important aspects Jung's extravert-introvert dichotomy. The introverted neurotic shows symptoms of anxiety, depression, and irritability; he has overly high levels of aspiration, overly high judgment discrepancies, is subject to response disorganization of the 'overactive' type, and tends to be of the leptomorph body build. This general syndrome we have called 'dysthymic', to avoid the faulty associations which the older term 'psychasthenic' (Janet, Jung) would call up. The extraverted neurotic is characterized by hysterical conversion symptoms; he has unduly low levels of aspiration, unduly low judgment discrepancies, is subject to response disorganization of the 'inert' type, and tends to be of the eurymorph type of body build. This general syndrome is identified with the 'hysteric' classification. Figure 22 gives a schematic picture of the relation of these two factors (neuroticism and extraversion-introversion) as operationally defined by our tests and measures.

In this volume we are concerned with the neuroticism factor only; extraversion-introversion has been discussed in detail in *Dimensions of Personality*, and further experimental work in connection with it will be reported at a later date. It has been mentioned here for two reasons: (1) The experimental data (particularly in connection with level of aspiration and response disorganization data) enforce at least a brief discussion of this factor, as otherwise the results become almost unintelligible, and (2) the general view underlying the employment of criterion analysis posits that the criterion group is not uniquely determined, but made up of a collection of groups which are themselves more homogeneous; the make-up of the criterion by means of a combination of such groups thus becomes itself an experimental and statistical experiment. The proof that the neurotic group is not homogeneous, therefore, strengthens the case for some type of criterion analysis, and is therefore discussed here.

We may conclude this brief survey by noting that all the evidence quoted is strongly in support of our heuristic hypothesis

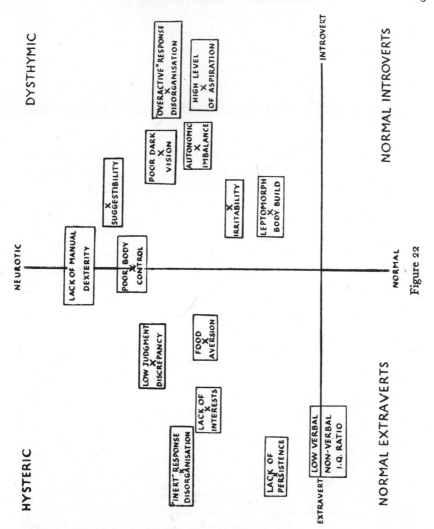

Figure 22

regarding the existence of a dimension of 'neuroticism' or 'stability' in personality research. We must now turn to a consideration of the possibility of the exact measurement of a person's position on the continuum posited.

Chapter Four

THE NEUROTIC DIMENSION: OBJECTIVE MEASUREMENT

IT is a well-known principle in scientific procedure that the qualitative and quantitative aspects of a problem tend to interact and that advances in the qualitative analysis of a complex field tend to be followed by improvements in quantitative measurement, which in turn lead to advances in qualitative analysis. Having in the previous chapter established the existence of a dimension of neuroticism and defined it operationally, we must now go on to discuss the possibilities of an exact quantitative measurement, and the reliability and validity of such measurement.

It is clear from the general approach adopted in this book that what we are concerned with is the 'internal' validity, i.e. the multiple correlation between a set of tests defining the factor of neuroticism with that factor. In addition, of course, we have an 'external' criterion, namely, the diagnostic distinction between normal and neurotic groups. The internal criterion, as has been pointed out in the second chapter, is defined partly in terms of the external by maximizing the correlation through rotation of the former; the external criterion, in turn, is modified in terms of the internal by selecting those clinical sub-groups in the general field of neurosis which maximize the correlation between factor and external criterion. In order to show how these various concepts interact, we will, in this chapter, describe an investigation carried out with particular reference to the solution of some of these problems which has not hitherto been reported. As this is the first research in which the full method of criterion analysis has been used, more details will be given of the statistical computations than would otherwise be required.

Two groups of male soldiers formed the experimental population in this research. The 'normal' group consisted of men who had had not less than six months' service, who were not re-enlistees (as far as possible), who had clean disciplinary records, and who, on the Matrices test of intelligence, had service grades other than 4 or 5. (This eliminates all those with I.Q.s of 90 or below.)[1]

The 'neurotic' group consisted of soldiers who were being discharged from the Army on neuropsychiatric grounds. Each of these had been seen by one of four psychiatrists, who diagnosed them under the three headings of hysteria, anxiety state, or psychopathy. No psychotics were tested and the psychiatrists agreed not to send patients with service grades of 4 or 5 unless they felt on clinical grounds that the patients were more intelligent than indicated by their test records.[2]

Certain deviations from the original plan, as outlined above, took place which must be noted. Regarding the controls, it was found impossible to obtain a large enough sample not containing re-enlistees, i.e. persons who rejoined the army after varying periods in civilian life. About 50 per cent of the normal subjects actually were re-enlistees, and if the assumption is justified that persons who rejoin the army in this fashion may be regarded as having failed in their adaptation to civilian life, and are therefore less stable and less well adapted than the average, then we must conclude that our normal group was slightly biased in the neurotic direction. Regarding the neurotic group, it was found on analysing the data later that the criterion requiring those who took part in the experiment to have selection grades of 3 or upwards was not fully followed. This led to there being a marked difference between controls and neurotics with respect to intelligence, the neurotics being very significantly inferior. (The exact data will be given later.)

---

[1] These men were sent from the Woolwich Garrison, and our thanks are due to the Commandant of the Royal Artillery Depot for having given permission for these men to be tested and for his interest and help in the project. The main work in connection with the administration of the project was carried out by Dr. S. Crown. Testing was carried out by Drs. A. Clarke (1950) and A. Gravely (1950), whose theses contain a detailed account of their work, by J. Standen, Dr. A. Lubin (1951), and G. Yukviss. To all these the writer is indebted for their skilled and competent contribution. In the description of the groups tested and the general set-up of the experiment the account given by Clarke (1950) has been followed very closely, and often verbatim. The number of cases used in Clarke's and Gravely's theses is smaller than that used in this chapter as the research went on beyond the point when these two started working up their results. In consequence some tests attained levels of significance they fell short of with the smaller number of subjects.

[2] Our thanks are due to Colonel Pozner for his invaluable help in making these arrangements and carrying them through, as well as to the other psychiatrists who took part in the selection procedure.

Another important reservation attaches to the diagnoses, particularly those of hysteria and anxiety states. In the many doubtful cases, one important variable factor is the personality bias of the interviewing psychiatrist. When there is some doubt as to the actual diagnosis, some psychiatrists will label a patient an hysteric, who in other hands might be called an anxiety state, and vice versa. Among the four psychiatrists who made the diagnoses, there existed certain diagnostic tendencies; thus, A had a strong tendency to diagnose hysteria, B had a slight tendency to diagnose hysteria, C thought that a good many of the cases came within the normal limits of emotional reaction to stress, but had a bias for anxiety states, and, finally, D when confronted with a doubtful case would always call it an anxiety state. The actual tabulation of diagnoses, as made by these four psychiatrists, strongly bore out these known biases, and consequently it is very doubtful whether the differential diagnoses between hysteria and anxiety states can be taken very seriously. We will give test results separately for these various groups so that the reader may be able to judge for himself the variations which do obtain between the different diagnostic groups. It should be noted that these reservations apply with less force to the diagnosis of psychopathy, which tends to be more clearly differentiated from the other two diagnoses.

All the experimental subjects—over 200 of them in the normal and over 120 in the neurotic group—were submitted to a battery of individual and group tests, including examples of all the main types of personality tests. The testing was carried out by members of the staff of the Psychology Department and by several Ph.D. students. Each subject was tested almost continuously for two full days, with suitable breaks for meals and rest pauses. The tests used will be briefly described in the next section, together with the main scores and variances on each test for the various groups. Also given in each case is the correlation ratio between each test and the fourfold classification into controls, anxiety states, hysterics, and psychopaths. Correlations significant at the 5 per cent level have been underlined once, correlations significant at the 1 per cent level twice, and correlations significant at the ·1 per cent level three times. In all cases where the correlation ratios are significant, biserial correlations are also given, for the tests concerned, for the dichotomy:normal versus hysteric + anxiety state, and the dichotomy:hysteric versus anxiety state.

As in most large-scale testing programmes it was impossible to carry out the testing in such a way that every subject completed every test. The cause lay partly in the breakdown of apparatus, the breakdown of the time schedule, late arrival of transport, and similar causes not dependent on the personality of the subject, and therefore not likely to have contributed any bias to the testing procedure. Together with the data relevant to each test are given, therefore, the number of cases in each of the groups involved. The first two variables: (1) physical age in years on day of testing, and (2) service grade on matrix test of intelligence, will show the way in which the data are set out.

(1) Age	Normals	Anxiety States	Hysterics	Psycho- paths	A. & H.	Correla- tion Ratio	Point Biserials	
							N. v. A. & H.	H. v. A.
No. of Cases	207	47	48	25	95	·298	302	95
Mean Score	25·54	23·36	21·12	21·64	22·23		·257	— ·212
Variance	36·01	31·37	23·00	19·07	28·12			

(2) Intelligence	Normals	Anxiety States	Hysterics	Psycho- paths	A. & H.	Correla- tion Ratio	Point Biserials	
							N. v. A. & H.	H. v. A.
No. of Cases	205	38	40	24	78	·506	283	78
Mean Score	2·84	4·10	4·18	4·42	4·14		— ·481	·026
Variance	0·88	1·50	2·10	2·43	1·78			

These figures show that, contrary to our intention, the normal group is differentiated from the neurotic group by being slightly older (a point which does not greatly matter as the difference is extremely slight, although statistically significant), and also a good deal more intelligent, as indicated by the higher score on the Matrices test. This failure to equate the two groups for intelligence has been pointed out before and the way in which it affects the results will be discussed later. It is possible that the matrix scores which determine the S.G. grading of the soldiers may not have been as valid a test as might be supposed, because in another test of intellectual capacity, the Mill Hill Vocabulary test, the differ- ence between the normals and the neurotics, while still significant, is considerably reduced. The figures for test 3, the Mill Hill Vocabulary, are given below.[1]

[1] A comparison of the ratio of verbal to non-verbal intelligence test results for anxiety states and hysterics confirms our previous finding that the ratio is *low* for hysterics (Eysenck, 1947; Himmelweit, 1945).

(3) Vocabulary	Normals	Anxiety States	Hysterics	Psycho- paths	A. & H.	Correla- tion Ratio	Point Biserials	
							N. v. A. & H.	H. v. A.
No. of Cases	205	45	47	25	92	·313	297	92
Mean Score	15·56	12·99	11·12	11·94	12·03		·294	−·154
Variance	24·24	39·04	35·00	46·13	37·46			

We are now ready to discuss the differences observed with respect to the various tests making up the battery proper. The first group of tests to be discussed is made up of personality inventories, questionnaires, and other written tests of the type described in the previous chapter. They are (4) the Crown Word Connection List:

(4) Word Connection List	Normals	Anxiety States	Hysterics	Psycho- paths	A. & H.	Correla- tion Ratio	Point Biserials	
							N. v. A. & H.	H. v. A.
No. of Cases	189	45	45	25	90	·316	297	90
Mean Score	12·36	15·51	17·38	16·76	16·44		−·295	·139
Variance	34·97	48·94	40·97	53·69	45·33			

The Maudsley Medical Questionnaire:

(5) M.M.Q.	Normals	Anxiety States	Hysterics	Psycho- paths	A. & H.	Correla- tion Ratio	Point Biserials	
							N. v. A. & H.	H. v. A.
No. of Cases	195	41	44	25	85	·596	280	85
Mean Score	10·30	23·24	20·44	19·04	21·79		−·596	−·169
Variance	42·87	52·50	83·57	67·92	69·76			

The Minnesota Multiphasic Personality Inventory, Hysteria Scale:

(6) M.M.P.I.	Normals	Anxiety States	Hysterics	Psycho- paths	A. & H.	Correla- tion Ratio	Point Biserials	
							N. v. A. & H.	H. v. A.
No. of Cases	200	45	44	25	89	·451	289	89
Mean Score	13·42	20·42	18·86	18·32	19·65		−·453	−·115
Variance	26·06	42·75	49·38	48·89	46·12			

The Minnesota Multiphasic Personality Inventory; O Score (this is the score on those items on the hysteria scale in which hysterics are supposed to answer in the same direction as normals):

1. Institute of Psychiatry, Maudsley Hospital (University of London).

2. Section of the Statistical Laboratory.

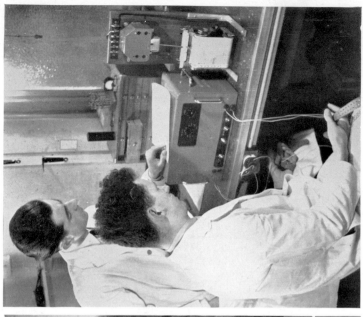

3. Punched-card equipment used for large-scale analyses.

4. Technical workshop for apparatus construction.

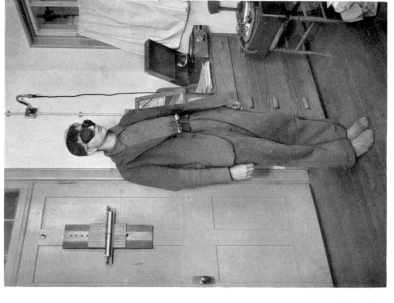

5. Body-sway test for suggestibility, with kymograph recording.

6. Body-sway test of suggestibility, with portable recording.

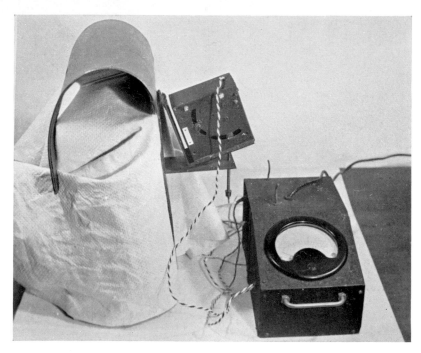

7. New electronic method of body-sway recording: the apparatus.

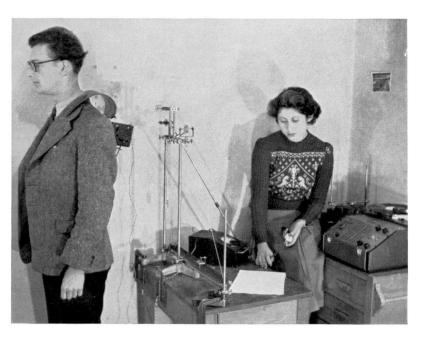

8. Apparatus shown in use.

9. Dark-vision test.

10. Cambridge Triple Tester, used for Level of Aspiration experiments.

11. Psycho-galvanic reflex apparatus, with electrodes.

12. Tracing board.

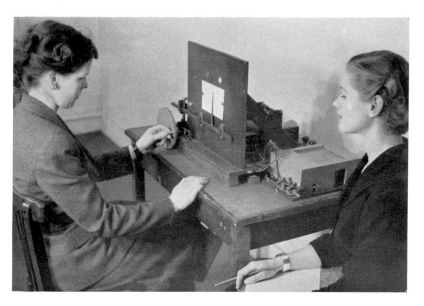

13. Davis choice-behaviour unit.

14. Maudsley adaptation of choice-behaviour unit.

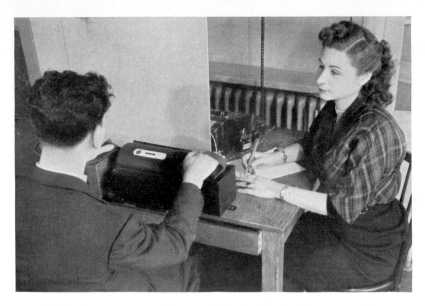

15. Luria apparatus, with automatic visual stimulus presentation.

16. Dynamometer persistence test.

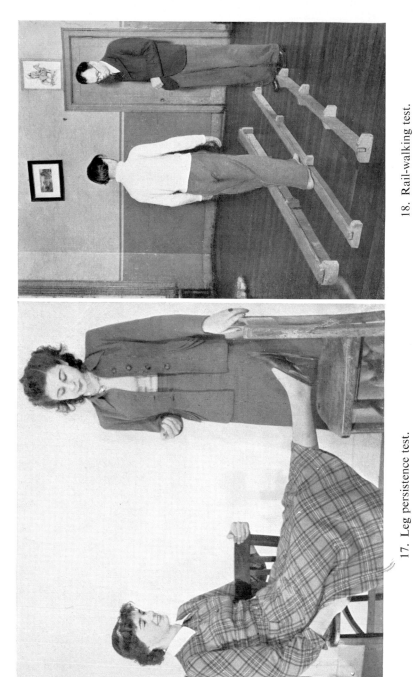

17. Leg persistence test.

18. Rail-walking test.

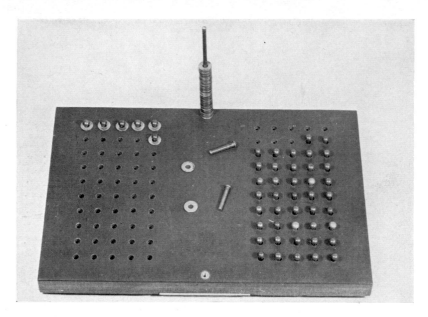

19. Finger dexterity test (U.S.E.S. battery).

20. Test in action.

21. Speed of decision test.

22. Dotting test.

24. Mirror-drawing test.

23. Manual dexterity test.

25. Needle-threading test.

26. Close-up view of needle-threading test.

27. Agility (water-carrying) test.

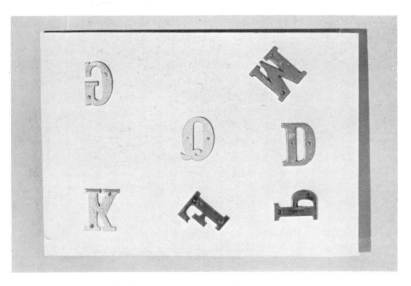

28. Kretschmer abstraction test.

1. Starting with **LIST A** put a check mark (√) beside the **four words** which **BEST** describe this person, and then put a cross (x) beside the **four words** which **LEAST** describe this person. **Then do the same for LIST B.**

LIST A		LIST B	
......Corrupt	......Depraved	......Obscene	......Mild
......Sunny	......Trustworthy	......Spirited	......Menacing
......Merciless	......Gentle	......Downcast	......Reticent
......Reposed	......Resigned	......Tricky	......Timid
......Terrified	......Subdued	......Steady	......Good
......Respectable	......Artificial	......Unafraid	......Boastful

2. Put a cross (x) at a point on the scale which best describes the intelligence of this person.

Dull	Below Average Intelligence	Average	Above Average Intelligence	Superior

3. Remarks: (write here just exactly what you think about this person).

....

....

....

....

....

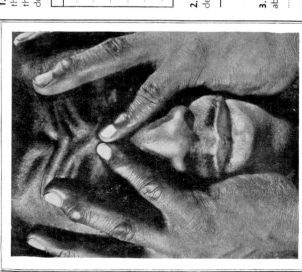

PICTURE VI

	a	b	c	d	e	f	T
A							
B							
T							

29. Character Interpretation test: sample page.

1. Starting with **LIST A** put a check mark (✓) beside the **four words** which **BEST** describe this person, and then put a cross (**x**) beside the **four words** which **LEAST** describe this person. **Then do the same for LIST B.**

LIST A		LIST B	
......Unassuming	......Straightforward	......Quiet	......Unnatural
......Unconcerned	......Decent	......Independent	......Deceiving
......Sociable	......Disdainful	......Self-pitying	......Despondent
......Depressed	......Spirited	......Jolly	......Quarrelsome
......Frightened	......Infected	......Understanding	......Untainted
......Insulting	......Treacherous	......Sluttish	......Constant

2. Put a cross (**x**) at a point on the scale which best describes the intelligence of this person.

Dull	Below Average Intelligence	Average	Above Average Intelligence	Superior

3. Remarks: (write here just exactly what you think about this person).

....
....
....
....

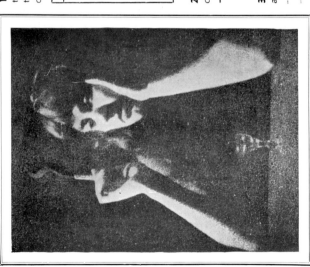

PICTURE XI

	a	b	c	d	e	f	T
A							
B							
T							

30. Character Interpretation test: sample page.

(7) M.M.P.I. O Score	Normals	Anxiety States	Hysterics	Psycho-paths	A. & H.	Correlation Ratio	Point Biserials	
							N. v. A. & H.	H. v. A.
No. of Cases	200	45	44	25	89		289	89
Mean Score	6·78	4·87	5·18	5·08	5·02	·237	·227	·046
Variance	12·44	12·39	11·46	11·83	11·82			

The Minnesota Multiphasic Personality Inventory; Lie-Score:

(8) Lie Score	Normals	Anxiety States	Hysterics	Psycho-paths	A. & H.	Correlation Ratio	Point Biserials	
							N. v. A. & H.	H. v. A.
No. of Cases	200	45	44	25	89	·105		
Mean Score	3·06	2·80	3·39	2·56	3·09			
Variance	3·96	3·48	6·24	3·26	4·88			

Annoyances (total number of annoyances picked from a list prepared especially for this battery and obtainable from the Institute of Psychiatry, Psychology Department):

(9) Annoyances	Normals	Anxiety States	Hysterics	Psycho-paths	A. & H.	Correlation Ratio	Point Biserials	
							N. v. A. & H.	H. v. A.
No. of Cases	205	47	47	24	94	·161	299	94
Mean Score	22·82	26·81	26·38	24·33	26·60		—·166	—·019
Variance	100·85	149·29	105·89	101·19	126·26			

Social Attitudes; Emphasis Score (this is the number of items on which the individual *agrees strongly* or *disagrees strongly*; the inventory of social attitudes used has been published elsewhere (Eysenck, 1947a)):

(10) Emphasis	Normals	Anxiety States	Hysterics	Psycho-paths	A. & H.	Correlation Ratio	Point Biserials	
							N. v. A. & H.	H. v. A.
No. of Cases	189	40	42	19	82	·148		
Mean Score	15·39	18·28	17·71	19·95	17·99			
Variance	89·40	129·02	108·84	118·05	117·30			

Worries (this is a Pressey X–O type of test especially made up for this experiment, copies of which may be had from the Psychology Department, Institute of Psychiatry):

(11) Worries	Normals	Anxiety States	Hysterics	Psychopaths	A. & H.	Correlation Ratio	Point Biserials	
							N. v. A. & H.	H. v. A.
No. of Cases	170	44	43	21	87	·272	257	87
Mean Score	17·55	26·34	24·63	22·86	25·49		−·278	−·059
Variance	149·28	226·37	203·38	239·83	213·25			

Number of Things Disliked (this is a Pressey X–O type of test, the score on which is the number of things disliked. It was especially made up for this experiment, and copies may be had from the Psychology Department, Institute of Psychiatry):

(12) Dislikes	Normals	Anxiety States	Hysterics	Psychopaths	A. & H.	Correlation Ratio	Point Biserials	
							N. v. A. & H.	H. v. A.
No. of Cases	177	44	39	23	83	·322	260	83
Mean Score	13·11	18·73	21·72	17·17	20·13		−·323	·116
Variance	57·53	143·97	194·73	112·79	167·99			

Number of Things Liked (this is a Pressey X–O type of test, the score on which is the number of things liked. It was especially made up for this experiment, and copies may be had from the Psychology Department, Institute of Psychiatry):

(13) Likes	Normals	Anxiety States	Hysterics	Psychopaths	A. & H.	Correlation Ratio	Point Biserials	
							N. v. A. & H.	H. v. A.
No. of Cases	184	44	41	25	85	·071	269	85
Mean Score	41·52	41·50	40·44	38·00	40·99		·017	−·037
Variance	231·23	207·98	201·95	261·33	202·92			

Discussion of Questionnaire Variables.—It will be seen that nearly all the questionnaires give a highly significant differentiation between the normal and the neurotic groups. The highest discrimination is given by the Maudsley Medical Questionnaire, which has a correlation ratio of ·60. One exception to this general conclusion is the emphasis score, which is insignificant, although all the three neurotic groups differ in the expected direction (greater emphasis) from the normal group. The other exception is of much greater interest and importance; item 8, the Lie Score, shows no differentiation between the normal and neurotic groups. This finding is of particular importance because the Lie Scale was constructed in order to determine whether or not a given subject completed the test in such a way as to try and show himself in a particularly good light. Such a tendency would be brought out very clearly by a high figure on the Lie Score, as has been shown experimentally by various investigators. Our finding that normals and neurotics do not differ with respect to the Lie Score would appear to go counter to claims often made that the normal group would be trying to make themselves appear in a good light, whereas the neurotic group would not, and that any differences on questionnaires such as the Maudsley Medical Questionnaire would be due to this tendency. No such interpretation is possible on the basis of our data. We may conclude that both neurotics and normals tend to give answers to the best of their ability and that these answers discriminate at a very high level of significance between the two groups.

It may be of interest to compare the scores of our groups with other normal and neurotic groups tested previously to determine whether they can be regarded as in any way representative. The two tests on which most standardization data are available are the Word Connection List and the Maudsley Medical Questionnaire. The average score for a normal group on the Word Connection List is about 10; for neurotic groups it is in the neighbourhood of 16. Our data would suggest that while the neurotic group is similar to those tested previously, the normal group is somewhat less stable than other groups tested, a conclusion well in line with the fact that this group included a large number of army re-enlistees, as pointed out above. With respect to the Maudsley Medical Questionnaire, the scores for the normal and neurotic groups respectively are very close to those of previous samples tested at various times. The scores given here may be compared with those quoted in an earlier chapter. On the whole, it seems likely that the groups tested in this research are fairly typical of normal and neurotic groups respectively.

The next group of tests to be discussed is made up of objective behaviour tests. Four of these, numbers 14, 15, 16, and 17, are manual dexterity tests, M, N, O, and P, taken from the United States Employment Service General Aptitude Battery. These tests are illustrated in several of the photographs in this book (numbers 19, 20, 23), and will therefore not be described in detail. The results obtained from them are given below, as well as a combined total score, number 18.[1]

(14) Dexterity Test M	Normals	Anxiety States	Hysterics	Psycho-paths	A. & H.	Correlation Ratio	Point Biserials	
							N. v. A. & H.	H. v. A.
No. of Cases	168	39	37	23	76	·315	244	76
Mean Score	77·29	71·59	72·16	71·39	71·87		·298	·033
Variance	60·72	57·51	96·97	74·34	75·77			

(15) Dexterity Test N	Normals	Anxiety States	Hysterics	Psycho-paths	A. & H.	Correlation Ratio	Point Biserials	
							N. v. A. & H.	H. v. A.
No. of Cases	168	39	37	23	76	·335	244	76
Mean Score	83·06	76·15	74·97	73·35	75·58		·301	− ·046
Variance	101·09	162·50	178·30	135·06	168·27			

(16) Dexterity Test O	Normals	Anxiety States	Hysterics	Psycho-paths	A. & H.	Correlation Ratio	Point Biserials	
							N. v. A. & H.	H. v. A.
No. of Cases	168	39	37	23	76	·277	244	76
Mean Score	26·22	24·18	23·00	24·22	23·60		·266	− ·141
Variance	20·18	16·68	18·78	11·63	17·82			

(17) Dexterity Test P	Normals	Anxiety States	Hysterics	Psycho-paths	A. & H.	Correlation Ratio	Point Biserials	
							N. v. A. & H.	H. v. A.
No. of Cases	168	39	37	23	76	·335	244	76
Mean Score	25·56	22·77	23·03	23·00	22·90		·324	·030
Variance	10·68	15·29	22·30	12·54	18·47			

(18) Dexterity Tests, Total Score	Normals	Anxiety States	Hysterics	Psycho-paths	A. & H.	Correlation Ratio	Point Biserials	
							N. v. A. & H.	H. v. A.
No. of Cases	168	39	37	23	76	·397	244	76
Mean Score	212·13	194·69	193·16	191·96	193·95		·375	− ·031
Variance	350·71	556·64	729·75	451·41	632·90			

[1] It should be noted that in order to save time these tests were not administered in exact conformity with the official instructions. Results given should, therefore, not be used in comparing our groups with others tested on the basis of the official instructions. The main difference lay in the curtailment of pre-test trials, and in different wording of instructions.

Test 19 is the Leg Persistence test, scored in terms or the number of seconds during which the leg is held out over a chair without touching down (illustrated in photograph 17).

(19) Persistence	Normals	Anxiety States	Hysterics	Psychopaths	A. & H.	Correlation Ratio	Point Biserials N. v. A. & H.	H. v. A.
No. of Cases	172	38	37	23	75	·148	247	75
Mean Score	60·17	48·95	48·65	52·61	48·80		·149	−·004
Variance	1184·20	1036·70	1612·00	983·80	1302·60			

Tests 20 and 21 are Speed of Tapping tests, in which the subject is required to tap on a piece of paper with the tip of his pencil for 15 seconds.

(20) Tapping I	Normals	Anxiety States	Hysterics	Psychopaths	A. & H.	Correlation Ratio	Point Biserials N. v. A. & H.	H. v. A.
No. of Cases	167	39	37	23	76	·055		
Mean Score	69·76	70·26	71·89	67·83	71·05			
Variance	365·00	413·10	254·70	381·40	332·20			

(21) Tapping II	Normals	Anxiety States	Hysterics	Psychopaths	A. & H.	Correlation Ratio	Point Biserials N. v. A. & H.	H. v. A.
No. of Cases	168	39	37	23	76	·071		
Mean Score	72·38	73·59	75·41	70·43	74·47			
Variance	332·00	297·30	181·10	349·80	238·40			

Items 22 and 23 relate to the amount of scatter produced by tapping with a pencil on a sheet of paper.

(22) Scatter I	Normals	Anxiety States	Hysterics	Psychopaths	A. & H.	Correlation Ratio	Point Biserials N. v. A. & H.	H. v. A.
No. of Cases	172	39	37	23	76	·192	248	76
Mean Score	58·43	93·33	67·84	49·13	80·92		−·154	·175
Variance	4073·00	6338·60	4217·40	3490·10	5400·50			

(23) Scatter II	Normals	Anxiety States	Hysterics	Psychopaths	A. & H.	Correlation Ratio	Point Biserials N. v. A. & H.	H. v. A.
No. of Cases	172	39	37	23	76	·235	248	76
Mean Score	54·36	101·28	69·73	43·91	85·92		−·196	−·187
Variance	4575·60	8558·80	5374·90	3606·70	7168·50			

Item 24 is the average scatter on both trials. Scatter is measured in terms of the length of the perimeter drawn around the dots in such a way that only convex and no concave lines are admitted.

(24) Mean Scatter	Normals	Anxiety States	Hysterics	Psycho-paths	A. & H.	Correla-tion Ratio	Point Biserials	
							N. v. A. & H.	H. v. A.
No. of Cases	172	39	37	23	76	·217	248	76
Mean Score	56·74	97·69	68·92	46·96	83·68		−·178	−·186
Variance	4164·80	7234·00	4593·20	3458·50	6079·60			

Numbers 25, 26, and 27 are scores derived from a Speed of Decision test, in which two cards are placed in front of the subject, face down, and he is asked to say which of the two will be the higher. If he is right he obtains one point; if he is wrong he loses one point; if he says he feels certain about being right he gains or loses two points respectively. The time for 10 decisions is measured and score number 25 is the longest time minus the shortest time. Score 26 is the total time on all 10 tests, and score 27 is the number of certainties. (See photograph no. 21.)

(25) Speed of Decision, L–S	Normals	Anxiety States	Hysterics	Psycho-paths	A. & H.	Correla-tion Ratio	Point Biserials	
							N. v. A. & H.	H. v. A.
No. of Cases	172	39	37	23	76	·045		
Mean Score	3·38	3·46	3·54	3·09	3·50			
Variance	5·59	5·04	12·81	2·90	8·71			

(26) Speed of Decision— total time	Normals	Anxiety States	Hysterics	Psycho-paths	A. & H.	Correla-tion Ratio	Point Biserials	
							N. v. A. & H.	H. v. A.
No. of Cases	172	39	37	23	76	·063		
Mean Score	21·24	21·26	18·92	19·61	20·12			
Variance	213·45	257·56	142·80	107·70	200·43			

(27) Speed of Decision— certainties	Normals	Anxiety States	Hysterics	Psycho-paths	A. & H.	Correla-tion Ratio	Point Biserials	
							N. v. A. & H.	H. v. A.
No. of Cases	172	39	37	23	76	·148		
Mean Score	8·30	7·97	7·65	6·96	7·82			
Variance	6·81	6·92	7·29	11·13	7·03			

Scores 28 to 31 are derived from the Track Tracer test, in which the subject is required to trace a path between two rows of holes with a metal stylus; if he touches one of the holes, a buzzer rings and an error is counted on an electric counter (illustrated in photograph 12). This test is given as a Level of Aspiration test, in the way described in *Dimensions of Personality* (1947), and the four scores given are 28—average goal discrepancy for the time scores; 29—average judgment discrepancy for the time scores; 30—average error score; and 31 longest time performance score.

(28) Goal Discrepancy: Total Score	Normals	Anxiety States	Hysterics	Psycho-paths	A. & H.	Correlation Ratio	Point Biserials	
							N. v. A. & H.	H. v. A.
No. of Cases	172	38	37	22	75	·148		
Mean Score	1·23	2·13	2·16	·59	2·15			
Variance	6·02	30·66	10·31	7·30	20·34			

(29) Judgment Discrepancy: Time Score	Normals	Anxiety States	Hysterics	Psycho-paths	A. & H.	Correlation Ratio	Point Biserials	
							N. v. A. & H.	H. v. A.
No. of Cases	172	38	37	22	75	·134		
Mean Score	−·59	·16	·51	−·23	·33			
Variance	5·27	26·95	14·15	7·14	20·09			

(30) Mean Error Score	Normals	Anxiety States	Hysterics	Psycho-paths	A. & H.	Correlation Ratio	Point Biserials	
							N. v. A. & H.	H. v. A.
No. of Cases	172	38	37	22	75	·167		
Mean Score	100·47	112·37	111·08	108·64	111·73			
Variance	920·30	807·80	1276·60	840·90	1025·30			

(31) Longest Time Score	Normals	Anxiety States	Hysterics	Psycho-paths	A. & H.	Correlation Ratio	Point Biserials	
							N. v. A. & H.	H. v. A.
No. of Cases	172	38	37	22	75	·161		
Mean Score	38·05	42·79	42·24	40·96	42·52			
Variance	151·20	104·17	238·02	115·76	167·96			

Scores 32, 33, 34 and 35 are derived from the Necker Cube Perceptual Reversal test, given the following four ways. First of all, the number of reversals during passive contemplation for 30 seconds (score 32); second, the number of reversals while trying to maximize the number of reversals (score 33); third, the number of reversals while trying to minimize the number of reversals (score 34); and lastly, the number of reversals while regarding the Cube passively, without trying to maximize or minimize the score (score 35).

(32) Cube Reversal— passive	Normals	Anxiety States	Hysterics	Psychopaths	A. & H.	Correlation Ratio	Point Biserials	
							N. v. A. & H.	H. v. A.
No. of Cases	178	41	44	25	85	·110		
Mean Score	6·16	5·78	5·09	6·88	5·42			
Variance	21·65	14·38	9·29	23·19	11·72			

(33) Cube Reversal— maximizing	Normals	Anxiety States	Hysterics	Psychopaths	A. & H.	Correlation Ratio	Point Biserials	
							N. v. A. & H.	H. v. A.
No. of Cases	178	41	44	25	85	·077		
Mean Score	11·93	10·76	12·32	13·16	11·56			
Variance	51·33	49·34	100·22	101·97	75·42			

(34) Cube Reversal— minimizing	Normals	Anxiety States	Hysterics	Psychopaths	A. & H.	Correlation Ratio	Point Biserials	
							N. v. A. & H.	H. v. A.
No. of Cases	178	41	44	25	85	·055		
Mean Score	3·67	3·66	3·36	3·20	3·51			
Variance	6·58	13·43	10·38	2·58	11·73			

(35) Cube Reversal— passive	Normals	Anxiety States	Hysterics	Psychopaths	A. & H.	Correlation Ratio	Point Biserials	
							N. v. A. & H.	H. v. A.
No. of Cases	178	41	44	25	85	·071		
Mean Score	6·49	6·39	5·64	6·64	6·00			
Variance	19·83	28·54	13·07	29·66	20·43			

Scores 36 and 37 are derived from attempts to measure the amount of pressure exerted on a pencil while doing the Mirror Drawing test (score 36), and while doing a test involving the writing of S and S reversed. The amount of pressure was measured in terms of the number of sheets of papers through which the pressure left a mark.

(36) Point Pressure, I	Normals	Anxiety States	Hysterics	Psychopaths	A. & H.	Correlation Ratio	Point Biserials	
							N. v. A. & H.	H. v. A.
No. of Cases	187	42	42	23	84	·176	271	84
Mean Score	7·37	7·67	8·14	7·22	7·90		—·153	·150
Variance	2·62	3·01	2·03	2·36	2·54			

(37) Point Pressure, II	Normals	Anxiety States	Hysterics	Psycho-paths	A. & H.	Correla-tion Ratio	Point Biserials	
							N. v. A. & H.	H. v. A.
No. of Cases	187	42	42	23	84	·167	271	84
Mean Score	7·13	7·40	7·69	6·74	7·55		—·132	·095
Variance	1·98	1·81	2·80	2·47	2·30			

Score 38 is the body sway in a Static Ataxia test scored in $\frac{1}{4}''$ units; score 39 is the body sway in the Suggestibility test (illustrated in photograph 8).

(38) Static Ataxia [1]	Normals	Anxiety States	Hysterics	Psycho-paths	A. & H.	Correla-tion Ratio	Point Biserials	
							N. v. A. & H.	H. v. A.
No. of Cases	177	42	46	25	88	·259	265	88
Mean Score	5·63	8·07	6·89	7·20	7·46		—·255	—·138
Variance	6·98	26·85	10·41	26·42	18·39			

(39) Body Sway Suggestibility [1]	Normals	Anxiety States	Hysterics	Psycho-paths	A. & H.	Correla-tion Ratio	Point Biserials	
							N. v. A. & H.	H. v. A.
No. of Cases	178	42	47	25	89	·161	267	89
Mean Score	14·63	23·00	21·70	22·68	22·32		—·159	—·023
Variance	375·67	839·07	750·56	845·31	783·70			

Scores 40 and 41 are in terms of answers to questions put at the end of the Static Ataxia and Suggestibility tests respectively, as to whether or not the subject had felt a tendency to sway or fall. Score = 2 points for 'Yes'. Answer, 1 point for 'No'.

(40) Ataxia Question	Normals	Anxiety States	Hysterics	Psycho-paths	A. & H.	Correla-tion Ratio	Point Biserials	
							N. v. A. & H.	H. v. A.
No. of Cases	176	42	47	25	89	·276	265	89
Mean Score	1·39	1·71	1·66	1·56	1·68		—·283	—·058
Variance	·24	·21	·23	·26	·22			

[1] Measurement of sway in these two tests was carried out by means of a device described in detail elsewhere (Furneaux, 1951) and illustrated in photograph 7.

(41) Suggesti-bility Question	Normals	Anxiety States	Hysterics	Psycho-paths	A. & H.	Correla-tion Ratio	Point Biserials	
							N. v. A. & H.	H. v. A.
No. of Cases	176	42	47	25	89	·138		
Mean Score	1·54	1·74	1·57	1·60	1·65			
Variance	·25	·20	·25	·25	·23			

Tests 42 and 43 were done with the use of the Luria test, score 42 being the number of verbal failures in the Association test, which constitutes a stimulus for the Luria, and score 43 being the amount of right-hand motor disturbance recorded on the kymograph (illustrated in photograph 15).

(42) Verbal Failures	Normals	Anxiety States	Hysterics	Psycho-paths	A. & H.	Correla-tion Ratio	Point Biserials	
							N. v. A. & H.	H. v. A.
No. of Cases	112	33	38	22	71	·197	183	71
Mean Score	3·73	5·33	6·34	4·09	5·87		—·195	·089
Variance	25·06	31·48	33·74	22·85	32·48			

(43) Right-hand Motor Disturbance	Normals	Anxiety States	Hysterics	Psycho-paths	A. & H.	Correla-tion Ratio	Point Biserials	
							N. v. A. & H.	H. v. A.
No. of Cases	89	30	31	18	61	·452	150	61
Mean Score	25·16	46·50	48·84	42·78	47·69		—·469	·048
Variance	334·84	652·47	560·34	659·24	596·92			

Scores 44 and 45 were derived from the Kretschmer Abstractions test, in which the subject is asked to look at a stimulus card on which are painted a number of coloured letters. He is told to memorize the letters and their exact positions and is tested on that after the cards have been withdrawn. He is then, without warning, asked what the colours of the different letters were. 44 is the number of colours remembered, 45 the number of letters.

(44) Colour Memory	Normals	Anxiety States	Hysterics	Psycho-paths	A. & H.	Correla-tion Ratio	Point Biserials	
							N. v. A. & H.	H. v. A.
No. of Cases	172	39	37	23	76	·126		
Mean Score	1·37	1·20	·89	1·17	1·05			
Variance	1·68	1·64	1·43	1·79	1·54			

(45) Letter Memory	Normals	Anxiety States	Hysterics	Psycho-paths	A. & H.	Correla-tion Ratio	Point Biserials	
							N. v. A. & H.	H. v. A.
No. of Cases	172	39	37	23	76	·274	248	76
Mean Score	15·51	12·72	13·16	13·65	12·93		·275	·052
Variance	16·70	18·89	19·14	18·24	18·81			

Tests 46, 47, and 48 are parts of a Concentration test in which a long series of numbers or letters is read out to the subject at the rate of one per second. At irregular intervals the series is suddenly interrupted and the subject is asked to reproduce the last six numbers of letters read out to him. Scoring is in terms of the numbers or letters repeated correctly in the right order. Score 46 is the score on the numbers test, 47 on the letters test, and 48 on the numbers and letters combined.

(46) Concen-tration: numbers	Normals	Anxiety States	Hysterics	Psycho-paths	A. & H.	Correla-tion Ratio	Point Biserials	
							N. v. A. & H.	H. v. A.
No. of Cases	170	39	37	23	76	·200	246	76
Mean Score	29·24	26·67	26·89	26·22	26·78		·183	·017
Variance	34·34	41·49	51·54	49·27	45·78			

(47) Concen-tration: letters	Normals	Anxiety States	Hysterics	Psycho-paths	A. & H.	Correla-tion Ratio	Point Biserials	
							N. v. A. & H.	H. v. A.
No. of Cases	170	39	37	23	76	·266	246	76
Mean Score	25·86	22·56	23·03	21·30	22·79		·231	·033
Variance	30·45	50·15	49·80	58·31	49·37			

(48) Concen-tration: total	Normals	Anxiety States	Hysterics	Psycho-paths	A. & H.	Correla-tion Ratio	Point Biserials	
							N. v. A. & H.	H. v. A.
No. of Cases	170	39	37	23	76	·259	246	76
Mean Score	55·11	49·23	49·92	47·52	49·57		·230	·028
Variance	103·42	159·76	146·58	178·08	151·42			

Test 49 is a Dark Vision test. The instrument used was an A.R.L. Adaptometer Mk. 1a, as produced at the Admiralty Research Laboratory. The instrument is illustrated in photograph 9. It consists of a rectangular box with a lamp at one end and a circular diffusing glass viewing screen at the other. The brightness of the screen can be varied by the insertion of sixteen graded apertures at a point about half-way between the lamp and the screen. The Adaptometer contains a movable filter holder which enables the user to insert any one of three filters. Thus a very wide range of illumination is at the experimenter's disposal, from $3 \cdot 961 \times 10^{-7}$ to $7 \cdot 847 \times 10^{-3}$ foot candles. Immediately in front of the viewing screen is a metal plate cut into the form of a sector which can be rotated into eight separate positions, being determined by a clicker mechanism. These positions may be described in hours as on a clock, i.e. 12 o'clock, 1.30, 3 o'clock, and so on, and the subject is asked to report on the position of the sector at each point of illumination of the screen. The apparatus operates on a 6-volt 40 ampere-hour battery and a rheostat can be adjusted so that the needle of an ammeter can be made to correspond with a calibration point on the meter dial. This latter is visible through a tiny inspection window and the reading is checked at least once during the course of testing. Performance on the test was scored after 3 minutes, after 6 minutes, and after 10 minutes, taking three readings of filter and aperture each time. Further details regarding the test are given by Gravely (1950).

(49) Dark Vision	Normals	Anxiety States	Hysterics	Psycho- paths	A. & H.	Correla- tion Ratio	Point Biserials	
							N. v. A. & H.	H. v. A.
No. of Cases	141	39	43	22	82	·249	223	82
Mean Score	13·57	15·00	15·35	15·27	15·18		−·252	·045
Variance	5·25	17·37	14·04	20·68	15·46			

The Flicker Threshold was measured with a Dawe Stroboflash (Type 1200 C). This instrument is a stroboscopic tachometer and is primarily used in engineering for measurement of shaft speeds, where the end of the shaft is inaccessible, or for the stroboscopic measurement of other moving objects. The Stroboflash consists essentially of a neon tube which can be made to flash intermittently at frequencies of from 600 to 14,500 flashes per minute, with an accuracy of $\pm \cdot 1$ per cent when the instrument is correctly calibrated. Calibration of the instrument was carried out before each testing session. Testing was carried out at the end of the Dark Vision test, which lasted a standard 10-minutes as the level of adaptation is known to influence results. Complete details regarding testing are given by Gravely (1950).

(50) Flicker Threshold	Normals	Anxiety States	Hysterics	Psycho-paths	A. & H.	Correlation Ratio	Point Biserials	
							N. v. A. & H.	H. v. A.
No. of Cases	154	36	45	23	81	·197	235	81
Mean Score	2589·0	2469·4	2531·1	2504·3	2503·7		·170	·142
Variance	59,810	20,470	68,100	10,440	47,360			

Tests 51 and 52 are different ways of scoring the Perseveration test. The subject is required to write S's as fast as he can for 15 seconds, and then S's reversed for 15 seconds. Then he is required to write S's and S's reversed alternately for 30 seconds. Score 51 is the number of symbols written during the first two periods combined over the number of symbols written in the third period. Score 52 is the total number of symbols written during all three periods.

(51) Per-severation	Normals	Anxiety States	Hysterics	Psycho-paths	A. & H.	Correlation Ratio	Point Biserials	
							N. v. A. & H.	H. v. A.
No. of Cases	174	40	40	22	80	·032		
Mean Score	1·67	1·69	1·74	1·72	1·71			
Variance	·58	·38	·28	·41	·32			

(52) Speed of Writing Symbols	Normals	Anxiety States	Hysterics	Psycho-paths	A. & H.	Correlation Ratio	Point Biserials	
							N. v. A. & H.	H. v. A.
No. of Cases	174	40	40	22	80	·268	254	80
Mean Score	61·37	55·70	50·18	54·04	52·94		·252	−·181
Variance	225·30	203·19	257·69	330·04	235·25			

Score 53 is derived from an experiment on the autokinetic phenomenon. The score is the number of seconds before the subject reports movement.

(53) Auto-kinetic Phenomenon	Normals	Anxiety States	Hysterics	Psycho-paths	A. & H.	Correlation Ratio	Point Biserials	
							N. v. A. & H.	H. v. A.
No. of Cases	126	37	42	23	79	·095		
Mean Score	44·41	57·46	45·17	48·35	50·92			
Variance	2436·76	3524·59	1888·58	2429·87	2657·56			

An examination of these objective behaviour test scores shows that quite a large number of them differentiate with considerable efficiency between the various groups. Among the more successful are those tests which previous work had indicated as being likely measures of neuroticism, i.e. the Manual Dexterity tests, Tapping Scatter, Static Ataxia, the Luria test, the Abstractions and Concentration tests, the Dark Vision, and the S test (score 52), which may be regarded as a test of personal tempo. There is one interesting divergence from the usual pattern, namely, the Body Sway Suggestibility test, which gives a barely significant differentiation between the normals and the hysteric plus anxiety state ($r = \cdot159$). This is lower than the differentiating capacity of the Static Ataxia test, which gives a comparable correlation of $\cdot255$. The lack of discriminating ability of the Body Sway test is probably due to the fact that in this case the suggestion record which had previously been used was substituted by a record made on a wire recording apparatus by an experimenter whose approach was the soft, ingratiating, persuasive, as opposed to the more direct, strong, dominating approach used in the ordinary record. It is also possible that the electronic method of recording body sway used may measure something rather different from the usual direct method. Correlations between the two different methods, taken on a different sample of 50 subjects, were found to be rather lower than anticipated.

The next group of tests to be discussed consists of measures of expressive movement. These have been described in considerable detail in another publication (Eysenck, 1951), and only brief descriptions will therefore be given here of each test. These tests are of particular interest, in spite of the fact that they universally fail to discriminate even at the 5 per cent level between the various groups tested, because, as will be shown later, it is precisely these tests which discriminate at very high levels of confidence between normals and psychotics. The importance of this finding, that those tests which give the best differentiation between psychotics and normals do not differentiate at all between neurotics and normals, will be obvious to the reader; it will be referred to again later in the text.

The first two tests (scores 54–63) are the 'Three Circles' and 'Three Squares' tests. The subject is handed a clean piece of paper and is asked to draw, first, three circles, and, second, three squares. No further directions are given and no questions answered.

Linearity. Scoring is as follows:
The three circles are touching or are concentric and linear, i.e.

a straight line can be drawn in such a way as to pass through all three circles. Score = 3 points.

The three circles are not touching and are not concentric. Score = 2 points.

The three circles are not linear. Score = 1 point.

The three circles are not scorable. Score = 0 points.

(54) 3 Circles: Linearity	Normals	Anxiety States	Hysterics	Psycho-paths	A. & H.	Correlation Ratio	Point Biserials	
							N. v. A. & H.	H. v. A.
No. of Cases	172	39	37	23	76	·114		
Mean Score	1·63	1·56	1·46	1·56	1·51			
Variance	·27	·25	·26	·26	·25			

Time taken to draw the three circles.

(55) 3 Circles: Time	Normals	Anxiety States	Hysterics	Psycho-paths	A. & H.	Correlation Ratio	Point Biserials	
							N. v. A. & H.	H. v. A.
No. of Cases	172	39	37	22	76	·071		
Mean Score	10·01	10·92	9·86	11·82	10·41			
Variance	63·72	103·07	44·56	95·58	73·90			

Smallest diameter of the three circles.

(56) Smallest Diameter	Normals	Anxiety States	Hysterics	Psycho-paths	A. & H.	Correlation Ratio	Point Biserials	
							N. v. A. & H.	H. v. A.
No. of Cases	172	39	37	23	76	·077		
Mean Score	31·51	33·08	31·62	27·39	32·37			
Variance	339·20	232·40	414·00	211·10	317·00			

Largest diameter of the three circles.

(57) Largest Diameter	Normals	Anxiety States	Hysterics	Psycho-paths	A. & H.	Correlation Ratio	Point Biserials	
							N. v. A. & H.	H. v. A.
No. of Cases	172	39	37	23	76	·071		
Mean Score	41·51	42·31	41·89	35·65	42·11			
Variance	703·00	518·20	499·10	389·30	502·20			

Average diameter of the three circles.

(58) Average Diameter	Normals	Anxiety States	Hysterics	Psycho-paths	A. & H.	Correla-tion Ratio	Point Biserials	
							N. v. A. & H.	H. v. A.
No. of Cases	172	39	37	23	76	·071		
Mean Score	36·34	37·18	36·76	31·74	36·97			
Variance	458·40	331·30	444·70	242·30	381·40			

Linearity score for the three squares. Scoring is as follows:

The three squares are touching or are concentric and linear, i.e. a straight line can be drawn in such a way as to pass through all three squares. Score = 3 points.

The three squares are not touching and are not concentric. Score = 2 points.

The three squares are not linear. Score = 1 point.

The three squares are not scorable. Score = 0 points.

(59) 3 Squares: Linearity	Normals	Anxiety States	Hysterics	Psycho-paths	A. & H.	Correla-tion Ratio	Point Biserials	
							N. v. A. & H.	H. v. A.
No. of Cases	172	39	37	23	76	·195	248	76
Mean Score	1·70	1·62	1·43	1·78	1·53		·160	—·183
Variance	·24	·24	·25	·27	·25			

Time taken to draw the three squares.

(60) 3 Squares: Time	Normals	Anxiety States	Hysterics	Psycho-paths	A. & H.	Correla-tion Ratio	Point Biserials	
							N. v. A. & H.	H. v. A.
No. of Cases	172	39	37	23	76	·095		
Mean Score	13·43	15·97	12·65	13·91	14·36			
Variance	106·98	158·50	89·51	65·99	126·07			

Smallest diameter of the three squares.

(61) Smallest Diameter	Normals	Anxiety States	Hysterics	Psycho-paths	A. & H.	Correla-tion Ratio	Point Biserials	
							N. v. A. & H.	H. v. A.
No. of Cases	172	39	37	23	76	·110		
Mean Score	37·33	36·15	38·11	29·13	37·11			
Variance	519·10	298·00	526·90	181·00	404·80			

Largest diameter of the three squares.

(62) Largest Diameter	Normals	Anxiety States	Hysterics	Psycho- paths	A. & H.	Correla- tion Ratio	Point Biserials	
							N. v. A. & H.	H. v. A.
No. of Cases	172	39	37	23	76	·110		
Mean Score	46·10	49·23	50·00	37·39	49·61			
Variance	838·00	723·10	961·10	411·10	827·80			

Average diameter of the three squares.

(63) Average Diameter	Normals	Anxiety States	Hysterics	Psycho- paths	A. & H.	Correla- tion Ratio	Point Biserials	
							N. v. A. & H.	H. v. A.
No. of Cases	172	39	37	23	76	·100		
Mean Score	41·63	43·33	43·24	33·91	43·29			
Variance	635·90	417·50	694·70	243·10	545·00			

It will be noted that the linearity score for the three squares has a significant F ratio and a corresponding correlation ratio of ·195. Similarly, the linearity score for the three circles is almost significant. It is interesting to note that these two scores are the only two in the battery of expressive movements which are *in*significant in discriminating between normals and psychotics.

Size estimation of a pound note (the subject is instructed to draw a rectangle the size of a pound note on a clean piece of paper. The score is the length of the diagonal. All measures are in millimetres):

(64) Diameter: Pound note	Normals	Anxiety States	Hysterics	Psycho- paths	A. & H.	Correla- tion Ratio	Point Biserials	
							N. v. A. & H.	H. v. A.
No. of Cases	172	39	37	23	76	·105		
Mean Score	154·53	156·67	157·57	149·13	157·11			
Variance	398·00	438·60	502·30	317·40	463·50			

Size estimation of a half-crown (the subject is instructed to draw the size of a half-crown piece. The score is the length of the diameter. All measures are in millimetres):

(65) Diameter: Half-crown	Normals	Anxiety States	Hysterics	Psycho- paths	A. & H.	Correla- tion Ratio	Point Biserials	
							N. v. A. & H.	H. v. A.
No. of Cases	172	39	37	23	76	·110		
Mean Score	35·14	36·31	35·38	33·61	35·86			
Variance	36·28	43·22	22·58	21·07	32·95			

Scores 66 and 67 are taken from the 'Fewness of Lines' test. The subject is given a clean sheet of paper with two parallel lines drawn on it, five inches apart. He is asked to draw lines across the sheet between the two lines given, and the time taken (score 66) and the number of lines drawn (score 67) constitute his score.

(66) Time taken	Normals	Anxiety States	Hysterics	Psycho-paths	A. & H.	Correlation Ratio	Point Biserials	
							N. v. A. & H.	H. v. A.
No. of Cases	171	39	37	23	76	·084		
Mean Score	37·68	44·03	30·70	38·70	37·54			
Variance	1266·03	5730·60	431·05	1120·58	3155·34			

(67) Number of Lines	Normals	Anxiety States	Hysterics	Psycho-paths	A. & H.	Correlation Ratio	Point Biserials	
							N. v. A. & H.	H. v. A.
No. of Cases	172	39	37	23	76	·173	248	76
Mean Score	14·06	13·38	10·92	10·96	12·18		·117	−·206
Variance	62·08	37·30	33·24	36·13	36·39			

Scores 68 and 69 are taken from the 'Waves' test, in which four V's are drawn on a sheet of paper in the four extreme corners of the sheet, pointing respectively downwards or sideways. The subject is instructed to trace the first one of these with his eyes open, and then to close his eyes when he comes to the end of the printed part and to trace another six V's the same size as the original one, with his eyes closed. The same is repeated with the other three. The two scores reported are the average amplitude and average wave-length over all four V's. (To measure the amplitude, draw a line across the top of the V and connect mid-point to the bottom of the V. This last line is the amplitude of the wave.) Scores were also calculated for the four sets of V's separately, but as they are completely lacking in significance they are not reported here.

(68) Average Amplitudes	Normals	Anxiety States	Hysterics	Psycho-paths	A. & H.	Correlation Ratio	Point Biserials	
							N. v. A. & H.	H. v. A.
No. of Cases	172	39	36	23	75	·095		
Mean Score	25·08	25·54	24·72	23·48	25·15			
Variance	25·96	36·78	27·69	25·44	32·15			

(69) Average Wave-length	Normals	Anxiety States	Hysterics	Psycho-paths	A. & H.	Correlation Ratio	Point Biserials	
							N. v. A. & H.	H. v. A.
No. of Cases	172	39	36	23	75	·110		
Mean Score	100·17	98·97	92·50	97·39	95·87			
Variance	509·30	709·40	562·10	492·90	640·80			

The last five scores are derived from the 'Measuring Distances' test. The subject is asked to indicate what he considered a 2 ft. distance to be by placing two matches 2 ft. apart on the table. Next, he is asked to indicate the distance of 1 ft., then one of 8 in. The distances are recorded only after he has finished the whole test. Scores 70, 71, and 72 are in terms of the distance between the two matches in $\frac{1}{4}$-inch units.

(70) Distance: 2 ft. test	Normals	Anxiety States	Hysterics	Psycho-paths	A. & H.	Correlation Ratio	Point Biserials	
							N. v. A. & H.	H. v. A.
No. of Cases	159	41	47	23	88	·055		
Mean Score	93·69	92·20	94·68	93·70	95·52			
Variance	170·19	264·96	226·14	205·49	242·94			

(71) Distance: 1 ft. test	Normals	Anxiety States	Hysterics	Psycho-paths	A. & H.	Correlation Ratio	Point Biserials	
							N. v. A. & H.	H. v. A.
No. of Cases	159	41	47	23	88	·071		
Mean Score	48·37	47·10	49·00	48·26	48·11			
Variance	56·17	57·64	61·91	60·84	60·15			

(72) Distance: 8 inches	Normals	Anxiety States	Hysterics	Psycho-paths	A. & H.	Correlation Ratio	Point Biserials	
							N. v. A. & H.	H. v. A.
No. of Cases	159	41	47	23	88	·100		
Mean Score	31·33	29·93	31·38	30·96	30·70			
Variance	23·44	23·27	32·07	29·77	28·19			

Scores 73 and 74 are the total overestimate and the total underestimate, respectively, i.e. a summation of all positive or negative errors respectively in $\frac{1}{4}$-inch units for the whole group concerned.

(73) Total Overestimate	Normals	Anxiety States	Hysterics	Psycho- paths	A. & H.	Correla- tion Ratio	Point Biserials	
							N. v. A. & H.	H. v. A.
No. of Cases	159	41	47	23	88	·071		
Mean Score	8·95	8·27	11·23	9·61	9·85			
Variance	134·88	167·20	308·23	252·52	242·06			

(74) Total Underestimate	Normals	Anxiety States	Hysterics	Psycho- paths	A. & H.	Correla- tion Ratio	Point Biserials	
							N. v. A. & H.	H. v. A.
No. of Cases	159	41	47	23	88	·077		
Mean Score	11·58	15·05	11·74	12·70	13·28			
Variance	261·30	328·35	165·76	204·68	241·36			

Another group of tests, namely, the so-called projective techniques, is represented in this study only by the Rorschach. Scores 75 and 76 are derived from a group Rorschach test given according to the group method developed by Harrower-Erikson. Score 75 is a neuroticism score based on seven of the Miale and Harrower-Erikson nine signs; score 76 is based on 15 of Davidson's seventeen signs. Absence of a given neurotic sign was scored + 1, so that the score is one of *normality*.

(75) Rorschach: Neuroticism	Normals	Anxiety States	Hysterics	Psycho- paths	A. & H.	Correla- tion Ratio	Point Biserials	
							N. v. A. & H.	H. v. A.
No. of Cases	157	35	42	21	77	·243	234	77
Mean Score	2·92	2·31	2·38	1·76	2·35		·177	·023
Variance	2·37	2·10	2·05	2·09	2·05			

(76) Rorschach: Davidson Score	Normals	Anxiety States	Hysterics	Psycho- paths	A. & H.	Correla- tion Ratio	Point Biserials	
							N. v. A. & H.	H. v. A.
No. of Cases	157	35	42	21	77	·205	234	77
Mean Score	6·54	5·83	6·02	5·14	5·94		·135	·050
Variance	4·66	3·97	3·73	2·93	3·80			

Of the measures reviewed above, twenty-eight were chosen for the purpose of a factorial analysis. These twenty-eight scores will be identified by the numbers which they received in the descriptions contained in the first part of this chapter; it will also be possible in this way to identify the direction of scoring for each test. Product-moment correlations were calculated between these

4								
)	−·054							
1	·085	·153						
3	−·135	·116	·211					
7	·099	−·051	·104	·026				
7	·149	·140	·307	−·023	−·018			
)	−·069	·089	−·234	−·198	−·154	−·151		
5	·087	−·261	−·185	−·203	·306	−·122	·246	
2	−·016	−·299	−·122	−·166	·169	−·019	·110	·716

variables; these correlations are given in Table XXV. In view
of the fact that not every subject had completed every test, it was
impossible to use the total number of subjects for this analysis.
Ninety-six subjects had done all except three of our twenty-eight
tests. Thirty-eight subjects had done all tests, including these three
(dark-vision, flicker threshold, and the Luria tests). Consequently
the great majority of the correlations in the table are derived
from N = 96; all correlations involving the above-mentioned three
tests are derived from N = 38. As pointed out above, there is no
reason to expect that failure of a subject to carry out one of the
tests was in any way correlated with that subject's personality or
motivation. All the subjects used for this analysis were of course
normals; no neurotic soldier was included in the correlations.

We may now proceed to analyse this matrix. Five factors altogether were taken out before the residuals could be regarded as
definitely insignificant. These centroid factors were then subjected
to criterion analysis. We may regard the 'Hysteria plus Anxiety'
group as our nuclear neurotic group, and in Table XXVI,
column 2, are given the biserial correlations of each of the 28 tests
with the normal-neurotic dichotomy, defining neurotic in terms of
the combination of hysterics and anxiety states.[1] In order to make
all these values positive, the signs of 14 tests were changed, as
indicated in the column headed 'Multiplier'. It is with these
changed signs that we will be dealing throughout the discussion
that follows.

Column 3 gives the saturations of each test with a factor
obtained by finding that vector which maximized correlation
between columns 2 and 3. This factor, therefore, is by definition
identified as a factor of 'neuroticism'. The correlation between
columns 2 and 3 is a good deal lower than in several other analyses
reported in this book; where usually the correlation between factor
and criterion column is between ·6 and ·8, it is only ·400 in the
present case. We do not have far to seek for a solution. As pointed
out before, the normal soldiers were considerably more intelligent
than the neurotic soldiers through an error in selection. But intelligence has not hitherto been found to have any close relation with
neuroticism. It follows that the intelligence test (test 2) has a high
correlation with the normal-neurotic dichotomy ($r = ·481$), but a
completely negligible factor saturation ($r = ·109$). Unfortunately

[1] Each of the correlations is based on the largest possible number of subjects
who had completed each test.

TABLE XXVI

Test Number	Multiplier	Correlation Between Tests and Normal-Neurotic Dichotomy I	Rotated Factor Solution I					Correlation Between Tests and Normal-Neurotic Dichotomy II	Rotated Factor Solution II				
	1	2	3	4	5	6	7	8	9	10	11	12	13
1		·257	—·121	—·027	·241	—·127	—·171	·313	·059	·090	·256	—·122	—·164
2	—1	·481	·109	—·070	·259	—·260	·138	·518	·229	·170	·123	—·219	·162
45		·275	·334	·115	·092	—·118	—·116	·257	·365	—·019	—·119	—·074	·090
46		·183	·178	·130	·573	·507	·162	·212	·414	—·030	·365	·568	·181
47		·231	·257	·101	·574	·378	—·068	·286	·499	·086	·310	·447	—·040
14		·298	·386	·479	—·204	—·412	·021	·328	·380	·424	·335	·390	·041
15		·301	·115	·497	·243	—·243	·145	·360	·393	·370	·185	·218	·162
16		·266	·305	·486	·197	—·225	—·104	·266	·511	·344	·032	·182	·130
17		·324	·427	·356	·074	—·209	·045	·343	·500	·236	—·156	—·158	·074
19		·149	·162	·070	·163	·390	—·186	·138	·297	·037	·032	·358	·160
24		·178	·249	·058	·253	·045	·195	·063	·051	·099	·339	·055	·197
3	—1	·294	·215	—·153	·405	·039	·268	·301	·318	·281	·167	·105	·298
4	—1	·295	·301	—·157	·067	·054	·045	·313	·224	—·216	—·153	·007	·070
5	—1	·596	·317	·315	·138	·110	·129	·563	·200	·374	—·126	·168	·154
6		·453	·324	·173	·219	·297	·536	·421	·179	·176	·345	·302	·534
7		·227	·071	—·433	·355	·282	·345	·242	·117	·520	·175	·222	·576
9	—1	·166	·556	—·387	—·093	·018	·057	·127	·252	·421	—·463	·087	·091
11	—1	·278	·380	—·374	—·087	·171	·090	·237	·103	·372	—·348	·218	·110
12		·323	·299	·265	·324	—·012	—·221	·271	·343	·397	·034	·054	·185
13	—1	·017	—·206	—·078	·106	—·093	—·206	·067	—·146	·075	·233	—·117	·214
52	—1	·252	·269	·077	·265	·481	·087	·243	·382	—·063	·086	·431	·122
38	—1	·255	—·119	·176	—·239	·006	·002	·219	—·170	·253	—·091	—·033	·018
39	—1	·159	—·149	—·097	·086	·189	—·003	·161	—·121	—·080	·148	·178	—·006
40	—1	·283	·178	·039	·152	·022	—·083	·236	·234	—·035	·015	·053	—·067
49	—1	·252	—·024	·167	·339	·104	·442	·233	·197	·281	·223	·075	·421
50	—1	·170	—·152	·379	·244	·176	·299	·198	·089	·333	·339	·170	·289
42	—1	·195	·481	—·516	·148	—·264	·117	·120	·320	—·616	—·250	—·176	·166
43	—1	·469	·455	—·381	·233	—·388	·147	·408	·401	—·516	—·151	—·299	·199

it is not only the intelligence test which is affected in this way, but every test which is correlated with intelligence. Thus the low criterion correlation appears to be due largely to an irrelevant sampling error. Fortunately, this error does not affect the main part of our argument, which is concerned not with the establishment of the fact that a factor of neuroticism exists, but rather with the question of whether the diagnosis of 'psychopathy' forms part of this factor.

Accordingly we have calculated a new criterion column (column 8), made up by correlating each test with a new criterion consisting of the old neurotic group (hysterics and anxiety states) and the psychopaths *weighted equally*. Column 9, then, is that factor which maximizes the correlation with column 8. If this correlation is equal to or larger than that found before ($r = \cdot400$), then it would follow that psychopathy forms part of our best possible criterion. In actual fact the correlation drops to $r = \cdot320$, thus indicating that psychopathy is not part of the nuclear concept of 'neuroticism', and hence not part of our best possible criterion. This conclusion is not influenced by the unfortunate selection error which introduced differences in intelligence between normal and neurotic groups, as both the hysteric-anxiety and the psychopathic groups are equally affected by this error. In the absence of repetition and confirmation of this finding it would be unwise to make too definite a statement, but the data strongly support the conclusion that psychopathy is likely to have projections on the neuroticism axis, but unlikely to lie on it. We cannot, on the basis of these data, say whether the proper position for psychopathy is in the space generated by those axes already located (psychoticism, extraversion-introversion), or whether a new dimension will be required to accommodate this particular set of personality traits. In the absence of factual information, it would be idle to speculate.

We may now turn to certain observations suggested by the results in Tables XXV and XXVI. We have only attempted to interpret the first factor extracted from our matrix, i.e. the 'neuroticism' factor: the question arises as to the nature of the other factors. As the experiment was set up with a definite problem in mind, and did not therefore include controls which would facilitate such interpretation of factors other than the first one, it is with considerable hesitation that we suggest the possible meaning of factors two and three, i.e. columns 4 and 5. The second factor appears to divide fairly clearly the verbal tests from the non-verbal, in a manner similar to that usually found in the analysis of batteries of intelligence tests. On the one side we have the flicker fusion, manual dexterity, finger dexterity, body sway, leg persistence, tapping, abstractions, and concentration tests; on the other the vocabulary, word connection list, Maudsley medical questionnaire, worries, likes, interests, and annoyances tests, as well as the Luria verbal failures and the Minnesota o scale. There are few exceptions to this rule, and those that stand out are perhaps not inexplicable. Thus the Luria test appears with the verbal tests, which is perhaps intelligible in terms of the exclusively verbal stimulation provided, and the verbal response required.

The emergence of this factor lends some support to an heuristic hypothesis formulated elsewhere in connection with a discussion of recent advances in personality testing (Eysenck, 1950). 'It is widely agreed that personality rests on a firm hereditary basis, but is also subject to great alterations through social and other environmental influences. It would appear, by and large, that personality tests of the objective performance type are related rather more closely to the inherited pattern of a person's conative and affective traits; tests of conditioning, of suggestibility, of autonomic imbalance, of sensory dysfunctioning and of motor expression appear so closely bound up with the structural properties of the nervous system and with the body build or the sensory equipment of a person that the likelihood of hereditary determination can hardly be gainsaid.

'On the other hand, tests employing unstructured material, and verbal reactions of the questionnaire type, would appear to reflect more the historical aspects of a person's life story and be subject to day-to-day fluctuations of mood and outlook. If we may use an analogy from physics we might say that tests of this type deal with problems of hysteresis rather than with those of structure.' As is well known, in the cognitive field also environmental influences are much stronger in connection with verbal than in connection with non-verbal tests. Further proof for the heuristic hypothesis advanced here will be given in a later chapter.

The third factor has reasonably high saturations in S.G. (Service Grade), as determined by the Matrices test of intelligence, concentration, and vocabulary test; it seems likely that we are dealing here with an intellectual factor of some kind. However, as the intellectual field has been mapped out so well already by factorial analyses properly planned for the purpose, there is little point in amplifying this suggestion. Nor will we attempt to interpret the other two factors extracted.

Interesting points are suggested by a comparison of columns 2 and 3. Apart from the main hypothesis regarding the causes of proportionality of these columns, there are certain subsidiary assumptions non-fulfilment of which may cause the correlation to drop quite considerably. One of these assumptions is that of linear regression of each test on neuroticism. Figure 23 will illustrate this point. Let the abscissa be the normal-neurotic continuum, divided at point Y into two parts, viz. our normal and neurotic groups respectively. Let A, B, and C be the regression lines of three tests of

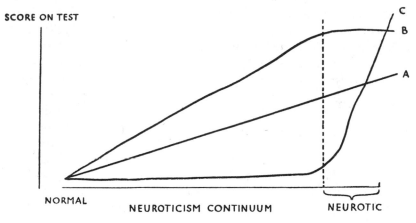

Figure 23

neuroticism. It will be seen that test C will give a good discrimination between normals and neurotics, but show very small correlation with other neuroticism tests in the normal group. Test B, conversely, will show good intercorrelations within the normal group, but will not give such good differentiation between normals and neurotics. Only test A, having a linear regression line, will show strict proportionality between discrimination and intercorrelation.

The figures in Table XXVI suggest that questionnaires of various kinds follow the regression line exemplified by test C; it will be seen that for both the Maudsley and Minnesota questionnaires the figures in column 2 are considerably higher than those in column 3. Tests of the Pressey X–O type and the 'Annoyances' kind, however, appear to follow the regression line of test B; the figures in column 3 are considerably higher than those in column 2.

The word connection list, the Concentration tests, the Luria motor disturbance, and the Leg Persistence test are examples of tests apparently following regression line A. It is difficult to generalize from these data, but it does appear reasonable to frame an heuristic hypothesis to the effect that verbal tests (both of the direct questionnaire and the indirect cross-out type) have curvilinear regression on neuroticism, while objective behaviour tests tend to have linear regression lines. Further research is urgently needed to provide more direct evidence on these points.

We must now face the question of the validity of various batteries of tests which might be constructed from those included in our battery. The most obvious method of ascertaining this value would perhaps be that of calculating a multiple correlation between all our tests and the neuroticism factor, which would thus constitute our criterion. This procedure is obviously fallacious; while it gives us the satisfyingly high R of almost ·90, we must regard this value with suspicion until the whole battery has been validated on another sample of normal and neurotic soldiers.

Instead, the following method was used in order to minimize the tendency of multiple correlations to capitalize on chance errors. Prior to any calculations being undertaken, two sets of eight tests each were designated as being most likely to have satisfactory correlations with the fact or of neuroticism; these judgments were based on long experience with the tests, and several previous analyses. These two sets of tests were called A and B, and included respectively tests 4, 5, 14, 16, 19, 39, 42, 47, and 9, 11, 15, 17, 24, 53, 45, 46. It was planned to calculate R for these two sets separately and in combination; it was thought that in thus making a choice of the tests to be used in advance, those chance factors which tend to inflate multiple R would have much less scope to assert their influence.

Subsequent to the completion of the experiment, test 39 was dropped from set A because for reasons explained above it was not comparable to the type of test on which our reasoning had been based, through the use of a different recording, and a different method of measurement. Subsequent to the completion of the analysis, test 9 was dropped from Set B because the correlation between this test and the factor was much higher than was usual in our experience, and because we wanted to avoid inflating the multiple R by the inclusion of a correlation patently too high. While this omission of two tests from the originally designated batteries may be criticized, it may be noted that the effect on the multiple R's is very small, and on the whole tends to lower rather than to raise them.

The values of R for these two batteries of seven tests, calculated according to the Lubin-Summerfield (1951) method, are ·755 and ·728 respectively; for the combined batteries R = ·817. These values may still be overestimates, but it seems unlikely that the true validity of either battery would be much below ·70, or that of the combined battery below ·80. As a check on this conclusion, another method of calculation was tried. Eighteen tests had been selected before completion of the calculations, and on the basis of previous experimentation, as most likely to correlate significantly with the neuroticism factor. Two of these had to be dropped for reasons already given (Body Sway suggestibility and Annoyances), so that we are left with sixteen tests—45, 14, 15, 16, 17, 19, 24, 4, 5, 6, 38, 11, 52, 49, 42, 43. A multiple R was then calculated, giving equal weights to all these tests, and making no use whatsoever of the statistical findings of the present analysis. In this way, both selection of tests and weighting system are unaffected by obtained results, and the resulting R should give an estimate of the lowest possible validity coefficient for our battery of tests. The value of R turned out to be ·77, a value which strongly supports our previous conclusion. Any reasonable system of weighting based on previous work, and not using the figures derived in the present research, would raise this figure to ·80 or over. It seems reasonable, then, to conclude that the battery of tests here assembled has a validity of approximately ·80 or thereabouts: it will be shown later that a similar battery has a reliability of at least ·85, and probably above ·90. These figures strongly support the argument advanced in Dimensions of Personality that in neuroticism we are dealing with a personality factor which can be measured as reliably and as validly as intelligence. In further support of this contention, a brief description will next be given of two experiments applying similar methods to those described to children. One of these experiments deals with objective and verbal tests, the other with the Rorschach.

Hitherto we have been dealing exclusively with adults, because most of the work done on emotional stability and neuroticism has been done with subjects over eighteen years old. If our general hypothesis of neuroticism as a kind of constitutional weakness be correct, however, it would appear essential that experiments with children, using analogous tests to those described above, should be shown to give similar results. From the practical point of view, too, the measurement of liability to breakdown in children is probably far more important than such measurement in the case of adults; preventive work is more likely to be successful at a relatively early age, and the possibility of 'screening' children who need psychiatric attention is a very inviting one. Two comparable studies have been reported from our laboratory, one using objective behaviour tests and pencil and paper tests, the other using projective material.

In the first of these studies (Himmelweit & Petrie, 1951), 50 normal and 50 neurotic children were matched on sex, age, and I.Q., and tested for five hours by means of individual tests and for three hours by means of group tests. Selection of normal children was carried out by asking head-teachers to select those children for testing who appeared relatively well adjusted, i.e. who showed no obvious signs of emotional maladjustment or scholastic backwardness. Selection of neurotic children was simply on the basis of choosing consecutive admissions to the Maudsley Child Guidance Clinic. These 'neurotic' children were later rated by the Senior Psychiatrist on a five-point scale for degree of adjustment; two were rated well-adjusted, and seven as only mildly maladjusted. It will be seen that the neurotic group was not ideal as a criterion group, and those who are familiar with school populations and teachers' ratings will agree that the school sample would contain some 5 to 10 per cent of questionable stability. It is likely that our criterion misclassifies about 10 to 15 per cent of all the children; this would tend to attenuate results considerably.

The tests used are described in detail elsewhere (Himmelweit & Petrie, 1951); it appears that neurotic children tend to differ from normal children in precisely those areas in which neurotic adults differ from normal adults. Thus neurotic children were observed to be more suggestible, less persistent, have less manual dexterity, worse body control, higher levels of aspiration, and slower speed. In addition they made a smaller number of attempts to deal actively with an aggressive situation of which they were onlookers in a Verbal Provocation test; they produced more critical, unhappy endings in a sentence completion test; they made fewer aggressive responses in a picture frustration test; showed more dislikes in a Word Liking test; showed characteristic patterns on expressive movements tests; had a weaker grip on a dynamometer test; and showed discontent on a questionnaire with their age and position in the family.

Fourteen tests showing the best discrimination were selected, and a discriminant function analysis performed. The method used was that originated by Penrose (1947) which gives a close approximation to the linear discriminant function when all intercorrelations are approximately equal. This method of discrimination requires the computation of a 'size' and a 'shape' score for each person. These scores are respectively the sum of the individual standard scores of each test, and the sum of individual scores suitably weighted, the weight being proportional for each test to the observed difference of the two group means for that test. The shape and size scores tend to be uncorrelated, and the linear function that best differentiates between the groups (i.e. reduces the number of misclassifications to a minimum) is then determined by calculating the multiple regression of the normal-neurotic dichotomy on the two scores.

Figure 24 shows the scatter diagram produced by plotting each child's score against the 'size' and 'shape' co-ordinates; each dot represents a neurotic child, each cross a normal child, while the diagonal line drawn through the cluster of points is the linear discriminant. It will be seen that nine maladjusted and ten well adjusted children are misclassified according to the criterion, giving a total misclassification of 20 per cent. This should be compared with a chance level of misclassification of 50 per cent. The quadratic discriminant was calculated, avoiding the assumption that the variance-covariance matrices within each group were the same, but did not aid significantly in correct classification.

The multiple correlation coefficient was found to be + ·70, a value which presumably capitalizes on chance errors to some extent, and is subject to shrinkage in future applications of the tests. However, it was found that 'neuroticism' scores calculated on this basis correlated significantly with the psychiatrist's ratings for the neurotic children, thus showing validity when applied to a sample which had not determined the actual weights used.

The second of these studies is very similar in design and treatment to the first one (Cox, 1951). Subjects were divided into an experimental group of sixty neurotic boys attending the Maudsley Child Guidance Clinic, twenty of whom were aged from 8 years to 9 years 11 months, twenty from 10 years to 11 years 11 months, and twenty from 12 years to 13 years 11 months, and a control group of 'normal' boys matched for age and intelligence. An individual Rorschach test was given to these children, as well as an individual intelligence test of the non-verbal type (Progressive Matrices). In scoring the Rorschach test, Beck's (1944) scoring categories were used, with minor additions from Klopfer and Kelly (1942).

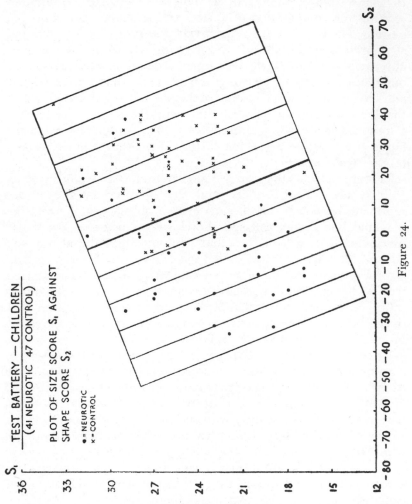

Figure 24.

Twenty-five indices were selected from the much larger number scored, and intercorrelated. Correlations were also formed between these variables and the intelligence test result (I.Q. in the table), and between the variables and the normal-neurotic dichotomy (the criterion). Five factors were extracted from the resulting matrix, which is reported in full elsewhere (Cox, 1951). The saturations for these factors of the twenty-seven items—twenty-five scoring categories, I.Q., and criterion—are given in Table XXVII. Also given are the correlations between the various items and the normal-neurotic criterion (cf. column 'D'.) The first value in the

TABLE XXVII

	I	II	III	IV	V	D
1. Criterion	265	734	208	−196	−121	(83)
2. A	484	−171	−441	−220	−139	−12
3. Ad.	360	503	−305	−184	226	43
4. Hds.	403	562	−182	127	218	49
5. Fire	392	−378	189	089	−178	−08
6. Geol. & mtns.	474	−188	342	397	084	03
7. Water	441	−505	174	056	−037	−10
8. Arch.	477	072	598	−110	−084	23
9. Mech. Sci.	362	398	417	084	−273	50
10. Misc.	140	−527	252	075	267	−47
11. Ws.	188	154	478	142	−332	25
12. D.	825	153	−183	−216	139	48
13. Dd.	602	257	−278	257	−050	25
14. F's.	942	154	−268	095	−089	34
15. F+'s	841	261	−094	058	−305	40
16. F−'s	661	−069	−264	337	382	−03
17. F+	731	435	−289	142	−157	40
18. F−	501	193	−330	197	508	18
19. FM	426	−128	−129	047	105	00
20. CF−	199	−477	324	−149	335	−33
21. C	484	−560	056	319	−050	−38
22. V & Y	575	−475	276	−363	169	00
23. I.Q.	030	254	512	257	−084	32
24. No.	897	−063	−354	149	−177	21
25. Av. time	−448	461	167	250	365	−08
26. Range	−451	420	161	337	489	−03
27. Failure	−811	−297	−036	516	−246	58

Decimal point properly preceding each entry omitted.

'D' column, which has been put in brackets, is the square root of the communality for the criterion, and is an estimate of the degree to which the total battery has succeeded in measuring the trait underlying the dichotomy, i.e. neuroticism.

The interpretation of these factors is relatively straightforward. The first factor appears to be one of productivity or number of responses, having its highest loadings on 'total number of responses' (·897) and total number of responses involving the use of form (·942), and its highest negative loading on 'failure to respond' (−·811).

The second factor appears to be the neuroticism factor one would expect to find very prominent in such a sample of children; it has its highest loading in the normal-neurotic criterion (·734), and is distinctly proportional in its loadings to the D column. The third factor appears as one of intelligence, with high loadings on I.Q. and cultured and unusual responses like architecture, mechanical and scientific, and geology.

The fourth factor depends for its interpretation so much on Rorschach mythology that only the most tentative explanation seems in order. It appears to contrast the individual who meets the environment either with a quick, often poor response, or violently, by emotional outbursts and point-blank refusal to co-operate, with the individual who experiences the environment without attempting to control it, being too absorbed in his personal difficulties. 'This interpretation is based on the implications in Rorschach terms of the Geology and Mountain response, which is suggestive of superficial evasiveness, common-place stereotypy and the pure Colour responses indicating crude emotionality. These characteristics may be conceived as opposed to the feelings of inferiority, anxiety, depression, and more generally apathy and passivity implied by the chiaroscura and vista responses.' The similarity of this 'dynamic' interpretation to the introvert-extravert dichotomy is obvious, but in view of the hazards of such inter-pretation no stress is laid on this factor. No interpretation is attempted of factor V, which may be entirely a statistical artefact.

Having thus shown the presence of a strong factor of neuroticism in the test data, a discriminant function analysis was carried out for the maximal differentiation of the two groups. Details of the method used will be found elsewhere (Cox, 1951); the final results are given in Figure 25, in a form comparable to Figure 24. It will be seen that the degree of misclassification on the basis of the Rorschach is greater than it had been in the case of the objective behaviour tests; nevertheless, the multiple correlation between factor scores and criterion reaches the respectable value of ·594 when all five factors are used, and ·566 when only the first two factors are used. (This difference is not statistically significant.) Again, it is probable that these values overestimate the size of the correlation one might hope to obtain on repeating the experiment, and that the values quoted are subject to shrinkage. However, it seems unlikely that there has been much maximization of error; indeed, the high saturations which the normal-neurotic dichotomy rating received in the factor analysis, i.e. in a type of analysis in which no such maximization of error takes place, suggests that our figures err if anything in underestimating the possible usefulness of this test for the detection of potential neurotics. It should also be borne in

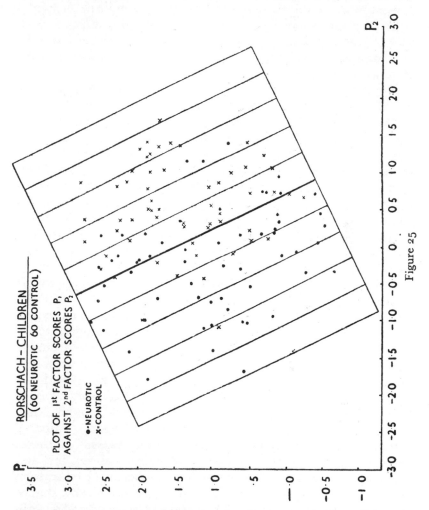

Figure 25

mind, of course, that the criterion itself was far from perfect and that higher validity coefficients could be expected if some way could be found to purify the criterion.

This analysis raises important theoretical points. Projective experts and Rorschach analysts will undoubtedly protest that by thus treating the Rorschach as an ordinary psychometric device, violence is done to the underlying principles of this technique. They will point out that when a record is being analysed, the meaning of a given score changes subtly in accordance with the context in which this score is found, so that we must never treat a given response 'analytically', i.e. in isolation, but must see it as part of a gestalt. Failure to do so robs the Rorschach test of its most distinctive features, and falsifies the picture which may be obtained from it.

The atomist's reply would of course be along familiar lines. He would point out that it is impossible statistically to get better prediction than that given by the multiple correlation formula, and that any departure from the weights given to any particular score by the regression formula according to the dictates of 'insight' or regard for the total gestalt can only lead to a lowering of predictive accuracy. The large-scale experiment on selection of clinical psychologists at Michigan provides empirical evidence on this point; it will be described in some detail elsewhere in this book.

In the present case, a very simple experiment suggests itself to test the validity of the theoretical position taken by the gestaltist. Given the criterion of allocating a group of children to either the normal or the neurotic side, we have already shown with what success this can be accomplished through the use of factorial analysis. Now if the gestaltist claim is justified, we would expect expert judgment based on the total record, and subject to no restrictions whatever, to be superior to the predictive accuracy achieved by the formal statistical analysis. Here indeed we would seem to have a crucial experiment on this very important theoretical point, and consequently two experienced Rorschach workers were asked to sort the hundred and twenty records into those they regarded as 'definitely neurotic', 'probably neurotic', 'probably normal', and 'definitely normal'. (For various reasons, the total number of records in the results given below is not always 120, and consequently a statement of the actual number involved in each case is given. One of the two Rorschach experts was given a chance to look at a sample of records for the sake of getting familiar with the particular local characteristics of the children; these are of course not included in the experiment.)

Below are given the results for expert M (Table XXVIIA). It will be noted that out of 116 children, 58·6 per cent are correctly identified, a result which is significant at the 5 per cent level when the one-tail test is used ($t = 1 \cdot 764$). 'Definitely' neurotic or normal identification is no better than 'probably' neurotic or normal identification. The correlation between prediction and actual status is ·17. These results are hardly encouraging.

TABLE XXVIIA

Classification by Expert M	Actual Classification		
	Neurotic	Normal	Correct
			%
Definitely neurotic	15	10	60
Probably neurotic	19	14	58
Probably normal	15	26	63
Definitely normal	9	8	47

Results from the other Rorschach expert show that of 96 children, 23 were correctly classified as normal and 23 as neurotic: 25 normal children were misclassified as neurotic, and 25 neurotic children disclassified as normal. The result, it appears, is slightly though not significantly worse than might be expected by chance. (It should be noted that when this expert sorted protocols without having to pay attention to the condition that 50 per cent of the children were normal and 50 per cent neurotic, he obtained very much better results, chi squared being 10·7. It is difficult to account for this difference.)

No finality is claimed for this comparison between the atomistic and the gestaltist methods of approach, nor do we claim that the overwhelming superiority of the atomistic method would necessarily be found in future work. This particular comparison was introduced as an afterthought, and did not form part of the original design of the experiment; consequently certain controls are lacking which would be essential if the results were to be regarded as in any sense definitive. It is included here mainly for the purpose of pointing out that theoretical points of view, such as those of the atomist and the gestaltist, can be settled on the empirical level, and are capable of being submitted to controlled experimentation; twenty years of verbal argument have not produced the consensus of opinion in this field which ought to follow a series of well-designed studies. It is, therefore, the method rather than the result of this research on which we wish to lay stress. Those who believe in the gestaltist approach, and want to remain in the realm of science, must sooner or later submit their hypotheses to a strict experimental test of the kind here outlined; semantic argument along well-worn lines is not likely to make their point of view acceptable to experimentalists who look rather for empirical demonstrations.

While these results and considerations make it appear feasible to consider techniques such as the Rorschach in terms of orthodox test construction, application, and validation, it should be stressed that in many respects these techniques fall behind legitimate requirements. Let us consider only one of these requirements, namely that of reliability. The literature here is in such a confused state that it is almost impossible to derive any agreed conclusions. Thus in one breath Rorschach experts claim that such devices as the split-half technique for measuring Rorschach reliability are inapplicable because the test must be considered as a whole, while in the next breath they quote with approval such applications of the split-half technique as have given acceptable values for Rorschach reliability. If the original objection to the use of the split-half method has any force, then surely the demonstration that nevertheless high reliabilities can be obtained must be taken to invalidate the hypothesis which has led to the original objection. This is but another example of the *ad hoc* use to which theories are being put in current clinical work, so that even when deductions made from these theories are shown to be falsified, this does not lead to any modification of the original theory.

However, if we take theoretical arguments against the use of the split-half method seriously, then we must fall back on the 'equivalent tests' procedure for measuring reliability. Fortunately there is a parallel form of the Rorschach test, constructed in such a way as to be strictly comparable to it, namely, the so-called Behn-Rorschach (Zulliger, 1941) or *Bero* test. The Bero and the Rorschach tests were given, in properly counterbalanced order, to one hundred normal and ninety-six abnormal subjects, in an attempt to obtain evidence on the reliability of the Rorschach scoring categories (Meadows, 1951). This procedure would seem to be unexceptionable from the point of view of Rorschach theory, provided the two versions are indeed strictly comparable.

The crucial test for the assumption of comparability consists in a comparison of the means and sigmas of the scoring categories of the two tests. If these are not significantly different, then clearly the two tests measure exactly the same personality areas; if they are significantly different, then it is impossible to maintain the hypothesis of comparability. Table XXVIII gives means and sigmas for eight scoring categories (R, W, D, M, F, C, A, and P), for the normal, abnormal, and total groups respectively. Comparison shows the close similarity of the figures for the two tests. In addition to the 8 scoring categories quoted, another 27 were in actual fact compared, for normals and abnormals separately,

TABLE XXVIII

MEAN RORSCHACH SCORES AND SIGMAS, AS COMPARED WITH MEAN BEHN-RORSCHACH SCORES AND SIGMAS, FOR NORMAL, ABNORMAL, AND TOTAL GROUPS

Scoring Category		$\overline{XR}$	$\overline{XB}$	σR	σB
R	N	24·40	25·62	12·17	11·25
	A	19·00	19·83	10·26	10·16
	T	21·80	22·76	11·59	11·10
W	N	8·02	8·24	3·36	3·58
	A	6·31	5·60	3·24	2·74
	T	7·20	6·94	3·41	3·46
D	N	15·05	16·06	10·07	9·26
	A	11·50	13·10	8·65	8·47
	T	13·40	14·55	9·61	9·01
M	N	2·08	1·82	1·44	1·68
	A	·99	1·12	1·21	1·11
	T	1·55	1·47	1·44	1·53
F	N	11·24	10·94	8·28	6·53
	A	8·25	9·15	6·31	6·04
	T	9·80	10·01	7·53	6·36
C	N	1·56	1·23	1·44	1·31
	A	·60	·63	1·02	1·07
	T	1·09	·93	1·34	1·24
A	N	7·89	10·08	4·15	4·68
	A	6·75	8·22	3·94	4·34
	T	7·33	9·15	4·09	4·61
P	N	4·48	4·23	1·62	1·69
	A	3·38	3·37	·67	·97
	T	3·99	3·80	1·65	1·66

making a total of 70 comparisons. Out of these 70 comparisons of values for the means, three were significantly different at or beyond the 5 per cent level. This is roughly what would be expected by chance (it is impossible to give an exact value to the chance hypothesis as the scoring categories are of course not independent); consequently there is little reason to assume that the two tests are not comparable.

TABLE XXIX

RELIABILITY COEFFICIENTS (RORSCHACH V. BEHN-RORSCHACH) FOR
NORMAL AND ABNORMAL GROUPS

Category		N :	A :	Category		N :	A :
R	(f)	·83	·86	FM	(f)	·36	·54
F	(f)	·78	·71	Art	(c)	·35	·51
Hd	(c)	·78	·41	Cl	(f)	·34	·52
D	(f)	·74	·81	m	(f)	·33	·52
Ad	(c)	·70	·54	AAt	(c)	·31	·62
S	(f)	·69	·40	C	(f)	·30	·58
A	(c)	·63	·80	FK	(f)	·30	·35
FC	(f)	·62	·25	Dd	(f)	·28	·62
H	(c)	·57	·57	A Obj.	(c)	·26	·57
W	(f)	·53	·60	Pl.	(c)	·26	·43
M	(f)	·52	·60	Blood	(c)	·20	·62
Fc	(f)	·50	·45	F-	(f)	·20	·59
Obj	(c)	·50	·70	Sm. Cl.	(c)	·18	·24
K	(f)	·47	·58	K	(f)	·14	·33
Geog.	(c)	·45	·52	c	(f)	·13	—·10
N	(c)	·40	·40	CF	(f)	—·04	·39
Sx.At.	(c)	·39	·65	Fire	(c)	—·05	·40
P	(f)	·36	·54				

f = formal score
c = content score

Table XXIX gives the correlations between the two tests, for all 35 scoring categories, and for normal and abnormal subjects separately.[1] These correlations may be regarded as reasonable estimates of the reliabilities, and as such are of considerable interest. It will be seen that not one correlation is as high as ·90 (customarily regarded as an acceptable level of reliability), and only the R category, i.e. the total number of responses, gives a correlation of over ·80 for both normals and abnormals. One

[1] It will be noted that the order of size for the reliabilities is very similar for the normal and abnormal groups, but that the reliabilities for the abnormal group are fairly consistently larger than those for the normal group.

further category (F) gives a correlation of over ·70 for both normal and abnormal groups, and one category (A) gives a correlation of over ·60. Five correlations (Ad., H, W, M, and Obj.) are over ·50 for both normals and abnormals. A considerable number of correlations is in the low twenties or below, and some are actually negative! These results should be borne in mind by those who base their interpretations on minute differences in Rorschach scores; the possibility that these differences are merely fortuitous, and of no fundamental importance, cannot be disregarded.

Indeed, if we were to advance an hypothesis to account for the superiority in the experiment described on page 163 of the statistical over the intuitive approach, it would be in terms of the tendency of the expert to pay attention to, and base his interpretation on, minute idiosyncrasies, odd phrasings, and slight deviations from the normal which have little reliability, and consequently little validity, while giving less weight to the more reliable and valid scoring categories which are picked out by the factorial—statistical approach. The same hypothesis has been advanced by Kelly and Fiske (1950) to account for a similar failing of the projective-intuitive approach in the large-scale Michigan experiment into the selection of Clinical Psychology students. 'The essence of clinical evaluation and integration of data involve permitting the clinician to assign to each item of opinion "beta weights", which vary from case to case according to the clinician's perceived patterning of the data. Our findings suggest that this technique may result in increasing the ratio of error variance to true variance with successive ratings based on increments of information. This may lead to a subjective feeling of increased knowledge about the assessee without a parallel awareness of the fact that many of the additional items of information are not actually correlated with the criteria, and hence should not be weighted in arriving at a prediction about the assessee.'

This chapter has shown us that at least one dimension in the non-cognitive field can be measured with sufficient accuracy to make it possible to proceed to more formal experiments on the causation and the correlates of 'neuroticism'; we must now turn to a detailed consideration of the available evidence in these fields.

Chapter Five

HEREDITY AND ENVIRONMENT

IT is commonly believed that heredity plays a considerable part in the determination of an individual's personality. If we accept the well-known definition of personality as 'the integrated organization of all the cognitive, affective, conative, and physical characteristics of an individual as it manifests itself in focal distinctness to others', we might expect that much research endeavour would have been dedicated to the discovery of hereditary influences on the cognitive, affective, conative and physical characteristics of the individual. A certain amount of such research there has been, but its emphasis has been curiously lopsided; we have some studies into inheritance of physical characteristics, and some into inheritance of cognitive abilities, but there has been little worth-while research into the conative and affective sides of personality.

The most favoured method of investigation has been the so-called 'twin method' developed in Germany (Siemens, 1924), which consists in comparing the average resemblance of identical twins with that of fraternal twins. The difference between identical twins, due to environment alone, is compared with the difference between fraternal twins, due to both heredity and environment; if differences between fraternal twins are much greater than between identical twins, heredity appears to be a powerful causative factor, while if differences are small or non-existent, the influence of heredity as a causative factor in individual differences is discounted. It is possible to give mathematical expression to the estimated contribution of heredity and environment to the variance of any given test, as well as of the interaction of heredity and environment (Shuttleworth, 1935), provided we are ready to make the assumption that the environment is as similar for a pair of fraternals as for a pair of identicals.

The large amount of research done along these lines into the inheritance of intelligence has been summarized adequately by Verschuer (1939), Schwesinger (1933), Newman, Freeman, and Holzinger (1937), Gottschaldt (1939), and Woodworth (1941).

The fairly universal conclusion has been that 'inter-family environmental differences account for a much smaller proportion of the variance in intelligence than do hereditary differences' (Shuttleworth, 1935). No equally comprehensive generalization has hitherto been made in the affective and conative fields, if we except the rather negative conclusions arrived at by Newman, Freeman, and Holzinger (1937) who say: 'In most of the traits measured the identical twins are much more alike than the fraternal twins, as indicated by higher correlations. This is true of physical dimensions, of intelligence, and of educational achievement. *The only group of traits in which identical twins are not much more alike consists of those commonly classed under the heading of personality.*[1] . . . The difference in resemblance of the two classes of twins is not the same in the different groups of traits. In general, the contrast is greater in physical traits, next in tests of general ability (intelligence), less in achievement tests, and least in tests of personality or temperament. In certain instances, viz. tapping, will-temperament, and neurotic disposition, the correlations of identical twins are but little higher than those of fraternal twins.'

A brief review of such experimental and observational data as are available will indicate some of the reasons for this failure to achieve positive results comparable to those achieved in the cognitive field, and will also make us familiar with certain dangers in twin research which have invalidated many conclusions confidently drawn from methodologically inadequate data.

Much the most extensive work on the inheritance of personality has been done in the field of mental illness, where twin studies of psychotic (and occasionally neurotic) patients have been widely accepted as a method for elucidating the influence of heredity on pathology. The work of Rudin (1930), Rosanof *et al.* (1935, 1941), Essen-Moeller (1941), Luxenberger (1928, 1930, 1933, 1934, 1935, 1940), Kallmann (1941, 1946), and Kallmann & Barrera (1942), leaves little doubt that concordance in identical twins is considerably more frequent than in fraternal twins, although still far from perfect. This type of work inevitably suffers from the subjectivity of psychiatric diagnoses, and the lack of reliability associated with all rating methods.

A quite different field, which also has attracted some attention, is that of criminal tendency. Lange (1931), Stumpfl (1936), Kranz (1936), and Borgstroem (1939), have shown that identical twins

[1] Italics not in original.

are more concordant in their criminality than are fraternal twins, even when complete separation has taken place. Popenoe (1936) concludes from a review of this material that 'we must ascribe to heredity a more important role in the production of crime than has hitherto been the case'.

When we come to the more definitely experimental type of study, we find that the relevance of the experiment to the question of heredity of personality is usually contingent on the theory of personality held by the investigator. Conditioning experiments appear important to the followers of Pavlov; eidetic imagery to those who agree with Jaensch's system; handwriting is studied by the 'expressive movement' school; autonomic patterns are investigated by the physiological experimenters; perseveration and fluency by the Spearman school; projective techniques are employed by the followers of Rorschach and Freud.

Much work has been carried out in the field of handwriting, both along subjective, interpretative lines and along objective, quantitative lines. The picture is somewhat confused. Bracken (1940a and b) found no hereditary determination for differences in handwriting pressure in 42 pairs of twins, while Carmena (1935b) and Miguel (1935) came to the opposite conclusion after experimenting on 50 pairs of twins each. Writing speed was found to be determined largely by heredity in Bracken's (1939a) study of 38 sets of twins, a conclusion confirmed in a later study by the same author (Bracken, 1940a) on 42 pairs of twins. Thelen (1939) conducted matching experiments which showed hereditary factors to be prominent in handwriting, while Hartge (1936) found handwriting to be of no diagnostic value in individual diagnosis of monozygoticity. Nicolay (1939) and Hermann (1939) agree in finding little hereditary determination in handwriting, with the exception of the writing angle. Saudek & Seeman (1932, 1933) emphasize both heredity and environment in the determination of writing and drawing. Newman, Freeman, & Holzinger (1937) support Galton's original finding, that there is surprisingly little resemblance between handwritings of identical twins. The one exception to this appears to be the quality of the handwriting (cf. also Kramer & Lauterbach (1928)).

Closely related to handwriting studies are three investigations of the Downey Will-Temperament test, which is based essentially on handwriting characteristics. Tarcsay (1939) reports negative conclusions, while Bakwin (1930) is more positive. Newman, Freeman, & Holzinger (1937) report findings which definitely disprove the hypothesis that heredity determines individual differences in reaction to this test; the intraclass correlations on the four scales of this test used by them are higher for fraternal than for identical twins! (The actual values are ·69, ·36, ·53, and ·51 as against ·45, ·31, ·51, and ·48.)

Perceptual factors in the personality of twins have been studied by Bracken (1939c), Hofstetter (1948) and Smith (1949). Eidetic imagery, which according to Jaensch's theories is closely connected with personality type, was shown by the last-named author to be strongly determined by hereditary factors, as was also reaction time. The other authors show that in the production of after-images, in the extent of visual illusions, and in accommodative convergence heredity plays a powerful part.

A beginning has been made in the study of conditioning in twins by Kanaev (1934, 1938, 1941), who used the Krasnogorsky modification of Pavlov's method to show remarkable similarities between identical twins. He links this approach to Pavlov's theories of personality, which are based on conditioning experiments, and it is unfortunate that his suggestive work has been left in a relatively undeveloped state where no certain conclusions can be drawn.

Another physiological variable which has been studied on the hypothesis that it might be found to be correlated with personality differences is the brain-wave pattern. Lennox et al. (·1945), Elmgren (1941), Davis & Davis (1936), and Gottlober (1938) have shown remarkable similarities between identical twins, and less marked similarity between fraternal twins; in the absence of any satisfactory theory linking brainwave patterns to personality, however, it is difficult to interpret these findings.

Of more definite relevance to personality are three studies of yet a third physiological variable, viz. the psycho-galvanic reflex. The important monograph by Wenger (1948) has definitely established the close connection between neuroticism and autonomic imbalance, and has shown that the P.G.R. is a good measure of autonomic imbalance. Carmena (1934, 1935a), working on 60 pairs of twins, showed that the P.G.R. is strongly influenced by heredity. Jost & Sontag (1944) supported this finding by using, in addition to the P.G.R., pulse pressure, salivation, heart period, respiration rate, vasomotor persistence time, and other autonomic measures. They conclude that an autonomic constitution may be at least partially inherited.

Ratings along the lines of the Vineland Social Maturity Scale have been carried out by Bracken (1939b), Troup & Lester (1942), and Wilson (1941); there is considerable agreement that whatever is measured by this scale is influenced to a considerable extent by heredity. While it is believed that the Social Maturity Scale measures personality factors additional to intelligence, it has not hitherto been possible to identify them, and therefore it is difficult to interpret the findings.

Motor skill has been studied by Brody (1937) and by McNemar (1933). Both authors find identical twins much more alike than fraternal twins, and conclude that the hereditary hypothesis is the most plausible explanation of individual differences in motor skills. This finding is relevant to personality research because it has been shown by Eysenck (1947) that motor skills correlate quite highly with neuroticism, so that hereditary determination of individual differences in skill give presumptive evidence for hereditary determination of individual differences in neuroticism.

Related to this work are the studies by Becker & Lenz (1939) and Pauli (1941) showing that differences in work curves are more pronounced in fraternal than in identical twins. Irregularities in work curves have also been shown to be diagnostic of neuroticism (Eysenck, 1947), so that this finding too supports the tentative hypothesis that neuroticism may be based on a hereditary foundation.

Perseveration has been studied by Yule (1935) and by Cattell & Molteno (1940). The former, using 115 twins, showed that on a battery of p tests of the Stephenson type heredity played an important part; the latter, using 84 pairs of twins, found that p tests gave no evidence of hereditary influence. Tests of F (fluency of association) were also given by Cattell & Molteno, who concluded that family-environmental differences 'are about 8 times as important as hereditary segregation of genes in accounting for individual differences in fluency'. This conclusion links up with the work of Carter (1938, 1939) and Sorensen & Carter (1940) on association in twins; it was found that identical twins are slightly more alike with respect to speed of association.

Most of the studies mentioned so far have had only tangential relevance to personality; more directly relevant might be work on questionnaires and projective tests. Carter (1933, 1935) has reported on the use of the Bernreuter Personality Inventory as applied to 133 pairs of twins. Identical twins were markedly more similar than fraternal twins with respect to neurotic tendency, self-sufficiency and dominance. This conclusion does not agree with the results published by Newman, Freeman & Holzinger (1937) with respect to another neuroticism questionnaire. The Rorschach technique has been used by Troup (1938), Eckle & Ostermeyer (1939), Marinescu *et al.* (1934), and Kerr (1936). Results are conflicting, Kerr's being essentially negative, Marinescu's positive, while the other reports are somewhat intermediate. No clear picture emerges from the combined results, however.

Certain techniques have been used by one investigator only, and while the connection between the test used and personality is not always clear, the results illustrate a point in methodology which we want to stress in the discussion. Szondi (1939) found greater similarity in identical twins when he applied the test that bears his name to 97 pairs of twins. Petö (1946) used psychoanalysis as his method of investigation, finding surprising identity of symptom in two identical twins. Malan (1940) found spatial orientation to be an inherited trait. Hunt & Clarke (1937) showed marked differences in the startle pattern of a pair of twins. Carter (1932) found occupational interests to be due in part at least to hereditary causes. Frischeisen-Köhler (1933) reports that personal tempo is definitely conditioned by heredity. Thompson (1943) showed determination of play-behaviour by heredity. Waardenburg (1929) showed greater similarity between identical twins with respect to likes and dislikes. Zilian (1938) found less variability for identical twins on imaginal and motor factors. Steif (1939) found great similarity in scribbling between identical, little similarity between fraternal twins, a result similar to Luchsinger's findings with respect to voice range (1940).

Certain obvious characteristics emerge even from this very brief review of the literature dealing with twin studies in personality research. (1) Objectively oriented investigations are mostly very limited in scope, dealing with traits of a low order of complexity such as scribbling, angle of handwriting, eidetic imagery, reaction times, or spatial orientation. (2) When an attempt is made to study higher-order concepts, such as criminality or psychosis, the concepts chosen are of a sociological-ethical, or psychiatric rather than of a psychological nature, and the investigation proceeds along lines far removed from the objectivity of psychometric testing procedures. (3) While on the whole most authors agree that identical twins are more alike than fraternal twins on most of the tests used so far, there are many inexplicable contradictions (e.g.

the studies of perseveration, of questionnaire tests, and of the Rorschach). (4) Most personality tests have such low reliabilities that results are almost bound to be disappointing; correction for attenuation is seldom attempted. (5) Even when results are clear-cut, they are often difficult to interpret due to our lack of knowledge of precisely what it is a given test is measuring.

Some of the conflicting results reported may be due to technical faults which vitiate many of the studies reported. Results are often stated as impressions, rather than being reported as objectively scored and statistically validated conclusions. Choice of twin-pairs to be tested is often based on faulty sampling practices, fraternal twins which look unlike each other being overlooked in favour of those who resemble each other. (Correct procedures are suggested by Verschuer (1939) and Rosanoff et al. (1937).) Diagnosis of monozygoticity or dizygoticity has often been faulty, even where the procedures adopted have been described in full. These and other technical faults are easily overcome by experimenters of reasonable competence. Two other criticisms are more fundamental, and must be discussed in some detail.

(1) In passing, we have noted that the whole procedure of twin research rests on the assumption that the environment is as similar for a pair of fraternal twins as it is for a pair of identical twins. Stocks (1930), Holmes (1930), Bracken (1933, 1934a, 1934b, 1935, 1936), Wilson (1934), and Jones & Wilson (1933) present reports indicating that identicals are treated more alike than are fraternals, a fact which would appear to invalidate this assumption. Blue-kercken (1935), Lohmeyer (1935), and Misbach & Stromberg (1941), on the other hand, show that often the very fact of the identicals' similarity leads to different development in the sense that they take on complementary roles. Schiller (1937) and New-man et al. (1937) have confirmed this point. Meumann (1935) and Bounterwek (1936) have shown a tendency for identical twins to select different occupations. Woodworth (1941) comments that 'such differentiation of roles as has been observed would probably cause identicals to differ in certain special abilities and personality traits. . . .' In any case, as Wilson (1934) has emphasized, while in many respects the identical pairs live under more similar conditions than the fraternals, 'this fact must be attributed ultimately to the influence of their heredity which led, or forced them to "select" more similar environments'. While it is impossible to be dogmatic on this point, it does appear that the argument against similarity

of environment for the two types of twins is speculative and hypo-thetical; there is no evidence to suggest that such differences as may exist are not themselves due to hereditarily determined selec-tion of environments, or that the small differences observed could account for the large differences in test results. Until more em-pirical evidence is produced by the critics we cannot concede that their arguments do much damage to twin research methodology.

(2) The following criticism of twin work has not to our know-ledge been made previously, although a solution to the problem posed by it has been published elsewhere (Eysenck, 1950). It is relevant not only to studies of temperamental traits, but equally so to work on intelligence and would seem to undermine the elaborate structure of argument built up on twin research. Essentially, this criticism concerns a conceptual jump which takes place when an argument is presented regarding the inheritance of *intelligence* from the intercorrelations of identical and fraternal twins on *a particular test*, say the Binet. We may generalize and say that a demonstration that individual differences in performance on a given test are due to heredity cannot be used as proof that a hypothetical trait or ability imperfectly measured by that test is inherited. The argu-ment can best be presented by using an algebraic model.

We may write the factorial equation of the Binet test in the following form:

$$\sigma^2 \text{BINET} = \sigma_g^2 + \sigma_V^2 + \sigma_N^2 + \sigma_{SP}^2 + \sigma_M^2 +$$
$$\sigma_C^2 + \ldots \sigma_X^2 + \sigma_S^2 + \sigma_E^2$$

where $\sigma^2\text{BINET}$ denotes the total variance of the Binet test, σ_g^2 the contribution to that total variance made by 'g' or intelligence, while $\sigma_V^2, \sigma_N^2, \sigma_{SP}^2, \sigma_M^2, \sigma_C^2 \ldots \sigma_X^2$ denote contributions to the vari-ance by verbal, numerical, spatial, memory, comprehension, and other group factors, and σ_S^2 and σ_E^2 stand for the contribution to the variance of specific and error factors. Using estimates derived from Burt & John's (1942) analysis of the Binet, the total variance contributed by 'g' or intelligence is only about 30 to 40 per cent, or less than half the non-error variance. McNemar's (1942) series of analyses attributes on the average 40 per cent of the total vari-ance to 'g', the proportion ranging from 35 to 50 per cent. If we neglect the error variance, which amounts only to about 5 per cent and of course cannot be said to be caused either by heredity or environment, but which is merely an error of measurement uncor-related with the abilities or traits the test is measuring, we can conclude by and large that one-half of the variance at most is due to 'g', while at least one-half is due to various other common factors or specifics.

It will be clear now how unjustified is the jump from the statement 'individual differences in Binet scores are accountable for in terms of heredity to the extent of 80 per cent, which, granted certain assumptions, is a statement of fact, to the much more usual statement that 'individual differences in intelligence are accountable for in terms of heredity to the extent of 80 per cent', which is a completely unwarranted generalization which could be made only if all the non-error variance were attributable to 'g'. It could be that all the group and specific factors hypothesized were completely determined by heredity, in which case heredity would play only a very minor part in the determination of 'g'; it could be that the group and specific factors were largely caused by environmental differences, in which case 'g' might be 100 per cent inherited. *Unless we can analyse the total variance of a test into its constituent parts, and measure these parts separately, no scientifically tenable conclusion can be drawn from the data.* If this criticism be justified, it follows that the whole literature on the inheritance of intelligence, perseveration, social maturity, motor skill, conditionability, personality type, or any other ability or trait, in so far as it is based on twin studies, must be considered invalid. This conclusion may appear harsh in the extreme, but it is difficult to see how it can be avoided on the evidence to hand.

It follows from what has been said above that if we want to measure the degree to which a particular trait or ability is inherited in a given sample, then we must study, not the individual test results, but rather the hypothetical underlying factors which generate the test variance. In studying intelligence, that would mean administering a battery of tests to the experimental population, intercorrelating these tests, factor-analysing the resulting factor matrix, and obtaining factor scores for each experimental subject on each factor isolated. We could then submit these factor scores to the mathematical treatment appropriate to our problem, and obtain data relevant not to one test only, but to intelligence, or verbal ability, or memory, or whatever our factors might turn out to be.

In the field of cognition, the main factors underlying test performance have been isolated by Spearman, Thurstone, Holzinger and other experimenters using the method of factorial analysis.

We know now what to measure, and we know how to measure it. In the fields of conation and affection, however, the position is less clear. There are numerous theories, but few facts; much is hypothesized, but little known. The problem thus arises as to the correct choice of the experimental variable.

Our choice has been determined largely by two considerations: (1) The social importance of the trait investigated, and (2) the existence of a sufficient body of knowledge regarding it. On both counts we had little difficulty in arriving at our decision to study the inheritance of the trait variously named neuroticism, emotional instability, or lack of integration, and discussed in detail in earlier chapters. We may state the hypothesis investigated in this paper in a formal manner: The trait of neuroticism, as operationally defined in terms of the pattern of intercorrelations between a specified set of objective personality tests, is in large part determined by heredity, and such individual differences with respect to it as appear in the experiment cannot be accounted for in terms of environmental influences.

The relevance of the experiment to the psychological and psychiatric fields needs little stressing; it may be worth while, however, to point out the importance attaching to the result from the point of view of the logic of factorial analysis. It will have been noted that our definition of neuroticism is essentially in terms of factorial analysis, i.e. in terms of the condensation of a set of observed correlations into a smaller number of hypothetical underlying variables or factors. This method has frequently been criticized on various grounds, and while some of these criticisms have not always been based on thorough knowledge of precisely what is implied in the method, it cannot be denied that some doubts could not be allayed in terms of statistical arguments alone. In particular, the fact that the resolution of a given matrix of intercorrelations into factors can be carried out in an infinite number of ways has perplexed many critics otherwise not hostile to this approach. Thurstone's method of overcoming this difficulty (a difficulty which is not faced at all by some writers like Burt and Stephenson) is well known; it consists essentially in overdetermining the solution. This method, while of the utmost importance in work on abilities, appears less well suited to the requirements of non-cognitive experimentation, and the method of 'criterion analysis' has been suggested as a plausible alternative (Eysenck, 1950).

However, proof has been lacking hitherto that factors thus

determined have any 'real' existence, and are something other than mere 'statistical artefacts'. In part the argument about 'real' existence is of course a philosophical and semantic one; in a very definite sense any scientific concept is an 'artefact' lacking 'real' existence. A concept, whether it be that of an electron, an instinct, a quantum of energy, a complex, or a sound wave, is an abstraction, and thus not 'real'; scientific concepts are 'artefacts' almost by definition. However, what critics usually mean by this objection is something quite different. They denote a factor an 'artefact' if it does no more than merely summarize existing knowledge, if it does not go beyond the circle of its own derivation.

Here the present experiment should be of crucial importance.[1] Having defined our factor of neuroticism in terms of the intercorrelations of a set of tests, we proceed to examine the biological unit of this factor by analysing the degree to which the factor *as a whole* is inherited. The crucial question, therefore, is this: Is the degree of hereditary determination of this factor greater than that of any single test contributing to the total factor variance, or is nothing gained by substituting the 'factor score' for the score on any of the tests which jointly define the factor? If the result shows that the factor is inherited to a more marked extent than any single test, it follows that we have succeeded in proving that the factor is no mere artefact, but has a certain degree of biological reality. As will be shown later, the considerable difference actually observed in hereditary determination between factor and best test encourages us to believe that we have succeeded in this demonstration.

In any study involving a comparison of identical and fraternal twins, care must be taken to avoid errors that might arise from unrepresentative samples. Many previous studies have been open to criticism because of their methods of sampling. If the selection of twins is carried out as in the study by Newman, Freeman and Holzinger (1937), by inquiry into local schools, there exists the possibility of overlooking those fraternal twins who are quite dissimilar, thus yielding an underestimate of the average difference between fraternal twins. This is because twins who are much alike

---

[1] The experiment was carried out by D. Prell and the writer in collaboration; a detailed description has been published elsewhere (Eysenck & Prell, 1951). We wish to record our indebtedness to Dr. R. R. Race and staff of the M.R.C., Blood Group Research Unit, the Lister Institute, for their kindness in performing the laboratory work on the determination of blood groups for the twins.

attract attention and are brought to the investigator's notice, while those differing considerably in appearance and behaviour may be overlooked. The questionnaire method of sampling is even more likely to yield a sample overloaded with fraternal twins who are very much alike. Probably the most adequate method of securing an unbiased sample is to use the birth record method (von Verschuer, 1939). This was the method used in the present study (Eysenck & Prell, 1951).

The birth records for five boroughs in south London were searched for all twins of the same sex, born during the period 1935–1937. The reason for selecting only like-sex twins was that identical twins of necessity belong to the same sex. If then, fraternal twins of the opposite sexes had been included, they would have introduced a possible complication due to sex differences. Concerning the age limits, the lower limit was set because children younger than 11 could not have taken all of the tests; the upper limit was set because a wide age-range necessitates statistical corrections for age which complicate the picture.

The survey of the birth records yielded the names of 130 pairs of like-sex twins. From these it was possible to locate 68 pairs who were living in the London area, close enough to be able to attend the Psychological Laboratory of the Institute of Psychiatry. The remainder were either living too far away, had died, or could not be located. In no case was parental permission to test refused. The twins were examined as they were located. After examination they were classified as identical or fraternal according to a procedure to be described presently.

Although there is no longer any doubt of the existence of two types of twins, efficient criteria are needed in order to effect a valid separation in all cases. Two methods of diagnosis have been used to group identical and fraternal twins: the foetal-membrane method and the similarity method. In view of the many criticisms made of the former, the latter was employed.

The similarity method involves the comparison of the members of a pair of twins in respect to numerous physical characteristics which are determined by heredity. As the number of characteristics is increased arithmetically, the chances of any two siblings not being alike on all the characteristics is increased geometrically. Therefore, if the chances of two children in the same family being alike in one such characteristic is one in two, the chances of their being alike in ten is one in one thousand.

In the present investigation the set of criteria upon which the diagnosis of zygosity was made is as follows:

(1) Close resemblance of ears, teeth and facial features.
(2) Iris pigmentation.
(3) Standing height.
(4) Presence or absence of mid-digital hair.
(5) Ability to taste phenyl-thio-carbamide.
(6) Scapular shape.
(7) To (14) Blood groups A_1A_2BO, Rh, MNS, P, Lewis, Kell and Lutheran.

(1) *Close resemblance of ears, teeth, and facial features* was rated on a three-point scale; no resemblance, *different* (D); pronounced resemblance, but *slight differences* (SD); and very pronounced resemblance rendering it almost impossible to distinguish the twins, *same* (S).

(2) The *resemblance* of the *iris pigmentation* was rated on a three-point scale; no resemblance, *different* (D); pronounced resemblance, but *slight differences* in one zone (SD);[1] and very pronounced resemblance, rendering it almost impossible to distinguish his twins, *same* (S).

(3) The *standing height* of each twin was measured to the nearest quarter of an inch.

(4) *Presense or absence of hair* on the dorsum of the mid-digital region of the fingers was determined by placing the subject's hand, half clenched and bent slightly backwards, between the investigator and a source of light. This was provided by a 100-watt electric light placed seven feet behind the subject's hand. Presence of any hair on one or more fingers was scored as: *hair* +.

(5) *Ability to taste phenyl-thio-carbamide* was ascertained by having the subject drink one-quarter teaspoonful of a 1/20,000 solution of PTC. The subject was asked what the substance tasted like. Any answer other than water was scored as: *taste* +.

(6) The *scapular shape* was found by running the hand over the inside edge of both scapulæ. The twins were classified as either *concave* (CC), *straight* (S), *convex* (CV), or *mixed* (M). The mixed

---

[1] In the majority of individuals, the iris is composed of two zones, an inner and an outer of different pigmentation. In fifty pairs of siblings studied by Rife (1943), no two pairs were found to have the same iris pigmentation in regard to both zones, although in ten pairs the outside zones were the same, and in four pairs the inside zones were the same.

type included any combination of the other three: (CC–CV), (CV–S), etc.

Grouping the Twins into MZ and DZ. Using the data on the 14 criteria, the twins were first classified into one of three groups: *definite-MZ, definite-DZ*, and *doubtful*. A pair of twins was considered *definite-MZ* if they had (S)'s in criteria (1) and (2); differed less than 1·5 inches in height on criteria (3);[1] *and* if the children agreed exactly on criteria (4) to (14) inclusive. Twins were considered as *definite-DZ* if they were rated (D) on both criteria (1) and (2); *or* if their height differed by more than 3·5 inches, criterion (3); *or* if they differed on *any one* of criteria (4) to (14) inclusive. Twins were considered *doubtful* if they had ratings of (SD) on both criteria (1) and (2), or a rating of (SD) on either (1) or (2) and a rating of (S) on the other; if they differed 3·5 inches or less on criteria (3); *and* if they agreed exactly on criteria (4) to (14) inclusive.

On the basis of the above procedure, 20 pairs of twins were classified as *definite-MZ*, 24 pairs as *definite-DZ*, and 6 pairs as *doubtful*.

When a pair of twins had been rated as *doubtful*, the blood groups of both parents were ascertained in order to effect a final classification.[2] The blood groups of the twins and their parents were then compared to determine the chances of the blood groups of two siblings from a known mating being alike on all of the blood groups. In five of the *doubtful* pairs, the chances of the two children being alike on all of the blood groups, taking into account the blood groups of their parents' blood, were: 1:256, 1:256, 1:1000, 1:1000, and 1:2000. Accordingly, these pairs of twins were classified MZ. In the other *doubtful* pair the chances were: 1:16, therefore this set was classified DZ.

The research design calls for a criterion group of neurotic children against which the factor extracted from the normal twins could be validated. Twenty-one children born between 1935 and 1937 were selected from out-patients at the Maudsley Child

---

[1] Newman, Freeman, & Holzinger (1937) found that 94 per cent of their 50 sets of MZ twins had pair differences in standing height of less than 1·5 inches; 53·8 per cent of their 50 pairs of DZ twins had pair differences of less than 1·5 inches. None of their MZ twins had a pair difference of over 3·1 inches; whereas 19·1 per cent of their DZ twins had a pair difference of over 3·1 inches.

[2] Blood group tests were not made for the parents of all 50 pairs of twins as it was feared that an attempt to persuade the parents to submit to a 'blood-test' might have resulted in a loss of the co-operation already secured.

Guidance Clinic. Great care was taken to exclude children with organic complications, or with possible psychotic traits, or who were not definitely considered 'unstable' by the examining psychiatrist. The resulting sample of twenty-one children approaches as closely as is possible at the present stage of psychiatric knowledge a 'pure' neurotic group, with relatively little mixture of other mental or physical disorders.

The following tests were used in this study: it should be remembered that the choice was made before our knowledge of this factor was as extensive as it is now, and that consequently a much better choice could be made at the present time than was possible when this experiment was being planned.

(1) Intelligence (Wechsler-Bellevue, Similarities and Digit Symbol sub-tests).
(2) Tapping Area (cf. p. 133).
(3) Tapping Speed (cf. photograph 22).
(4) Level of Aspiration.
(5) Motor Speed Test (Track Tracer, cf. photograph 12).
(6) Speed of Decision (choice of 'higher' of two playing cards, lying face downwards on the table; cf. photograph 21).
(7) Static Ataxia.
(8) Body-Sway Suggestibility.
(9) Dynamometer Strength of Grip.
(10) Word Dislikes.
(11) Brown Personality Inventory (Adapted).
(12) Lie Scale (adapted from M.M.P.I.).
(13) Flicker Fusion.
(14) Autokinetic Movement.
(15) Autokinetic Suggestibility.
(16) Speed of Writing S's backwards.
(17) Fluency.

(A detailed description of the tests is given in Eysenck & Prell, 1951; short descriptions of most of them will be found in other chapters of this book.)

The intercorrelations between the 17 tests are reported in Table XXX for the 100 twins, as well as correlations with zygosity, sex, and age. Table XXXI records saturations of the tests for three significant factors, which leave only insignificant residuals. Also given in Table XXXI are the correlations of each test with the

TABLE XXX

	Zygosity (V1)	Sex (V2)	Age (V3)	1 Intelligence	2 Tapping Area	3 Tapping Speed	4 Level of Aspiration	5 Motor Speed Test	6 Speed of Decision	7 Static Ataxia	8 Body Sway Suggestibility	9 Grip	10 Word Dislikes	11 Personality Inventory	12 Lie Scale	13 Critical Flicker Fusion	14 Autokinetic Movement	15 Autokinetic Suggestibility	16 Backward 'S'	17 Fluency
V1		−·121	·002	−·147	−·013	−·007	−·068	−·012	−·005	−·107	·068	−·021	·133	·225	−·292	−·084	·067	·020	−·055	·016
V2	−·121		−·394	·152	−·053	−·006	−·033	−·080	·014	·046	·025	−·278	·177	−·031	−·051	−·163	−·058	−·023	·214	·065
V3	·002	−·394		·188	·073	·305	·008	·337	−·025	·077	·025	·466	−·101	−·063	−·156	·131	−·032	−·034	·248	−·073
(1)	−·147	·152	·188		−·058	·130	−·078	−·010	−·151	−·094	−·015	−·075	·065	·144	·277	·132	−·203	−·133	·354	·181
(2)	−·013	−·053	·073	−·058		·027	·123	−·115	−·107	−·043	−·018	·022	·081	·103	−·072	·010	·029	·095	−·014	·078
(3)	−·007	−·006	·305	·130	·027		−·033	−·075	−·007	−·022	−·004	·290	−·234	−·127	−·029	−·070	−·007	−·395	·331	·136
(4)	−·068	−·033	·008	−·078	·123	−·033		·017	−·071	−·033	−·015	−·015	−·040	−·088	−·072	−·050	−·007	·177	−·126	·143
(5)	−·012	−·080	·337	−·010	−·115	−·075	·017		−·072	−·015	·091	·188	·075	·189	−·006	−·035	−·081	−·012	−·176	·045
(6)	−·005	·014	−·025	−·151	−·107	−·007	−·071	−·072		·135	−·035	−·076	−·084	−·069	−·034	−·113	−·080	·100	−·109	−·038
(7)	−·107	·046	·077	−·094	−·043	−·022	−·033	−·015	·135		·621	−·028	−·083	−·043	−·104	−·190	·382	·047	·092	−·142
(8)	·068	·025	·025	−·015	−·018	−·004	−·015	·091	−·035	·621		−·049	−·054	−·016	−·012	−·146	·130	·155	·035	−·167
(9)	−·021	−·278	·466	−·075	·022	·290	−·015	·188	−·076	−·028	−·049		−·220	−·174	−·100	−·016	−·160	·048	·200	·032
(10)	·133	·177	−·101	·065	·081	−·234	−·040	·075	−·084	−·083	−·054	−·220		·102	−·029	−·023	·225	·089	−·081	·174
(11)	·225	−·031	−·063	·144	·103	−·127	−·088	·189	−·069	−·043	−·016	−·174	·102		·296	·020	·027	·048	−·156	·091
(12)	−·292	−·051	−·156	·277	−·072	−·029	−·072	−·006	−·034	−·104	−·012	−·100	−·029	·296		·102	−·296	−·092	−·014	−·192
(13)	−·084	−·163	·131	·132	·010	−·070	−·050	−·035	−·113	−·190	−·146	−·016	−·023	·020	·102		·225	−·131	·002	·242
(14)	·067	−·058	−·032	−·203	·029	−·007	−·007	−·081	−·080	·382	·130	−·160	·225	·027	−·296	·225		·045	·062	·047
(15)	·020	−·023	−·034	−·133	·095	−·395	·177	−·012	·100	·047	·155	·048	·089	·048	−·092	−·131	·045		−·042	·149
(16)	−·055	·214	·248	·354	−·014	·331	−·126	−·176	−·109	·092	·035	·200	−·081	−·156	−·014	·002	·062	−·042		·110
(17)	·016	·065	−·073	·181	·078	·136	·143	·045	−·038	−·142	−·167	·032	·174	·091	−·192	·242	·047	·149	·110	

criterion [1] (these are biserial correlations; all others are product moment correlations). Items 13 has been omitted from further calculations as it was impossible to give this test to the neurotic group. In order to rotate the factors so as to obtain maximum correlation with the criterion, those tests which showed negative correlations with the criterion were multiplied by − 1 as indicated in Table XXXI; this is merely a device which reverses the direction of scoring of the tests affected, and leaves the data unchanged in any material way. The last column of Table XXXI gives the rotated factors. The new factor 1 correlates ·758 with the criterion column, having been rotated into maximum agreement with it. Factor II was then rotated in such a manner as to preserve orthogonality with Factor I, and to take up all the remaining variance on the intelligence test. Factor III is irrelevant to our purpose, and no interpretation of it will be attempted. Interpretations of Factors I and II are straightforward and dictated by the results: Factor I is a factor of neuroticism, Factor II one of intelligence.

Table XXXII gives the means and variances for the neurotic children, the identical twins, and the fraternal twins, on all 17 tests and also on the factor score for the 'neuroticism' factor. The first three columns give the means for the three groups; only two of the differences between identical and fraternal twins are significant at the 5 and 1 per cent levels respectively, viz. the Neurotic Inventory and the Lie Scale. It is difficult to interpret these results, particularly in view of the fact that the inventory did not discriminate at all between normal and neurotic children. Why identical twins should be more given to lying than fraternal twins we cannot explain! The next three columns give the variance for all the children as individuals; the only difference, at the 2 per cent level of significance, is on the Static Ataxia test, where identical twins are more variable than fraternal twins. (Only differences between the two types of twins are reported, as no particular interest attaches to differences between normals and neurotics, apart from the correlation of each test with this dichotomy, which is given in Table XXXIII.)

The last two columns give variances for identical and fraternal twins taken as pairs. In sixteen out of eighteen cases the identical

[1] The criterion, of course, is the difference for each test of the scores between the 100 normal twins and the 21 neurotic children who form the control group.

TABLE XXXI

Test	Centroid Factor Saturations			Correlation with Criterion	Score multiplier for Rotation	Rotated Factor Saturations		
	I	II	III			I	II	III
1. Intelligence	·520	·203	·149	-·053	-1	-·010	·577	·028
2. Tapping Area	-·038	·210	-·107	-·244	-1	·156	·006	·181
3. Tapping Speed	·432	·129	·099	·088	1	·049	-·458	-·028
4. Level of Aspiration	-·130	·190	-·360	-·056	-1	·095	-·159	·385
5. Motor Speed Test	-·123	-·249	·245	·215	1	·071	·121	·343
6. Speed of Decision	-·158	-·120	·111	-·172	-1	·007	-·148	-·173
7. Static Ataxia	-·467	·437	·258	-·304	-1	·656	-·184	-·106
8. Body Sway Suggestibility	-·358	·355	·225	-·183	-1	·529	-·126	-·097
9. Strength of Grip	·326	·246	·339	·052	-1	-·052	·271	·454
10. Word Dislikes	-·250	·115	·131	-·237	-1	·250	-·142	-·102
11. Personality Inventory	-·157	-·094	·209	-·064	-1	·061	-·108	-·249
12. Lie Scale	-·121	-·091	-·160	-·008	-1	-·076	-·188	·086
13. Flicker Fusion	·245	·031	·113	—	—	—	—	—
14. Autokinetic Movement	-·271	·346	·138	-·167	-1	·454	·079	-·011
15. Autokinetic Suggestibility	-·394	·061	-·283	·045	1	-·129	·415	-·223
16. Backward 'S'	·391	·393	·063	·065	1	-·176	-·502	-·168
17. Fluency	·250	·161	·334	·027	1	-·136	-·379	·191

TABLE XXXII

Description of Test	Means			Variances					
				Individuals			Pairs		
	Neurotics	Identicals	Fraternals	Neurotics	Identicals	Fraternals	Identicals	Fraternals	
1. Intelligence	14·86	14·82	13·52	14·02	24·48	14·46	47·50	24·48	
2. Tapping Area	19·05	12·42	12·66	181·80	95·06	67·54	113·86	57·36	
3. Tapping Speed	43·33	45·34	45·22	71·62	65·33	71·56	102·90	91·13	
4. Level of Aspiration	32·86	31·74	29·84	151·38	144·64	255·69	192·26	277·70	
5. Motor Speed Test	49·05	59·95	59·50	223·06	402·08	338·42	693·62	441·12	
6. Speed of Decision	3·94	3·02	3·00	7·54	2·54	4·33	3·43	3·80	
7. Static Ataxia	3·07	2·10	1·81	1·36	2·61	1·12	4·94	1·74	
8. Body Sway Suggestibility	4·74	3·10	3·50	8·55	7·30	10·26	12·86	11·59	
9. Strength of Grip	68·57	68·74	68·32	85·46	98·40	107·49	185·26	159·33	
10. Word Dislikes	10·81	8·36	9·12	21·11	9·09	7·33	13·90	10·30	
11. Personality Inventory	12·86	10·70	13·14	35·10	34·38	22·74	47·42	29·10	
12. Lie Scale	1·33	1·66	·96	1·43	1·58	1·10	2·36	1·29	
13. Flicker Fusion	*	2657·64	2613·64	*	71769·81	62204·32	124436·59	76820·54	
14. Autokinetic Movement	21·74	15·95	17·50	101·29	131·27	136·92	231·06	168·88	
15. Autokinetic Suggestibility	1·43	1·48	1·50	·26	·26	·26	·40	·29	
16. Backward 'S'	9·90	11·24	10·58	26·23	35·66	37·02	61·92	55·78	
17. Fluency	10·05	10·28	10·40	16·69	18·66	11·63	25·50	13·04	
18. Factor Score (Neuroticism)	13·34	23·20	22·96	12·60	91·55	41·47	172·67	50·83	

* Test 13 could not be applied to the neurotic children.

twin variance is larger; two of these differences are significant at the 2 per cent level (Static Ataxia and Neuroticism Factor Score). There seems to be little doubt that in our sample identical twins and fraternal twins have almost identical means with respect to neuroticism (23·20 and 22·96 respectively),[1] but that the identical group contains pairs of twins tending to be more extremely unstable, and more extremely stable, than the fraternal twin group.

Table XXXIII shows the raw intraclass correlations between twins of both types, correlations with age, and the partial correlations resulting from eliminating age differences. It will be seen that age plays little part in determining scores, and that correction leaves the correlations very much as they were before. The last column of Table XXXIII gives Holzinger's h^2 values, i.e. the extent to which each test variance is determined by heredity. It will be seen that the test of intelligence has an h^2 (·676) which is almost identical with the h^2 values given by the best neuroticism tests: static ataxia (·692), autokinetic movement (·648) and suggestibility (·701).

As the last step in this procedure, factor scores on the neuroticism factor were calculated for each twin and h^2 values calculated for these 'neuroticism scores'.

$$h^2 = \frac{r_i - r_f}{1 - r_f} = \frac{(1 - r_f) - (1 - r_i)}{(1 - r_f)}$$

where r_i = intraclass correlation for identical twins and r_f = intraclass correlation for fraternal twins. It follows that

$$(1 - r_i) = \frac{\text{'within' } i \text{ variance}}{\text{'total' } i \text{ variance}} = \frac{13\cdot680}{91\cdot551} = \cdot149, \text{ from which}$$

$r = \cdot851$. Similarly, $(1 - r_f) = \dfrac{\text{'within' } f \text{ variance}}{\text{'total' } f \text{ variance}} = \dfrac{32\cdot480}{41\cdot468}$

$= \cdot783$, from which $r_f = \cdot217$. It follows that $h^2 = \cdot810$.

This value is considerably higher than that given by any single test, and indicates that the factor constitutes a biological unit which is inherited as a whole.

The h^2 technique used in this paper gives the percentage of twin difference variance attributable to nature providing that

[1] These mean scores of the normal children should be compared with the mean score for neurotic children (13·34). There is relatively little overlap between the two distributions of scores, and the difference between the normal and neurotic group means is significant at a very high level.

TABLE XXXII

RAW INTRACLASS CORRELATIONS BETWEEN TWINS, CORRELATIONS OF TRAITS WITH AGE, AND RESULTING PARTIAL CORRELATIONS

Trait	Identical Twins			Fraternal Twins			Hereditary Determination h^2
	Between Twins	With Age	Partial	Between Twins	With Age	Partial	
1. Intelligence	·905	·208	·890	·670	·168	·660	·676
2. Tapping Area	·193	·187	·164	−·148	−·068	−·144	·269
3. Tapping Speed	·557	·105	·552	·266	·508	·011	·547
4. Level of Aspiration	·320	−·256	·272	·084	·218	·038	·243
5. Motor Speed Test	·700	−·399	·643	·296	−·265	·243	·528
6. Speed of Decision	·340	−·046	·339	−·122	−·009	−·122	·193
7. Static Ataxia	·857	·066	·856	·537	·101	·532	·692
8. Body Sway Suggestibility	·737	·104	·734	·128	−·045	·110	·701
9. Strength of Grip	·850	·580	·774	·468	·354	·392	·628
10. Word Dislikes	·512	−·060	·510	·394	−·152	·380	·210
11. Personality Inventory	·369	·081	·365	·273	−·046	·257	·145
12. Lie Scale	·485	−·090	·481	·167	−·254	·109	·418
13. Flicker Fusion	·709	·110	·705	·229	·157	·209	·627
14. Autokinetic Movement	·734	−·210	·722	·228	·151	·210	·648
15. Autokinetic Suggestibility	·534	·011	·534	·141	−·081	·135	·461
16. Backward 'S'	·711	·333	·708	·491	·161	·477	·423
17. Fluency	·357	−·077	·353	·118	−·068	·114	·270
'Neuroticism' factor:	·851			·217			·810

certain assumptions are met. Two of these assumptions are that nurture influences are the same for both types of twins, and that differences due to nature are uncorrelated with differences due to nurture. It is probable that these assumptions are not completely met, and that consequently our estimate is too high. On the other hand, another assumption, viz. that the variance due to errors of measurement is negligible, is quite certainly not fulfilled, and in view of the known unreliability of personality tests we must assume that errors of measurement may play a considerable part. This would lead one to believe that the found h^2 would be an under-estimate of the true value, and it seems not impossible that this factor may cancel out the two previously mentioned. It is perhaps permissible, therefore, to argue that the h^2 found is a rough and ready estimate of the contribution which heredity makes to individual differences in neuroticism.[1]

Our conclusion regarding the size of this contribution is not in agreement with that arrived at by Newman, Freeman, & Holzinger (1937). Where they find that 'the only group of traits in which identical twins are not much more alike consists of those commonly classed under the heading of personality . . .', we have shown that identical twins show a correlation on neuroticism of ·851, while fraternal twins show a correlation of only ·217. From this it was concluded that individual differences with respect to neuroticism, stability, integration, or whatever we may wish to call this trait or factor, are determined to a very marked extent by heredity, and very much less markedly by environment. This conclusion, of course, applies only in the general type of environment from which all our twins came, and might not be applicable under conditions of more extreme environmental variation such as may obtain in other cultures.

Having demonstrated how strong an influence heredity exerts in at least one field of personality, we cannot close this chapter without drawing attention to certain important theoretical points which would seem to be directly related to this demonstration. These points arise largely out of what to us appears a somewhat unhealthy tendency in current psychological literature to repeat in the field of affection and conation the errors and misinterpreta-tions which vitiated the early work on intelligence. We are referring, of course, to the unconquerable tendency among certain writers to

[1] We have used Holzinger's h^2 statistic in our estimates because no better estimate of the contribution of heredity to the total variance is available.

interpret their results in terms either of hereditary or environmental influences, although the methodology of their research does not permit any conclusions to be reached on this point. We have learned through the lost labours of many years that an experimental observation to the effect that dull parents have dull children is irrelevant to the question: To what extent are intellectual differences innate? We know now—as we should always have realized—that both hereditary and environmental causes may with equal facility be invoked to explain the observation. But we do not appear to have learned to use 'transfer of training' and apply this lesson to other fields than the intellectual. The literature is replete with papers in which the fact that trait A in a group of children is found to be correlated with trait X in their mothers is used as an argument to the effect that the behaviour characterized by trait X is directly causative of the behaviour characterized by trait A. No appeal to the elementary text-book principle that correlation *does not* and *cannot* prove a direct causal relation appears sufficient to stem this flood of environmentalistic interpretation, and even otherwise critical reviews often fail to point out the fact that both trait A and trait X may be due to a third variable, namely, an inherited tendency to behave in this manner, and may be completely unaffected by environmental manifestations.

Such neglect of caution in interpreting results could perhaps, according to current psychiatric thinking, be traced back to emotional causes and tie-ups which the present writer is not competent to disentangle. It is perhaps significant that both behaviourism and psychoanalysis, divergent as their paths otherwise appear to be, are at one in this respect; indeed, even the apparent differences between the democratic ideals of the U.S.A. and the U.K., and the dialectical authoritarianism which characterizes the 'dictatorship of the proletariat' in the U.S.S.R. melt away before this belief in the 'equality of man'. Slater (1950) has put this criticism into particularly strong, but entirely justifiable terms. 'There has . . . been an increasing tendency among clinicians to minimize the effects attributable to genetical causes, and to teach a psychiatry in which they receive little or no mention. This tendency has been marked in Britain, but it has assumed formidable strength in the U.S.A. Instead of a harmonious development, in which the psychoses and neuroses, constitution and environment, psychogenesis and physiogenesis receive their due share of attention, interest among practical workers has been devoted more and more exclusively towards psychotherapy, psychoanalysis, social psychiatry, personnel selection, group therapy, and preoccupations with anthropology, sociology, and political theory. In its one-sidedness, this development is not healthy.

'It is a sign of bad omen that it is possible for text-books of clinical psychiatry to appear, with claims for comprehensiveness, in which no mention is made of the established facts of genetics and of the hereditary element in mental disorder. Their authors appear to feel, though in fact this view depends on a misapprehension, that recognition of a hereditary factor implies a therapeutic nihilism; and that an energetic and optimistic attitude towards treatment calls for a neglect of hereditary factors, just as a due appreciation of the patient as an individual demands forgetfulness of nosological entities. One suspects that the prime motivation is derived from the philosophy of Dewey, which is no doubt over-simplified in the notion that one should accept as true that which has convenient practical applications.

'It would not perhaps be putting it too high to say that we are witnessing the manifestation of an anti-scientific tendency which is winning an increasing number of supporters. The customary canons of scientific reasoning are ignored by these schools. Uncomfortable facts are left unconsidered. Hypotheses are multiplied regardless of the principle of economy. Explanations which may be valid for certain members of a class of phenomena are regarded as true for the class as a whole. Interpretations which conform with theory, and which might be true, are regarded as established. Possible alternatives are not considered, and no attempt is made to seek for evidence of critical value which shall decide between them. Criticisms from outside are ignored, and only the initiate may be heard. Utterance is dogmatic and arrogant, and lacks scientific humility and caution. These are the mental mechanisms which we associate with the growth of a religious orthodoxy, and not with the progress of science. The movement is of significance to genetics, because it is likely adversely to affect the personnel and facilities for research, and to lead to a psychiatry without biological foundation and divorced from contact with the other natural sciences.'

We may perhaps with some advantage analyse in some detail one particular study to see how this particular idol of the marketplace can find its way into the conclusion of what is otherwise an admirable experiment.

The experiment chosen for this purpose may justifiably claim to be the first attempt to apply factor analysis to psychoanalytic hypotheses; indeed, apart from serving as our demonstration model the work to be discussed has many claims to be included in this volume for the sake of the positive contribution it has to make. It would have been easy to find a much more obvious and vulnerable piece of work; we have chosen on purpose to deal rather with a particularly subtle and well-controlled experiment.

The study under review deals with the influence of breast feeding on character-formation (Goldman-Eisler, 1948, 1950, 1951). The very first sentence sets the pattern: 'The description of adult character in terms of childhood experience is one of the basic principles of psychoanalytic characterology, and indeed the genetic approach (in the sense of *ontogenetic*, or referring to childhood experience) to human personality is the essence of the theory and method of psychoanalysis.' The particular hypothesis chosen in this experiment is concerned with oral character traits and their origin, as outlined more particularly by Karl Abraham (1916, 1924, 1942) and E. Glover (1925). Oral character traits are believed to originate from repressed or deflected oral impulses which are dominant during the nursing period and which have undergone transformation into certain permanent behaviour patterns by the processes of reaction-formation, displacement, or sublimation. Two main syndromes are posited by these writers to emerge from the experiences of gratification or frustration attached to the oral stage of libido development. One of these is the orally gratified type (late weaning), who is supposed to be distinguished by an unperturbable optimism, generosity, bright and sociable conduct, accessibility to new ideas, and ambition accompanied by sanguine expectation. The other, the orally ungratified type (early weaning) is characterized by a profoundly pessimistic outlook on life, sometimes accompanied by moods of depression and attitudes of withdrawal, a passive-receptive attitude, a feeling of insecurity, a need for assurance, a grudging feeling of injustice.

We thus have two hypotheses: (1) Certain traits tend to correlate together in a well-defined way so as to give rise to a factor of 'orality', and (2) the position of a person on the continuum defined by this factor is determined by his experiences of early or late weaning. The first of these hypotheses is clearly testable by means of a factorial analysis; the second is subject to a more direct test using analysis of variance. One hundred and fifteen middle-class

TABLE XXXIV

(Reliability coefficients are presented in parentheses following the description of each trait.)

Optimism: Optimism and pessimism are antithetical expressions in character-formation of an omnipotent and magical relation to reality. Optimism deriving from this unconscious source would be upheld by the individual against reasonable expectation $(r = \cdot 90)$.

Pessimism: Inability to accept frustrating experiences as part of reality. Defence against disappointments through summary and advance resignation, anticipation of disappointment $(r = \cdot 74)$.

Passivity: Passive-receptive attitude, hedonism, indolence, self-indulgence $(r = \cdot 81)$.

Desire for the Unattainable: Intense desire to climb combined with a feeling of unattainability, of difficulty in achievement, of the insuperable, grudging incapacity to get on $(r = \cdot 78)$.

Displaced Oral Aggression (Verbal): Aggressive use of speech, 'omnipotent valuation of speech', 'incisive speech'.

Aggression: The desire to injure or inflict pain, to overcome opposition forcefully, to fight, to revenge an injury, to attack, to oppose forcefully $(r = \cdot 78)$.

Aloofness: Negative tropism for people, attitude of rejection $(r = \cdot 73)$.

Ambition: Tendency to overcome obstacles, to exercise power, to strive to do something difficult as well and as quickly as possible, to attain a high standard, to excel one's self $(r = \cdot 68)$.

Autonomy: Those who wish neither to lead nor to be led, those who want to go their own way, uninfluenced and uncoerced. Independence of attitude $(r = \cdot 88)$.

Dependence: Tendency to cry, plead or ask for nourishment, love, protection or aid. Helplessness, insecurity $(r = \cdot 56)$.

Guilt: 'Conscience', inhibiting and punishing images, self-torture, self-abasement $(r = \cdot 90)$.

Change: A tendency to move and wander, to have no fixed habitation, to seek new friends, to adopt new fashions, to change one's interests and vocation. Inconsistency and instability $(r = \cdot 71)$.

Conservatism: Adherence to certain places, people, and modes of conduct. Fixation and limitation. Enduring sentiments and loyalties, persistence of purpose; consistency of conduct; rigidity of habits $(r = \cdot 56)$.

Impulsion: The tendency to act quickly without reflection. Short reaction time, intuitive or emotional decisions. The inability to inhibit an impulse $(r = \cdot 82)$.

Deliberation: Inhibition, hesitation and reflection before action. Slow reaction time, compulsive thinking $(r = \cdot 87)$.

Exocathexis: The positive cathexis in practical action and co-operative undertakings. Occupation with outer events: economic, political, and social occurrences. A strong inclination to participate in the contemporary world of affairs $(r = \cdot 72)$.

Endocathexis: The cathexis of thought or emotion for its own sake. A preoccupation with inner activities, feelings, fantasies, generalizations, theoretical reflections, artistic conceptions, religious ideas; withdrawal from practical life $(r = \cdot 73)$.

Nurturance: Tendency to nourish, aid, and protect a helpless object. To express sympathy, to mother a child, to assist in danger $(r = \cdot 79)$.

Sociability: Tendency to form friendships and associations; to join, and live with, others. To co-operate and converse socially with others. To join groups $(r = \cdot 70)$.

S.S.P.   O adults constituted the experimental population; for all of these statements from their mothers regarding process and time of weaning were available. Nineteen scales, mainly of a questionnaire type, were constructed or modified from existing scales, to measure traits which according to the hypothesis under investigation were related to 'orality'. Table XXXIV gives the titles of these scales, together with a split-half reliability coefficient for each scale. (The average number of items in each scale was 8; average reliability was ·76.) The full scales are published elsewhere (Goldman-Eisler, 1951).

These 19 scales were intercorrelated, and the resulting table is given below (Table XXXV). A factor analysis was carried out, and the saturations for two factors are reported in Table XXXVI. It will be seen that the first factor does indeed resemble the hypothetical 'oral' type—aloofness, pessimism, endocathexis, conservatism, deliberation, guilt, and aggression forming the 'ungratified' type, and exocathexis, optimism; nurturance, sociability, change, and impulsion forming the 'gratified' type. So far, then, the hypothesis appears to be confirmed. (We shall not here discuss the interpretation of the second factor, as this would take us too far afield. The interested reader is referred to the original paper (Goldman-Eisler, 1951).)

We must now turn to the second hypothesis, linking this type with early or late weaning. An analysis of variance was carried out on 'early weaners' and 'late weaners', defining these in terms of weaning at not later than four months of age, and not earlier than five months of age respectively. This reduced the number of cases to 89. A second analysis of variance compared 'early weaners', as defined above, and 'very late weaners', defined as having been weaned at not earlier than nine months of age. Scores for this analysis were estimates of factor scores. The analyses are given below in Tables XXXVII and XXXVIII. It will be seen that in both cases the results are in the expected direction, and that in both cases they are significant at the 1 per cent level. The correlation between 'early weaning' and 'gratified orality' is ·271 according to the first analysis, and ·305 according to the second analysis.

An alternative method for assessing the correlation between type and weaning is available. We can include 'early weaning' in our factor analysis, and establish its saturation with the first factor. This turns out to be ·337, thus confirming the previous result which shows a correlation of approximately ·3 between oral type and

TABLE XXXV

	Opt.	Exo.	Nur.	Soc.	Amb.	Change	Unatt.	Delib.	Imp.	Cons.	Dep.	Guilt	Aggr.	Auto.	Endo.	Oral	Aloof.	Pass.
Opt.																		
Exo.	·51																	
Nur.	·46	·35																
Soc.	·20	·31	·17															
Amb.	·27	·14	−·17	−·11														
Change	·16	−·05	·30	·21	·01													
Unatt.	−·34	−·22	·06	−·01	·22	·32												
Delib.	−·11	·05	·00	−·15	−·26	−·35	·02											
Imp.	−·38	−·16	−·05	·08	·04	·44	·13	−·75										
Cons.	·21	−·19	−·11	−·50	−·15	−·50	−·14	·42	−·39									
Dep.	−·10	−·15	−·22	·39	·32	·04	·11	·19	−·36	·06								
Guilt	−·15	·00	−·02	−·20	−·09	·12	·24	·23	−·17	·21	·47							
Aggr.	−·31	−·16	−·27	−·17	·00	·00	·28	−·38	·35	−·05	−·05	·16						
Auto.	−·23	−·47	−·29	−·20	·07	·17	·07	−·12	−·19	−·20	−·11	−·47	·01					
Endo.	−·29	−·60	−·16	−·40	·16	−·04	·32	·08	·04	·20	·21	·05	·08	·31				
Oral	−·36	−·07	−·19	−·19	−·23	−·02	−·07	·42	·12	−·14	−·08	−·13	·33	·10	·60			
Aloof.	−·37	−·55	−·65	−·50	−·09	−·29	−·02	·05	·00	−·20	−·07	·05	·24	·41	·33	·12		
Pass.	−·48	−·34	−·43	−·01	−·40	−·01	−·25	−·16	·21	·02	·17	−·01	·32	·06	·03	·37	·44	
Pessim.	−·63	−·55	−·22	−·34	·05	−·14	−·02	·27	−·10	·16	−·02	·38	·11	·13	·20	·11	·37	−·03

TABLE XXXVI

Trait	Factor Saturations		Trait	Factor Saturations	
	I	II		I	II
Optimism	−680	−298	Guilt	208	−352
Pessimism	542	−041	Change	−272	267
Passivity	376	214	Conservatism	370	−436
Unattainable	050	209	Impulsion	−104	761
Oral Aggression	−156	303	Deliberation	227	−766
Aggression	209	479	Exocathexis	−678	−316
Aloofness	750	234	Endocathexis	477	160
Ambition	−192	153	Nurturance	−573	−201
Autonomy	156	560	Sociability	−499	−031
Dependence	245	−296			

TABLE XXXVII

Source	Degrees of Freedom	Sum of Squares	Mean Square
Within weaning group	88	22·267	·253
Between early and late weaning group	1	2·033	2·033
	89	24·300	·2730

$F = 8·04$ Epsilon = ·271

TABLE XXXVIII

Source	Degrees of Freedom	Sum of Squares	Mean Square
Within weaning group	64	16·271	·254
Between early and very late weaning group	1	1·904	1·904
	65	18·175	·280

$F = 7·50$ Epsilon = ·305

weaning. We might thus conclude that both hypotheses had been verified; we have found the hypothetical type to exist roughly as posited, and we have found this type to be related to weaning in the predicted direction at a high level of confidence. It is at this point that we must bring our criticism to bear.

Let us first of all look closely at the traits characterizing the oral type. Comparison with results of factorial analyses published elsewhere in this volume will show that the structure of traits found here is very similar to that which has given rise to the hypothesis of an introvert-extravert dichotomy; the results of the factorial analysis agree with this interpretation at least as well as they do with that made by Goldman-Eisler. This, of course, is not entirely unexpected; when experienced psychologists and psychoanalysts set down syndromes of trait resemblances which they have observed in their experience it is not unlikely that they should agree in their observations, even though they may give different names to the syndromes thus isolated. It is important, though, to remember that for Jung and his followers extraversion or introversion are largely determined by constitution, while for Freud and his followers the 'oral' type is determined entirely in terms of early childhood experience. Thus the results of the factorial study do not confirm Freud any more than they confirm Jung; as far as the crucial difference between them is concerned the results are neutral.

What can we say of the correlation of this typology with weaning? Surely the existence of a correlation as small as ·3—even though it be fully significant—cannot under any circumstances be given a causal interpretation. It is equally plausible to suggest that introverted mothers tend to have introverted children by the action of genetic factors; that introverted mothers tend to wean their children earlier because of their lack of 'exocathexis'; and that consequently there will arise a correlation between early weaning and child's introversion which can all too easily mislead the investigator to believe in some principle of direct causation.

There is an obvious objection to this line of argument. It may be maintained that in criticizing the experiment we have left out a crucial part. Did not the investigator set out to test the predicted consequences of a clearly formulated theory? What more can a single experiment do than to verify such a deduction? Is not too high a standard being applied to experiments of this kind, a standard which contradicts the logic of scientific methodology?

The answer to this objection is very simple. The deduction from a theory the testing of which may serve as a confirmation of the theory must refer to phenomena *which themselves are as yet unknown*. This essential requirement is not fulfilled in the present case. Abraham and Glover based their hypothesis on the observation that among their patients there appeared to be a close concomitance between personality and certain weaning practices in their childhood. From this observation they erected the hypothesis of the oral type. But clearly this hypothesis cannot be tested simply by confirming the original observation of a correlation between oral type and weaning! To test it would require a deduction different from the original observation. Such a deduction should preferably be made in such a way as to provide a crucial experiment between the two rival hypotheses outlined above. In the absence of such an experiment, all that the Goldman-Eisler study has done is to confirm in a very impressive manner Abraham's and Glover's original observation of a correlation. The interpretation of that correlation is not affected in any way by her experiment, and it would be indicative of 'environmentalist' prejudice to interpret it as favouring the Freudian view, just as it would be evidence of a 'hereditarian' prejudice to interpret it as favouring the Jungian view.

It is because the former prejudice is so widespread and so insidious that we have included this extended discussion here. Implicit assumptions which govern interpretation of data in the absence of factual evidence may be far more harmful to a science than explicit errors which can easily be put right. The environmentalist assumption underlies the greater part of contemporary work in the field of personality, and still determines interpretation of strictly neutral material in the complete absence of confirmatory evidence. This does not mean that the environmentalist hypothesis is necessarily false; we have no knowledge on which to base an opinion. The need, as always, is for well designed experiments which will enable us to cease arguing, and substitute fact for interpretation.

Chapter Six

THE PSYCHOTIC DIMENSION

IN *Dimensions of Personality* the writer has discussed briefly the possible relationship between the factor of extraversion-introversion isolated there, and the schizothymia-cyclothymia typology advocated by Kretschmer. It was felt that the facile equation of the introvert with the schizothyme, which many writers in the field of personality have assumed as a fact, could not be maintained in view of the explicit statements by Jung (1923) and Kretschmer (1948) regarding the position of the hysteric in their respective typologies. For Jung, the hysteric is a prototype of the extrovert; for Kretschmer, the hysteric has close affinities to the schizophrenic and belongs, therefore, quite definitely to the schizothyme group. As it is clearly impossible for the hysteric to be both extroverted and schizothymic; if we equate introversion with schizothymia, it is impossible to regard these two typologies as identical. In view of the absence of independent evidence on this point, no positive suggestions were made regarding the position of Kretschmerian types in our own dimensional system of personality. However, clearly, this was an unsatisfactory position and an experimental integration of the two systems became a priority in our experimental programme.

Another problem arose in this connection which also demanded an empirical answer. As will be shown, Kretschmer's hypothesis of a cyclothymia-schizothymia dimension of personality is dependent on the assumption of an essential continuity between normal and psychotic mental states; in other words, he postulates a normal-psychotic continuum, or a factor of 'psychoticism'. In the same way, Jung implies a factor of 'neuroticism' in making neurotic syndromes prototypes of his normal typology. The question arises whether these two dimensions of neuroticism and psychoticism are identical (assuming they both exist), or whether they must be regarded as clearly separate and unrelated. Existing theories are not at all helpful on this point. Freud, who posits a general factor of regression, would identify the neuroticism and psychoticism factors, describing the psychotic as one who has regressed most severely, and the neurotic as one who has regressed less severely; the normal person, presumably, showing signs of regression. Most orthodox psychiatrists seem to assume that neuroticism and psychoticism are situated along two unrelated dimensions; however, their actual practice in diagnosing patients does not seem to follow their theoretical point of view. A patient is diagnosed, for instance, either as a schizophrenic or as an hysteric. If these two labels are considered to lie on orthogonal axes, there is no reason why a patient should not be diagnosed as suffering from both these disorders, just as a patient might be an hysteric and intelligent, or a schizophrenic and tall. This current procedure could only be defended if we assumed that psychotic and neurotic states were qualitatively different from the normal, a belief held more frequently with respect to psychotics than with respect to neurotics. It will be clear that the field is in a somewhat chaotic state and that not only do different writers flatly contradict each other, but that the same author at different times will follow different and often contradictory hypotheses. Again an empirical clarification is essential.

This chapter, then, is devoted to a description of the Kretschmerian system and to a report on our experimental results, which were sufficiently clear-cut to permit at least a preliminary and provisional interpretation. The account of Kretschmer's system will be somewhat more detailed than may appear necessary at first glance; the reasons for this detailed description are threefold. In the first place, Kretschmer's system is known to the Anglo-Saxon world almost entirely through the translation of a very early edition of his book; the important revisions and the large amount of experimental evidence accumulated since by Kretschmer and his students is hardly ever mentioned or taken into account. This means, as the writer has shown elsewhere (1950c, 1951), that critics are still busy demolishing a position which Kretschmer himself left about thirty years ago, and fail to appreciate the important advances which he has made since. An up-to-date exposition of Kretschmer's system, therefore, seems an absolute necessity for an adequate understanding of the problem involved.

In the second place, Kretschmer has been dealing for a long time with methodological problems in the field of typology which are of great importance in connection with the general aim of this book and which have again hardly received the attention which they deserve, although the writer does not believe that the methods which Kretschmer suggested and used in the 1920's are as powerful and convincing as the factorial methods introduced since. They are of great interest and importance, nevertheless, and deserve more critical appreciation and discussion than they have received hitherto.

In the third place, Kretschmer and his students have originated subsidiary hypotheses and have constructed tests to investigate these hypotheses, which appear to the writer far in advance of most of the work being carried out in the field of personality research in other countries, using much more sophisticated statistical methods. Indeed, to anyone surveying personality research dispassionately, it will be only too obvious that there exists a rather high negative correlation between, on the one hand, psychological insight, astute framing of hypotheses, and general understanding of personality structure, and, on the other hand, statistical sophistication, ability in the construction of experimental tests for the testing of hypotheses, and expert knowledge of methods of ascertaining validity and reliability. Kretschmer, although his approach is deficient in the elaborate statistics which have recently been the vogue, nevertheless combines these two indispensable sides of personality research to an unusual degree, and his work deserves to be better known than it is. It is not good for science that a stereotyped view of a man's contribution should obscure aspects of that contribution which do not fit in with the stereotype. It is in the hope of destroying certain erroneous notions and aiding a better appreciation of Kretschmer's real contribution that the first part of this chapter has been written.

Kretschmer's system is a typology, but it would be very wrong to imagine that his conception of 'type' is similar to that so frequently criticized in elementary text-books. In this simplified kind of presentation, the concept of 'type' is often contrasted with the concept of 'trait' and it is suggested that the 'type' approach implies a bimodal type of distribution, whereas the 'trait' approach implies a unimodal type of distribution. The argument is often advanced that as most human characteristics can be shown to vary unimodally, the 'type' approach must be erroneous. This argument is, of course, fallacious, as the *observed* distribution of scores on a test which has no rational metric underlying it has no necessary connection with the true distribution of scores. All we have available with psychological tests are the observed distributions, of course, and to argue from those to the 'true' distributions is not admissible.

In any case, regardless of the validity of the argument from distribution, the concept of 'type' as being essentially bimodal is not in accord with Kretschmer's own definition (or, indeed, with that of Jung or most other Continental typologists). Kretschmer makes his meaning quite clear. 'The concept of type is the most important fundamental concept of all biology. Nature . . . does not work with sharp contrasts and precise definitions, which derive from our own thought and our own need for comprehension. In nature, fluid transitions are the rule, but it would not be true to say that, in this infinite sea of fluid empirical forms, nothing clear and objective could be seen; quite on the contrary. In certain fields, groupings arise which we encounter again and again; when we study them objectively, we realize that we are dealing here with focal points of frequently occurring groups of characteristics, con- centrations of correlated traits. . . . What is essential in biology, as in clinical medicine, is not a single correlation, but groups of correlations; only those lead to the innermost connections. It is daily experience in the field of typology, which can be deduced quite easily from the general theory, that in dealing with groups of characteristics one obtains higher correlations than with single characteristics. . . . What we call, mathematically, focal points of statistical correlations, we call, in more descriptive prose, con- stitutional types. The two are identical; it is only the point of view which differs. . . . A true type can be recognized by the fact that it leads to ever more connections of biological importance. Where there are many and ever new correlations with fundamental bio- logical factors, for instance, in the constitutional types dealt with here, we are dealing with focal points of the greatest importance.' It will be seen that the conception of type which Kretschmer has elaborated here is very similar to the one given by the writer, who regards types as 'observed constellations or syndromes of traits', and traits as 'observed constellations of individual action tend- encies' (1947). This use of the term type, which is not far removed from the conception discussed by Murphy and Jensen (1932), appears to be free from the defects which the concept of type is often alleged to possess.

The particular system of correlations which Kretschmer chooses as a starting point lies in the constitutional field, i.e. in the field of body types, where he contrasts, as is well known, the pyknic and the leptosomatic types, with a third one, the athletic, considered sometimes intermediate and sometimes definitely divergent from the other two. In addition, he has dysplastic types and a certain proportion of unassignable doubtfuls. While Kretschmer's approach is not exactly along statistical lines, a number of factorial studies of intercorrelations between bodily dimensions, reviewed by the writer (Eysenck, 1947), have shown that essentially there is a main dichotomy corresponding closely to his pyknic-leptosomatic type, and there can, therefore, be little doubt that this first step in his typology is eminently sound, although it may be suggested that greater statistical sophistication might have enabled him to purify his concepts rather more, and also to arrive at better indices of body build than those elaborated in his book.

The position of the athletic type raises important points here, a consideration of which cannot be deferred. Kretschmer and Enke (1936) consider the athletic type as being essentially different from both the others rather than as being intermediate between them. This position appears unacceptable to us. In the first place, there is no independent statistical proof, such as only factor analysis could supply: in our own work we found no evidence of a factor of this kind (Eysenck, 1947). In the second place, in the large body of experimental work in which Kretschmer and his followers have tried to differentiate the three body types with respect to psychological functions, it will be found in almost every case that the athletics are intermediate between pyknics and the leptosomatics, though somewhat closer to the latter. This suggests very strongly that they are not in a separate group, but are, in truth, intermediate. The attempt of Kretschmer and Enke to create a third type from the athletics often leads to rather disingenuous arguments. Finding usually that leptosomatics and athletics differ very little in their test results and are opposed to the pyknics, they have to argue that the causes which lead to the test results of leptosomatics are different from those which lead to the test results of the athletics, although no evidence of any kind is given to support these *ad hoc* arguments. The reader will be able to judge this point from the experiments quoted elsewhere (Eysenck, 1951), and detailed data are given there for all three groups separately.

If the pyknic-leptosomatic typology is not only justified, but also fruitful, we should expect to find a large number of correlations of psychological importance. However, it may be noted that there are also a large number of physiological correlations, particularly in the field of autonomic functioning and of endocrinology, which deserve some mention; these have been summarized briefly by the writer elsewhere (Eysenck, 1950c, 1951).

Having laid his foundation in terms of body build, it is well known that Kretschmer proceeds to point out that there is close affinity between the manic-depressive type of insanity and pyknic body build on the one hand, and between schizophrenic disorders of all kinds and the leptosomatic (and to a smaller extent the athletic) type on the other. He also points out the particular affinity obtaining between athletic body build and epilepsy, basing himself, in part, on Dubitscher's work with the Rorschach Test (1932), who found among athletics reactions very similar to those found by Rorschach among epileptics. Westphal (1931) gives a table embodying over 8000 cases showing these relations fairly clearly (Table XXXIX).

TABLE XXXIX

Body Build	Schizophrenics: 5233 cases	Manic Depressives: 1361 cases	Epileptics: 1505 cases
	%	%	%
Pyknic	13·7	64·6	5·5
Athletic	16·9	6·7	28·9
Leptosomatic	50·3	19·2	25·1
Dysplastic	10·5	1·1	29·5
Doubtful	8·6	8·4	11·0

The writer has reviewed the literature with respect to these somatopsychic relations elsewhere (Eysenck, 1947) and will not repeat his conclusions; by and large, we may accept the main points made by Kretschmer—i.e. the prevalence of leptosomatic body build among schizophrenics and of pyknic body build among manic-depressives. It is known, however, that Kretschmer goes beyond the correlation of psychotic disorders and body types; he believes that schizophrenia and manic depressive insanity are merely extremes of contrasted psychological trait syndromes, which he calls the cyclothyme and the schizothyme, respectively. He holds that what is true of the extremes is also true, if to a lesser extent, of the less exaggerated, more normal members of each type. As he says: 'Only when this viewpoint is pursued into the field of normal psychology will we be able to appreciate the problem of constitution in its full importance. There is no jump in thus going over into normal psychology, but as we follow the threads between body build and psychological peculiarity from the psychotic, step by step, through all types of psychopathic personality and get further and further away from those great mental disturbances which form the beginning of our investigation—lo and behold—suddenly, we find ourselves among healthy people, among well-known faces. Here we recognize as familiar, normal features those traits which previously we had seen in caricature. We find the same types of facial structure, the same stigmata of bodily constitution, and we find that behind the same exterior dwell the same psychological forces.'

This general theory may, perhaps, be introduced by reference to Figure 26. This figure shows the distribution of the whole popula-

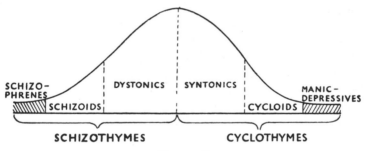

Figure 26

tion in terms of a normal curve of distribution, ranging from one extreme (schizophrenia) to the other (manic-depressive insanity). All persons left of the mean would be schizothymic, meaning by that merely that their personality make-up has in common certain elements which are grotesquely exaggerated in those psychotic patients whom we label schizophrenics, whereas all those to the right of the mean would be cyclothymics, meaning by that that their personality make up has in common certain elements which are grotesquely exaggerated in manic-depressive patients. Persons who are definitely abnormal but not yet psychotic Kretschmer calls schizoid or cycloid respectively, whereas the large number of persons in the centre of the distribution he calls syntonic, if they are on the cyclothymic side, and dystonic if they are on the schizothymic side. It is possible that Kretschmer would object to the use of a normal curve to depict the relation between schizothymes and cyclothymes but little importance can be attributed in any case to the form of distribution when the underlying metric is unknown; just as in the case of the distribution of intelligence, the normal curve must be regarded merely as a convenient device rather than an accurate representation of actuality.

We believe that in all essentials, Figure 26 brings out accurately the main points of Kretschmer's views. We see, therefore, that Kretschmer is suggesting a definite dimension of personality, which we may call cyclothymia-schizothymia, but it would seem to follow from his writings that another dimension is also implied, ranging from normality to psychotic disorder and orthogonal to the first, so that his theory can best be represented in terms of two orthogonal axes, one measuring schizothymia-cyclothymia, the other normality-psychotic abnormality or 'psychoticism'. Indeed, if we were to follow him faithfully, we would have to add two further dimensions, namely, the diathetic and the psychasthetic scales. In his view, cyclothymes vary among themselves on a scale ranging from humorous, vivacious, quick-witted, to the quiet, calm, serious —the so-called diathetic scale; whereas schizothymes vary from shy, nervous, sensitive, to dull, stupid, torpid—the so-called psychasthetic scale. As, however, there is no experimental evidence in Kretschmer's work regarding these scales, and as he makes little use of them and does not define their relation to each other in any way, we have thought it better to simplify the problem by concentrating on his major hypothesis rather than on these subsidiary ones. The student of this problem, however, should keep them in mind.

Attempts have been made by Kretschmer (1948), Van Der Horst (1916, 1924), Kibler (1925), and Zerbe (1929) to make direct tests of the association between mental type and physical type, assessing the former by means of interviews or questionnaires, and statistical tests applied to these figures by the writer have shown that the results are in accordance with the hypothesis at a high level of confidence (Eysenck, 1950c). However, Kretschmer, quite rightly, lays most stress on a somewhat indirect procedure which is derived from Van der Horst. 'There always appeared a marked correlation between the normal leptosomatic subject and the schizophrenic patient on the one hand, and the normal pyknic subject and the manic-depressive subject on the other. This suggests a close relation between the psychological make-up of the leptosomatic and the schizophrene and a firm concordance between the psychological structure of the pyknic and the manic-depressive.' Put in other words, Van de Horst and Kretschmer try to show the general validity of the concept of schizothymia and cyclothymia beyond the psychotic realm by using body build as a *tertium quid*; their method of proof is to show that normal people of leptosomatic or pyknic body build react to certain psychological experiences in a manner similar to that of schizophrenes and manic-depressives, who are known to be also leptosomatic or pyknic on the average. This is an ingenious method which deserved careful consideration. Some of the results from it, particularly those of Van der Horst himself (1916, 1924) and of Kibler (1925) are very impressive indeed. Fundamentally, however, it has certain weaknesses which make it doubtful whether any definite conclusions can be derived in this way. As a methodology it follows only partly the rules of the hypothetico-deductive method, as the results deduced from the hypothesis are not stated in a rigorous enough fashion to make proof or disproof possible. This is particularly so in view of the fact that the authors quoted do not state their results in terms which are amenable to proper statistical treatment. However, in spite of these criticisms, it should be realized that here we have a method which could be made into an extremely powerful tool by slight changes in methodology and procedure, and when it is realized that the work to be described was carried out at a time when the research genius of the rest of the world was still gazing upon the Bernreuter Inventory as a *non plus ultra* of personality tests, it will be clear that here we are dealing with a serious effort to come to grips with a problem of fundamental importance at a time when its very existence was realized by very few other workers.

We shall return to these methodological considerations later on and attempt to suggest an improved method for solving the very difficult problem which Kretschmer set himself, by means of a modification of the factorial approach. Before doing that, however, we shall briefly summarize various researches falling under this general heading. As has been mentioned before, Kretschmer's conception of type implies the discovery of certain correlations between traits. Thus, the schizothyme in his view would be found to be dissociative, form-reactive, high in personal tempo, better in motor co-ordination, more perseverative, and with greater autonomic reactivity. It is the intercorrelation of these (as well as many other) traits which define the schizothyme pole of the type continuum as opposed to the cyclothyme pole, which would be characterized by traits showing him to be integrative, colour reactive, low in personal tempo, poorer in motor co-ordination, less perseverative, and with less autonomic reactivity. The experimental evidence for these various assertions has been discussed at some length elsewhere (Eysenck, 1950c, 1951); here we may take one of these traits as an example of the treatment which Kretschmer gives to these concepts. For this purpose, the trait which he calls '*Spaltungsfaehigkeit*' has been chosen, i.e. a trait characterized at the one pole by an ability to *dissociate*, at the other pole by a tendency to *integrate* diverse mental content. As is the case with most of Kretschmer's work, the hypothesis is derived originally from a close clinical study of large numbers of subjects. It is then given an operational definition by the elaboration of a number of objective tests which are conceived to measure the particular trait hypothesized. These measures are then applied to groups of schizophrenes and manic-depressives and normal leptosomatics and pyknics, and the hypothesis is considered to be verified if observed differences lie in the expected direction, at a reasonable level of statistical confidence.[1]

Kretschmer holds that the concept of dissociation (*Spaltung*) is of fundamental importance in understanding the mentality of the schizothyme, just as its opposite, integration, is important for the understanding of the cyclothyme mentality. His concept of dissociation goes further than that of Warren (1934): 'The breaking up of a combination of any sort into its constituents.' He means by it, 'The ability to form separate and partial groupings within a single act of consciousness: from this results the ability to dissect complex material into its constituent parts.' This tendency towards dissociation characterizes the schizothyme and when exaggerated puts the *schiz* into *schizophrenia*! The absence of this ability to dissociate leads to a concrete, synthetic way of looking at the mental content which characterizes the cyclothyme and, in exaggeration, the manic-depressive.

A brief description of some of the experiments performed by Kretschmer and his students to quantify this concept will make the discussion more realistic.

(1) In a complex reaction-time experiment, it is possible to

---

[1] Kretschmer does not himself give calculations to assess the significance of his findings but these calculations have been made in connection with the experiments discussed and are given in detail in the paper already referred to (Eysenck, 1950c, 1951); here, we need only note that for each of the experiments to be described now statistical significance was adequate at the ·01 level.

measure the disturbing effect of various agents such as noise, a flashing light, etc. These distracting stimuli, according to the hypothesis, should lengthen the reaction-time of manic-depressives and of normal pyknics much more than that of schizophrenics or of normal leptosomatics, as the schizothyme group should be able to keep the two mental contents (experimental stimulus and disturbance) separate to a much greater extent than the cyclothymes, for whom one should interfere much more with the other.

(2) In another experiment, the subject has to remember the numbers of differently coloured squares on a card which is being presented to him, one row at a time, the theory underlying the experiment being that the schizothyme, with his dissociative ability, would easily be able to carry in his mind the number of different categories into which to classify these various coloured squares, and that he would be quicker and more accurate in the total task.

(3) In this experiment, coloured groups of nonsense syllables are shown to the subject in a tachistoscope with instructions to observe either the colours or the letters. He is later questioned about both letters and colours. The hypothesis underlying the experiment would require the schizothyme, with his higher abstractive ability, to be able to observe what is required and to pay no attention to other features of the stimulus, whereas the cyclothyme would remember more of what he was not asked to observe and less of what he was asked to observe.

(4) Long, unfamiliar words are presented tachistoscopically, being shown 10 times in succession so as to facilitate reading of the word, which could not be completed at one exposure. There are two ways of getting at the meaning of the word: (i) the abstractive, analytic, dissociative method, in which the total word is built up by reading successive letters and syllables and constructed as a whole from these parts, and (ii) the global, synthetic, integrative method in which a single impression is obtained and then elaborated in successive exposures. The first of these methods would be expected to characterize the schizothyme, the second the cyclothyme.

(5) In this experiment, an attempt is made to study the effect of mental addition of twenty numbers on the regular rhythm of ergograph work. It is hypothesized that schizothymes would be capable more easily than cyclothymes to keep these two different tasks separate, so that they would give more correct answers in the one and have less disruption of the regular rhythm in the other task.

(6) On the Rorschach test we would expect schizothymes and cyclothymes to show marked differences when a comparison is made between the number of whole (W) versus the number of detailed (D, d) answers, an expectation borne out in actual fact.

These are only six of a much larger number of experiments carried out by Kretschmer, but they do illustrate the underlying hypothetical trait of dissociative ability, and as each of these experiments has been shown to differentiate significantly in at least one case between extreme groups on the schizothymia-cyclothymia continuum, it must be admitted that there is, at least, some evidence here which favours the Kretschmerian hypothesis. In an unpublished factorial analysis involving the tests mentioned, as well as an intelligence test and a measure of body type (the Rees-Eysenck index of body-build described in *Dimensions of Personality*), the writer was able to show that a general factor was present in all these tests and in the measure of body type, even when intelligence had been partialled out. This experiment was only done on a small number (N = 44) of unselected university students at the University of Pennsylvania and until results from a replication, at present in progress with much larger numbers, are available, it cannot be considered anything but suggestive. However, it can be seen that as far as experimental results go, they do not contradict but tend to support the Kretschmerian hypothesis.

What has been said of this particular trait appears to be true, *mutatis mutandis*, of the other traits described by Kretschmer. Available evidence has been discussed in detail elsewhere (Eysenck, 1950c, 1951); in the absence of factorial studies dealing with these traits, we cannot admit that they have been definitely shown to exist and be measurable by means of the tests developed by Kretschmer. Nevertheless, the consistent results obtained by him and other workers suggest that at least we have here an available source of hypotheses, theories, and well formulated research projects.

Kretschmer's methodological procedure, however, must be regarded as faulty. While defining, as does the present writer (1947), a type as 'an observed constellation or syndrome of traits', Kretschmer does not draw the obvious conclusion that we must first identify our traits and then isolate the type by means of the observed intercorrelation of traits; instead, he tries to prove the existence of the traits by arguing from the existence of a type. In other words, he shows that the one test of perseveration discriminates between cyclothymes and schizothymes and that another test of perseveration also discriminates in the same way; this he seems to regard as sufficient proof that both tests measure perseveration, which is, of course, a logical fallacy. The writer has shown that a test of suggestibility discriminates between neurotics and normals and that a test of persistence also discriminates in this fashion, and that accordingly the two tests correlate (Eysenck, 1947). It does not follow from this that persistence is the same thing as suggestibility, and, indeed, the proof that the tests in question are tests of persistence or suggestibility has to be given in terms of separate factorial studies embodying different types of suggestibility and persistence tests.

While Kretschmer places much importance on these traits, as we may, perhaps, call them in conformity with modern psychological usage, the mainstay of his whole system, of course, is the cyclothymic-schizothymic dichotomy. We must criticize his method of proving that this dichotomy, whose existence in the psychotic field few would deny, can and should be accepted in the normal field. A more direct method than the one used by him, which relies on the possibility irrelevant *tertium quid* (the pyknic-leptosomatic dichotomy) is required for this purpose, and is to be found in the method of criterioanalysis. Although Kretschmer shows that there is a correlation between body-build and the two main types of functional psychotic disorder, that correlation is not very high, and the writer has shown elsewhere (Eysenck, 1947) that body-build is correlated with other variables (neuroticism, extraversion-introversion) which are unrelated to the Kretschmerian concepts. If that be so, then clearly many of Kretschmer's findings, which appear superficially to support his views, may in reality have quite a different explanation. To give just one example, Kretschmer has shown that leptosomatics are slow and accurate while pyknics are quick and inaccurate. This may be interpreted in terms of his system; however, an alternative explanation is also possible as we have shown that hysterics tend to be more of a eurymorphic (pyknic) body-build than are dysthymics, who tend to be leptomorphic in body-build. It has also been shown that hysterics tend to be quick and inaccurate, whereas dysthymics tend to be slow and accurate. It follows from this that there should be a correlation between body-build and a speed-accuracy test, but the interpretation of the experiment may be in terms quite different from those advanced by Kretschmer, using concepts essentially alien to his system. It is because of the danger of indirect proof exemplified in this case that a more direct method of examining Kretschmer's hypothesis becomes necessary. Let us turn then to a more direct test of Kretschmer's hypothesis, using the method of criterion analysis.

In order to use the hypothetico-deductive method in this field, it is particularly important to state the hypotheses to be tested quite clearly, and to make deductions from them which can be tested empirically. As explained before, there are two main hypotheses involved in Kretschmer's system: (1) The functional psychoses (schizophrenia and manic-depressive insanity) are not qualitatively different from normal mental states, but form one extreme of a continuum which goes all the way from the perfectly normal rational to the completely insane, psychotic individual. All possible intermediate stages are represented on this continuum. (2) The two main functional psychoses (schizophrenia and manic-depressive insanity) show patterns of traits which are observable in non-psychotic persons also, although in a less extreme degree, and which give rise to a continuum running from the extreme schizothyme to the extreme cyclothyme, again with all intermediate steps being represented on this continuum. These continua are presumed to be orthogonal to each other.

A third hypothesis is frequently identified with Kretschmer's system, but does not appear essential to it, although Kretschmer himself has made considerable use of it in his own attempt to supply proof of his general system. This is the hypothesis that the schizothymic-cyclothymic continuum is correlated with body-build, schizothymes being leptosomatic, cyclothymes being pyknic with respect to their bodily habitus. The third hypothesis, being logically independent of the other two, will not be tested in the present experiment.

We have attempted to state Kretschmer's hypotheses in such a way that a statistical and experimental test of them becomes possible; while we believe that in stating them in this fashion we have not misrepresented him in any way, and while we believe that these views are held by him, explicitly or implicitly, it should be borne in mind that in thus reducing a complex and difficult system to two brief fundamentals we may have done violence to this system. Whether this be so or not, the reader must decide for himself on the basis of Kretschmer's own writings.

We may outline briefly how criterion analysis will be used in conjunction with the problem posed by Kretschmer's hypothesis. Let the line AB in Figure 27 represent the normal-psychotic continuum, and let the line I,I' cut off at point X that part of the continuum containing mental states conventionally diagnosed 'psychotic' by psychiatrists. (The distribution of the total population has been tentatively included in the figure in the form of a normal curve of distribution. As the actual form of the distribution is irrelevant to the argument, which merely hypothesizes a continuous distribution, any other form of rectilinear or curvilinear distribution might be substituted for the normal form without affecting the argument.) Let n objective psychological tests (a, b, c, ... n) be given to the two populations separated by the line I,I', i.e. to a normal group and to a psychotic group. (The term

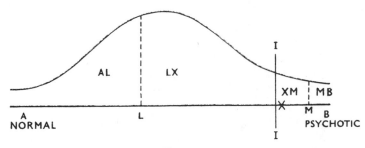

Figure 27

'normal' here means nothing but 'not under psychiatric care for mental disorders'; it does not imply anything more positive than this absence of demonstrable and demonstrated mental disorder.) Let us assume that each of these n tests distinguishes significantly between the normal and the psychotic groups. (In actual practice, $n + x$ tests would have to be given in all, so that tests not distinguishing at the chosen level of significance could be rejected.)

Now let us divide the normal group into two parts, by making a cut at point L on the line AX; similarly, let us make a cut at point M on the line XB, thus subdividing the psychotic group also. (Points L and M may be anywhere between A and X, and X and B, respectively; there is no implication that they should divide the respective populations into equal halves.) On the hypothesis that AB represents a true continuum, we have now divided both the normal and the psychotic groups into two parts, one of them more normal, the other more psychotic. Group AL is more normal than LX; group XM is more normal than group MB. If AB is a true continuum (the hypothesis to be tested), and if each of our n tests is related to that continuum in a linear fashion (supplementary hypothesis), then it would follow that on these n tests group AL would differ from group LX in the same way that group AX differed originally from group XB. Similarly, group XM would differ from group MB in the same way that AL differed from LX.

We may put these arguments in a form which permits of their being tested. If tests a and b differentiate significantly between groups AX and XB, then it would follow according to our hypothesis that they should differentiate also between AL and LX. Similarly, they should differentiate between XM and MB. This deduction, unfortunately, does not permit of any direct test, as there is no known method of determining points L and M, and therefore of differentiating the groups under discussion. However, we can transform the concept of 'differentiate' into the concept of 'correlate', and test our hypothesis in this fashion. If on tests a and b the normal group does better than the psychotic group, it would follow, as explained above, that group AL should do better on both tests than group LX. Similarly, group XM should do better on both tests than group MB. But these statements are synonymous with saying that *for both the normal and the psychotic groups separately, there should be a positive correlation between tests a and b.*

This argument can be extended to n tests, and implies as one consequence that *tests which differentiate significantly between normals and psychotics should give positive intercorrelations when these correlations are run for the normal or the psychotic groups separately.* Here then we would have a possible test of our hypothesis. But we can refine this test a little by pointing out that not only should these correlations be positive, but also that they should be proportional to the power of each test to differentiate between the normal and psychotic groups originally. We may express this differentiating power in terms of a biserial correlation for each test with the normal-psychotic dichotomy, denoting the column of n correlations between tests and criterion the *Criterion Column* $(C_{n,p})$. We may then say that the average of the intercorrelations of a test with all the other tests in the battery, for either the normal or the psychotic group, should be proportional to the correlation of that test with the criterion, i.e. the normal-psychotic dichotomy.

Instead of averaging correlations, it would appear more suitable to perform a factor analysis on the intercorrelations between our n tests. Let us assume that we extract two factors from each of our two matrices, the sets of intercorrelations for the normal and the psychotic groups respectively, which we may call F_p and F_p' for the psychotic and F_n and F_n' for the normal group. It would follow from our hypothesis and our selection of tests that F_n and F_p should be proportional to each other, and to our Criterion Column, $C_{n,p}$. Here, then, we have reached the final and crucial test. We have made a hypothesis as to the existence of a general factor underlying the pattern of variances and covariances of test performances of normal and psychotic groups, and deduced certain consequences which would follow if our hypothesis were true, and which would not follow on any tenable counter-hypothesis. In so far as these deductions are verified, we may consider our hypothesis as supported; in so far as these deductions are not verified, we may consider our hypothesis as disproven.

It will be clear that a similar procedure could be used with respect to our second hypothesis. What would be required there would be a set of n tests which discriminate between schizophrenic and manic-depressive patients; the Criterion Column in this case would consist of the biserial correlations of each test with this new criterion. Apart from these changes, the procedure as outlined above is applicable to just the same extent as it is in respect to our first hypothesis. The continuum in question is shown in diagrammatic form in Figure 26; on the basis of Kretschmer's hypothesis we would expect factors F_n' and F_p' to be proportional to each other, and also to the new Criterion Column, $C_{s,d}$.

Both hypotheses can be tested at the same time, using n tests which differentiate significantly (using Fisher's F test) between the three groups involved, the normal, schizophrenic, and manic-depressive. The two criterion columns, $C_{n,p}$ and $C_{s,d}$, could then be calculated quite easily by running biserial correlations between each of the n tests and the normal versus psychotic dichotomy for $C_{n,p}$ (using the combined schizophrenic and manic-depressive groups to form the psychotic group), and by running biserial correlations between each of the n tests and the schizophrenic–manic-depressive dichotomy for $C_{s,d}$. Product-moment correlation would then be run between the n tests for the normal and the psychotic groups separately, thus giving us two separate matrices. These, when factor analysed according to either the centroid or the summation method, or indeed any of the current methods, should result in two factors each, F and F', which would be proportional to each other, and to the respective criterion columns.

This, in brief, is the method which has been used in the present experiment. The experimental population consisted of 100 normal subjects and 100 psychotic subjects divided into two equal groups consisting of 50 manic-depressives and 50 schizophrenics.[1] Altogether, 84 sets of scores were derived from over 30 independent objective tests given to these three groups, of which the great majority were significant when the F test was applied to the scores of these three groups. The tests used included four tests of fluency, the Crown Word Connection List, a work-curve test, a colour-form test, a mirror-drawing test, a social-attitude test, two level of aspiration tests, a concentration test, 11 tests of expressive movements, two tests of perseveration, one test of dissociation (*Spaltungsfaehigkeit*), one test of tapping, four tests of oscillation, one speed-accuracy test, one suggestibility test, one tracing test, and one persistence test. Results of these various tests are given in detail elsewhere (Eysenck, 1951). The results may be summarized verbally, drawing attention to the following points. In the first place, the large number of significant differences found shows that the three groups tested are very unlikely to have come from a single universe; there is good reason to believe that the selection procedures have been successful in giving us subjects showing much greater heterogeneity than would have been expected by chance.

In the second place, it appears that on the majority of tests, the schizophrenic group scores somewhere between the normal and the manic-depressive group. Out of 38 test results significant at the ·1 per cent level, only six show exceptions to this general tendency. In other words, it would appear as if we were dealing with one continuum, ranging from normal through schizophrenic to manic-depressive. This point will be taken up again later, when further data are being adduced to throw some light on it.

In the third place, it is clear even from a casual inspection of the data that the variances in the psychotic groups are considerably larger than those in the normal groups; there is also a tendency, although less strongly marked, for variances in the manic-depressive group to be larger than in the schizophrenic group.

[1] Further details regarding population and other features of the experimental group will be found elsewhere (Eysenck, 1951).

In the fourth place, it is interesting to note that those tests which had in past work been shown to have high correlations with neuroticism, or to discriminate well between normals and neurotics, do not show even a tendency to discriminate between normals and psychotics. We might mention here such tests as persistence, body sway (with and without suggestibility), perseveration, work curve inversions, and the word connection list.

In the fifth place, it is clear that neither the colour-form test nor the dissociation test gives results which support Kretschmer's hypotheses. There are no significant differences with respect to these tests, and the actual figures are not even suggestive of any such differences as he predicts. It is possible that the tests used by us were unsuitable for a relatively high-grade group of subjects, and that with tests better suited to the level more significant results might have been obtained. While this argument cannot be gainsaid, there is no evidence to favour such speculation in our results.

In the sixth place, it is apparent that there are a number of personality traits which distinguish the normal from the psychotic group at or below the 1 per cent level. We may perhaps briefly summarize these, emphasizing of course that the terms used here should be understood to bear the operational connotation imposed upon them by the actual tests used. We find then that psychotics are less fluent, perform poorly in continuous addition, perform poorly in mirror drawing, show slower oscillation on the reversal of perspective test, are slower in tracing with a stylus, are more undecided with respect to social attitudes, show poorer concentration, have a poorer memory, tend to make larger movements and to overestimate distances and scores, tend to read more slowly, to tap more slowly and to show levels of aspiration much less reality adapted (Eysenck, 1950, 1951). Those who would argue that of course psychotics are poorer in all tasks than are normals, and that consequently these results are hardly surprising, will have to explain why no such differences were observed with respect to the tests enumerated under point four above.

In the seventh place, no differences were observed with respect to a number of tests other than those mentioned under number four. These are: social attitudes, such as radicalism, time of writing, number of lines drawn. Occasionally, tests under the same general classification gave conflicting results; thus, under the heading of 'Fluency', tests 'Flowers' and 'Words' showed no significant differences, while tests 'Birds' and 'Animals' did. Similarly, when both the best and the worst of a series of scores on a test were scored separately, different results were sometimes obtained. As an example, we may select test 7, 'Concentration', where two subtests are used, 'Letters' and 'Numbers', each consisting of eight separate scores which are added to give total scores. For both 'Letters' and 'Numbers', the lowest scores do not give significant differences, while the highest scores give significant differences. This phenomenon could with advantage be studied separately; its implications are, presumably, that while normals often do as poorly as psychotics on a single trial, psychotics hardly ever do as well as normals, even on a single trial.

This completes our brief summary of the isolated results of the experiment, and we must turn now to the study of the patterns of intercorrelations by means of criterion analysis.

In view of the fact that not all the tests used gave highly significant results, and as many of the scores used were not experimentally independent of each other, twenty tests in all were selected for the factorial study. These tests are given in Table XL. Also given in this table are the biserial correlations of each test

TABLE XL

	I $r_{c,d}$	II $r_{c,s}$	III $r_{s,d}$	IV $r_{c,p}$
1. Overestimation in distance judgment	$-\cdot160$	$-\cdot325$	$\cdot159$	$-\cdot233$
2. Fluency—animals	$\cdot323$	$\cdot203$	$\cdot189$	$\cdot293$
3. Social attitudes—zero responses	$-\cdot189$	$-\cdot255$	$\cdot070$	$-\cdot222$
4. Reading prose—time in secs.	$-\cdot364$	$-\cdot332$	$-\cdot031$	$-\cdot335$
5. Three circles—time in secs.	$-\cdot322$	$-\cdot254$	$-\cdot140$	$-\cdot268$
6. Concentration—numbers	$\cdot274$	$\cdot279$	$-\cdot037$	$\cdot278$
7. Tapping—15 secs.	$\cdot197$	$\cdot280$	$-\cdot081$	$\cdot244$
8. Mirror drawing—J scores, average	$-\cdot364$	$-\cdot237$	$-\cdot228$	$-\cdot301$
9. Perspective reversal—slow	$\cdot290$	$\cdot089$	$\cdot208$	$-\cdot199$
10. Perspective reversal—normal	$\cdot193$	$\cdot224$	$-\cdot016$	$\cdot229$
11. Abstractions—letters remembered	$\cdot379$	$\cdot195$	$\cdot207$	$\cdot301$
12. Three squares—diameter	$-\cdot397$	$-\cdot271$	$-\cdot041$	$-\cdot322$
13. Tracing test—J scores, average	$-\cdot274$	$-\cdot265$	$\cdot016$	$-\cdot257$
14. Work curve—lowest score	$\cdot376$	$\cdot262$	$\cdot129$	$\cdot309$
15. Size estimation—half-crown	$-\cdot253$	$-\cdot332$	$\cdot106$	$-\cdot294$
16. Numbers 1–20; length of writing	$-\cdot250$	$-\cdot063$	$-\cdot216$	$-\cdot162$
17. Expressive movements—length of waves	$-\cdot459$	$-\cdot213$	$-\cdot279$	$-\cdot341$
18. Expressive movements—amplitude	$-\cdot556$	$-\cdot242$	$-\cdot339$	$-\cdot402$
19. YEAR—length of writing	$-\cdot353$	$-\cdot228$	$-\cdot097$	$-\cdot275$
20. Suggestibility	$-\cdot005$	$-\cdot042$	$\cdot039$	$-\cdot025$

with the following dichotomies: (1) Controls versus depressives; (2) controls versus schizophrenics; (3) schizophrenics versus depressives $(C_{s,d})$; (4) controls versus psychotics $(C_{n,p})$. The product-moment intercorrelations for these twenty tests were calculated for the normal (control) group, and separately for the psychotic group. The tables are given in Eysenck (1951).

These two tables were factor analysed by means of Thurstone's centroid method. Thurstone's method of sign reversal was used until all the column sums were positive; this was followed by reflection of pairs of columns in accordance with Holley's criterion (1947). Two factors were extracted from each of the tables; this number was decided by means of the following method. (1) A one-factor solution was assumed and iterations made until the communalities from the last two iterations were all within $\pm \cdot 005$, when the first factor residuals were calculated. 28 and 22 of these were above the $\cdot 05$ level of significance in the two tables, where 19 would have been expected by chance; 12 and 8 respectively were above the $\cdot 01$ level, where 4 would have been expected. It was therefore decided to extract a second factor. (2) A two-factor solution was assumed and iterations carried out until the last two agreed within $\pm \cdot 001$. The second-factor residuals were then calculated, and in both tables 8 and 2 respectively were found to be significant at the $\cdot 05$ and $\cdot 01$ levels, where 19 and 4 would have been expected by chance. The analysis was terminated at this point. Factor saturations are given in Table XLI together with the communalities.

We now have available the data with which to test our hypothesis. As shown in section one, Kretschmer's hypothesis requires that the two sets of factor saturations should be proportional to each other. We must therefore correlate F_n with F_p, and F_n' with F_p'; the hypothesis requires that these two correlations should be significantly positive. In actual fact they are $+ \cdot 868$ and $+ \cdot 746$; it appears therefore that this deduction is borne out by the facts. Both factor patterns are remarkably alike.

The next deduction to be tested relates to our Hypothesis I, and states that F_n and F_p should both be proportional to $C_{n,p}$. The respective correlations are $+ \cdot 895$ and $+ \cdot 954$. Again we find our deduction verified, and it would appear that psychotic states do in fact form a continuum with normal mental states. Our last deduction relates to Hypothesis II, and requires that F_n' and F_p' should both be proportional to $C_{s,d}$. The correlations in question are

TABLE XLI

	Normal Group			Psychotic Group		
	F_n	F_n'	$h_n{}^2$	F_p	F_p'	$h_p{}^2$
1	·043	·184	·036	·170	·044	·031
2	— ·202	·342	·158	— ·379	·361	·274
3	·119	·048	·016	— ·060	·183	·037
4	·498	— ·198	·287	·363	— ·165	·159
5	·383	·052	·149	·396	·196	·195
6	— ·334	·705	·609	— ·375	·432	·327
7	— ·176	·157	·056	— ·290	·226	·135
8	·355	— ·055	·129	·276	— ·330	·185
9	— ·263	— ·215	·115	— ·373	— ·228	·191
10	— ·152	— ·129	·040	— ·373	— ·064	·143
11	— ·241	·391	·211	— ·448	·170	·230
12	·623	·417	·562	·174	·171	·060
13	·329	— ·053	·111	·425	— ·124	·196
14	— ·428	·260	·251	— ·497	·142	·267
15	·084	·288	·090	·244	·121	·074
16	·063	·508	·262	·183	·357	·161
17	·240	·156	·082	·509	·156	·283
18	·315	·054	·102	·537	·120	·303
19	·107	·169	·040	·202	·579	·376
20	·007	— ·060	·004	— ·034	— ·099	·011

+ ·029 and + ·085, and it will be clear that in this case the deduction is not verified. It would appear to follow that schizothymia-cyclothymia does not exist as a separate dimension of personality.[1]

Before accepting this negative conclusion, however, it would appear desirable to study the possible effects which rotation might have on the emergence of a factor of the kind we are looking for. As has been pointed out in the original paper on criterion analysis (1950), one feature of this method is the rotation of factors, not into simple structure as in Thurstone's system, but into maximum correlation with the criterion column. As we have two criterion columns in the present study, two separate and different rotations are possible for each of the two matrices: (1) rotation such that

[1] No attempt is made here to interpret F_n' and F_p'. Such interpretation could be speculative at best, and could serve little useful purpose. The possibility that this second factor may be related to the personality dimension extraversion-introversion (Eysenck, 1950c, 1951) has been considered, but until the tests most highly saturated with factor two have been included in the same battery with other tests known to measure E–I no such view could be put forward with any confidence.

a vector is found which, in the two-factor space, coincides as nearly as possible with the projection of the $C_{n,p}$ column on that space, and (2) rotation such that a vector is found which, in the two-factor space, coincides as nearly as possible with the projection of the $C_{s,d}$ column on that space. In either case, the second factor is calculated by keeping it orthogonal to the factor first extracted. When these rotations are carried out the following results are obtained:

Correlations between $\hat{F}_n$ and $\hat{F}_p$ and $\hat{F}_n{}'$ and $\hat{F}_p{}'$ are now + ·858 and + ·769 respectively. Correlations of $\hat{F}_n$ and $\hat{F}_p$ with $C_{n,p}$ are now + ·894 and + ·951 respectively, while correlations of $\hat{F}_n{}'$ and $\hat{F}_p{}'$ with $C_{s,d}$ are still quite insignificant. Rotations according to (2) are rather more interesting. Correlations between (F_n) and (F_p) and $(F_n{}')$ and $(F_p{}')$ are now + ·830 and + ·793 respectively. Correlations of (F_n) and (F_p) with $C_{s,d}$ are now + ·548 and + ·679 which seemingly indicates that here we do have some justification for speaking of a schizothymia-cyclothymia factor. But this putative factor can be shown to have no real meaning when we compute the correlation between $C_{n,p}$ and $C_{s,d}$, which turns out to be + ·559. This is simply a confirmation of a point made before, viz. that differences between schizophrenics and manic-depressives tend to be in the same direction as differences between normals and schizophrenics, and that therefore the schizophrenic group tends to be intermediate between the others. In other words, the correlations of (F_n) and (F_p) with $C_{s,d}$ appear due entirely to the correlation of $C_{s,d}$ with $C_{n,p}$, and again we find no evidence whatever for the existence of a schizothymia-cyclothymia factor.

This conclusion, like others in this chapter, should not be taken as in any way definitive. It is possible that a selection of tests which gave more scope to schizophrenic-depressive differences might produce results more in line with Kretschmer's hypothesis, although the fact that tests of his which were included did not succeed in producing this discrimination makes it somewhat unlikely that very different results would be reached with a different selection of tests. It is perhaps significant that wherever results in this experiment are positive, they are very decidedly so, and where they are negative, they are equally decidedly negative; the support for the first hypothesis investigated, and the failure to find any support for the second hypothesis, are equally impressive in their decisiveness.

We have shown, so far, that neither neurotics nor psychotics are something *sui generis*, qualitatively different from normal people; instead, we have been able to show that there exists a 'neuroticism' continuum linking normals with neurotics, and a 'psychoticism' continuum, linking normals with psychotics. The question immediately arises: Are these two continua identical, or are they independent of each other? Identity would presumably be assumed by the Freudian theory of 'regression', according to which there is a continuum ranging from the normal, well-adapted personality, through the neurotic, partly regressed patient, to the psychotic, almost completely regressed. Independence would be assumed by most of the psychiatric textbooks written along Kraepelinian lines. The problem is clearly an important one, indeed it is fundamental for any useful taxonomic system. There is no doubt that it is eminently amenable to a systematic experimental attack.

There are certain fairly obvious clinical findings which make the assumption of one common continuum somewhat unlikely. If we were dealing with one single continuum, normals developing a psychosis should pass through a state of neurotic disorder first; similarly, neurotics should be far more susceptible to the development of a psychotic illness than normals. Neither of these deductions appears to be verified by psychiatric observations. Somewhat more definite are certain findings from military experience. There is a clear, monotonic rise in neurotic breakdown rate with increasing length of military service; there is no such rise in psychotic breakdown rate. There is a clear drop in neurotic breakdown after the cessation of hostilities, of between 60 and 70 per cent; there is no change in psychotic breakdown at all.[1] Clearly, neurotic and psychotic breakdown respond quite differently to environmental stress, a fact which makes it difficult to maintain the 'single dimension' hypothesis.

These data, derived as they are from observation rather than from experiment, support but do not prove the hypothesis that here we are dealing with two dimensions rather than one. The rest of this chapter is devoted to a somewhat more formal proof of this proposition. Let us first of all consider the type of deduction which may be made from the two hypotheses between which we are trying to decide. On the 'single continuum' hypothesis, we are

1 I am indebted to W. A. Hunt for pointing out the facts to me, and for allowing me to consult the figures on which the above conclusions are based.

dealing with three groups—normals, neurotics, psychotics—whose mean 'regression' scores lie in that order along a single continuum or dimension. We would, therefore, expect that those tests which discriminate significantly between normals and neurotics should also discriminate with even greater significance between normals and psychotics. We have already seen that this is not so. Tests like suggestibility, static ataxia, persistence, and the Word Connection List discriminate between normals and neurotics at a high level of

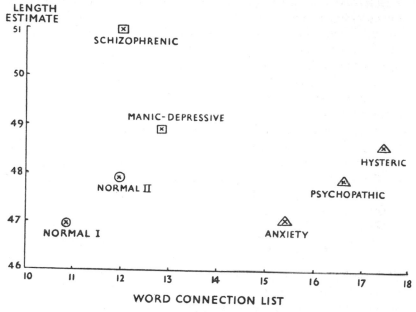

Figure 28

significance, but fail completely to discriminate between normals and psychotics. Other tests, like the large selection of expressive movement tests described in Eysenck (1950c, 1951), discriminate at a high level of confidence between normals and psychotics, but fail to discriminate between normals and neurotics. These results have already been mentioned in passing. It may be more enlightening to present comparisons based on a few selected tests in diagrammatic form.

Figure 28 shows a plot in which the ordinate and the abscissa respectively represent scores on two tests (the Word Connection List and a test of Length Estimation, scored for amount of overestimation), the first of which discriminated very significantly

between normal and neurotic groups, while the second discriminated very significantly between normal and psychotic
groups. Plotted in the diagram are the mean scores of two normal
groups who were given the two tests, two psychotic groups (one
manic-depressive, the other schizophrenic), and three neurotic
groups (one hysteric, one psychopathic, and the third suffering
from anxiety). On the basis of the 'single continuum' hypothesis,
we would expect these means to lie on a more or less straight line,

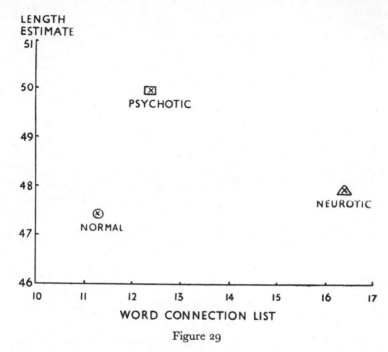

Figure 29

with the normal groups at one end, the psychotic groups at the
other, and the neurotic groups intermediate. It will be seen that
the facts do not bear out the hypothesis. It is impossible to regard
the results as compatible with a single-dimension hypothesis; we
need at least two dimensions to accommodate the triangular
normal-psychotic-neurotic grouping. This is even more apparent
in Figure 29, where the average results are plotted for the normals,
psychotics, and neurotics respectively, using total groups not split
up into their constituent parts. Figures 30 and 31 bear out this
impression; using two other sets of tests (suggestibility and an
expressive movement test described in Eysenck (1950c) in the one,

and tapping rate and static ataxia in the other) we find that in
neither case can the three means be arranged in a linear form,

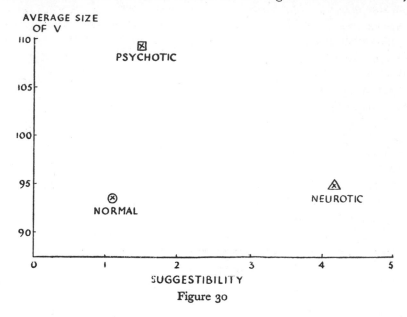

Figure 30

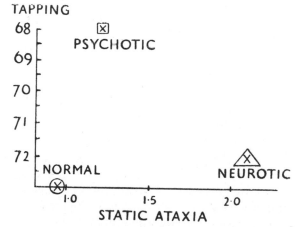

Figure 31

suggestive of one underlying dimension or continuum; in each case
a two-dimensional space is required.

These fairly clear-cut examples do not of course constitute a formal proof; no effort has been made to apply formulæ to these results and show the statistical significance of the deviations from a straight line. As a demonstration *ad oculos*, these diagrams appeared sufficiently striking to demonstrate the logic of the argument underlying our proof; for the proof itself we must turn to a somewhat more formal demonstration. Two such demonstrations will in fact be given, the first more definitely experimental, the second more statistical in nature.

The experimental study alluded to was carried out by F. Freeman (1951), using the Character Interpretation test illustrated in photographs 29 and 30. The nature of the test will be apparent from these reproductions. Twelve photographs of human faces—male and female, adult and child—are given to the subject, together with a set of 24 adjectives for each. The various sets of adjectives are divided into two lists of 12 each, called List A and List B; instructions are to put a check mark beside the four words in List A which best describe the person shown in the picture, and then to put a cross beside the four words in List A which least describe the person. The same is then done for the adjectives in List B.

The twelve adjectives in each List are selected according to a scheme which is identical for all the pictures. Two adjectives relate to feelings of (*a*) hostility, two to feelings of (*b*) self-importance, two to (*c*) immorality (other than sexual), two to (*d*) sexual immorality, two to (*e*) depressive feelings, and two to (*f*) fearfulness and insecurity. One of the two terms in each case is worded positively, the other negatively; 'virtuous' and 'loose' would thus form a contrasting pair of words in the sexual category, 'uneasy' and 'undisturbed' would form a similar pair in the fearful-insecure category. The adjectives in each case were chosen so as to have some apparent relevance to the particular picture in question. Negative (unfavourable) reactions (either putting a check mark beside an unfavourable adjective, or putting a cross beside a favourable one) are given higher scores than positive (favourable) reactions (either putting a cross beside an unfavourable reaction, or putting a check mark beside a favourable one).

Scoring generally is done on several levels. At the lowest level, each adjective is scored separately. At the second level, the two adjectives forming a pair in a particular list are combined. At the third level, corresponding pairs in Lists A and B are combined. At the fourth level, all categories for a picture are combined, giving a general index of liking or disliking for that picture. And at the highest level, all these indices are combined in a grand total, expressing an individual's liking or disliking towards all the pictures.

The general hypothesis underlying this test will be apparent from the description. Differences between subjects in assigning character traits to the people whose pictures constitute the test may be presumed to be related to the personalities of the subjects themselves; if that be true, it would follow that the scores of men would differ from the scores of women, or that the scores of neurotics would differ from those of psychotics, and those of both groups from the scores of normal subjects.

These conclusions would only follow, of course, if our system of scoring possessed a certain amount of reliability; like any objective scoring system for what is essentially a projective test (properly so called in this instance, as the mental mechanism hypothesized is that of projection) the one employed here may be putting together on *a priori* grounds scores which psychologically are quite unrelated. Reliabilities were calculated at various levels of combination, and are sufficiently high to show that such a criticism would not be entirely justified. Reliabilities at the third level (List A versus List B for pairs of adjectives) for 100 normal male subjects average around ·40. At a higher level, we compare total 'like' score for a particular category in List A for a given picture with total 'like' score for a particular category in List B for the same picture. Below are given the reliabilities, averaged over all 12 pictures, for 100 normal, 50 psychotic, and 50 neurotic subjects, all of them male. The values are: ·67, ·68, and ·67. Considering the small number of choices which makes up each score, these reliabilities are rather encouraging. Neither age nor intelligence were found to be correlated with the scores.

We may now return to the main reason why we introduced a discussion of the Character Interpretation test into this chapter. If our assumption is justified that normal, psychotic and neurotic subjects will react differently to the stimuli provided, and that their reactions are the product of fundamental personality traits, then it would follow that on the Freudian hypothesis of a single normal-neurotic-psychotic dimension the psychotic deviations from the normal pattern should be in the same direction as the neurotic deviations, but more strongly marked. If no such generalization could be derived from the data, then the 'single continuum' hypothesis would appear to be invalidated.

In order to avoid the necessity of quoting the extremely lengthy and complex material relating to all the pictures in this test, we shall give details only for the two pictures reproduced in this book as photographs 29 and 30. The pictures represent a male negro and a white woman respectively. In the case of the negro, the scores for categories a to f, summed over Lists A and B, are as follows: 26·56 for 100 normal male subjects; 23·00 for 50 male psychotics; and 28·84 for 50 male neurotics. Two of the three differences are significant (normals versus psychotics) or very significant (psychotics versus neurotics), and it will be noticed that neurotics and psychotics differ from normals in opposite directions; the psychotics give more 'like', the neurotics more 'dislike' responses than the normals. On the other picture, the scores of the same three groups are respectively 30·26, 25·52, and 29·72; the normal-psychotic and the psychotic-neurotic differences are both very significant. In this case the psychotics again have higher 'like' scores than the other two groups, but the neurotics are not in any way differentiated from the normals.

Results from these pictures are typical of all the others: there is no tendency for results to fall into the normal-neurotic-psychotic arrangement called for by the Freudian hypothesis. Other sequences, such as neurotic-normal-psychotic, or normal-psychotic-neurotic, appear much more frequently, thus suggesting that we are dealing with more than a single continuum.

At the conclusion of the test, the subjects were asked to endorse a similar set of adjectives as applied to themselves, first as seen by the person whose photograph they liked best, and then as seen by the person whose photograph they liked least. The actual instructions for this test are reproduced on the opposite page. The construction of the sets of adjectives, and the method of scoring, are the same for these two tests as they were for the twelve picture test items. On the first test (adjectives marked as by the person liked best) the sequence of scores is normals (12·58), psychotics (15·04), and neurotics (17·80); all these differences are significant or very significant. Normals, apparently, consider themselves liked best, neurotics consider themselves liked least, with psychotics in between. On the second test (adjectives marked as by the person liked least) the sequence of scores is normals (21·06), psychotics (21·32), and neurotics (24·84); neurotics differ significantly from both normals and psychotics. Here again, normals consider themselves liked best, neurotics consider themselves liked least, with

CHARACTER INTERPRETATION TEST

1. Each picture is numbered. In the Table below, put the number of the person you liked BEST under Rank No. 1, next best under No. 2, and so on until the person you liked LEAST, whose number goes under Rank No. 12.

RANK	1	2	3	4	5	6	7	8	9	10	11	12
PICTURE												

2. What would the person you ranked No. 1 say about **you**? Which four words would that person say applied **BEST** (√) to **you**, and which four words would apply **LEAST** (x)?

LIST A		LIST B	
....Nervous	....Considerate	....Boastful	....Moody
....Virtuous	....Modest	....Kind	....Immoral
....Dishonest	....Sincere	....Dependable	....Unreliable
....Affected	....Unfriendly	....Amusing	....Natural
....Happy	....Degenerate	....Dependent	....Idealistic
....Sad	....Relaxed	....Critical	....Assured

Remarks: (Just exactly what would this person you ranked No. 1 say about **you**?)

....

	a	b	c	d	e	f	T
A							
B							
T							

3. What would the person you ranked No. 12 say about **you**? Which four words would that person say applied **BEST** (√) to **you**, and which four words would apply **LEAST** (x)?

LIST A		LIST B	
....Cheerful	....Reliable	....Unsure	....Confident
....Worried	....Unhappy	....Unassuming	....Moral
....Perverted	....Reserved	....Snobbish	....Insincere
....Normal	....Sociable	....Suspicious	....Evil-minded
....Calm	....Conceited	....Honest	....Friendly
....Malicious	....Designing	....Downhearted	....Humorous

Remarks: (Just exactly what would this person you ranked No. 12 say about **you**?)

....

	a	b	c	d	e	f	T
A							
B							
T							

psychotics in between. These results also fail to support the 'single continuum' hypothesis, at a high level of statistical significance.

We must now turn to a somewhat more statistically oriented study. The method used in it has already been alluded to in our discussion of the work of Rao and Slater, in which they showed that psychiatric ratings of hysterics, psychopaths, obsessionals, anxiety states, and normals on thirteen points could be explained entirely in terms of one dimension (identifiable with neuroticism), without requiring any other continuum than differences in severity of neurosis to account for diagnostic differences between the groups. The method to be used has been developed independently by several workers including C. R. Rao (1948) and is based on Fisher's maximum likelihood principle; it has obvious similarities with the independently developed solution of Penrose (1947) and Smith (1947), and falls under the general heading of discriminant function analysis. Rao & Slater (1949) essentially used certain linear discriminant functions called 'canonical' to give a geometrical representation of the differences between various neurotic sub-classifications; their method requires an answer to the dimensional problem—how many dimensions are sufficient to represent all the groups measured?—and supplies a test of significance which is unfortunately lacking in the traditional factorial approach to this question. Lubin (1950) has put Rao's method into a form in which it can more easily be understood by workers in the psychological field, and has also carried out the analysis on which this section is based.[1]

We have already shown that both 'neuroticism' and 'psychoticism' are continuous variables, ranging all the way from the extremely well adjusted, mature, stable type of personality to the extremes of neurotic or psychotic abnormality. Yet for certain purposes it is desirable to classify individuals into groups—normal, psychotic or neurotic—for various social and administrative reasons. A person has to be certified as psychotic; this is an all-or-none decision. A person is rejected from the army because of neurotic disability; this again is an all-or-none decision. Diagnosis as neurotic or psychotic may determine the course of treatment—the neurotic may receive psychotherapy, the psychotic may receive

---

[1] The psychological interpretation of Lubin's results given on the pages below was made by the writer; Lubin's thesis is concerned only with the statistical issues involved.

E.C.T., or be subjected to leucotomy. In a similar way, although intelligence is generally considered to be a continuous variable, the decision to label a person as 'mentally defective' is in essence based on a system of classification in which everyone is either 'normal' or 'subnormal'. Categorical decisions are essential in practice; it is the task of science to aid in the correct choice of categories, and to minimize the number of misclassifications.

The best available method for classifying individuals into mutually exclusive categories on the basis of quantitative scores is Fisher's discriminant function (1936, 1938). It is applied in the present case to three groups of subjects—50 normals, 50 psychotics, and 50 neurotics—of roughly equal age and sex distribution. None of the psychotics were certified, and none were of the chronic, deteriorated type. The normals were chosen on the usual negative criterion of not being to our knowledge under treatment for mental disorders of any kind. It is almost certain that the criterion is far from perfect, and that if the whole group of 150 subjects were to be seen and diagnosed by a psychiatrist ignorant of their previous diagnosis, a correlation of less than unity would be found. This fact will seriously attenuate our results, but is unlikely to lead to exaggerated claims as to the value of the method. Four tests of manual dexterity were given to all the subjects, the tests chosen being tests M, N, O, and P from the General Aptitude Battery of the United States Employment Service, whose kindness in allowing us to use their tests is acknowledged with gratitude. (The tests are illustrated in photographs 19, 20, 23.) Again, the choice of tests was such that our findings would constitute a minimum rather than a maximum claim; it is well known that the higher the intercorrelations between tests, the less likely are they to make independent contribution to a multiple selection problem. It will be clear that if normals, psychotics, and neurotics can be discriminated successfully on the basis of four manual dexterity tests, then much better discrimination could be achieved on the basis of a larger number of more diversified tests. However, we are here concerned more with the method than with the results, and even with the restrictions imposed on the solution by the choice of tests and subjects, results will be shown to be markedly positive and in accord with our hypothesis.

The first step in the procedure requires the condensation of the four tests into the two canonical variates that will best differentiate the three groups in two dimensions;[1] the second step requires the application of Rao's likelihood solution for classification. Table XLII shows the results of the first step; in it are given the means, variances, and correlation ratios of the two canonical variates, Y_1 and Y_2. It will be seen that Y_1 has a correlation of ·64 with the trichotomous classification, while Y_2 has a correlation of ·45 with it. The first of these is the largest possible correlation ratio of any linear combination of the four tests with the criterion, while the second is the largest possible correlation ration of any linear combination of the four tests which at the same time correlates zero with Y_1. In combination, Y_1 and Y_2 correlate with the criterion to the extent of ·78.

TABLE XLII

	Normals	Neurotics	Psychotics	Correlation Ratio
Y_1	78·240	66·540	59·420	·64
Y_2	40·660	48·560	39·280	·45
S_1^2	79·166	55·192	136·167	
S_2^2	56·596	67·639	64·247	

Before calculating Y_1 and Y_2, we must of course test the latent roots for significance. It is always possible to represent the group means in m-1 dimensions; before using this number of dimensions, however, (two in this case) we must show that the means do not lie along one dimension, or coincide at one point. In other words, we must show (1) that there are significant differences between the groups, and (2) what the minimum number of dimensions is which is required to represent the differences between the group means. It is the possibility of such a test of significance that constitutes the main claim of this procedure to our interest. According to Bartlett's (1938) test, both roots are significant at the P = ·001 level. We may therefore conclude that two dimensions are necessary and sufficient to account for our observed test data. Interpretation of Y_1 and Y_2 will be attempted later on; here we may

[1] The canonical transformation of the original variables is not a necessary step (Slater, 1948); the likelihood that an individual belongs to any one of the groups can be calculated by using likelihood functions based on the original test results directly. This latter method cannot be less efficient than the former, and it may occasionally be significantly more efficient. However, it is very much more laborious. Both solutions were calculated, and the difference between them found to be insignificant.

point out simply that inspection of the values in Table XLII suggest that Y_1 is identical with our 'psychoticism' factor, and Y_2 with our 'neuroticism' factor.

If we wish to go on and assign our 150 subjects to their appropriate class on the basis of their test scores, we must transform the canonical variates, Y_1 and Y_2, into likelihood functions of the Rao type. This procedure, which will minimize the proportion of misclassifications, consists of calculating the likelihood for each individual of belonging to each of the three groups, and then assigning him to that group for which he has the maximum likelihood. Table XLIII gives the results: it will be seen that 71 per

TABLE XLIII

		Psychotic	Neurotic	Normal	Total
Predicted	Psychotic	34	9	3	46
Group	Neurotic	9	32	6	47
Membership	Normal	7	9	41	57
					150
Percentage correctly classified:		68%	64%	82%	71·3%

cent of all cases are correctly classified.[1] A non-parametric test of significance (Lubin, 1950) applied to this table shows that misclassifications are very significantly fewer than chance ($P < ·001$).

As was pointed out earlier, the quadratic likelihood solution using the canonical variate scores is not the only one possible. We may use a linear rather than a quadratic solution, and we may use the original test scores rather than the canonical variates based on them. These various methods give rather similar results. Results of the various methods are compared in Table XLIV.

A visual presentation of the data is given in Figure 32. The two canonical variates, Y_1 and Y_2, constitute the ordinate and the abscissa: the mean values of the 150 subjects are plotted according to their scores on Y_1 and Y_2. The three lines which split the diagram into three parts are the discriminant function lines, giving

[1] It will be seen that the total number classified into each group does not correspond with the number known to be in that group. This is an obvious difficulty of this method which has received a proper solution only recently (Rao, 1948).

TABLE XLIV

Method of Solution	Variables Used	Percentage Correctly Classified			
		Total	Normal	Neurotic	Psychotic
			%	%	%
Quadratic	Canonical variate	71·3	82	64	68
Linear	Canonical variate	68·7	78	58	70
Quadratic	Test scores	72·7	80	66	72
Linear	Test scores	68·7	80	68	68

Predicted group membership on the basis of the quadratic likelihood canonical variate scores.

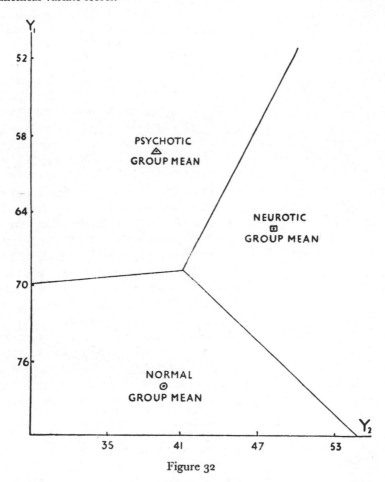

Figure 32

the lowest degree of misclassification. The resemblance·of the positions of the three groups to those of the three groups in Figures 29, 30, and 31 will be noted. It will also be noted that the position of the psychotic and normal means, which are parallel to the Y_1 axis, justifies our interpretation of this canonical variate as 'psychoticism', while the fact that Y_2 discriminates the neurotic mean from the two other means may serve as justification of our interpreting this canonical variate as one of 'neuroticism'.

Not too much importance is attributed to the actual discrimination achieved. It is well known that statistical combinations of several scores in order to give maximum correlation with a criterion tend to give spuriously high values because of the utilization of chance errors which happen to correlate with the predicted variables. The fact that the zero-order correlation ratios are relatively high—being equal to ·50, ·57, ·56, and ·51 respectively for tests M, N, O, and P—makes it unlikely that the multiple R would drop very much on repetition of the experiment (two such repetitions are under weigh at the moment). Also it is clear that a more careful selection of subjects, and a more varied selection of tests, would result in substantial improvement on the figures given here. However, our main purpose in quoting this study lay not in the demonstration of the possibilities for differential diagnosis of objective tests (welcome as this proof may be); it lay in the demonstration that two dimensions are required in order to account for the distribution of scores made by normal, psychotic, and neurotic subjects. This conclusion agrees with that derived from our factorial studies, and adds the important element of statistical significance; where previously our results had to be evaluated more or less on an impressionistic basis, they can now be stated in terms of exact P values.

Chapter Seven

APPLICATIONS OF DIMENSIONAL ANALYSIS

IN this chapter a number of investigations are described in which an attempt has been made to apply the dimensional approach to various practical problems. Included are studies into the after-effects of prefrontal leucotomy, into the employability of mental defectives, into work adjustment and productivity of un-skilled factory workers and into the selection of students and nurses. These studies extend our knowledge in two directions. They make use of populations—mental defectives, nurses, factory workers, teachers—which are quite unlike those on whom our dimensions were first established; the fact that very similar results appear in these new populations to what we had observed in the original groups lends strong support to the universality of the phenomena. And secondly these studies bring into the universe covered by our tests concepts and variables not previously dealt with. Productivity, work adjustment, social relations and ability to get on with people, popularity—these are only a few of those used in these studies. Nor have we failed to follow the dictates of the hypothetico-deductive method even when dealing with these severely practical problems. In each case a definite hypothesis was stated, and the investigation designed in such a way as to provide evidence for or against the hypothesis.

(1) Post-operative Effects of Leucotomy

Perhaps the most interesting and important of the series of studies summarized in this chapter is the investigation of the after effects of leucotomy, carried out by A. Petrie (1952). Its import-ance lies not only in the practical necessity of knowing just what sort of personality change may be expected to occur after the fibres connecting the frontal lobes with the thalamus have been sec-tioned; it sheds light on theoretical issues of fundamental interest. At the same time, this study illustrates very well a point on which stress has been laid before, namely, the importance of making full use of the hypothetico-deductive method in psychological investigation. Too much work has been done on the after-effects of leucotomy in a spirit of blind empiricism, of trying any test that came to hand that might be relevant; the almost completely negative results of this approach will be familiar to most readers, and are catalogued in Crown's very able survey of the field (1951). What is required, surely, is first of all an hypothesis, couched in operational terms, as to what after-effects would be expected, followed by an experimental design which permits unambiguous verification or refutation of deductions made from this theory. Even if unsuccessful, such a procedure would increase our knowledge far more than any number of *ad hoc* empirical tests based on no clear underlying hypothesis.

The results of the almost universal failure to make use of this method have been rather melancholy. Bronfenbrenner (1951) has stated the position admirably: 'It is difficult for the would-be theorist to avoid being forced in one of two dissociated directions. If he covets his reputation as a scientist, he is under pressure to confine himself to the analysis of relatively simple phenomena where the variables are few, discrete, and susceptible to rigorous experimental control. The most significant aspects of human behaviour, however, are not likely to be found in this category, for they are characteristically elusive and multideterminate. To wrestle with these at a realistic level and at the same time to face up to the expectations and criticisms of fellow-scientists take more time, energy, patience, and self-integration than many able men command. It is far easier to remain free from such demands by doing one's theorizing in a non-scientific context. As a result, it is perhaps possible to say—with only moderate exaggeration—that the study of human behaviour in America shows a bimodal distribution with undisciplined speculation at one mode and rigorous sterility at the other.' This study will illustrate how it is possible to achieve scientific rigor, while avoiding *rigor mortis*, through the use of the hypothetico-deductive method.

The first two hypotheses advanced by Petrie are illustrated in Figure 33. Taking her cue from the isolation of the two personality dimensions of neuroticism and introversion-extraversion, she posits that (1) *neurotic patients after leucotomy will show a decrease in neuroticism*, and (2) that *neurotic patients after leucotomy will show an increase in extraversion*. An additional hypothesis relates to another personality dimension, this time in the cognitive field, and states that (3) *neurotic patients after leucotomy will show a decrease in intelligence*. It should be noted that these predictions apply to *neurotic* patients only; the changes to be expected with psychotics will be discussed later in connection with the experimental work of Crown (1950).

The use of such terms as *neuroticism, extraversion,* and *intelligence* presupposes some sort of operational definition, as otherwise no testable deductions from these hypotheses are possible. Six tests, taken in the main from *Dimensions of Personality,* were used to measure neuroticism: body-sway suggestibility, manual dexterity,

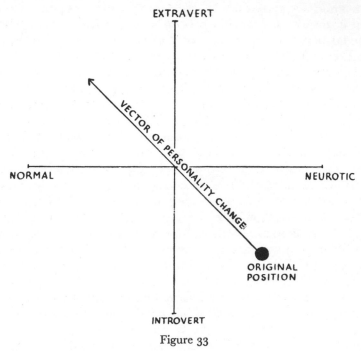

Figure 33

smoothness of work-curve, self-rating scales, tempo of handwriting, and disposition-rigidity. The prediction made on the basis of the original hypothesis requires the following changes after leucotomy: decrease in suggestibility, improvement in manual dexterity, greater smoothness of work-curves, less self-criticism and fewer inferiority feelings on self-rating scales, greater speed of handwriting, and less disposition-rigidity.

Another set of six tests was used to measure introversion: accuracy/speed ratio, intropunitiveness, relative dislike of sexual humour, verbal/non-verbal intelligence test ratio, persistence, and a preoccupation with the past rather than with the present or the future. The prediction made on the basis of the original hypothesis requires the following changes after leucotomy: lower speed/accuracy ratio, decrease in intropunitiveness, increase of sex-humour appreciation, lowering in the verbal/non-verbal intelligence test ratio, lessening in persistence, and a lessening in pre-occupation with the past.

Regarding the changes in intellectual capacity, the Wechsler-Bellevue and the Porteus Mazes tests were used, as well as the 'Proverbs' test from the Revised Stanford-Binet test. The direction of changes to be expected will be self-evident from the original hypothesis.

Two separate types of operation were performed. The first of these is the so-called Posterior Standard Leucotomy, described in detail elsewhere (McKissock, 1943). The other type of operation, the Anterior Rostral Leucotomy, is an open bilateral operation, carried out through a pair of burr holes under direct vision. It is more anterior, and therefore presumably less damaging, than the Posterior Standard Leucotomy; full details will be found elsewhere (McKissock, W., 1949). Two further hypotheses were based on the differences between these two types of operation. In view of the fact that the Rostral operation is less far-reaching, it was posited (4) that *the same changes would be found as in the Standard operation, but that their extent would be less extreme.* The other deduction is based on the assumption that the great variability in the after-effects of the Standard operation may be due to operative variability consequent upon lack of visual control, a lack not present in the open Rostral operation. It would seem to follow, if this reasoning be correct, that (5) *there should be less variability in the after-effects of the Rostral operation.*

The patients operated upon were severe neurotics, primarily those suffering from obsessional symptoms and from anxiety; they would in the main fall into the category of 'dysthymics' as described in *Dimensions of Personality.* The same principle of selection was followed in choosing patients for either type of operation, and there is little reason to suspect the group of patients who were given the Standard operation to have been different in any important respect from the group of patients who were given the Rostral operation: 20 patients in the Standard group were tested before the operation, and retested three and nine months after the operation; 15 patients in the Rostral group were tested befoie the operation, and retested six months after the operation. Some additional patients in the Standard group only received one retest; some additional patients in the Rostral group received only unilateral incisions. Results from the main groups only are summarized here; a full report will be found elsewhere (Petrie, 1952).

The results of the tests as applied to the Standard operation group of patients are given in Tables XLV, XLVI, XLVII; these figures, it should be noted, are merely a brief summary of the many lengthy and detailed tables given by Petrie. Regarding the predicted decrease in neuroticism, it will be seen that the direction of the change for all six tests is as predicted; this is true both for the three-months and the six-months retest. Most of the C.R.s are fully significant, and for every test there is at least one significant change in the predicted direction—either after three or after nine months. We may conclude that with respect to this dimension of personality, the original hypothesis is fully borne out.

TABLE XLV

CHANGES AFTER LEUCOTOMY: CRITICAL RATIOS

	3 *months*	9 *months*
(1) *Neuroticism*		
(a) Body sway suggestibility	2·33	2·91
(b) Manual dexterity	6·14	3·95
(c) Smoothness of work curves	2·34	N.S.
(d) Self-rating scale	N.S.	2·86
(e) Tempo of handwriting	N.S.	2·43
(f) Disposition-rigidity	1·90	2·12

With respect to the Introversion-Extraversion dimension, the results are equally clear. Again all tests change in the predicted direction, and with one exception all the changes are significant at a high level of confidence. (It would have been permissible in all cases to use the one-tail test. In order to avoid any possibility of arbitrary statistical manipulation of data, however, Petrie used the two-tail test in connection with computations arising from the Standard operation, thus reducing the chances of finding significant differences.)

With respect to intelligence, again the figures are very clear. The only test which does not show any declines after the operation is the Wechsler Performance scale; the Verbal scale, the Full scale, and the Porteus Mazes test all show the predicted decline at a highly significant level. Certain points ought to be borne in mind here, however. It is somewhat artificial to divorce the cognitive functions from personality as a whole, and the fact that the ratio of verbal to non-verbal performance on intelligence tests is a good measure of introversion (Himmelweit, 1945) shows the close relation which obtains between temperament and intelligence. The

TABLE XLVI

CHANGES AFTER LEUCOTOMY: CRITICAL RATIOS

	3 months	9 months
(2) *Extraversion-Introversion*		
(a) Speed/Accuracy ratio	1·10	1·75
(b) Intropunitiveness	2·53	3·34
(c) Sex humour liking	Significant *	Significant *
(d) Verbal/non-verbal Intelligence test	Significant *	Significant *
(e) Persistence	2·82	2·42
(f) Preoccupation with past	Significant *	Significant *

* Data in original significant but not expressed in terms of C.R.

differential decline here found—marked with respect to verbal intelligence, non-existent with respect to performance—is exactly what would have been predicted on the basis of Petrie's second hypothesis. The Porteus test also involves personality factors outside the purely cognitive field; according to hypothesis (2) speed and accuracy on this test should change after the operation, and

TABLE XLVII

CHANGES AFTER LEUCOTOMY: CRITICAL RATIOS

	3 months	9 months
(3) *Intelligence*		
(a) Wechsler Verbal	4·81	3·09
(b) Wechsler Performance	0·24	1·04 (improved)
(c) Wechsler Full Scale	4·02	2·23
(d) Porteus Mazes	3·14	1·67

indeed both changes are observed (C.R.s 2·47 and 3·25 respectively for the three months' retest). No figures are given for the Binet Proverbs test, but qualitative observation of responses leaves little doubt of considerable deterioration in ability to generalize.

These three tables then verify in almost every detail the prediction made, and suggest very strongly that in this type of patient a marked change takes place with respect to his position on the three dimensions of personality involved. Much additional information is given in Petrie's book which supports this conclusion, but we have no space to discuss it in any greater detail. Instead, we must now turn to the changes which follow after the open Rostral type of operation.

These changes are summarized in Table XLVIII; they are in the same direction as those reported in connection with the Standard operation, and most of them will be seen to be significant. Affecting any direct comparison is the fact that the number of patients submitted to the two types of operation is unequal; it will be remembered that 20 patients had the Standard operation done, while only 15 had the Rostral operation done. When this qualification is borne in mind, there remains little doubt that the non-cognitive changes observed after the Rostral operation are identical in direction, but smaller in extent, compared with the changes observed after the Standard operation. Thus hypothesis (4) is seen to be verified, and in so far as the results are relevant to hypotheses (1) and (2) they must be regarded in the nature of a replication of the first experiment, thus establishing our faith in the reproducibility of these results on a much firmer basis.

TABLE XLVIII

CHANGES AFTER ROSTRAL LEUCOTOMY: CRITICAL RATIOS

(1) *Neuroticism*
    (a) Body sway suggestibility   2·27
    (b) Manual dexterity   2·64
    (c) Smoothness of work curves   N.S.
    (d) Self-rating scale   2·93
    (e) Tempo of handwriting   4·67
    (f) Disposition-rigidity   1·85

(2) *Extraversion-Introversion*
    (a) Speed/Accuracy ratio   N.S.
    (b) Intropunitiveness   2·07
    (c) Sex humour liking   Significant *
    (d) Verbal/Non-verbal Intelligence test   N.S.
    (e) Persistence   N.S.
    (f) Preoccupation with past   Significant *

(3) *Intelligence*
    (a) Wechsler Verbal   1·12
    (b) Wechsler Performance   1·65
    (c) Wechsler Full Scale   1·21
    (d) Porteus Mazes   0·33

* Data in original significant but not expressed in terms of C.R.

This confirmation only applies to the non-cognitive changes, i.e. to changes along the dimensions of neuroticism and extraversion-introversion. Changes in intelligence level do not follow the pattern observed after Standard operations; the obvious loss found in patients operated on according to the Standard procedure is absent in patients operated on according to the Rostral procedure. This result argues in favour of a specific location hypothesis with respect to certain aspects of intellectual functioning, and may thus explain the contradictory reports on intellectual after-effects of leucotomy which have characterized the literature (Crown, 1951). While this finding thus opens up exciting new research prospects, it is not intimately connected with our main theme, and will not therefore be pursued further.

One way of illustrating the fact that in the cognitive field the effects of the two operations are dissimilar, while in the non-cognitive field they are similar, is to calculate correlation coefficients between the critical ratios of the differences in test scores following on the two operations. Comparing the first Standard operation retest with the Rostral operation retest, the correlations for cognitive and non-cognitive test C.R.s are respectively $-$ ·400 and $+$ ·211; comparing the second Standard operation retest with the Rostral operation retest, the correlations are $-$ ·143 and $+$ ·369 respectively.[1] Thus after the longer period the changes in temperament and character had become increasingly similar in the two operations, while the dissimilarities between the cognitive after-effects on the two operations had decreased. (It is quite justifiable to use C.R.s in this fashion, although the number of patients in the two groups is different.)

We may now turn to the fifth hypothesis, which used the obvious differences between an open and a closed operation to predict greater variability of after-effects in the closed operation. To investigate this hypothesis, the S.D.s of the differences in tests on which significant changes were found after both types of operation were compared. The results favour the hypothesis strongly with respect to measures of introversion-extraversion, but are ambiguous with respect to measures of neuroticism. We can only regard this hypothesis as partially confirmed, therefore, and must await a repetition of the experiment, possibly with larger numbers of

---

[1] The number of tests involved in these correlations is 19 and 32 respectively for the first retest, and 19 and 41 for the second retest. The other tests included are fully described in Petrie (1952).

subjects, before deciding definitely either for or against it. It should be remembered, in this connection, that while Meyer (1949, 1950) and others have shown that there is considerable variation in the incisions made in the Standard operation, it has not yet been ascertained that the open Rostral operation does actually lead to more precise results. Possibly part of the variation in the cut may be due to the elasticity of the brain tissue, and part to hæmorrhage and interference with blood supply. This is a complex problem, and no final conclusion can be claimed.

In summary of this research, we may say that a large number of highly significant changes has taken place after prefrontal leucotomy, a finding which in itself contrasts markedly with the usual dearth of positive results in this field. These changes are in almost every case in the direction predicted by the original hypothesis, and the results obtained with the Standard operation are duplicated by the results obtained with the Rostral operation, although in a less marked manner. This decrease in extent of change is itself in line with the original hypothesis. Variability of effects is somewhat more marked after the closed than after the open operation, but although this result is in line with the original hypothesis it cannot be regarded as firmly established. The failure to find any change on cognitive tests after the Rostral operation, although considerable changes were found after the Standard operation, was not predicted, and must await confirmation before it can be accepted as a fact.

These results, it will be remembered, were obtained on neurotic subjects, and the predictions were made with reference to neurotic subjects only. What hypotheses could one advance in the psychotic field? Clearly, changes along the dimensions of neuroticism and extraversion-introversion would only be expected to occur in a very attenuated form, if at all. Changes in intelligence level cannot be predicted in terms of our dimensional system, as cognitive processes have not yet been linked up properly with psychoticism. The main prediction, therefore, would be a shift along the psychoticism axis, in the direction of greater normality. It would be easy to translate this prediction into operational terms by reference to the tests which have been shown to define a factor of psychoticism; unfortunately no research is available in which these tests have been used. There is some evidence that our prediction with respect to neuroticism and extraversion-introversion is fulfilled, however, in Crown's study of the effects of prefrontal leucotomy on 36 psychotic patients, retested three months after the original operation (1951).

Relevant results include a slight tendency towards lower intelligence test scores. 'Post-operative changes on tests of speed-accuracy, persistence, level of aspiration, and on the Rorschach "experience type" gave no consistent support to the hypothesis that a psychotic group becomes more extraverted after leucotomy.' 'There were no significant changes after leucotomy in the scores of tests designed to measure Eysenck's . . . factor of personality organization. The general direction of the changes which occurred on tests of suggestibility, static ataxia and on the oscillation test suggested an increase in the "normality" of the group.'

When one is dealing with definite hypotheses, negative results may be as important as positive results. In terms of our conception of the psychotic axis as running orthogonal to the neuroticism and extraversion-introversion axes, it is quite easy to understand why results found on a group of neurotic patients cannot be duplicated on a group of psychotic patients; indeed, any other result would have thrown doubt on the general theory. Similarly, we may add to our positive forecast regarding the shift of psychotic patients on the psychoticism axis a negative one, viz. that no such shift would take place in neurotic patients. Both predictions are easy to test, and refutation or verification should only be a matter of time.

(2) *The Employability of Mental Defectives*

The work here described was undertaken to study the employability of mental defectives; this severely practical aim has theoretical implications of great importance, however, which were clearly brought out by the two investigators, J. Tizard and N. O'Connor, in a series of papers describing their investigation (1950a, 1950b, 1950c, 1951, Tizard, 1951, O'Connor, 1951). The present account is concerned only with that section of their data which is relevant to our general hypothesis of a 'neuroticism' factor; for more detailed descriptions the reader is referred to the papers quoted above.

It is widely believed that mental defectives, certified as such and segregated in special institutions, are characterized by I.Q.s well below the somewhat arbitary but widely accepted limit of 70 originally suggested by Terman. Some writers have suggested lower limits than this, and most authorities would consider that factors other than the I.Q. should be considered in certification;

however, it is widely agreed that although individuals having I.Q.s of over 70 may occasionally be certified, only very exceptional circumstances would justify such a step. This general picture is not in agreement with results obtained on 104 high-grade institutionalized male mental defectives, who were given 5 tests of general intelligence. The tests used, together with the mean I.Q.s obtained by the group, are given in Table XLIX; it will be seen quite clearly that the average level of ability of this group is represented by an I.Q. level of about 75. Thus the average score of this group is well above what one would normally have expected to be the maximum score. Indeed, scores as high as I.Q. 120 and above were recorded by isolated individuals on the Koh's Block Design test, the Binet Vocabulary test, and the Porteus Mazes test!

TABLE XLIX

Test	Mean I.Q.
Koh's Block Design, Alexander Version	75
Progressive Matrices, 1938, untimed	75
Binet Vocabulary Test	71
Porteus Mazes Test, Vineland Revision	83
Cattell Non-Verbal Test, Form I.B.*	73

* S.D. adjusted to 16 from 25 as given by Cattell, so as to make the results comparable with other tests.

Several different interpretations are possible of these data. Certification may be at fault, in not giving sufficient weight to test results, and particularly by relying on one single test (Binet vocabulary) to the exclusion of other tests less subject to environmental influences. Indeed, it might plausibly be argued that the assessment of an individual's intelligence should never be undertaken on the basis of a single test, but that a battery of tests, administered and interpreted by an expert in diagnostic testing, constitutes the only safe basis for such an assessment. Even if we assume that the original testing was carried out competently, and that the average I.Q. of our group at that time was around the 50 level, the statistical fact of regression (assuming a correlation of about ·50 between original test and retest—a figure which is more likely to be an overestimate than an underestimate, in view of the low observed intercorrealtions of the five tests in Table XLIX) would have caused the average to rise considerably in the years intervening between the original and the final testing. Disregard of the facts of

regression in assessing intellectual status and development is undoubtedly a potent cause of aberrant I.Q. values in samples of
high-grade mental defectives.

However, in addition to these two possible explanations of the
rather puzzling facts reported by Tizard, we must consider the
possibility that certification is carried out on the basis, not merely
of intellectual defect, but of a combination of mental defect and
neuroticism. The child that is merely dull, with an I.Q. of 60 or
65, may easily escape certification; the child that is less dull, but is
also suffering from emotional instability, is far more likely to be
found an unbearable nuisance by Society, and to be certified as a
mental defective. On this hypothesis, 'mental deficiency' of high-
grade defectives would be regarded as a combination of intellectual
deficit and emotional instability, weighted differently by different
certifying officers. High emotional stability could then counter-
balance a low I.Q., while low stability would offset even a
moderately high I.Q.

On the basis of these considerations one would be able to make
two predictions regarding the employability of high-grade defectives. The first prediction would be that they would be rather
variable with respect to neuroticism, the second that neuroticism
would play a more important part than intelligence in their success
or failure to adjust successfully to their employment. One further
prediction may be made, namely that neuroticism in defectives can
be measured objectively with the same tests used with normals.
These three predictions, or hypotheses, form an interlocking system
which can easily be tested empirically.

The first hypothesis to be tested is clearly the one related to the
applicability to defectives of the tests of neuroticism found to be
valid in normals. The subjects used in this study were 104 high-
grade mental defectives; they were consecutive admissions to
Darenth Park, with cases with physical handicaps, or with I.Q.s
below 50 excluded. Mean age was 21 years, with an S.D. of 4·6.
The following tests of neuroticism were used: (1) Body Sway test of
Suggestibility; (2) Heath Rail Walking test; (3) Manual Dexterity
(U.S.E.S. tests M and N); (4) Finger Dexterity (U.S.E.S. tests O
and P); (5) Speed on the Track Tracer test. Also included was a
measure of intelligence, namely the Matrices test. In addition to
these tests, a four-point rating of stability was used, based on the
social behaviour of the defectives tested. Each subject was rated by
three judges, a psychiatrist and two psychologists, who were equally

familiar with the subjects. Intercorrelations of judges' ratings averaged ·6; a combined rating was obtained in which complete agreement of the three judges was required. The four points of the rating scale were defined in detail (O'Connor, 1951); briefly they were: (1) Markedly stable, (2) Stable but immature, (3) Rather unstable, (4) Markedly unstable. Numbers of defectives in these four categories were respectively 45, 15, 29, and 15.

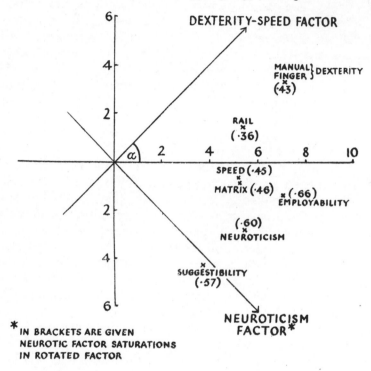

Figure 34

Intercorrelations of tests and rating are given in Table L, together with factor saturations for two factors. These are centroid factors, and as the diagram shown in Figure 34 reveals, require rotation before they can be considered meaningful. After rotation through angle alpha, it can be seen quite clearly that the major factor is one of neuroticism, defined by the neuroticism rating and the suggestibility test. The other neuroticism tests also have reasonable saturations (manual and finger dexterity, speed, and rail walking), and intelligence will be seen to correlate with neuroti-

TABLE L

	1	2	3	4	5	6	7	8	Centroid Factor Saturations I	Centroid Factor Saturations II	Neuroticism Factors Rotated
(1) Neuroticism Rating	( )	·32	·30	·24	·29	·23	·20	·47	·52	−·28	·60
(2) Body Sway Suggestibility		( )	·09	·20	·20	·24	·24	·33	·40	−·40	·57
(3) Rail Walking Test			( )	·45	·44	·20	·22	·44	·55	·19	·36
(4) Manual Dexterity				( )	·66	·35	·40	·45	·74	·33	·43
(5) Finger Dexterity					( )	·39	·37	·39	·74	·32	·43
(6) Matrices (I.Q.)						( )	·32	·34	·52	−·07	·46
(7) Speed-Track Tracer							( )	·28	·51	−·05	·45
(8) Employability Criterion *								( )	·72	−·12	·66
(9) Persistence—Leg	−·01	·14	·02	·06	·04	·05	·05	·00			
(10) Persistence—Dynamometer	·21	·00	·04	·08	·01	−·03	·06	−·04			

* Employability Criterion: 53·3 per cent of total variance accounted for by 2 factors.

cism to the extent of ·46. This is slightly higher than the value given for the correlation between intelligence and neuroticism in normal groups, but the difference is not significant, and may be due to sampling errors. The second factor is not to be regarded as a pure factor, but appears to be loaded largely with tests requiring muscular co-ordination—rail walking, manual and finger dexterity, speed test. The possibility that such a factor may exist cannot of course be gainsaid; it is merely doubted whether it can justifiably be postulated on the basis of these results. It is of interest, however, that suggestibility has no loading on this factor; thus it does not appear that lack of muscular co-ordination is responsible for body sway in the suggestibility test.

We may conclude then that our hypothesis regarding the usefulness of tests validated on intellectually normal groups for the measurement of neuroticism in defectives may be regarded as strongly supported. An interesting exception to this statement is the persistence test, which was also applied to the 104 defectives. This test was given in two forms, the leg persistence test, in which the subject is required to hold out his leg unsupported as long as he can, and the dynamometer test, in which he is required to hold a dynamometer grip at 2/3 maximum pull for as long as he can. This type of test had always given good results with intellectually normal subjects in differentiating the neurotic from the normal subjects. With the defectives, however, discrimination was very poor; when the two tests were included with the others in Table L and the combined Table factor analysed the saturations of the persistence tests, while in the right direction, were below the ·20 level. This curious tendency of persistence tests not to give acceptable results with mental defectives had already been noted previously (Eysenck, 1947; Brady, 1948), and an explanation of this odd phenomenon would be of great interest. It illustrates to perfection the truth of the often neglected statement that while we may measure such traits as suggestibility, persistence, and intelligence in isolation, the assumption of linear regression, independence, and normal distribution are liable to fail us once we go beyond the middle range, and deal with the extremes of the distribution.

We must now turn to our other hypotheses, viz. those dealing with the employability of defectives. Between nine months and a year following the testing of the 104 defectives, their work success, or employability, was estimated by a Social Worker on the basis of the scales shown in Table LI.

TABLE LI

	Rating Scale	N
Conspicuous all-round success on daily licence	7	6
Settled down well in first job in daily licence	6	13
Satisfactory on daily licence after not more than two replacements	5	17
Settled on daily licence after several trials	4	30
Failed consistently on daily licence	3	16
Successful in institution work, but unlikely to be considered for licence	2	14
Unsuccessful in Institution workshop	1	8

This employability criterion was incorporated in Table XLIX, and it will be seen from Figure 33 that it had a factor saturation for neuroticism of ·66, as well as a slight correlation with the motor co-ordination factor (·31). It appears, then, that our original hypothesis is borne out by the results; employability of mental defectives is forecast with considerable accuracy by neuroticism tests. Employability is forecast by both factors in combination to the extent of a correlation of ·73. Considering the unreliability of the criterion (no data are available on this, but a general knowledge of the many chance factors entering into a person's success in employment under the general conditions of this experiment suggests an upper bound to reliability in the neighbourhood of ·8) this must be regarded as a remarkable success. The conclusion seems justified that neuroticism is a very important factor in the employability of defectives. It will be seen from Table L that the influence of intelligence on employability is very much less important; the correlation between employability and score on the Matrices test is only ·34, so that only about one-fourth as much predictive power is given by intelligence tests as by neuroticism tests.

The social consequences of these findings are considerable. It will be remembered that this group of 104 defectives was not selected but constituted successive admissions of physically not handicapped persons with I.Q.s over 50. Two-thirds of this group was suitable for employment in the community, at wages averaging £4 10s. od., and going up to £7 on occasions. A further 29 per cent were suitable for institution employment. Only 8 per cent were unemployable custodial cases. Both society and the defectives themselves would benefit from the introduction of routine testing along the lines suggested of all high-grade defectives, and a vigorous policy of licensing and work-placement. It hardly needs emphasizing, however, that all such work should be supervised and controlled by fully qualified clinical psychologists, well acquainted with the problems, both psychological and statistical, which arise in mental testing, and specially trained in the administration of objective performance tests of personality. Untold harm could be done by the use of psychological tests in unskilled hands; indeed it is only too obvious that the indiscriminate use of such tests as the Binet by those whose background training has not included a considerable amount of mental testing and statistics is doing much harm to the whole mental testing movement. How much greater could be the harm resulting from the indiscriminate use of the much more complex and difficult tests used in personality measurement!

(3) Work Adjustment of Unskilled Factory Workers

Among the fields studied by industrial psychologists, those of productivity and work adjustment are recognized to be of paramount importance. Most of the published work has dealt with the relation of abilities to those concepts. A pioneer study was carried out by Markowe, Heron, and Barker, respectively a psychiatrist, a psychologist, and an economist, into the relationship obtaining between productivity and work adjustment on the one hand, and various temperament and character traits on the other. Their work is of particular interest as it extends the type of research described in this book to unskilled factory workers, a group not previously investigated. It is natural that in the brief summary of their work here given, most stress will be laid on the psychometric aspects, so that for the majority of the facts and calculations mentioned we are indebted to Alastair Heron, whose own account of the experiment should be consulted for further details (1951).

The research was carried out in the main factory of a co-ordinated group of manufacturing and trading firms in the chemical and light engineering industry manufacturing a range of lead-acid accumulators. The medical member of the team was the first to make direct contact with the firm, and spent several months 'working his way' round the various factory departments. This preliminary period of getting acquainted constituted an indispensable part of the general approach. Having ensured general co-operation from management, and from worker representatives through the Works Committee, meetings were held with selected officials, including the Chief Shop Steward, to discuss the research project.

Meetings were also held with the men who constituted the experimental group, and an outline given of the aims and objects of the investigation.

The experimental group selected consisted of grid-casters in the Moulding Department. No selection took place; all eighty-five men who constituted the entire population of grid-casters were approached. Of these, one refused to co-operate, one was transferred to another factory, and three left of their own accord before the conclusion of the project. Thus the experimental group consisted of eighty persons. These were subjected to a variety of psychiatric, medical, and psychological procedures.

(1) Height, weight, vision and hæmoglobin measurements were made routinely, as were also lumbar pull dynamometer tests and the Schneider test of cardio-vascular efficiency. Clinical examination of special systems was performed when indicated or requested.

(2) A medical and psychiatric interview was carried out by the psychiatrist, and ratings made on the basis of this interview and the measures described under (1) combined for: (a) Past health, (b) Recent mental health, and (c) Recent physical health, using 4-point scales; also rated were thirteen personality traits, on 3-point scales. These health and personality ratings were made by the psychiatrist quite independently, without the aid of supervisors' ratings, productivity data, or absenteeism records.

(3) Most of the psychological tests given have already been discussed in connection with other researches. They included the following tests of intellectual ability: The Dominoes test, which is probably the purest 'g' test yet devised, the U.S.E.S. Paper Form Board, the Mill Hill Vocabulary test, and a letter series test. Tests of temperament used were the following: Crown Word Connection List, Hand Dynamometer persistence, Cattell's '237' test of perseveration, a 'Worries' inventory, the U.S.E.S. Peg and Finger Boards, the Track Tracer, Static Ataxia, Leg Persistence, an 'Annoyances' inventory, an 'Interests' inventory, the Rees-Eysenck Index of Body Build, a 'Food Dislikes' inventory, and a Level of Aspiration test. An individual Rorschach test was also administered, but results have not been analysed in conjunction with the other tests and will not be discussed here. Total time of administration was in excess of two hours per subject.

Having described the predicting variables, we must now turn to the predicted variables, i.e. the criteria for this particular research. It is well known that in industry good criteria are hard to find, and much research was devoted to finding reliable and valid criteria of Work Adjustment and of Productivity.

(1) Work Adjustment. A panel of six raters was established, consisting of the foreman, a former chargehand now in the departmental office and in daily contact with all the men, and the four chargehands, who rotate independently of the three piecework shifts worked by the men. Two sets of ratings were obtained from the raters, an interval of five weeks elapsing between the two ratings. The method used is rather original, and is fully described by Heron (1951).

'Will you please listen carefully to the explanation which I read to each of the six supervisors who are taking part in this section of the research project.

'The object of this exercise is to classify the eighty men whom we have seen in the Moulding Department with respect to their *apparent adjustment to the total demands of the job-situation.*

'It is important to make it quite clear from the outset, first of all, that these classifications will remain strictly confidential to the members of the Team; and secondly, that we do NOT want a rating which is based solely or mainly on a man's rate of production as compared with others.

'In front of you are three trays; in my hand is a set of cards, each card bearing the name and clock number of one of the eighty men who are taking part in the research.

'In a few moments I shall place a large card at the head of each tray, and after giving you an opportunity to read what they say, and to observe that the two *side* ones describe *extremely* different people, I shall start handing you one small card at a time. If you feel that the man whose name and clock number is on the card is correctly described by EITHER of the two *side* trays, then place his card in that tray. If you feel that the description is too extreme for that particular man, or if you don't know him well enough, then drop his card in the CENTRE tray, marked 'Average'. On this first sorting, there will be very many more in the *centre* tray than in the two side ones put together. Is that clear?'

(PAUSE. ANSWER ANY QUESTIONS.)

(PLACE LARGE CARDS AT HEAD OF TRAYS. PAUSE TO LET HIM STUDY THE DESCRIPTIONS. ANSWER ANY QUESTIONS.)

'I shall hand you a fresh card every 5 seconds, like this.'

(DEMONSTRATE WITH THREE BLANKS.)

'Right, let's begin, and keep up a steady pace.'

(When the first sorting is complete, take the cards from the 'VERY WELL-ADJUSTED' tray and if they exceed TEN in number, ask the rater to look through them, and to pick out 'the *best* 8 or 10'. Place rejects in centre tray; repeat for 'BADLY-ADJUSTED' if necessary, asking him to pick out 'the *worst* 8 or 10'. Now place second pair of large cards in side trays, take pack from *centre* tray in hands and say:)

'Now we are going to sort out the cards of the *average* men. The procedure will be the same as before, except that this time as the end trays are *not* such extreme descriptions, we can expect to have about a *quarter* of the cards in each of them, and about half in the middle tray. Right?'

(REPEAT SORTING PROCEDURE.)

(When the second sorting is complete, adjust the contents of the side trays to about 14–20 cards each if possible, but DO NOT FORCE AN INCREASE OR DECREASE against the rater's selection if he seems satisfied.)

MATERIAL ON LARGE CARDS

Rating

I	Thoroughly settled down
	Never have to worry about him
	No trouble to me at all
	Well-adjusted to the job

⎫
⎬ First two cards in end trays.
⎭

5	Has never really settled down
	Always having to keep him in mind
	One of my headaches
	Badly-adjusted to the job
	Has settled down *better* than average

2
    Seldom need to worry about him
    Not much trouble to me

    Fairly-well adjusted to the job
                                    Second two
                                    cards in
                                    end trays.
    Has settled down *less* well than average
    Quite often have to keep him in mind

4
    Is quite some trouble to me
    Not very well adjusted to the job

3
    AVERAGE
                                      (Used in
                                    middle tray
                                    on both
                                    sortings.)

Product-moment correlations were calculated between each pair of raters on each occasion, as well as between the ratings of each rater from one occasion to the other. The average inter-correlation between the six raters was ·483, indicating a validity of the average rating of approximately ·90 (Eysenck, 1939). The average reliability of the raters was ·781. A factor analysis of the table of intercorrelations was carried out, yielding a single general factor which accounted for 50·5 per cent of the variance, and leaving no residuals greater than the S.E. of a zero correlation. The total variance may therefore be apportioned as follows: Com-munality = 50·5 per cent, Specificity = 27·6 per cent, Unreli-ability = 21·9 per cent. In view of the prominence of one general factor in these ratings, the twelve ratings for each individual rated were combined into a single average rating, which constitutes the Work Adjustment Rating defined as the measure of concern caused to the supervisors by the worker.

(2) Productivity. A performance index was used, in which the number of grids produced, multiplied by the agreed rate of pro-duction expressed as a number of 'standard minutes' per hundred, is divided by the actual clock minutes worked, thus showing the value of a worker's time in terms of his actual production. Various

calculations showed that this index, which had been in use for a long time in connection with a wage incentive system, could be regarded as a reasonable one, within the limits set to high individual production rates by the general feeling of solidarity in the workshop. As is well known, fear of 'overproduction' resulting in unemployment, opposition to high taxation, which affects high earnings due to high production, and tensions created by out-producing less able members of the group all tend to impose a level of uniformity on production which keeps it below the maximum possible without undue exertion. All variations in productivity are therefore considerably attentuated, and much smaller than they would be if each individual were working 'full out'. The difficulties introduced into the analysis by these extraneous factors are likely to reduce any correlations which might be found between productivity and other factors almost to vanishing point.

Product-moment intercorrelations were calculated between all the variables. In view of the fact that age correlated significantly with several of the variables, partial correlations were calculated and the resulting table of correlations (with age partialled out) submitted to a factorial analysis. The results of the centroid analysis are given in Table LII, together with the rotated solution.[1] To facilitate interpretation, a diagram has been prepared of the position of the various tests on the plane formed by factors I and II (Figure 35). It will be seen that factor I is characterized by the four intelligence tests (Dominoes, Letter Series, Vocabulary, and Paper Form Board), and by two speeds of writing tests, which in a group of this composition are known to correlate quite highly with intelligence. No other test has a high positive correlation with this factor, which is clearly identifiable with intelligence.[2]

The second factor is characterized by all those tests which had been found previously to be good measures of neuroticism: many worries, many annoyances, high static ataxia, poor persistence (on both tests), many food aversions, neurotic score on Word Connection List, poor mental health rating. Poor job adjustment also has a projection on this factor, which encourages us to interpret it with a fair measure of confidence as neuroticism. It should be

[1] The rotated solution shown here differs slightly from that given by Heron himself. This difference, however, is not material to the argument.

[2] The Word Connection List, a measure of neuroticism, has a high negative saturation in intelligence in this analysis. Previous work has not disclosed any reason for this surprisingly high correlation.

TABLE LII

| No. | Variable | Scoring Direction | Factor Loadings ||||||||
| | | | Unrotated |||| After Rotation ||||
			k_1	k_2	k_3	k_4	I	II	III	IV
1	Dominoes	High score	62	−21	34	−32	81	00	−01	−01
2	Paper Form Board	" "	47	06	32	17	55	09	13	16
3	Vocabulary	" "	39	−21	21	−30	56	−05	01	−11
4	Writing '237' and reversed (total)	" "	59	25	42	−21	65	14	30	30
5	Grip	Strong	26	26	−04	01	11	−09	15	31
6	Finger Dexterity	High score	35	27	24	25	21	21	03	47
7	Track Tracer, first time	Fast	35	11	00	31	13	01	−16	43
8	Manual Dexterity	High score	21	33	05	27	00	09	07	46
9	Absolute Goal Discrepancy	Low	17	−06	27	27	16	27	−20	20
10	Hand Persistence	Short	−18	45	21	−17	−10	21	51	04
11	Leg Persistence	"	−23	42	17	−17	−15	18	48	00
12	Static Ataxia	High	−11	08	38	20	−02	45	00	07
13	Word Connection List	High 'neurotic' score	−48	48	−09	10	−56	12	36	10
14	Annoyances	Many	−21	−12	35	18	−06	43	−12	−11
15	Worries	Many	−23	02	50	−12	07	47	18	−23
16	Interests	Many	−28	−17	31	24	−13	44	−20	−13
17	Track Tracer, choice	Speed	−20	−19	09	27	−17	22	−27	−06
18	Approach to timed test	Quick	26	27	03	29	03	03	07	41
19	Index of Body Build	Short/round	−07	−03	21	23	−04	29	−12	06
20	Psychiatric rating of M. Health	Good	08	−16	22	26	10	24	−26	09
21	Productivity	High	24	26	04	19	06	05	05	39
22	Supervisors' ratings, 'job adjustment'	Poor	−36	−22	35	−11	−03	36	00	−42
23	Letter Series	High score	56	−27	31	−26	74	00	−08	−03
24	Writing S-S-SS (Total)	High score	47	24	27	−19	49	05	28	26
25	Food Aversions	Many	−17	35	15	−23	−07	11	45	−05

pointed out, however, that there are a few anomalous findings which contradict previous work, and which can at the moment only be ascribed to the fact that this group is very different in composition and background to any of those hitherto studied. Thus

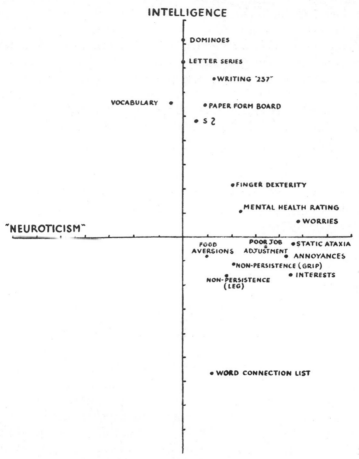

Figure 35.—Note: some items near origin omitted

the item 'Many interests' has a positive correlation with neuroticism; eurymorphic body-build, and good finger dexterity, also show positive correlations with neuroticism, although at such a low level that sampling errors might be responsible for these findings. However, it would not be wise to dismiss findings contrary to hypothesis in any cavalier manner, and it may even be one of the most fruitful ways 'of developing our knowledge in this field to follow up discrepant results and attempt to find an explanation for them.

The third factor is much more difficult to identify, although the fact that one pole is characterized by low persistence, many food aversions, high score on the Word Connection List, and speed of writing suggests that possibly we may here be dealing with the extraversion-introversion factor, in somewhat attenuated form. The tests mentioned characterize the prototype of the extravert, the hysteric, as opposed to the prototype of the introvert, the dysthymic, and although not much reliance can be placed on this identification it is well in line with previous work, although here again by no means all the individual tests can be said to confirm the suggestion made.

Factor four is rather easier to identify; it is characterized essentially by manual and finger dexterity, speed in carrying out a co-ordination test, strong grip, speed in writing, and other tests indicative of speed and co-ordination. In a job depending so much on motor co-ordination, it is perhaps small wonder that 'poor job adjustment' is negatively correlated with this factor, and 'high productivity' positively.

Certain interesting features of Table LII may be worthy of comment. It will be seen that the item: 'Psychiatric rating of mental health' is almost completely uncorrelated with any other item, and has only negligible factor saturations. Its saturation on the neuroticism factor is probably too small to be significant, but in so far as attention may be paid to it its direction will be seen to be contrary to expectation: individuals with a 'good' rating on mental health will be found to have high neuroticism scores on the whole, and vice versa. This somewhat surprising result is unlikely to be due to deficiencies in the examining psychiatrist; it may with some confidence be said to be the result of the very unusual situation in which the ratings were made. In the normal clinical situation, the psychiatrist is sought out by the patient, who readily confides in him. In addition, the psychiatrist has available data concerning the work history of the patient, and other information which is helpful to him. In the experiment under discussion, the psychiatrist requests the subject to see him, thus arousing suspicion and perhaps hostility in a working-class population not entirely oblivious of periods of unemployment and lay-offs, when any personal deficiency was something to be hidden from the employer or what might be considered his representatives. Also, records of past work-history and the like would of course have contaminated the psychiatrist's rating, which was to be correlated with items of this very kind, and consequently no information on these points was made available to him. It is not surprising that under these conditions, so different from those under which he is accustomed to exercise his skill, the psychiatrist's rating contributed little to the prediction of either criterion, or to the measurement of any factor.

The supervisor's rating of 'poor job adjustment', on the other hand, shows high saturations on the neuroticism factor (in the expected direction), and also on the motor speed factor. Productivity shows high saturations only with the motor speed factor. It is interesting that intelligence has no saturations of any size on either of the two criteria; it is perhaps less surprising that introversion-extraversion should be neutral with respect to work adjustment and efficiency.

The data quoted above show that (1) personality tests of the type advocated in this book can be given effectively in an industrial situation; (2) they show patterns of personality organization in unskilled workers very similar to the patterns shown by other groups hiterto studied; (3) they are applicable in conditions which severely restrict the proper functioning of psychiatrists; (4) they have a certain validity in predicting work adjustment and efficiency, even under conditions which make the assessment of these two criteria rather difficult.

In support of points (1) and (2), another study may be mentioned which was carried out on yet anotlier group of subjects differing in many important respects from those studied previously. As part of an enquiry into miners' rheumatism, Miss Braithwait administered the following five tests of neuroticism to a group of colliery workers, consisting of 84 miners, 45 maintenance workers and 45 office-workers: (1) Word Connection List; (2) Maudsley Medical Questionnaire; (3) Leg persistence test; (4) Annoyances test; (5) Finger dexterity test. These tests were intercorrelated by Alastair Heron, and a factorial analysis performed which resulted in one general factor. The data are given in Table LIII; it will be seen that all the saturations are positive and in the expected direction; the saturation of the persistence test is as high as ·519, that of the Maudsley Medical Questionnaire ·419, while the Annoyances test has the lowest discriminatory power (·225). Multiple R, indicating the accuracy with which these five tests, suitably weighted, would measure the general factor they define, is ·686; it must be realized, of course, that this value is subject to shrinkage due to the well-known tendency of R to capitalize on chance errors of measurement. Nevertheless, the results strongly support the view that the tests used measure one underlying factor of neuroticism, even in a group of subjects very unusual in psychological enquiries.

TABLE LIII

N = 174   S.E. zero r = ·076

		1	2	3	4	5	k_1	$k_1{}^2$
1	r Residuals			+·128 −·012	+·086 −·087	+·040 −·035	+·148 +·064	·333	·111
2	r Residuals				+·221 +·004	+·139 +·045	+·013 −·092	·419	·176
3	r Residuals					+·103 −·014	+·156 +·026	·519	·269
4	r Residuals						−·009 −·065	·225	·051
5								·251	·063

Key: 1. Word Connection List
2. Maudsley Medical Questionnaire
3. Leg Persistence Poor
4. Many Annoyances
5. Poor Finger Dexterity

$R_{12345 \cdot \text{FACTOR}}$ = ·686

(4) Student and Nurses' Selection

In a review of the literature on student selection by means of psychological tests, Eysenck (1947c) pointed out the promising start which had been made by Munroe (1945) and others in attempting to use personality tests of a non-cognitive kind to forecast success at University, and maintained that the more widespread use of tests of this type would add considerably to the usefulness of student selection. In particular, he stressed the relevance of the concept of neuroticism as applied in this field, the hypothesis being that students with a high score on neuroticism would be less likely to succeed than students with a low score, and of comparable intelligence. Some experimental efforts have been made to investigate this hypothesis, and although results obtained so far are less direct and less convincing than those related to other hypotheses discussed in this chapter, they are presented here for the sake of completeness.

The first study to be mentioned was carried out by Petrie (1948) on 49 male and 8 female students at a Medical School. The necessity of using group tests eliminated *ab initio* most of those tests which in the past had been found to be good measures of neuroticism, and left three measures which with some misgivings were applied to the students. These three measures were: (1) Word Connection List, (2) Maudsley Medical Questionnaire, and (3) the Index of Inaccuracy. This index, originally used as a measure of neuroticism by Himmelweit (1950), was calculated by dividing the number of false answers in all the cognitive tests by the total number of answers attempted, and was hypothesized to be correlated with neuroticism in terms of the theory that emotional maladjustment interferes with smooth mental functioning. Correlations between the Index of Accuracy and the two other tests were significantly positive for the students investigated ($r = \cdot43$ and $\cdot40$ respectively), and we may therefore regard the hypothesis that the Index of Inaccuracy is a measure of neuroticism as supported. In addition to these three neuroticism tests, several cognitive tests were given, including tests of Vocabulary, classification, rote memory, sentence completion, fluency, decoding, and form perception. (The fluency test might of course also be regarded as a personality test, in view of the fact that low fluency has been shown to correlate with neuroticism (Eysenck, 1947) and other traits.)

To obtain a criterion superior to the usual one of examination results, two independent judges were chosen by the Dean, who rated the students on a five-point scale with respect to their medical ability. The combined rating was found to have a reliability of $\cdot80$. Correlations of the neuroticism measures with the rating were all in the expected direction, but disappointingly low. For the two verbal tests (Maudsley Medical Questionnaire and Word Connection List) correlations were $-\cdot16$ and $-\cdot08$ respectively; for the Index of Inaccuracy the correlation was $-\cdot27$, and for the Fluency test it was $\cdot29$. Except for the latter two tests, the correlations are too low to be of any practical use. A multiple R of $\cdot63$ was found from the battery as a whole, excluding sentence completion and Word Connection List; this R is of course a slight overestimate in view of the well-known fact that multiple R tends to capitalize on chance errors. However, later work done with these tests has shown that the correlations observed in this sample are typical of other groups as well, and that a predictive accuracy of between ·5 and ·6 can easily be reached. Given the present selection ratio obtaining in medical schools, it can be shown that by the use of tests the failure rate could easily be reduced from its present level of 18 per cent to between 1 and 2 per cent. Similarly, the number of students rated 'very good' could be increased from the present level of 10 per cent to between 30 and 40 per cent. While non-cognitive tests did not contribute to any considerable extent to this prediction, the discovery that the Index of Inaccuracy is a measure of neuroticism must be counted as a valuable addition to our knowledge of the operational meaning of this term.

Another attempt to use non-cognitive tests was made by Himmelweit (1950, 1951), though on a rather larger scale. This study is of particular interest because it contains a comparison in predictive accuracy between several different types of information, such as interviews, cognitive tests, temperament tests, biographical information, and achievement tests. In scope and thoroughness, this study is without doubt the outstanding British contribution to the experimental investigation of student selection.

Students tested were first of all submitted to the usual admission procedure, which consisted of an interview, a general essay paper, and a paper on paraphrase and précis. Interviews were conducted by a number of Interviewing Boards, consisting of members of the Academic Staff. According to the memorandum circulated to the Boards the objectives of the interview were as follows:

(1) 'The interview is to be considered as an independent factor to be subsequently correlated with the candidate's paper qualifications and Entrance Examination results. Nevertheless, it is desirable to obtain a grasp of the candidate's paper qualifications and background before the interview, so as to be able to relate the form and course of the interview to the candidate's particular circumstances.

(2) The main object of the interview is to assess the candidate's suitability to pursue a course of study at . . , special consideration being given to the following factors:

(a) General intelligence.
(b) Previous education, training and experience.
(c) Interests and motivation.
(d) Personality and character.

(3) 'Interviewing Boards are asked to make a single general assessment of the candidate's claims, not to sum up the results of separate assessments under each of the above headings.'

The Boards were asked to make the overall assessments on a nine-point scale.

Students were tested with a battery of cognitive tests, similar to that used by Petrie, but more extensive. They were also given a set of general knowledge tests, and tests measuring their aptitude in reading Tables, Charts, and Graphs. A detailed biographical questionnaire was also completed. Last, the following tests of non-cognitive personality qualities were given: (1) Shipley Inventory, Form C. (2) Ranking Rorschach test, an adaptation of the Harrower-Erickson Multiple Choice Group Rorschach described by Eysenck (1947). (3) Level of Aspiration test, in connection with a cancellation test. (4) Level of Aspiration test in connection with a decoding test. (Tests 3 and 4 are attempts to make use of the level of aspiration technique in a group situation.) (5) Speed test—decoding. (6) Speed test—cancellation. (7) Index of Inaccuracy. (8) Introversion test. (This consisted of the difference in standard scores between the vocabulary and the paper formboard test, a score which had been shown previously to be diagnostic of introversion (Himmelweit, 1945).)

The criterion against which tests, interviews, and other data were validated consisted of the Intermediate and the Finals examinations. An attempt was made to assess the reliability of these examinations, using Guilford's equation 205 (1936) in order to obtain a minimum estimate of the reliability of the constituent part measures, and using the Kuder-Richardson Formula (1937) to obtain a minimum reliability of their sum. Average estimates of examination reliability are ·74 for the Final examination, and ·80 for the Intermediate. While this is a minimum estimate, an application of Eysenck's formula for estimating the true reliability of the ratings of judges (1939) gave figures very similar to the above, which may therefore be accepted as being reasonable estimates of the true reliabilities. The papers in intermediate and final examinations were correlated for a set of 245 students, and the resulting matrix factor-analysed. A general factor, accounting for 37 per cent of the total variance, was first extracted, followed by a bipolar factor, accounting for 6 per cent of the variance, which divided the papers into two sets—those given in the intermediate, and those given in the final examination. It is clear that what is common to the two examinations is more than six times as important as what is specific to each.

This finding suggests the possibility of correlating the two examinations themselves in order to find a maximum possible prediction—it is very unlikely that a test can predict an examination better than another examination very similar to the one serving as criterion. This correlation turned out to be very slightly in excess of ·60. The lowness of this figure reflects in part the unreliability of the two examinations; when the observed correlation is corrected for attenuation, the corrected value approaches ·80, which is a better estimate of the true correlation between the two examinations, assuming both to be perfectly reliable.

Test prediction of examination results is inevitably lower than the observed inter-examination correlation, and amounts to ·46 for the intermediate examination and ·55 for the final examination ($n = 232$ for the former, and 114 for the latter).[1] Correction for lack of reliability in the criterion would raise both correlations approximately to the ·6 level, but of course this figure is of purely theoretical interest. Of more interest is the finding that, using the obtained correlations only as indicators of predictive success, it can be shown that the use of tests as selection criteria would reduce the number of failures from over 20 per cent to something like 5 per cent, under the selection conditions actually obtaining at the same time.

Having noted the general results of the testing procedure, we may now return to the non-cognitive tests. Some of these, like the Inventory and the Group Rorschach, failed to give significant correlations. The two level of aspiration tests gave results in the expected direction, i.e. showing greater failure rates among those having high aspiration scores; correlations for the Aspirations test (cancellation) and Aspiration test (decoding) were − ·20 and − ·11 (Final and Intermediate examination respectively), and − ·15 and − ·10. The Index of Inaccuracy again gave the best result, showing correlations of ·51 and ·26 with the two examinations. While because of its mode of derivation this Index correlates with the tests of ability from which it is derived, these correlations are too low to account for more than a small proportion of its

[1] Application of the regression weights derived from this sample of students to another batch gave a correlation of ·42 with final success, thus showing the usual decline in predictive accuracy associated with multiple R when applied to new groups.

predictive variance. The speed score on the decoding test gave significant prediction, while the speed score on the cancellation test failed to do so; all these correlations are too low to be of any interest.

As would have been expected from the general hypothesis linking Inaccuracy and high Level of Aspiration scores with neuroticism, these tests intercorrelate positively. The two Level of Aspiration tests intercorrelate ·47; Inaccuracy correlates ·20 and ·09 with the other two tests. While these correlations are very small, they are derived from tests which are themselves very unreliable, and if individual tests had been given higher correlations would almost certainly have been found.

We may now turn to a comparison of the test results with the interview results. In the first place, correlations of interview ratings with all tests of intelligence are insignificant; indeed, the majority are negative. If the tests are accurate measures of intelligence, the interview would appear to tend to give preference to the duller, rather than to the brighter students. In the second place, the interview shows negligible correlations with the other Entrance Examinations ($r = -$ ·02 and ·10). Thirdly, the interview predicts examination success to the completely insignificant extent of ·07. It can be seen that although the non-cognitive tests used in this investigation did not predict success with anything like the accuracy one might have hoped for, nevertheless they were markedly superior to interviewing procedures of the kind described. This failure of the interview is only one of many instances showing the impossibility of achieving reliable and valid prediction on the basis of subjective ratings, personal impressions, and clinical insight; many other examples have been discussed in an earlier chapter. However rudimentary our objective methods of personality investigation, and however difficult their application in the group situation—even now they can be said to give results superior in reliability and validity to the interview.

It should be borne in mind, in assessing the contribution of the interview, that the interviewing board had at its disposal the paper qualifications and background of the candidate. American experience has shown that these data alone would normally give predictions considerably higher than those made by the Board. It would appear, therefore, that the contribution of the interview may well be negative in sign, as well as small in extent.

If temperamental factors play a part in the achievement of

University students, it would appear even more likely that such factors would influence the work of nurses and others who are in constant contact with people of one kind or another, and whose academic achievement is only in part related to their professional proficiency. An experiment to test this hypothesis was carried out by Petrie and Powell (1950), who tested 126 nurses at one of the well-known London hospitals. Petrie paid particular attention to the question of a suitable criterion, as the choice of a criterion is of the utmost importance in all prediction testing.

A special rating scale was devised, based on available English and American scales intended for nursing and allied professions. It asked for a 5-point rating on each of 18 personality and ability traits. The rating was carried out after the nurses had been in training in the hospital for at least eighteen months. Each nurse was rated by three independent judges who knew her well. The average intercorrelation between these three judges (matron, ward sister, and sister tutor) was ·649. A *total rating* was derived for each nurse, consisting of the sum of the ratings given by the three judges on the eighteen traits.

The ratings on the eighteen traits (averaged for the three judges) were intercorrelated for the 126 nurses, and a factorial analysis was carried out. This gave evidence of two factors, accounting for 55 and 12 per cent respectively of the variance. The first factor has positive saturations throughout, and might best be described as a general factor of nursing efficiency. The second factor is bipolar and contrasts the following sets of traits:

(1) Knowledge of underlying principles of nursing practice and nursing skills.

(2) Ability to adapt these to the individual needs of the patient. Imagination; foresight; ability to anticipate requirements of new situations.

(3) Ability to rise to the occasion in emergency. Initiative; resource; ability to stand up to difficult situations.

(4) Ability to plan, organize and time duties successfully. Management of own work and others.

These four traits are clearly characterized by their close relationship to intellectual capacity and learning ability. They are contrasted with another four traits which are characterized by their relationship to social attitudes and ability to deal with other human beings. These traits are:

(1) Co-operation with other members of the ward team. Influ-

ence on associates and juniors; relationship with other members of the Staff.

(2) Satisfactory relationship with the patients. Ability to gain their co-operation. Patience; understanding; kindness and sympathy.

(3) Satisfactory attitude to patients' families and visitors to the ward. Thoughtfulness; kindness and tact; courtesy.

(4) Loyalty to the standards of the Training School and the Hospital. Co-operation with authority; ability to accept criticism.

It appears, therefore, that our hypothesis regarding two quite different types of demand being made of a good nurse is justified. One demand is that she should have enough mental ability to cope with her work; the other that she should have the kind of temperament that allows her to make the maximum use of her ability in this profession. The two sets of ratings listed above as having the highest positive and negative saturations with the bi-polar factor were summed for each nurse, and the totals, representing respectively intellectual and social relationship traits, were correlated with the tests administered to the nurses.

Correlations of the tests used with the *total rating* criterion are given in Table LIV. It will be seen that for the cognitive as well as

TABLE LIV

List of Tests and their Correlation with the Criterion: r

1. Accurate clerical observation. Minnesota Clerical Test. Number of mistakes in comparison of figures. ·325 *
2. Accurate clerical observation. Minnesota Clerical Test. Number of mistakes in comparison of names. ·309 *
3. Manual dexterity. Average score on O'Connor Tweezer Test. ·289 *
4. Persistence at a task. Productivity in word building test. ·263 *
5. Persistence at a task. Time spent in word building test. ·156
6. Kent-Shakow Performance Intelligence Test. Intelligence score. ·173 *
7. Kent-Shakow Performance Intelligence Test. Number of mistaken moves. — ·240 *
8. Non-verbal Intelligence. Penrose Pattern Perception Test. ·209 *
9. Maudsley Word Association Test. 'Neurotic' score. — ·193 *
10. Adaptation of Interest Test Pressey X–O. ·178 *
11. Adaptation of Annoyance Test Pressey X–O. — ·132
12. Verbal Intelligence. Mill Hill Vocabulary Test. ·128
13. Speed Accuracy Preference. Number of mistakes in trial on track tracer when accuracy is stressed. — ·175 *
14. Concentration Test. ·152
15. Distractibility Test. Number of mistaken answers. — ·121
16. Strength of maximum grip on the Dynamometer. ·142

* Starred correlations are significant at the 5 per cent level. Most of the others are in the predicted direction and would be significant if the one tail test were applied.

for the non-cognitive tests all the correlations are in the expected direction, and that most of them are significant. A multiple R of above ·6 was obtained from a combination of 12 of these tests. Correlations of selected tests with the 'intellectual ability' and the 'personal relationship' criteria are given in Table LV. It can be seen that some of the tests are more closely related to the 'ability' criterion, others to the 'personal relationships' criterion. For example, both the non-verbal and the verbal tests of intelligence are closely related to the ratings on 'ability', but not at all to those on 'personal relationships'. The score on the Word Connection List, which is a neuroticism test, is more highly correlated with the 'human relationships' criterion than with the 'ability' one. On the

TABLE LV

CORRELATIONS OF INTELLECTUAL 'ABILITY' AND 'PERSONAL RELATIONSHIP' TRAITS WITH SOME OF THE TESTS USED

	Intellectual Ability Traits	Personal Relationship Traits
O'Connor Tweezer. Average number on two trials	+·286	+·207
Word Building. Number of words produced	+·302	+·136
Kent-Shakow Form Boards—number of mistaken moves	−·306	−·132
Penrose Pattern Perception Test. Number correct	+·270	+·042
Maudsley Word Connection List. Neurotic score	−·160	−·219
Educational Status	+·369	+·131
Mill Hill Vocabulary Test	+·269	−·086
Nursing Examination—theoretical	+·482	+·152
Nursing Examination—practical	+·358	+·363

manual dexterity test, which we have shown elsewhere to be a test of neuroticism as well as a test of ability, scores appear to be related to both types of criteria. It is also in line with our hypothesis that when the examination marks of the nurses are correlated with the two criteria, the theoretical examination is found to correlate ·482 with the 'ability' criterion, but only ·152 with the 'personal relationships' criterion, while the practical examination correlates equally well with both criteria ($r = ·358$ and ·363 respectively).

The outstanding results of this experiment are (1) the relatively small role played in nursing efficiency by intelligence (particularly as measured by verbal tests—correlation of Vocabulary with the total rating was not significantly different from zero), and (2) the relatively important role played by temperamental factors, as measured by various tests of neuroticism. None of the zero-order correlations are very high, but in combination they predict efficiency in nursing better than a battery of purely cognitive tests.

(5) *Sense of Humour and Popularity in Teachers*

So far in this chapter, we have discussed the position in factorial space of concepts such as employability, job satisfaction, job efficiency and others having occupational reference. The same technique of dimensional analysis, of course, can be applied to concepts having no such reference, and as an example an experimental study of the position of 'sense of humour' with respect to intelligence and neuroticism will be quoted. This investigation, carried out by F. Loos (1951), made use of several types of test to measure five separate meanings of the term, 'sense of humour'.

(1) Sense of humour may be looked at from the point of view of appreciation; a person is considered to possess this trait if his appreciation of the relative funniness of jokes, films, events, etc. agrees with our own, or with that of the majority. (2) Again, a person may be considered to possess 'sense of humour' if he appreciates a large number of jokes, witticisms, etc., or laughs a great deal about many things, irrespective of the order of funniness into which he would put these jokes, events, etc. (3) Alternatively, sense of humour may be looked at from the point of view of creation; a person is considered to possess this trait if he is constantly making jokes, drawing attention to amusing features of the situation, or in other ways creating merriment. (4) A fourth method of looking at sense of humour would emphasize the 'social stimulus' quality of the person, and rely on ratings by others of his 'sense of humour'. (5) Lastly, sense of humour may be defined in terms of self-ratings. These five definitions may give rise to tests which are highly correlated, but it is quite possible that they may point to quite unrelated aspects of personality.

The following tests were included in the research to measure the five aspects of 'sense of humour'. (1) A Limerick Ranking test, in which twelve limericks have to be ranked in order of funniness; the score is the amount of agreement with the average ranking of the whole group. (2) Limerick Liking test, in which the subject has to indicate how many of the limericks he considers funny; this number is his score. Both these tests were taken from an earlier paper by Eysenck (1943). (3) With respect to the 'creative humour' aspect, two tests were included. In the first of these, captions had to be written for cartoons from which the original captions had been eliminated; in the second, social situations were outlined to the subjects who had to find an amusing ending for each situation. Scoring of these creative efforts was carried out by judges who did not take part in the experiment. The validity of the average of twenty judges' ratings, using a formula developed elsewhere (Eysenck, 1939), was found to be in the vicinity of ·90, so that scores on these two tests are reasonably objective. (4) Social humour rating. This consisted of an averaged rating of the subjects' sense of humour, made by her colleagues. (5) In addition to these tests and ratings, each subject was asked to give a self-rating of her own sense of humour. In addition, a 'popularity rating' was obtained for each girl.

To assess the position of each girl on the intellectual dimension, Thurstone's Primary Mental Abilities tests were given to the girls; we thus obtain scores on the space, verbal, reasoning, number, and word fluency factors. To assess neuroticism and other possible temperamental factors, a group Rorschach was given,[1] as well as the Word Connection List, and the Worries, Likes, and Dislikes tests mentioned earlier in the book. Also used was the Rosenzweig Picture Frustration test, scored for Impunitiveness and for Extrapunitiveness minus intropunitiveness.

The subjects were 76 girls in a teachers' training college, with an average age of 19. Scores on the nineteen tests used were intercorrelated for the whole population, and a factorial analysis performed. Four significant factors were extracted. Factors I and II are plotted in Figure 36. The five Thurstone tests define factor I as an intelligence factor; the four neuroticism tests (Word Connection List, worries, word likes and dislikes) define the second factor as one of neuroticism. The results threw some interesting light on the relation of sense of humour to intelligence and neuroticism. Let us take the Limerick Ranking test first. Agreement with the average here is indicative of lack of neuroticism, as might have been expected; the slight positive saturation of this test with intelligence is also not contrary to expectation. The Limerick Liking test is also correlated with neuroticism, in the sense that the more stable girls tend to like a larger number of limericks. This test has no appreciable saturation with intelligence. We may conclude that

[1] The Rorschach was scored for neuroticism 'by means of the sign' method. Individual correlations were calculated between sense of humour tests and the various Rorschach categories; these correlations were all insignificant.

the more stable subjects like more limericks, and agree in their preferences more with the average judgment, than do the less stable girls.

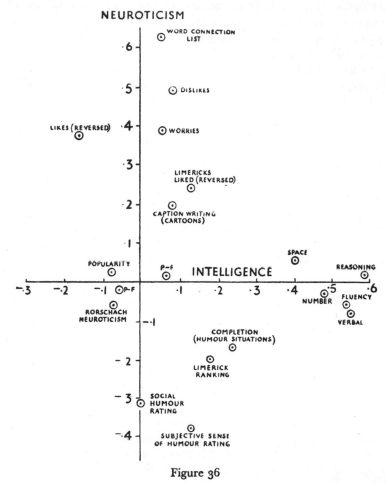

Figure 36

As regards the two creative humour tests, it will be seen that they both have slight correlations with intelligence, as might have been expected. Their saturations with the neuroticism factor are small and opposite in sign to each other, so that we cannot posit any relation between neuroticism and creative humour as measured here. This lack of relation may be a mere artefact, due to the imperfection of the tests used.

The social humour rating, and the subjective sense of humour rating, both show marked saturations with the neuroticism factor, in the expected direction, and fail to show correlations with the intelligence factor. It is interesting in this connection to see that the popularity rating is unrelated to either neuroticism or intelligence; in other words, an unstable girl, or an unintelligent one, is just as likely to be popular as a stable, or a bright one. But an unstable girl is not likely to be thought of as having a good 'sense of humour', nor is she likely to consider herself as possessing this trait. This agreement between self-judgment and poor rating is surprising in view of the frequent claims made in the literature that few people admit to having a poor sense of humour; perhaps the imperative demand for this quality in the American culture is more pressing than it is in England!

A third factor was clearly identified by the popularity rating, the social humour rating, and the subjective sense of humour rating; the only other test having a loading of above ·3 for this factor was the 'creative sense of humour' score on the Cartoon Caption Writing test. The other 'creative sense of humour' score was in the same direction, but insignificant, as is also the Limerick Ranking score. As the fourth factor consists merely of a 'double', namely the two Rosenzweig Picture-Frustration test scores, it follows that in this analysis there is no evidence that the different types of humour test used define a general factor of 'sense of humour'. Instead, we seem to be dealing mainly with relatively independent variables, whose variances are in part determined by intelligence and neuroticism. The only exception to this rule, interestingly enough, is the 'social stimulus value' concept of sense of humour; this 'social humour rating', as we have called it, forms a separate factor with popularity and with self-rating on 'sense of humour'. Apparently then it is the stable, popular girl who is considered to have a good sense of humour, and who considers herself to possess this quality; it is the unstable, unpopular girl who is lacking in sense of humour, and who knows herself to be defective in this respect. As far as the evidence goes, this 'social stimulus' concept of sense of humour is related slightly to both the creative and the appreciative aspect of sense of humour through the factor of neuroticism. This relation might appear somewhat stronger if better tests of these qualities were available.

It must be left to the reader to judge to what extent a research such as the present one may be said to have clarified the concept it

APPLICATIONS OF DIMENSIONAL ANALYSIS

was designed to analyse. Clearly the results cannot be regarded as in any sense final; different sets of tests, different populations, different culture patterns might easily produce results differing widely from those reported. Nevertheless, it is only through comparisons of different experiments, carried out in different conditions, that we can learn about the influence of those aspects of the experimental situation over which we have no control. At the very least, this research would seem to have confirmed the suspicion expressed by many writers that the concept of 'sense of humour' is not a unitary one, but that we are dealing rather with a multitude of independent aspects which must be quantified and studied separately. This research marks the beginning of a taxonomic study of the position of these various aspects within the total personality space.

Chapter Eight

THE ORGANIZATION OF PERSONALITY

ALL through this book, the reader will have noted that implicitly or explicitly a stand has been taken on a very important theoretical issue. In the field of personality research, as in the more strictly experimental fields of perception and memory, there are two fundamental ways in which we can order our thinking, and along which we can plan our experiments and construct our theories. The first of these is that of atomism or elementalism; the other is that of wholeness or gestalt—the organismic way. The great majority of psychologists who deal with the concept of personality either experimentally or clinically have adopted the organismic point of view; the present book, like its predecessor, takes an outspokenly atomistic, elementalistic point of view. Here and there, throughout this volume, we have taken up this argument with respect to individual issues; now we must come to grips with it on a somewhat more fundamental level.

First of all, let us see precisely what is meant by the 'organismic' approach in personality study. We cannot do better than to quote from a book which has put the wholistic point of view better and more clearly than any other, namely, the *Assessment of Men* (O.S.S. Staff, 1948). Apparently, it was 'one of the noteworthy features of the O.S.S. assessment system that it recognized explicitly the necessity of relating all observations to each other, not in a mechanical way, but by an interpretive process aiming at the discovery of general patterns and action systems, and made this the guiding principle of all its operations'. Underlying this feature of O.S.S. work we have a clearly stated hypothesis: 'Organismic assessment is based on the hypothesis that a trained psychologist or psychiatrist, with a fund of additional facts at his disposal, is, today, capable of improving to a significant degree the accuracy of mechanical prediction derived from test scores alone.' Apparently, 'the elementalistic approach calls for accurate quantitative measurements of partial, isolated processes, whereas the organismic approach comes down to inaccurate estimations of total integrated processes'. It follows from this that 'for a short over-all assessment the interview is probably the best and only indispensable method we have'. In contrast, 'the elementalistic method is abstract and unrealistic, since no attempt is made to reproduce the conditions under which the men will eventually perform. . . . In adopting this method . . . the psychologist makes a radical subjective judgment at the very start by electing constituent processes, testing for these separately, and then *adding* the scores to arrive at a final rating. He does this even though he knows that in actual life the mind does not *add* sequences of elementary processes to produce results, but *organizes* them into effective forms.'

Clearly, the organismic point of view is a *tenable* one; there are no internal contradictions which would make the system of beliefs briefly presented here illogical and mutually contradictory. Nor can the elementaristic point of view be dismissed on logical grounds. It follows that we must turn to the experimental evidence to decide between these two contradictory systems. Such evidence may be sought at three levels: (1) The level of total assessment, as in the O.S.S. programme itself; (2) an intermediate level, as in the case of Rorschach test interpretation along statistical or intuitive lines; (3) a fundamental level, as in perceptual organization, for instance.

At the level of total assessment, we have already quoted very briefly the Michigan study (Kelly, 1949, 1947; Kelly and Fiske, 1950). 'The large number of subjects studied, the very large number of techniques of measurement and assessment used, and the excellence of the experimental design would have made the findings from this programme outstanding, even if they had been less revolutionary in their import. From every point of view, the final results are a devastating comment on and criticism of the clinical methods of interviewing and projective testing current in most applied personality work. It was found that the most efficient clinical predictions in terms of both validity and economy of data are those based only on the matters contained in the credentials file and in the objective test profiles. The addition of autobiographical and projective test data appears to have contributed little or nothing to the validities of the assessment rating. Neither the initial nor the intensive interview made any apparent contribution. In fact, the predictions based on the credentials and objective tests are better than those made at the end of the programme on the basis of test procedures and observations! This consistent trend would seem to be all the more significant in view of the fact that assessment staff members tended to be uniformly of the opinion that the interview contributed most to their 'understanding of the case', followed by either the projective test or an autobiography' (Eysenck, 1951).

Kelly and Fiske (1950) point out that 'predictions based on individual projective tests as well as those based on an integration of data from all four projective tests yielded relatively low correlations with the rated criteria. Scores from a single objective test obtainable by mail at little cost predicted each of several criteria as well as all the clinical judgments made in the entire assessment programme.' They go on to say that 'many who have seen our results have been disturbed by the findings regarding the validity for this selection problem of specific techniques, which are felt by many professional psychologists to have a high degree of face validity (or is it faith validity?). Thus, it was the firm conviction of the staff of the O.S.S. Assessment Programme that the global evaluation of a person permits much more accurate predictions of his future performance than can possibly be achieved by a more segmental approach. . . . Our own findings to date serve to raise doubts concerning the validity of this general proposition. . . . Although the unstructured interview is one of the most widely used tools in personnel selection, the writers know of no evidence in the literature to suggest that such interviews have other than extremely low validity, which hardly justifies the degree of confidence and esteem with which they are held by users of the interview. One aspect of our findings is most disconcerting to us: the inverse relationship between the confidence of staff members at the time of making a prediction and the measured validity of that prediction.'

We see then that the only study hitherto carried out in such a way as to permit a comparison of the organismic and the elementaristic approach has completely failed to support the point of view of the organismic psychologists, although the psychiatrists and clinical psychologists who were actually carrying out the procedures and made the predictions were very largely supporters of this point of view. The elementaristic method of *adding* scores along well-known lines of multiple prediction is shown to be conspicuously superior to the organismic method of *organizing* data into a meaningful dynamic pattern for each subject. This finding does not, of course, constitute a universally valid disproof of the organismic position, but clearly the onus of proof is now with the organismicists, and it may be added that such proof must be experimental in kind—semantic arguments from supposedly higher general principles are not sufficient to controvert empirical findings.

At the second level, comparatively little research has been carried out; the small-scale experiment comparing statistical and intuitive diagnostic procedures with respect to the Rorschach test, which is outlined on page 163 of this book, may serve as an isolated example. This neglect of a very promising approach is rather odd; few psychologists have the facilities needed for a large-scale inquiry such as would be required at the highest level of complexity, but most research workers would find it very easy to set up an experiment at this level of complexity. Much useful information could be gained in this way regarding the efficacy of these two approaches; as far as our data are concerned the outcome of the experiment is again hostile to the organismic approach.

It is at the lowest level of complexity, however, in connection with the processes of perception or memory, that gestalt writers have been able to support the organismic view most strongly, and it is at this level that their view has achieved its greatest success. Consequently, experimentation specially planned to test the rival hypotheses in this field also is of particular interest and importance. If the organismic hypothesis fails here too, then we may say with some degree of confidence that it is unlikely to stand up to careful experimentation in more complex fields. We turn next, therefore, to an experiment which superficially may seem to have little to do with the study of personality, but which throws much light on the principles underlying the construction of psychological models of *organization*. This experiment, reported by Granger (1950), deals with æsthetic appreciation; it covers a field, therefore, which saw the original gestalt hypotheses grow (as in the work of Ehrenfels), and which is still regarded as the strongest fortress into which to retire for a last stand by many organismicists.

Granger took his stimuli from the Munsell Colour System (1921), which is organized around three dimensions: Value (more usually called lightness, i.e. the scale of greys from white to black); Chroma (more usually called saturation); and Hue (i.e. the special qualitative attribute which distinguishes red from blue, or green from yellow). Each dimension is intended to form a scale of perceptually equidistant steps. Three sets of tests were made up: (1) Hue tests, of which there were 24, made up in such a way as to hold value and chroma constant within each test. As far as possible, all ten hues were sampled in each case at all levels of the colour solid. (2) Value tests, of which there were 24, made up in such a way as to hold hue and chroma constant. (3) Chroma tests, of which there were 11, made up in such a way as to hold hue and value constant. The coloured chips which constitute the stimuli for each of these tests were presented to 25 male and 25 female subjects, screened for colour-blindness by means of three standard tests, under carefully controlled conditions against a medium grey background, with instructions to rank them in order of preference.

In the statistical treatment, Granger made use of Kendall's (1948) coefficient of concordance ('W'), which for all practical purposes may be considered equivalent to an average intercorrelation between the rankings of a number of subjects. All the 120 W-values calculated (for men and women separately, and for all the tests) are positive, thus showing that there is general agreement among the subjects on the rank-order of the stimuli. W-values average around ·5 for hue, ·2 for value, and ·4 for chroma. It is interesting to note that on an additional test, containing ten fully saturated hues, the W-values for men and women were much smaller than for other hue tests; this is presumably due to the fact that whereas the colours in the other hue sets differed only in respect of hue, those in the fully saturated set differed also in value and chroma. This decrease in agreement with increase in number of dimensions is of course a general proposition of dimensional analysis, but its empirical confirmation may be of some interest.

Not only do individuals agree with respect to their rankings of the stimuli on each of the 60 tests, but it can also be shown that the hue tests correlate with each other ($\overline{W} = ·34$), the value tests correlate with each other ($\overline{W} = ·44$), and the chroma tests correlate with each other ($\overline{W} = ·44$). Further than that, when each subject is given a score in terms of his correlation with the general order for the hue, value, and chroma tests, it can be shown that these rankings agree to the extent of $\overline{W} = ·64$, so that a subject who has a high score on one set of tests will also tend to have a high score on the other sets of tests. A last important demonstration is that *the order of preference for all three attributes of colour remains invariant from level to level, throughout the colour solid.*

These preference judgments would seem to have a firm objective basis in certain properties of the stimulus objects. To take but one example, namely, hue, Granger has shown that there exists a correlation of ·81 between the order of preference and the dominant wavelength of the colours, in the sense that the hues of shorter wavelength are preferred to those of longer wavelength.

We have given, very briefly, some of the facts regarding the æsthetic appreciation of the simplest possible stimulis, viz. a single colour. Can we use these results to forecast appreciation of colour combinations? Here we come against our first crucial problem. According to the atomistic or elementaristic type of analysis, we would expect the following considerations to determine preferences for colour combinations: (1) Preferences for the individual colours contained in the combination. If we took combinations of two colours and had these ranked, then we should expect the resulting ranking to show substantial agreement with a ranking carried out simply on the basis of the summed preference ratings for the single colours making up each dyad. (2) Relations between the colours contained in the combination. Thus if we take the hue circle, we might find that liking for a given combination of two colours increases as the distance between them on the colour circle increases. This rule also could easily be translated into a numerical, 'additive' rule which would specify exactly in each case which of two colour dyads should be preferred. (3) Specific and error factors. We are unlikely to find perfect test-retest correlations; indeed, reliabilities of simple preference tests are seldom above ·7 to ·8.

According to the gestalt hypothesis, these notions would be considered subject to criticism. Preferences for colour combinations are *emergent qualities*, essentially unlike the constituent qualities which determine preferences for single colours, and impossible to predict from any knowledge of single colour preferences, or from any quantitative relations obtaining between the colours.[1]

Here, then, we would appear to have an experimental model which may be expected to produce quite clear evidence for or against the holistic approach. Prediction of preferences for colour combinations is in principle possible on the basis of knowledge of (a) preferences of the single colours, and (b) knowledge of the objective relations obtaining between them along the dimensions of the colour solid; that is the bald statement of the atomistic

---

[1] It is interesting to note that the first psychologist to maintain this gestalt view was the arch atomist Wundt (1910), who maintained that preferences for colour combinations would be determined by a 'Totalgefühl', an emergent configuration with unique properties over and above those of the component stimuli. Külpe (1909) and Titchener (1912) held a contrary view, more in line with that advanced here.

position. Prediction based on these principles is impossible—what is involved are emergent qualities which cannot be reduced to known properties of the stimuli considered apart; that is the bald statement of the organismic position. We must now turn to the experimental evidence.

The first demonstration relates to the question of relation between stimuli, i.e. the hypothesis that colour combinations are preferred in terms of the distance between the component colours on the colour circle. The correlation, when a standard colour was presented together with a variable colour, was found to vary from ·93 to unity in different experiments, so that we may assume that the hypothesis is essentially correct. (In a similar experiment by Clarkson *et al.* (1950), correlations of ·96 and ·99 were observed, thus lending support to this generalization.)[1] Orders of preference for colour combinations correlated highly from subject to subject, for hues, values, and chroma. $\overline{W}$ coefficients average around ·6 to ·7, thus showing marked agreement. Not only do individuals agree with respect to their rankings of the stimuli on each of the tests, but it can also be shown that the hue tests correlate with each other ($\overline{W} = ·26$), the value tests correlate with each other ($\overline{W} = ·46$), and the chroma tests correlate with each other ($\overline{W} = ·37$). And lastly, the rankings of the subjects on the hue, value, and chroma tests correlate to the extent of $\overline{W} = ·64$, i.e. to an extent identical with that found when single colour stimuli were used.

When scores are calculated for each subject on the single colour rankings (combining scores on the hues, values, and chromas tests), and correlated with similar scores on the combined colours rankings (again taking into account hues, values, and chromas) we find a correlation of ·826. In other words, those subjects who agree most with the average order when ranking single colours also agree most with the average order when ranking colour combinations. This very high correlation indicates very strongly that the laws governing one type of ranking are essentially identical with those governing the other, thus arguing against the gestalt idea of emergent properties.

We now come to the main test of the hypothesis. Twenty colour combinations were ranked in order of preference, as were also the

[1] We are discussing here only hue combinations, but similarly high correlations were found for value (·94) and chroma (·90) tests, indicating that preferences for these types of combinations are also directly dependent on objective relation between component colours along their respective dimensions.

individual colours making up the combinations. Then correlations were run between the observed ranking of the colour combinations (O), the hypothetical ranking derived entirely from the preference judgments for the component colours (C), and the hypothetical ranking derived entirely from the colour intervals of the components (I). The correlation between O and C is ·631, and that between O and I is ·554: C and I are of course uncorrelated ($r = ·004$). When C and I are combined, they predict the final ranking to an extent indicated by a correlation of ·84. When corrections for reliability are introduced it can be shown that the predictive accuracy of the combination of C and I is not far short of 100 per cent. Thus the final preference judgments of colour combinations are determined entirely by the elements entering into the combination, and the relations between these elements as determined by simple algebraic addition. It is difficult to see how the gestalt hypothesis could be invalidated more conclusively.

We can, however, take one further step. Even colour combinations may be said to be at a relatively low level of complexity. What would happen if we correlated score on the colour ranking test with score on some much more complex test of art appreciation, such as the Maitland Graves Design Judgment test (1948), in which judgments have to be made between good and poor designs of considerable complexity? This test, which has been shown to have considerable validity and good reliability, is entirely in black and white, so that colour plays no part in it. It is easy to see that on the gestalt hypothesis no positive prediction could be made; here again those elusive *emergent properties* would prevent any application of knowledge gained from less complex stimuli. If we take our stand, however, on the demonstration of a general factor of æsthetic judgment (Eysenck, 1940), a demonstration based entirely on an atomistic view, then we would predict a sizeable correlation between these variables. In fact, correlations of ·59 and ·73 were observed when the Maitland Graves test was correlated with results from the single colour test and the colour combination test. (It should be noted that these correlations are not due to differences in intelligence; only very small correlations were found between intelligence and the colour ranking tests.) Here again, then, the atomistic view is supported by the test results, and the gestalt hypothesis discredited.

As in connection with previous demonstrations, we do not wish to imply that this particular study has once and for all settled the theoretical conflict between associationism and gestalt. We have reported it in some detail because it is only by constantly bringing these complex theoretical issues into direct contact with experimental data that we can hope to arrive at a meaningful and scientifically worth-while conclusion. If those who follow the organismic line of argument would similarly subject their concepts and arguments to empirical testing then we might see a considerable growth in the area of agreement between different schools of psychology, and an abatement in the purely semantic discussion which so often passes for theorizing. As in so many other areas of social psychology, 'the same old concepts and words are tumbling around in the same old empty drum to the resounding echo of excessive verbalization' (Eysenck, 1951d).

How, then, it may be asked, does the atomistic psychologist view the problem of personality organization? We may perhaps attempt to answer this question by reference to an urgent psychiatric problem, namely, that of diagnosis. Reference has already been made in an earlier chapter to the conflicting views, and the often self-contradictory pronouncements, of psychiatrists and clinical psychologists. In their terminology, they regard the patients under their care as falling into one of a number of different classes (hysteria, schizophrenia, neurasthenia, etc.), a view which is only permissible if these different disorders are regarded as *qualitatively* different; yet in much of their writing and even more so in their practice they regard these different classes as blending into one another, as being mutually overlapping, as being in fact differentiated along *quantitative* lines. Clearly the qualitative and the quantitative aspects must be reconciled in some way, but little guidance is to be found in the text-books.

The answer to this problem is implicit in the experiments described in the previous chapters of this book: we must determine the required number of dimensions, locate them accurately, and measure them with a given degree of reliability and validity. Figure 37 may serve as a very rudimentary model of the kind of structure we have in mind. Using our experimentally demonstrated three factors of neuroticism, psychoticism, and extraversion-introversion as three axes of a co-ordinate system, we can now locate a given patient in terms of his exact position within this system. Leaving out of account the extravert dimension for the moment, we can see that the average person would lie in the centre of the diagram, at A; a strongly psychotic person, undifferentiated with respect to neuroticism, would be located at P, while a strongly neurotic patient, undifferentiated with respect to psychoticism, would be located at N. A person suffering from both psychotic and neurotic disorders would be found at point P + N. In terms of this diagram, the question: 'Is this person psychotic or neurotic?' becomes as unreasonable as the question: 'Is this patient intelligent or tall?' 'Two orthogonal vectors, like neuroticism and psychoticism, generate a plane on which the position of an individual has to be indicated by reference to *both* vectors; we can only describe an

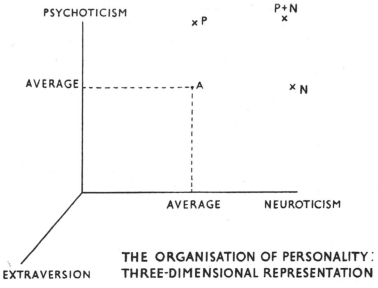

THE ORGANISATION OF PERSONALITY:
THREE-DIMENSIONAL REPRESENTATION

Figure 37

individual by giving both his I.Q. and his height, or by giving both his degree of neuroticism and of psychoticism. All positions on the plane thus generated are possible locations for a given individual, and it will be seen that *mixed cases* are far more likely than *pure cases*—we are more likely to find individuals in the plane of the diagram than on the ordinate or on the abscissa. This preponderance of mixed cases of course agrees well with clinical experience. Diagnosis on this showing should consist in the accurate determinations of an individual's position on the plane, rather than, as is now usual, in a simple either-or judgment' (Eysenck, 1951*b*).

It is not hypothesized, of course, that the three dimensions dealt with in this book are the only ones into which personality can be analysed, and along which measurement should take place. To take but one example, there is the case of intelligence, operationally defined in terms of Thurstone's second-order factor, which is approximately orthogonal to all the dimensions so far discussed. In due course, other dimensions will no doubt be isolated and measured, and much prospecting has already been done by Cattell (1946) into possible lines of progress. But regardless of the actual number of independent dimensions which our picture of personality may require, it is clear that categorical diagnosis of the 'either-or' kind are not warranted by the experimental findings; what is required is a separate assessment and measurement of each dimension in turn. It is not claimed that more than a beginning has been made in this complex, time-consuming, and difficult proceeding; it is believed, however, that results to date are fully in agreement with the general model of personality on which our procedures have been predicated.

We have then a general outline into which to fit such facts as future research may discover. It is clearly a static outline, in the same sense in which the periodic system of the elements is static; however, movement can easily be introduced into this outline when developmental facts can be experimentally controlled. As examples we may point to the studies on identical twins and on the after-effects of leucotomy summarized in earlier chapters.

The construction of such a general frame-work, of course, does not release us from the obligation to investigate separately the various factors which go to make up the structure, and to advance psychological hypotheses regarding their nature. Similarly, careful experimental studies are called for to investigate individual tests known to have high saturations for any of the factors postulated. Such work, however, must follow the establishment of the main dimensions of personality; it cannot precede it. Consequently, we have little to add on these counts; it must be left to future work to fill in these lacunæ.

Even so, however, certain theoretical speculations may be of some interest, and they are advanced here with the explicit warning that much experimental work will be required before we can assess their value. These speculations relate particularly to the neuroticism factor—possibly because more is known empirically regarding this factor than about any other; they are based on certain obvious analogies between neurotic illness and such physical events as, for instance, the fracture of metals—analogies which have passed into the very way in which we talk about neurotic 'breakdown', being under 'stress', reaching 'breaking-point', or having a 'brittle' personality. This analogy can be pushed a good deal further, and as long as it is recognized as an analogy and nothing more than that, it may throw some interesting light on our explorations of those weaknesses in personality which give rise to neurotic break-downs.

It may come as a shock to many psychologists not well versed in physical theory and knowledge that present-day knowledge of fractures of metals and their causes is far from satisfactory, and that there are various theories in the field none of which has as yet succeeded in providing direct experimental support for its contentions. Again, as in psychology, we have the historical and the ahistorical approach, as well as the controversy between the adherents of a 'dynamic' and those of a 'static' method of analysis. A brief description of current physical thought on this subject may provide a frame-work for our subsequent discussion.

'The basic scientific problem of the general conditions which determine the ductile and brittle failure of metals is still largely unsolved' (Sachs, 1948). Two main avenues of approach are being used to investigate these phenomena. The *micro-mechanical* method is being used to study the effect of various factors such as lattice imperfections, and the formation, reorientation, and growth of cracks. The *phenomenological* method studies the general macroscopic laws underlying fracture. 'Eventually the two types of investigations will be correlated to provide a single self-consistent theory for fracturing of metals' (Dorn, 1948). Most of our knowledge concerning the effect of stress on the fracture of metals has been obtained from the phenomenological approach. There is a direct complement here with psychological work, particularly with the distinction drawn between the molar and the molecular approach. The micro-mechanical method would find its analogue in detailed neurological work, or in the kind of work summarized by Selye under the revealing title of 'Stress' (1950). The phenomenological method would find its analogue in the molar approaches favoured by most psychologists nowadays. We may indicate this correspondence in the form of a Table:

Physical methodology:	*Psychological methodology:*
(1) Micro-mechanical method.	(1) Molecular method.
(2) Phenomenological method.	(2) Molar method.

It used to be assumed in physics that there were two general criteria for fracture: (1) Fracture occurs when a critical state of strain is achieved, and (2) fracture occurs when a critical state of stress is achieved. It is now accepted on the basis of recent investigations that the critical strain and critical stress laws for fracture are individually incorrect, and that we must follow Bridgman in postulating (3) that the stress level for fracture depends upon the entire stress and strain histories preceding fracture. Here we have another analogue with psychological theory, contrasting the historical with the constitutional point of view. And again the resolution is similar—a recognition of both elements, and an attempt to obtain quantitative estimates of the influence of both.

A geometrical representation in many ways similar to that provided by factor analysis in psychology may render the position in the physical field a little clearer. It can be shown that 'the state of stress in a homogeneous isotropic metal is completely defined by the three principal stresses. Therefore, the stress state at fracture can be represented by a stress surface in three-dimensional cartesian co-ordinate stress space as shown in Figure 38. Whenever the stresses are less than the values on the limiting surface, the metal

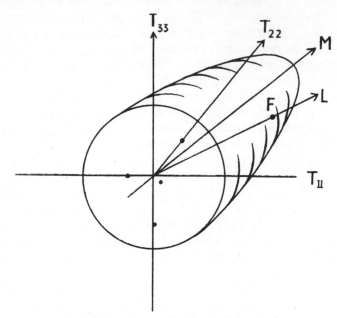

Figure 38.—Fracture Surface in Stress Space

will not fracture. But when the stress state reaches the limiting surface, fracturing will take place. Stressing along line OL, therefore, will not lead to fracture until a state of stress represented by point F on the fracture surface is reached.'[1]

It must, of course, be realized that this fracture surface is in no way to be regarded as rigid; its shape and size are determined by the previous stress or strain history of the metal, and alter with it. It resembles a flexible membrane whose distortion is dictated by the stress or strain history. For homogeneous isotropic metals, only certain shapes of the stress surface are theoretically possible. The surface must be symmetrical about line OM which makes equal angles with the positive directions of the three principal stresses. Furthermore, the surface must be independent of the orientation of the X, Y, Z co-ordinate axes of the parts being stressed. Therefore, the function of the principal stresses representing the fracture surface of a homogeneous isotropic metal must be invariant relative to rotations of the co-ordinate axes in the past.

This concept of 'fracture surface' has no equivalent in psychology, but potentially it would appear to have considerable heuristic value. Presumably axes having the properties mentioned above could be located through factorial studies, based on controlled observation in the case of human subjects, and based on experiment in the case of animals. The total size of the fracture surface would presumably be identifiable with our 'neuroticism' factor.

Our discussion so far may appear theoretical and remote because in actual fact the metals we work with are neither homogeneous and isotropic, and certainly in the psychological field anisotropy and non-homogeneity are more prevalent. However, science advances from the simple to the complex, and what has been said so far may serve as a first approximation. We must now try to encompass certain complicating factors.

The three axes along which we plotted the fracture surface are strictly arbitrary in their location, although conventionally one would presumably orient them in relation to direction of the application of the stress. When the same treatment is applied to anisotropic material, certain positions of the axes become prefer-

---

[1] The metal under discussion has been taken as essentially homogeneous and isotropic because the detailed variations in stress from grain to grain or even from point to point in a single grain of polycristalline metal are not known at present. Most studies on fracture in polycristalline metals have neglected the complications arising from the crystalline structure of the metals.

able; these can be determined by the differential reaction to stress of different parts of the material, by differing historical conditions of different parts of the material, or both. Similarly, it is the existence of inhomogeneity in human behaviour which decides us to prefer one set of factor axes to another—although even then no 'absolute' value attaches to such a position.

One important change in our picture which must accompany the shift from isotropic to anisotropic material is the inclusion of time as an additional dimension. It has been known for a long time that brittle solids may support a static stress for long periods of time without the slightest evidence of approaching failure, which then occurs with great suddenness. Experimental evidence shows that there is a definite relation between the intensity of the stress to which the brittle solid is subjected, and its duration necessary to produce a fracture. It was found that 'the duration of the stress required to obtain the failure decreased very sharply as the intensity of the applied stresses was increased' (Poncelet, 1948).

This phenomenon of 'static fatigue' cannot be reconciled with any of the classical theories of strength of brittle solids, which do not take the duration factor into consideration. The first step towards a solution of this dilemma was taken by Inglis (1913), whose observation that scratches or cracks reduce the strength of hardened steel plates, through the considerable intensification of the applied stresses at the crack tips, was taken up by Griffith (1921, 1924) in his famous 'crack' theory. According to this view, the notorious weakness of brittle solids to tensile stresses is attributed to the existence of indefinite 'flaws' in the solids; these flaws he believed to be in essence submicroscopic cracks. He assumed the structure to be continuous and developed his views along thermodynamic lines.[1] 'This new approach . . . introduced the factor time in the expression which determines the breaking stress . . . of brittle solids, and gives an intelligible interpretation of the phenomenon of static fatigue' (Poncelet, 1948). It also explains why the average stress required for the fracture of solids is many times smaller than that calculated from the forces acting between the atoms.

How is all this relevant to psychology? The application is sur-

[1] This creates a difficulty regarding the explanation of these flaws which can be sidestepped by assuming the structure of the solids to be particulate, and composed of ions. In this way the phenomenon is brought into the field of general statistical mechanics.

prisingly direct. Let us recall for a moment Thomson's so-called 'sampling theory' of intelligence. He explains the observed pattern of intercorrelations between intelligence tests in terms of *bonds*. 'Each test calls upon a *sample of the bonds* which the mind can form . . . some of these bonds are common to two tests and cause their correlation.' While not venturing to suggest in detail what the bonds might be, Thomson believes that 'they are fairly certainly associated with the neurones or nerve cells of our brains, of which there are approximately one hundred thousand million in each normal brain'. We may easily consider a theoretical equivalent to Thomson's cognitive hypothesis in the affective and conative sphere by postulating that the observed pattern of intercorrelations between neuroticism tests can be explained in terms of *faults*. Each test calls upon a *sample of the faults* which are inherent in the mind . . . some of these faults are common to two tests and cause their correlation. No neurological locus will be suggested for these hypothetical faults, although it would not be difficult to find many possible claimants, particularly in the autonomic sphere. Here, then, we have a concept directly related to our previous discussion, because clearly these hypothetical faults are strictly analogous to Griffith's submicroscopic cracks.

Certain other similarities may be stressed. One of these is the almost complete failure of classical theories to predict empirical results. There is little cause to document this statement with respect to psychology; in the physical field we may quote Slater's statement that 'we have been upset in modern times that materials so eminently "ductile" as mild steel, as revealed by our old-fashioned tensile test, have proved so undeniably and catastrophically brittle on many momentous occasions' (1948). Indeed, the failure of classical theory is perhaps more noticeable in the physical field because nature calls the scientist's bluff more clearly and definitely there than it does in the mental field. The ship sinks; the bridge breaks; the steel tower topples—these are events which cannot be explained away. But the patient who does not improve under psychoanalytic therapy, or who does not react to E.C.T.: the prediction of combat success or academic achievement that is not borne out in fact; the clinical diagnosis that is refuted by later developments—these can be argued away in a facile, semantic fashion. Physics lives in the world of the reality principle; psychology and psychiatry have not altogether emerged from the world of the pleasure principle.

Yet some at least of the failures of the psychologist must be laid at the door of those who determine the problems which he is to be set, and the conditions under which he shall attempt to solve them. It is quite customary to ask the psychologist to predict success of a group of people without specifying the exact nature of the situation in which success or failure will be decided. Thus the subjects who passed successfully through the O.S.S. assessment programme might be detailed to do one of a large number of very dissimilar jobs, ranging all the way from putting on propaganda shows in oriental countries to being dropped as secret agents into enemy-occupied territory. This situation would find an analogue in the physicist's being asked which of a large number of metal bars were likely to fracture, but without his being given any information as to the precise stress which would be applied to each of these bars. His 'prediction', if indeed he agreed to furnish one under such impossible conditions, would amount to little more than a statement of the present strength of the various bars. The success of his prediction would depend far more on the conditions to which these specimens would be exposed later, than on the accuracy of his measurement.

Again, while the physicist's failures are spectacular, they do furnish a criterion which does not admit of argument. The psychologist's criterion is only too often unreliable, illogical, and determined by extraneous considerations; low predictive accuracy is more often due to faults in the criterion than to faults in the predicting variables. What is worse, administrative action often interferes with his attempts to establish proper controls, so that it becomes quite impossible to evaluate properly the results of his procedures. In comparing forecasting accuracy of physical and psychological tests, these considerations must always be borne in mind.

Similar considerations apply to the situation in which the psychologist is called in to 'advise' on certain problems. He is usually expected to give his advice on the basis of general principles, and to do so more or less on the spot. Even in physics, where general principles have been established to a much greater extent than in psychology, such a demand would be deprecated, and an actual experimental investigation of the applicability of such principles to the particular situation insisted on. The psychologist, however, is seldom given the opportunity of carrying out such investigations, although in his case they are even more vital; he is expected, instead, to advise on problems of the utmost complexity on the basis of such very limited data as may be available—indeed, he must count himself lucky if there are any data at all. Until those who pose the questions gain some insight into the methods of science, and learn to provide suitable conditions for an experimental determination of the answer, psychology will continue to operate at a low level of scientific respectability.

Given the existing external circumstances, however, the psychologist can make a maximum contribution by (a) isolating the main dimensions of personality, and (b) improving the accuracy with which they can be measured. It is with these two aims in view that the experiments described in this book have been carried out. To what extent may they be said to have been achieved? The isolation of three main dimensions—neuroticism, psychoticism, extraversion—may be said to have been accomplished at a reasonably high level of confidence, although it would seem most desirable that all of this work should be repeated independently at other institutions; it is unfortunate that psychology has not adopted the practice widespread in the physical sciences where new claims are routinely tested by several institutions. Only in this way can we hope to build up a stock of verified trustworthy facts and principles; the single experiment may be of outstanding interest, but it can never be definitive. At the same time this procedure ensures that one of the most important of scientific requirements is met, namely reproducability of experimental conditions. Identifiability of groups, of sampling, of experimental procedure; repeatability of diagnoses, of tests, of treatments—all these must be ensured if an experiment is to be accepted as being of scientific value. And there is no better proof of reproducability of conditions than reproduction of results, although the inverse of this relationship does not of course hold. Subject, then, to such repetition we may claim to have made a contribution to our first task.

Regarding the actual measurement of these dimensions, we have shown in the text that neuroticism can be measured with a reliability in excess of ·85 and a validity of about ·80: these figures are minimum rather than maximum estimates, and are certainly encouraging. No exact figures can be given for the other two dimensions, as less work has been done in connection with them; there is no reason to believe that measurement there should be inherently less exact or less reliable. There are, however, certain warnings which long experience with work of this kind makes desirable in order to avoid disappointment.

In the first place, while on most of the groups studied exactly the same tests are found to correlate together to define a given factor—neuroticism, say—it is quite common to find that for one particular group one particular test will fall out of line. Some examples of this tendency have been mentioned already in the text. Thus for middle-class groups the Crown Word Connection List has a high saturation with neuroticism, and low correlations with intelligence; for a group of unskilled workers studied by Heron (1951) this test was found, however, to have only relatively low saturations with neuroticism, but high saturations with intelligence. This change can of course be explained in terms of different standards of literacy, nevertheless it indicates that results from one group cannot immediately be extended to other groups differing from the original one with respect to intelligence, social status, or in other important ways. Again, while for groups of normal intelligence the persistence test usually has good saturations with neurotics, it has been found quite consistently (Brady, 1948; O'Connor, 1951) that in mental defectives there is hardly any correlation between persistence and neuroticism. No obvious explanation of this difference suggests itself, and a special experiment would be required to study this discrepancy. Indeed, it is quite likely that a great deal may be learned about the nature of the factors involved by the careful study of such discrepant results.

A second difficulty which should not be underrated is related to the problem of test standardization. We have ample evidence that even slight changes in the test may produce profound changes in the results. Thus changing the method of recording sway on the body sway test, or changing the record on which the suggestion to 'sway forward' is made, may have a profound influence on the results obtained. Whether the subject can see the apparatus on entry or not, and whether he is frightened or not; the degree of reassurance given to him, and the reasons advanced for making him submit to being tested at all; whether the tester is a pretty young girl, a domineering male, or a mature, sympathetic woman —all these influences may, and in some cases do, affect a person's scores. They are difficult to control, particularly as the same stimulus—a pretty young girl as tester, for instance—may mean quite different things, and arouse quite different emotions, in subjects differing in age, sex, and marital happiness. Standardization is not impossible, but it is much more difficult with tests of this type than it is with tests of intellectual capacity. When what we are trying to measure are those somewhat intangible things—ego involvements, motivation, strength of drives—then we cannot in any simple way control the physical properties of our stimuli and assume equivalence. Here again, differences in results from one experiment to another may at first be disheartening; if they are regarded less as experimental failures, but rather as leads to definite hypotheses, and stimuli to further experimentation devoted to a solution of the particular problem created by these inconsistencies, they may actually be of considerable use and importance.

A third difficulty is connected with the one just mentioned. From many points of view, it would be desirable to keep tests identical from one experiment to another, so that cross-comparisons can be made. But if that is done we miss our opportunity to improve existing tests, and make use of such knowledge as we may have acquired during the course of our experiments. These two requirements have to be carefully balanced, and a decision is not always easy. Premature standardization may serve merely to crystallize poor and ineffective practices; constant changes may make all useful comparisons impossible. In the past we have laid greater emphasis on improvement and change; in the future we shall lay greater emphasis on standardization. But this problem cannot be settled by any facile generalization, and it is likely to arise whenever a particular experiment is being devised.

This point is closely related to the question of the amount of stress which the experimenter is to lay on the main two aspects of his work. He may either use many rough-and-ready tests, in order to isolate the main dimensions along which he intends to work; or he may carry out careful and detailed experimentation on a small number of tests, in the hope of refining these sufficiently to derive meaningful scores from them. An example may make clear the difference between these two approaches. We have used in our work raw scores on tests such as the Body Sway Suggestibility test, or the fluency test, and shown that these tests correlate significantly with the neuroticism factor. While such findings are interesting and important, they must nevertheless leave the investigator somewhat dissatisfied. Performance on even such relatively simple tests is certainly highly complex, and it is difficult to interpret findings psychologically. Thus Bousfield and Sedgewick (1944) made a detailed study of fluency tests, and found that curves of output could be described by an exponential equation: $N = C(1 - e^{-mt})$, where N is the number of words written up to a given time, t; C is the upper limit that the curve approaches asymptotically, presumably identifiable with the total supply of the kind of words called for by the instructions, while e is the base of the natural logarithms, and m measures the rate of depletion of the supply of words. These writers have also shown that the mathematically derived constants have psychological as well as mathematical meaning. When their subjects were given preliminary practice in naming automobiles the rate constant (m) increased, but not the supply of names constant (C). In another experiment, Bousfield & Sedgewick (1944) found that the theoretical supply of pleasant words was considerably larger than the supply of unpleasant words, but that the rate constant was the same. These findings make psychological sense, and suggest that this theory can be applied to individual differences in fluency. The number of words written in a given time is of course the raw score conventionally used as a measure of an individual's fluency; C and m are analytical or derived scores which in conjunction with each other determine the raw scores.

If we accept this theory, we see immediately that intercorrelations of raw scores, factor analyses of such intercorrelations, and correlations of raw scores with outside criteria, all cease to have any interpretable meaning. Observed correlations may be due to the influence of the C constant, the m constant, or any combination of the two; they would fluctuate in an unpredictable manner according to such variables as type of material selected, or length of test. (Clearly the raw score on a short test depends more on M, on a long test more on C.) In other words, analysis of raw scores would be psychologically meaningless, and give much less promising results than might be got from analysis of the C and m scores.

Similar considerations apply to the body sway test of suggestibility. A psychological analysis of this test (Eysenck, 1947) showed that at least two separate factors determine the raw score: the strength of the ideomotor connections within the individual who is being tested (his 'aptitude'), and his ability to resist this tendency. His raw score, therefore, would be something in the nature of a ratio of the two. Now the hypothesis advanced to explain the correlation of suggestibility with neuroticism depends only on one of the elements in this ratio, viz. the subject's ability to resist; there is no reason to expect neurotics to differ from normals with respect to their 'aptitude'. Consequently, 'aptitude' simply serves to exert a confusing and complicating influence on the score when we want to correlate neuroticism with 'ability to resist suggestion'. However, as we cannot at the moment measure 'aptitude' separately, and thus derive a score for 'ability to resist' directly, we must remain content with the raw score, which will be considerably attenuated by the influence of 'aptitude'. Work is proceeding at the moment to obtain separate measurements for the two parts of the ratio separately, but whatever the result of these endeavours, it must be clear that the raw score, in spite of its apparent simplicity, is in reality quite a complex resultant of several unrelated forces.

What is true of these two tests is presumably true, to a greater or lesser degree, of all our tests. Although superficially simple, yet in reality they are quite complex, and the raw score may bear no very constant or high relation to any of the forces which determine it. This fact may explain the comparatively low correlations which are usually found between tests of neuroticism; we are correlating raw scores, each of which is the resultant of several forces of which only one may be relevant to our analysis. If we could carry our analysis further, and obtain direct measures of these relevant forces, the attenuation of our correlations would be much reduced, and presumably the size of the correlation would be increased.

At the same time we might in this way obtain evidence regarding the contradictory findings which characterize so much of the literature on personality testing. Let us assume, for instance, that experimenter A finds that a test of fluency has a high saturation for intelligence, but a low saturation for neuroticism, while B reports that his test of fluency has low saturation for intelligence, but high saturation for neuroticism. These results obtained from the raw scores appear contradictory and inexplicable. Now let us assume, as is quite likely, that the 'total fund of relevant words'—C—is highly correlated with intelligence while the 'rate of production'—m—is highly correlated with neuroticism. A short test would depend more on m than on C, and would thus be a test of neuroticism more than of intelligence. A rather longer test would depend more on C than on m, and would thus be a test of intelligence rather than one of neuroticism. Thus by simply varying the length of the test, experimenter B might obtain superficially discrepant results from A. By working with analytical scores, both experimenters should find that C had high saturations on intelligence, m on neuroticism, regardless of the length of test used. Similar considerations, of course, apply to other variables, such as level of education, age, type of stimulus material, or sex; superficially discrepant results obtained from raw scores should be reconcilable in terms of analytic scores.

The conclusion might be drawn from this discussion that the most urgent task in the psychology of personality is the detailed analysis of individual tests and techniques along these lines. This conclusion would, in our view, be as false as the opposite one that the isolation of the main dimensions must precede such detailed analysis. In our view, both procedures must go hand in hand; promising tests are discovered in terms of their correlation with neuroticism, or psychoticism, or extraversion; they must then be analysed in detail, purified, and the new analytical scores used in order to determine with even greater accuracy the relevant factor. It is this interplay of statistical and experimental procedures which in our view will lead to important developments in the future.

BIBLIOGRAPHY

1. ABRAHAM, K. The first pregenital stage of the libido. In: *Selected Papers*. London: Hogarth Press, 1916.
2. —— A short study of the development of the libido viewed in the light of mental disorders. In: *Selected Papers*. London: Hogarth Press, 1924.
3. —— The influence of oral erotism on character-formation. In: *Selected Papers*. London: Hogarth Press, 1942.
4. AIR MINISTRY. *Psychological Disorders in Flying Personnel of the R.A.F.* Air Ministry: Publication 3139. London: H.M.S.O., 1947.
5. ALBINO, R. C. The stable and labile personality types of Luria in clinically normal individuals. *Brit. J. Psychol.*, 1948, **39**, 1, 54–60.
6. ALEXANDER, F. *Five year report of the Chicago Institute for Psychoanalysis.* 1932–7, 30–43.
7. ALLPORT, G. W. *Personality. A Psychological Interpretation.* New York: H. Holt & Co., 1937.
8. ASH, P. The reliability of psychiatric diagnoses. *J. abnorm. & Soc. Psychol.*, 1949, **44**, 272–6.
9. BAKWIN, R. M. Similarities and differences in identical twins. *J. genet. Psychol.*, 1930, **38**, 373–97.
10. BARNACLE, C. H., EBAUGH, F. G., & LEMERE, F. Association-motor investigations of the psychoneuroses. *Amer. J. Psychiat.*, 1935, **91**, 925–37.
11. BARTLETT, M. S. Further aspects of the theory of multiple regression. *Proc. Camb. Phil. Soc.*, 1938, **34**, 33–40.
12. BECK, S. J. *Rorschach's Test. I. Basic Processes.* New York: Grune & Stratton, 1944.
13. —— *Rorschach's Test. II. A Variety of Personality Pictures.* New York: Grune & Stratton, 1945.
14. BECKER, P. E., & LENZ, F. Die Arbertskurve Kraepelins und ein psychomotorischer Versuch in der Zwillingsforschung. *Z. ges. Neurol Psychiat.*, 1939, **164**, 50–68.
15. BELL, J. E. *Projective Techniques. A dynamic approach to the Study of Personality.* London: Longmans, Green & Co., 1948.
16. BENNETT, A. E., & SEMRAD, E. V. Common errors in diagnosis and treatment of the psychoneurotic patient—a study of 100 case histories. *Nebraska Med. J.*, 1936, **21**, 90–2.
17. BENNETT, E. Some tests for the discrimination of neurotic from normal subjects. *Brit. J. med. Psychol.*, 1945, **20**, 271–7, 280–2.
18. BLUEKERCKEN, J. Concerning the development of twins. *Internat. J. Indiv. Psychol.*, 1935, **1**, 73–81.
19. BOND, E. D., & BRACELAND, F. J. Prognosis in mental disease. *Amer. J. Psychiat.*, 1937, **94**, 263–74.

20. BORGSTROEM, C. A. Eine serie von Kriminellen Zwillingen. *Arch. Rass. Ges. Biol.*, 1939, **33**, 334–43.

21. BOUSFIELD, W. A., & SEDGEWICK, C. H. W. An analysis of sequences of restricted associative responses. *J. genet. Psychol.*, 1944, **30**, 149–65.

22. BOUTERWEK, H. Erhebungen an eineiigen Zwillingspaaren über Erbanlage und Umwelt als Charakterbildner. *Z. f. mensch. Vererbungs. u. Konstituionslehre*, 1936, **20**, 265–75.

23. BRACKEN, H. v. Psychologische Untersuchungen an Zwillingen. *Indus. Psychotechn.*, 1933, **10**, 351–2.

24. —— Mutual intimacy in twins: types of social structure in pairs of identical and fraternal twins. *Character and Personality*, 1934a, **2**, 293–309.

25. —— Psychologische Untersuchungen an Zwillingen. *Ber. Kongr. Dtsch. Ges. Psychol.*, 1934b, **13**, 117–19.

26. —— Zwillingsforschung und Psychologie des Gemeinschaftslebens. *Ber. Kongr. Dtsch. Ges. Psychol.*, 1935, **14**, 138–40.

27. —— Verbundenheit und Ordnung im Binnenleben von Zwillingspaaren. *Z. pedag. Psychol.*, 1936, **37**, 65–81.

28. —— Das Schreibtempo von Zwillingen und die sozial-psychologischen Fehlerquellen der Zwillingsforschung. *Z. mensch. Vererb.—u. Konst. Lehr.*, 1939a, **23**, 278–98.

29. —— Untersuchungen an Zwillingen über die Entwicklung der Selbständigkeit im Kindesalter. *Arch. ges. Psychol.*, 1939b, **105**, 217–42.

30. —— Wahrnehmungstäuschungen und scheinbare Nachbildgrösse bei Zwillingen. *Arch. ges. Psychol.*, 1939c, **103**, 203–30.

31. —— Erbbiologische Untersuchungen über die Handschrifteigenart. *Dtsch. Z. ges. gerichtl. Med.*, 1940a, **33**, 64–72.

32. —— Untersuchungen an Zwillingen über die quantitativen und qualitativen Merkmale des Schreibdrucks. *Z. angew. Psychol.*, 1940b, **58**, 367–84.

33. BRADY, M. Suggestibility and Persistence in Epileptics and mental defectives. *J. Ment. Sci.*, 1948, **94**, 444–51.

34. BRIDGMAN, P. W. *Dimensional Analysis*. New Haven: Yale Univ. Press, 1931.

35. BRODY, D. Twin resemblances in mechanical ability with reference to the effects of practice on performance. *Child Development*, 1937, **8**, 207–16.

36. BRONFENBRENNER, U. Toward an integrated theory of personality. In: *Perception—an Approach to Personality*. Ed. Blake, R. R., & Ramsey, C. V. New York: Ronald Press Co., 1951.

37. BURT, C. General and specific factors underlying the primary emotions. *Rep. Brit. Ass.*, 1915, **69**, 45.

38. —— The analysis of temperament. *Brit. J. Med. Psychol.*, 1937, **17**, 158–88.

39. —— The factorial study of the emotions. In: *Feelings and emotions. The Mooseheart Symposium in cooperation with the University of Chicago*. Ed. Reymert, M. L. New York: McGraw Hill Book Co. Inc., 1950.

40. BURT, C., & JOHN, E. A factorial study of Terman Binet Tests. *Brit. J. educ. Psychol.*, 1942, **12**, 139–87.
41. BURTT, H. E. Motor concomitants of the association-motor reaction. *J. exp. Psychol.*, 1936, **19**, 51–64.
42. CARMENA, M. Ist die personliche Affektlage oder 'Nervosität' eine ererbte Eigenschaft? *Zsch. f. d. ges. Neur. u. Psychiat.*, 1934, **150**, 434–45.
43. —— Is personal tranquillity or nervousness a property of hereditary origin? *Arch. Neurobiol.*, 1935*a*, **15**, 79–92.
44. —— Schreibdruck bei Zwillingen. *Z. ges. Neurol. Psychiat.*, 1935*b*, **103**, 744–52.
45. CARMICHAEL, H. T., & MASSERMAN, T. H. Results of treatment in a psychiatric outpatients' department. *J. Amer. Med. Assoc.*, 1939, **113**, 2292–8.
46. CARTER, H. D. Twin similarities in occupational interests. *J. educ. Psychol.*, 1932, **23**, 641–55.
47. —— Twin similarities in personality traits. *J. genet. Psychol.*, 1933, **43**, 312–21.
48. —— Twin similarities in emotional traits. *Character and Personality*, 1935, **4**, 61–78.
49. —— A preliminary study of free association. 1. Twin similarities and the technique of measurement. *J. Psychol.*, 1938, **6**, 201–15.
50. —— Resemblance of twins in speed of association. *Psychol. Bull.*, 1939, **36**, 641.
51. CATTELL, R. B. *The Description and Measurement of Personality*. New York: World Book Co., Yonkers, 1946.
52. ——, & MOLTENO, E. V. Contributions concerning mental inheritance. V. Temperament. *J. genet. Psychol.*, 1940, **57**, 31–47.
53. CLARKE, A. D. B. *The Measurement of Emotional Instability by means of Objective Tests. An Experimental Inquiry.* Ph.D. thesis. Univ. London Lib., 1950.
54. CLARKSON, M. E., DAVIES, O. L., & VICKERSTAFF, T. Colour Harmony. In: *Colour.* Imperial Chemical Industries Ltd. (Dyestuffs Division). Manchester: 1950.
55. COMROE, B. I. Follow-up study of 100 patients diagnosed as 'neurosis'. *J. nerv. & ment. Dis.*, 1936, **83**, 679–84.
56. COON, G. P., & RAYMOND, A. *A Review of the Psychoneuroses at Stockbridge.* Stockbridge, Mass., Austen Riggs Foundation, Inc., 1940.
57. COVILLE, W. J. A study of the effectiveness of the Maritime Service Inventory as a screening device at the United States Maritime Service Training Station, St. Petersburg, Florida. In: *The Psychobiological Program of the War Shipping Administration.* Ed. Killinger, G. G. California: Stanford Univ. Press, 1947.
58. COX, S. A factorial study of the Rorschach responses of normal and maladjusted boys. *J. genet. Psychol.*, 1951, 79, 95–115.
59. CROSLAND, H. R. *The Psychological Methods of Word-association and Reaction Time as Tests of Deception.* Univ. Oregon Publ. Psychol. Series, 1931, **1**, No. 3 (Abstract).
60. CROWN, S. A controlled association test as a measure of neuroticism. *J. Personality*, 1948, **16**, 198–208.

61. CROWN, S. *Psychological changes following prefrontal leucotomy.* Ph.D. thesis. Univ. London Lib., 1950.
62. —— Psychological changes following prefrontal leucotomy; a review. *J. Ment. Sci.*, 1951, **97**, 49–83.
63. —— The Word Connection List as a diagnostic test: norms and validation. *Brit. J. Psychol.*, 1952. To appear.
64. CURRAN, D. The problem of assessing psychiatric treatment. *Lancet*, 1937, **2**, 1005–9.
65. DAVIS, D. R. *Pilot Error—Some Laboratory Experiments.* London: H.M.S.O., 1948.
66. DAVIS, H., & DAVIS, P. A. Action potentials of the brain in normal persons and in normal states of cerebral activity. *Arch. neurol. Psychiat.*, 1936, **36**, 1214–24.
67. DENKER, P. G. Prognosis and life expectancy in the psychoneuroses. *Proc. A. Life Insur. M. Dir. America*, 1937, **14**, 179.
68. —— Results of treatment of psychoneuroses by the general practitioner. A follow-up study of 500 cases. *New York State J. Med.*, 1946, **46**, 2164–6.
69. DOERING, C. R. Reliability of observation of psychiatric and related characteristics. *Amer. J. Orthopsychiat.*, 1934, **4**, 249–57.
70. DORN, J. E. The effect of stress state on the fracture strength of metals. In: *Fracturing of metals.* Amer. Soc. for Metals: Cleveland, Ohio, 1948.
71. DREYER, J. L. E. *History of the Planetary Systems from Thales to Kepler.* London: Cambridge Univ. Press, 1906.
72. DUBITSCHER, F. Der Rorschacshe Formdeuteversuch als Diagnotisches Hilfsmittel. *Zts. ges. Neurol. Psychiat.*, 1932, **138**, 515–35.
73. ECKLE, C., & OSTERMEYER, G. Erbcharakterologische Zwillingsuntersuchungen. *Beih. Z. angew. Psychol.*, 1939, **82**, 255.
74. EDDINGTON, A. S. *Nature of the Physical World.* London: Cambridge Univ. Press, 1928.
75. ELKIN, F. Specialists interpret the case of Harold Holzer. *J. abnorm. & Soc. Psychol.*, 1947, **42**, 99–111.
76. ELLIS, A. The validity of personality questionnaires. *Psychol. Bull.*, 1946, **43**, 385–440.
77. ——, & CONRAD, L. S. Validity of personality inventories in military practice. *Psychol. Bull.*, 1948, **45**, 385–426.
78. ELMGREN, J. Quelques notions sur l'électrencéphalogramme humain. *Göteborgs Högsk. Årsskr.*, 1941, **47**, 24.
79. ESSEN-MOELLER, E. Psychiatrische Untersuchungen an einer Serie von Zwillingen. *Acta Psychiat. Neurol.*, 1941, Suppl. 23, 7–200.
80. EYSENCK, H. J. The validity of judgments as a function of the number of judges. *J. exp. Psychol.*, 1939, **25**, 650–4.
81. —— The general factor in aesthetic judgments. *Brit. J. Psychol.*, 1940, **31**, 94–102.
82. —— An experimental analysis of five tests of 'appreciation of humour'. *Educ. & Psychol. Measmt.*, 1943, **3**, 191–214.
83. —— *Dimensions of Personality.* London: Kegan Paul, 1947.
84. —— Primary social attitudes: 1. The organization and measurement of social attitudes. *Internat. J. Opin. & Attit. Res.*, 1947a, **1**, 49–84.

85. EYSENCK, H. J. Screening out the neurotic. *Lancet*, 1947*b*, April 19, 530.
86. —— Student selection by means of psychological tests. A critical survey. *Brit. J. educ. Psychol.*, 1947*c*, **17**, 20–39.
87. —— Uses and limitations of factor analysis in psychological research. In: *Proceedings of the 1949 Invitational Conference on Testing Problems.* Princeton, N.J. Educational Testing Service, October 29, 1949.
88. —— Criterion analysis—an application of the hypothetico-deductive method to factor analysis. *Psychol. Rev.*, 1950, **57**, 38–53.
89. —— Personality tests 1944–9. In: *Recent Progress in Psychiatry.* Ed. Fleming, G. W. T. H. London: J. & A. Churchill Ltd., 1950*a*.
90. —— War and aggressiveness: a survey of social attitude studies. In: *The Psychological Factors of Peace and War.* Ed. Pear, T. H. London: Hutchinson, 1950*b*.
91. —— Cyclothymia and schizothymia as a dimension of personality. I. Historical review. *J. Personality*, 1950*c*, **19**, 123–53.
92. —— Cyclothymia and schizothymia as a dimension of personality. II. Experimental. *J. Personality*, 1951. To appear.
93. —— Les dimensions de la personnalité et la conception du problème neurotique. In: *Proc. de la Semaine Internationale d'Anthropologie Différentielle.* Paris: Press·Universitaires, 1951*a*. To appear.
94. —— The organization of personality. *J. Personality*, 1951*b*. To appear.
95. —— Uses and abuses of factor analysis. *J. appl. Stats.*, 1951*c*. To appear.
96. —— Personality. *Ann. Rev. Psychol.*, 1951*d*. To appear.
97. ——, & PRELL, D. B. The inheritance of neuroticism. An experimental study. *J. ment. Sci.*, 1951. To appear.
98. FENICHEL, O. *Ten years of the Berlin Psychoanalysis Institute.* 1920–30, 28–40.
99. FISHER, R. A. Use of multiple measurements in taxonomic problems. *Ann. Eug.*, 1936, **7**, 179.
100. —— The statistical utilization of multiple measurements. *Ann. Eug.*, 1938, **8**, 376.
101. FRANZEN, R., & BRIMHALL, D. R. Problems of consistency arising from CAA medical examinations. *Rep. Div. Res. Civ. Aeronaut. Adm.*, 1942, **1**, 20.
102. —— —— Analysis of physical defects found by the armed services in pilots certified to be without disqualifying defect by civil pilot training examination. *Rep. Div. Res. Civ. Aeronaut. Adm.*, 1942, **2**, 18.
103. FREEMAN, F. *An experimental study of projection among normal and abnormal groups in a structural situation.* Ph.D. thesis. Univ. London Lib., 1951.
104. FRIESS, C., & NELSON, M. J. Psychoneurotics five years later. *Amer. J. Ment. Sci.*, 1942, **203**, 539–58.
105. FRISCHEISEN-KÖHLER, I. The personal tempo and its inheritance. *Character and Personality*, 1933, **1**, 301–13.
106. FURNEAUX, W. D. An apparatus for measuring bodily sway. *Amer. J. Psychol.*, 1951, **44**, 271–4.
107. GALILEO. *Dialogues concerning Two Great Systems of the World.* London, 1661.
108. GARDNER, J. W. An experimental study of the Luria technique for detecting mental conflict. *J. exp. Psychol.*, 1937, **20**, 495–505.

109. GLOVER, E. The significance of the month in psychoanalysis. *Brit. J. med, Psychol.*, 1924, **4,** 134–55.

110. —— Notes on oral character-formation. *Internat. J. Psycho-anal.*, 1925, **6,** 131–53.

111. GOLDMAN-EISLER, F. Breastfeeding and character formation. *J. Personality,* 1948, **17,** 83–103.

112. —— Breastfeeding and character formation: the etiology of the oral character in psychoanalytic theory. *J. Personality,* 1950, **19,** 189–96.

112a. —— The problem of 'orality' and of its origin in early childhood. *J. ment. Sci.*, 1951, **97,** 765–82.

113. GOTTLOBER, A. B. The inheritance of brain potentials. *J. exp. Psychol.*, 1938, **22,** 193–200.

114. GOTTSCHALDT, K. Phänogenetische Fragestellungen im Bereich der Erbpsychologie. *Z. indukt. Abstammungs—u. Vererbungslehre,* 1939, **76,** 118–57.

115. GOUGH, H. G. An additional study of food aversions. *J. abnorm. & Soc. Psychol.*, 1946, **41,** 86–8.

116. GRANGER, G. W. *An experimental study of colour preferences.* Ph.D. thesis. Univ. London Lib., 1950.

117. GRAVELY, A. *An investigation of perceptual tests as measures of temperament.* Ph.D. thesis. Univ. London Lib., 1950.

117a. GRAVES, M. *Design Judgment Test Manual.* New York: Psychol. Corp., 1948.

118. GRIFFITHS, A. A. The phenomena of rupture and flow in solids. *Phil. Trans. Roy. Soc. London, Series A,* 1921, **221,** 163–98.

119. —— Theory of rupture. *Proc. 1st Internat. Cong. Appl. Mech.* Delft, 1924.

120. GUILFORD, J. P. Unitary traits of personality and factor theory. *Amer. J. Psychol.*, 1936, **48,** 673–80.

121. —— *Psychometric Methods.* New York: McGraw Hill, 1936.

122. GUTTMAN, L. The Cornell Technique for scale and intensity analysis. *Educ. & Psychol. Measmt.*, 1947, **7,** 247–79.

123. HAMILTON, D. M., VANNEY, I. H., & WALL, T. H. Hospital treatment of patients with psychoneurotic disorder. *Amer. J. Psychiat.*, 1942, **99,** 243–7.

124. HAMILTON, D. M., & WALL, T. H. Hospital treatment of patients with psychoneurotic disorder. *Amer. J. Psychiat.*, 1942, **98,** 551–7.

125. HARDCASTLE, D. H. A follow-up study of one hundred cases made for the Department of Psychological Medicine, Guy's Hospital. *J. Ment. Sci.*, 1934, **90,** 536–49.

126. HARRIS, A. The prognosis of anxiety states. *Brit. Med. J.*, 1938, **2,** 649–54.

127. HARRIS, H. I. Efficient psychotherapy for the large out-patient clinic. *New England J. Med.*, 1939, **221,** 1–5.

128. HARTGE, M. Eine graphologische Untersuchung von Handschriften eineiiger und zweieiiger Zwillinge. *Z. angew. Psychol.*, 1936, **50,** 129–48.

129. HERMANN, E. Messungen an Handschrift-proben von Zwillingspaaren unter 14 Jahren. *Z. Psychol.*, 1939, **147,** 238–55.

BIBLIOGRAPHY

130. HERON, A. *A psychological study of occupational adjustment.* Ph.D. thesis. Univ. London Lib., 1951.
131. HIMMELWEIT, H. T. The intelligence-vocabulary ratio as a measure of temperament. *J. Personality*, 1945, **14,** 93–105.
132. —— Speed and accuracy of work as related to temperament. *Brit. J. Psychol.*, 1946, **36,** 132–44.
133. ——, & PETRIE, A. The measurement of personality in children. *Brit. J. educ. Psychol.*, 1951, **21,** 9–29.
134. —— Student selection—an experimental investigation: I. *Brit. J. Sociol.*, 1950, **1,** 328–46.
135. ——, & SUMMERFIELD, A. Student selection—an experimental investigation: II. *Brit. J. Sociol.*, 1951, **2,** 59–75.
136. HOFSTETTER, H. W. Accommodative convergence in identical twins. *Amer. J. Optom.*, 1948, **25,** 480–91.
137. HOLLEY, J. W. A note on the reflection of signs in the extraction of centroid factors. *Psychometrika*, 1947, **12,** 263–8.
138. HOLMES, S. J. Nature versus nurture in the development of the mind. *Sci. Mon.*, 1930, **31,** 245–52.
139. HOUTCHENS, H. M. A study of mental conflict in delinquent and non-delinquent boys. *J. Juv. Res.*, 1935, **19,** 180–92.
140. HOVLAND, C. I., LUMSDAINE, A. A., & SHEFFIELD, F. D. *Experiments on Mass Communication. Vol. III.* Princeton: Princeton Univ. Press, 1949.
141. HUDDLESON, J. H. Psychotherapy in 200 cases of psychoneurosis. *Mil. Surgeon*, 1927, **60,** 161–70.
142. HUNT, W. A., & CLARKE, E. M. The startle pattern in children and identical twins. *J. exp. Psychol.*, 1937, **21,** 359–62.
143. ——, & WITTSON, C. L. Some sources of error in the neuropsychiatric statistics of World War II. *J. Clin. Psychol.*, 1949, **5,** 350–8.
144. ——, WITTSON, C. L., & BURTON, H. W. A validation study of naval neuropsychiatric screening. *J. consult. Psychol.*, 1950, **14,** 35–9.
145. HUSTON, P. E., SHAKOW, D., & ERICKSON, M. H. A study of hypnotically-induced complexes by means of the Luria technique. *J. genet. Psychol.*, 1934, **11,** 65–97.
146. INGLIS, C. E. Stresses in a plate due to presence of cracks and sharp corners. *Proceed. Inst. Naval Architects*, March 13, 1913.
147. JACOBSON, J. R., & WRIGHT, K. W. Review of a year of group psychotherapy. *Psychiat. Quart.*, 1942, **16,** 744–64.
148. JANET, P. *Les Nev roses.* Paris: 1909.
149. JONES, E. *Decennial Report of the London Clinic of Psychoanalysis.* 1926–36, 12–14.
150. JONES, H. E., & WILSON, P. T. Reputation differences in like-sex twins. *J. exp. Educ.*, 1933, **1,** 86–91.
151. JOST, H., & SONTAG, L. W. The genetic factor in autonomic nervous system function. *Psychosom. Med.*, 1944, **6,** 308–10.
152. JUNG, C. G. *Psychological Types.* London: Routledge & Kegan Paul, 1923.
153. KALLMANN, F. J. The scientific goal in the prevention of hereditary mental disease and racial inferiority. *Proc. Genet. Cong.*, 1941, 172.
154. —— The genetic theory of schizophrenia. An analysis of 691 schizophrenic twin index families. *Amer. J. Psychiat.*, 1946, **103,** 309–22.

155. KALLMANN, F. J., & BARRERA, S. E. The heredoconstitutional mechanisms of predisposition and resistance to schizophrenia. *Amer. J. Psychiat.*, 1942, **98**, 544–50.

156. KANAEV, I. I. Concerning conditioned reflexes in uniovular twins. *Arkh. biol. Nauk.*, 1934, **34**, 569.

157. —— Physiology of the brain in twins. *Character and Personality*, 1938, **6**, 177–87.

158. —— On the question of lability of conditioned reflexes in twins. *C. R. Acad. Sci.*, 1941, **30**, 856–8.

159. KELLY, E. L. The selection of clinical psychologists. *Progress Report, Univ. Michigan*, Dec. 1949, 1–14.

160. —— Research on the selection of clinical psychologists. *J. clin. Psychol.*, 1947, **3**, 39–42.

161. ——, & FISKE, D. W. The prediction of success in the V.A. Training Programme in Clinical Psychology. *Amer. Psychol.*, 1950, **5**, 395–406.

162. KENDALL, M. G. Partial rank correlation. *Biomet.*, 1942, **32**, 277.

163. —— *Rank correlation methods.* London: Griffin, 1948.

164. ——, & BABINGTON SMITH, B. The problem of rankings. *Ann. Math. Stats.*, 1939, **10**, 275–87.

165. KERR. M. Temperamental differences in twins. *Brit. J. Psychol.*, 1936, **27**, 51–9.

166. KESSEL, L., & HYMAN, H. T. The value of psychoanalysis as a therapeutic procedure. *J. Amer. Med. Ass.*, 1933, **101**, 1612–15.

167. KIBLER, M. Experimentalpsychologischer Beitrag zur Typenforschung. *Z. ges. Neurol. Psychiat.*, 1925, **98**, 524–44.

168. KLOPFER, B., & KELLY, D. *The Rorschach technique.* London: G. Harrap & Co., 1942.

169. KNIGHT, R. O. Evaluation of the results of psychoanalytic therapy. *Amer. J. Psychiat.*, 1941, **98**, 434–46.

170. KRAMER, E., & LAUTERBACH, C. Resemblance in the handwriting of twins and siblings. *J. educ. Res.*, 1928, **18**, 149–52.

171. KRANZ, H. *Lebensschicksale Krimineller Zwillinge.* Berlin: Springer, 1936.

172. KRAUSE, L. S. Relation of voluntary motor pressure (Luria) to two other alleged complex indicators. *J. exp. Psychol.*, 1937, **21**, 653–61.

173. KRETSCHMER, E. *Korperbau und Charakter.* Berlin: Springer-Verlag, 1948.

174. ——, & ENKE, W. *Die Persönlichkeit der Athletiker.* Leipzig: Threime, 1936.

175. KUDER, G. F., & RICHARDSON, M. W. The theory and estimation of test reliability. *Psychomet.*, 1937, **2**, 151–60.

176. LANDIS, C. Statistical evaluation of psychotherapeutic methods. In: *Concepts and Problems of Psychotherapy.* Ed. Hinsie, S. E. London: Heineman, 1938.

177. LANGE, J. *Crime as Destiny.* London: Allen & Unwin, 1931.

178. LENNOX, W. G., GIBBS, E. L., & GIBBS, F. A. The brain-wave pattern, an hereditary trait; evidence from 74 'normal' pairs of twins. *J. Hered.*, 1945, **36**, 233–43.

179. LOHMEYER, G. The upbringing of twins. *Int. J. indiv. Psychol.*, 1935, **1**, 113–17.

180. Loos, F. M. *A study of the interrelations of sense of humour with some other personality variables.* Ph.D. thesis. Univ. London Lib., 1951.

181. Lubin, A. *Some contributions to the testing of psychological hypothesis by means of statistical multivariate analysis.* Ph.D. thesis. Univ. London Lib., 1951.

182. —— Linear and non-linear discriminating functions. *Brit. J. Psychol.* (Stat. Section), 1950, **3**, 90–103.

183. Lubin, A., & Summerfield, A. A square-root method of selecting a minimum set of variables in multiple regression. *Psychomet.*, 1951, **16**, 271–84.

184. Luchsinger, R. Die Sprache und Stimme von ein-und zweieiigen Zwillingen in Beziehung zur Motorik und zum Erbcharakter. *Arch. Klaus—Stift.*, 1940, **15**, No. 4.

185. Luff, M. C., & Garrod, M. The after-results of psychotherapy in 500 adult cases. *Brit. J. Med. Psychol.*, 1927, **7**, 57.

186. Luria, A. R. *The Nature of Human Conflicts.* New York: Liveright, Inc., 1932.

187. Luxenburger, H. Vorläufiger Bericht über psychiatrische Serienuntersuchungen an Zwillingen. *Z. Neur. Psych.*, 1928, **116**, 297–326.

188. —— Psychiatrisch-neurologische Zwillingspathologie. *Zentralb. Neur. Psych.*, 1930, **56**, 145–80.

189. —— Über einige praktisch wichtige Probleme aus der Erbpathologie des zyklothymen Kreises. Studien an erbgleichen Zwillingspaaren. *Z. Neur. Psych.*, 1933, **146**, 87–125.

190. —— Die Manifestationswahrscheinlichkeit der Schizophrenie im Lichte der Zwillingsforschung. *Z. Psych. Hyg.*, 1934, **7**.

191. —— Untersuchungen an Schizophrenen Zwillingen und ihren Geschwistern zur Prüfung der Realität von Manifestationschwankungen. *Z. Neur. Psych.*, 1935, **154**, 351–94.

192. —— Die Zwillingsforschung als Methode der Erbforschung beim Menschen. *Handb. Erbbiol. d. Menschen. II.* Berlin, 1940.

193. Mach, E. *The Science of Mechanics.* La Salle (Ill.), 1942.

193a. McKissock, W. The technique of pre-frontal leucotomy. *J. Ment. Sci.*, 1943, **89**, 194–8.

194. —— Recent techniques in psychosurgery. (Disc.) *Proc. Roy. Soc. Med.*, 1949, **42**, Suppl. 13.

195. McNemar, Q. Twin resemblances in motor skills, and the effect of practice thereon. *J. genet. Psychol.*, 1933, **42**, 70–99.

196. —— *The Revision of the Stanford-Binet Scale.* Boston: Houghton Mifflin, 1942.

197. Malan, M. Zur Erblichkeit der Orientierungsfähigkeit im Raum. *Z. Morph. Anthrop.*, 1940, **39**, 1–23.

198. Marinescu, G., Kreindler, A., & Copelman, L. Essai d'une interprétation physiologique du test psychologique de Rorschach. Son application à l'étude de la dynamique cérébrale des jumeaux. *An Psihol.*, 1934, **1**, 14–26.

199. Marquis, D. G. Research planning at the frontiers of science. *Amer. Psychologist*, 1948, **3**, 430–8.

308 BIBLIOGRAPHY

200. MASSERMAN, T. H., & CARMICHAEL, H. T. Diagnosis and prognosis in psychiatry. *J. Ment. Sci.*, 1938, **84,** 893–946.
201. MATZ, P. B. Outcome of hospital treatment of ex-service patients with nervous and mental disease in the U.S. Veteran's Bureau. *U.S. Vet. Bur. M. Bull.*, 1929, **5,** 829–42.
202. MAYER-GROSS, W., MOORE, J. N. P., & SLATER, P. Forecasting the incidence of neurosis in officers of the Army and Navy. *J. Ment. Sci.*, 1949, **95,** 80–100.
203. MEADOWS, A. W. An investigation of the Rorschach and Behn tests. Ph.D. thesis. Univ. London Lib., 1951.
204. MEUMANN, I. Testpsychologische Untersuchungen an ein-und zweieiigen Zwillingen. *Arch. ges. Psychol.*, 1935, **93,** 42–82.
205. MEYER, A. *Anatomical lessons from prefrontal leucotomy. A report based on the investigation of 122 brains.* Congrès Internat. de Psychiatrie, Paris, 1950.
206. MEYER, A., & McLARDY, T. Clinico-anatomical studies of frontal lobe function based on leucotomy material. *J. ment. Sci.*, 1949, **95,** 403–17.
207. MIGUEL, C. Schreibdruck bei Zwillingen. *Z. ges. Neurol. Psychiat.*, 1935, **152,** 19–24.
208. MILES, H. H. W., BARRABEE, E. L., & FINESINGER, J. E. Evaluation of psychotherapy. *Psychosom. Med.*, 1951, **13,** 83–105.
208a. MILLER, D. R. Responses of psychiatric patients to threats of failure. *J. abnorm. soc. Psychol.*, 1951, **46,** 378–87.
209. MISBACH, L., & STROMBERG, R. N. Non-separation as a source of dissimilarities between monozygotic twins: a case report. *J. genet. Psychol.*, 1941, **59,** 249–57.
210. MOORE, T. V. The empirical determination of certain syndromes underlying praecox and manic-depressive psychoses. *Amer. J. Psychiat.*, 1930, **9,** 719–38.
211. MORGAN, M. I., & OJEMAN, R. H. A study of the Luria method. *J. appl. Psychol.*, 1942, **26,** 168–79.
212. MUNROE, R. L. Prediction of the adjustment and academic performance of college students by a modification of the Rorschach method. *Appl. Psychol. Monogr.*, 1945, **7,** 104.
213. MUNSELL, A. H. An introduction to the Munsell system. In: *A Grammar of Colour.* Mittineague, Mass.: Strathmore Paper Co., 1921.
214. MURPHY, E., & JENSEN, F. *Approaches to Personality.* New York: Coward-McCamus, 1932.
215. NEUSTATTER, W. L. The results of fifty cases treated by psychotherapy. *Lancet*, 1935, **1,** 796–9.
216. NEWMAN, H. H., FREEMAN, F. N., & HOLZINGER, K. J. *Twins: a Study of Heredity and Environment.* Chicago: Univ. Chicago Press, 1937.
217. NICOLAY, E. Messungen an Handschriftproben von Zwillingspaaren uber 14 Jahren. *Arch. ges. Psychol.*, 1939, **105,** 275–95.
218. NUNBERG, H. On the physical accompaniments of association processes. In: *Studies in Word Association.* Ed. Jung, C. G. London: W. Heinemann, 1918.

219. O'CONNOR, N. *Personality variables which affect the vocational and social efficiency of high grade defectives.* Ph.D. thesis. Univ. London Lib., 1951.
220. OLSON, D. M., & JONES, V. An objective measure of emotionally-toned attitudes. *J. genet. Psychol.*, 1931, **39**, 174–6.
221. ORBISON, T. J. The psychoneuroses: psychasthenia, neurasthenia and hysteria, with special reference to a certain method of treatment. *California & West. Med.*, 1925, **23**, 1132–6.
222. O.S.S. ASSESSMENT STAFF. *Assessment of Men.* New York: Rinehart & Co., 1948.
223. OSTWALD, W. *Natural Philosophy.* London: Williams & Norgate, 1911.
224. PAULI, R. Die Arbeitskurve in der psychologischen Zwillingsforschung. *Arch. ges. Psychol.*, 1941, **108**, 412–24.
224a. PEARSON, K. *The Grammar of Science.* London: Buck, 1911.
225. PENROSE, L. S. Some notes on discrimination. *Ann. Eug.*, 1947, **13**, Part 4, 228–37.
226. PĚTO, E. The psychoanalysis of identical twins—with reference to inheritance. *Int. J. Psychoanal.*, 1946, **27**, 126–9.
227. PETRIE, A. The selection of medical students. *Lancet*, August 28, 1948, 325.
228. —— *Personality and the Frontal Lobes.* London: Routledge & Kegan Paul, 1952.
229. PETRIE, A., & POWELL, M. B. Personality and nursing. An investigation into selection tests for nurses. *Lancet*, Feb. 25, 1950, 363.
230. PONCELET, E. F. A theory of static fatigue for brittle solids—the nature of static fatigue. In: *Fracturing of Metals.* Cleveland, Ohio: Amer. Soc. for Metals, 1948.
231. POPENOE, P. Twins and criminals. *J. Hered.*, 1936, **27**, 388–90.
232. RAO, C. R. Utilization of multiple measurements in problems of biological classifications. *J. roy. Stat. Soc.*, B, 1948, **10**, 159–203.
233. ——, & SLATER, P. Multivariate analysis applied to differences between neurotic groups. *Brit. J. Psychol.*, 1949, **2**, 17–29.
234. REES, L. Body build, personality and neurosis in women. *J. ment. Sci.*, 1950, **96**, 426–34.
235. REYBURN, H. A., & RAATH, M. J. Primary factors of personality. *Brit. J. Statist. Psychol.*, 1950, **3**, 150–8.
236. REYMERT, M. L., & SPEER, G. S. Does the Luria technique measure emotion or mere bodily tension? *Character and Personality*, 1938, **7**, 192–200.
237. RIFE, D. C. Handedness and dermatoglyphics in twins. *Hum. Biol.*, 1943, **15**, 46–54.
238. ROSANOFF, A. J., HANDY, L. M., & PLESSETT, I. R. The etiology of manic-depressive syndromes with special reference to their occurrence in twins. *Amer. J. Psychiat.*, 1935, **91**, 725–62.
239. —— —— —— The etiology of mental deficiency with special reference to its occurrence in twins. *Psychol. Monog.*, 1937, **48**, 137.
240. —— —— —— The etiology of child behaviour difficulties, juvenile delinquency, and adult criminality, with special reference to their occurrence in twins. *Psychiat. Monog.*, 1941, **1**, 187.
241. ROSS, T. A. *An Enquiry into Prognosis in the Neuroses.* London: Cambridge Univ. Press, 1936.

242. RÜDIN, E. Praktische Ergebnisse der psychiatrischen Erblichkeitsforschung. *Die Naturwiss.*, 1930, **18**, 273–80.

243. RUNKEL, J. E. Luria's motor method and word-association in the study of deception. *J. genet. Psychol.*, 1936, **15**, 23–37.

244. RUSSELL, B. *Human Knowledge—Its Scope and Limits.* London: Allen & Unwin, 1948.

245. SACHS, G. *Introduction to 'Fracturing of Metals'.* Cleveland, Ohio: Amer. Soc. for Metals, 1948.

246. SARGENT, H. Projective methods: their origins, theory, and application in personality research. *Psychol. Bull.*, 1945, **42**, 257–93.

247. SAUDEK, R., & SEEMAN, E. *Handschriften und Zeichnungen eineiiger Zwillinge.* Berlin: 1933.

248. SCHILDER, P. Results and problems of group psychotherapy in severe neuroses. *Ment. Hyg.*, 1939, **23**, 87–98.

249. SCHILLER, M. Zwillingsprobleme dargestellt auf Grund von Untersuchungen an Stuttgarter Zwillingen. *Z. f. mensch. Vererbungs. -u. Konstitutionslehre*, 1937, **20**, 284–337.

250. SCHWESINGER, G. C. *Heredity and Environment.* New York: Macmillan, 1933.

251. SCOTT-BLAIR, G. W. *Measurement of Mind and Matter.* London: Dobson, 1950.

252. SEEMAN, E., & SAUDEK, R. The self-expression of identical twins in handwriting and drawing. *Character and Personality*, 1932, **1**, 91–128.

253. SELYE, H. *The Physiology and Pathology of Exposure to Stress.* Montreal: Acta Inc., 1950.

254. SEN, A. *A study of the Rorschach test.* Ph.D. thesis. Univ. London. *Brit. J. Psychol.* (Stat. Section), 1949, **19**, 142–3.

255. SHARP, D. L. Group and individual profiles in the association-motor test. *Univ. Ia. Stud. Child Welf.*, 1938, **15**, 97–171.

256. SHUEY, H. An investigation of the Luria technique with normal and psychotic subjects. *J. abnorm. soc. Psychol.*, 1937, **32**, 303–33.

257. SHUTTLEWORTH, F. K. The nature versus nurture problem. *J. educ. Psychol.*, 1935, **26**, 655–81.

258. SIEMENS, H. W. *Die Zwillingspathologie.* Berlin: Springer, 1924.

259. SLATER, E. Psychiatric Genetics. In: *Recent Progress in Psychiatry.* Ed. Fleming, G. W. T. H. London: Churchill, 1950.

260. SLATER, I. G. Metallurgical aspects of brittle fracture phenomena in mild steels. In: *Fracturing of Metals.* Cleveland, Ohio: Amer. Soc. for Metals, 1948.

261. SLATER, P. The psychometric differentiation of neurotic from normal men. *Brit. J. med. Psychol.*, 1945, **20**, 277–9.

262. —— Discussion. In: Utilization of multiple measurements in problems of biological classifications. *J. Roy. Stat. Soc.*, B, 1948, **10**, 159–203.

263. —— The factor analysis of a matrix of 2 × 2 tables. Supplement. *J. Roy. Stat. Soc.*, 1947, **9**, 114–27.

264. SMITH, C. A. B. Some examples of discrimination. *Ann. Eug.*, 1947, **13**, 272.

265. SMITH, G. *Psychological Studies in Twin Differences: with reference to afterimag and eidetic phenomena as well as more general personality characteristics.* Lund: Gleerup, 1949.

266. SORENSON, M. I., & CARTER, H. D. Twin resemblances in community of free association responses. *J. Psychol.*, 1940, **9**, 237-46.
267. SPEARMAN, C. *The Abilities of Man.* London: Macmillan, 1927.
268. SPEER, G. S. The measurement of emotions aroused in response to personality test items. *J. Psychol.*, 1931, **3**, 445-61.
269. STEBBING, L. S. *A Modern Introduction to Logic.* London: Methuen & Co., 1930.
270. STEIF, A. Similarity of scribbling in twins. *Psychol. Stud. Univ. Bp.*, 1939, **3**, 51-66.
271. STOCKS, P. A biometric investigation of twins and their brothers and sisters. *Ann. Eug.*, 1930, **4**, 49-108.
272. STOUFFER, S. A., SUCHMAN, E. A., DEVINNEY, L. C., STAR, S. A., & WILLIAMS, R. M., Jr. *The American Soldier: Adjustment during Army Life.* Vol. I. Princeton: Princeton Univ. Press, 1949a.
273. STOUFFER, S. A., LUMSDAINE, A. A., & M. H., WILLIAMS, R. M., Jr., BRESTER SMITH, M., JANIS, I. L., STAR, S. A., & COTTRELL, L. S., Jr. *The American Soldier: Combat and its Aftermath.* Vol. II. Princeton: Princeton Univ. Press, 1949b.
274. STOUFFER, S. A. *The American Soldier: Measurement and prediction.* Vol. IV. Princeton: Princeton Univ. Press, 1950.
275. STUIT, D. B. *Personnel Research and Test Development in the Bureau of Naval Personnel.* Princeton: Princeton Univ. Press, 1947.
276. STUMPFL, F. *The Source of Crime. Based on the Histology of Twins.* Leipzig: Thieme, 1936.
277. SYMONDS, P. M. *Adolescent Fantasy.* New York: Columbia Univ. Press, 1949.
278. SZONDI, L. Instinct and education. Experimental researches on the instinct tendencies of twins. *Psychol. Stud. Univ. Bp.*, 1939, **3**, 79-111.
279. TARCSAY, I. Testing of will-temperament in twins. *Psychol. Stud.*, 1939, **3**, 36-50.
280. THELEN, E. Zuordnungsversuche an Schriftproben von Zwillingen. *Z. Psychol.*, 1939, **147**, 215-37.
281. THOMPSON, M. The modifiability of play behaviour with special reference to attentional characteristics. *J. genet. Psychol.*, 1943, **62**, 165-88.
282. THORLEY, A. S., & CRASKE, N. Comparison and estimate of group and individual method of treatment. *Brit. Med. J.*, 1950, **1**, 97-100.
283. THURSTONE, L. L. *The Vectors of the Mind.* Chicago: Univ. Chicago Press, 1935.
284. TITCHENER, E. B. *A Textbook of Psychology.* New York: The Macmillan Co., 1912.
285. TIZARD, J. *An experimental study of the vocational adjustment of subnormal boys.* Ph.D. thesis. Univ. London Lib., 1951.
286. ——, & O'CONNOR, N. The employability of high-grade mental defectives. Part 1. *Amer. J. Ment. Def.*, 1950a, **54**, 563-76.
287. —— —— The employability of high-grade mental defectives. Part II. *Amer. J. Ment. Def.*, 1950b, **55**, 144-57.
288. —— —— The abilities of adult and adolescent high-grade male mental defectives. *J. Ment. Sci.*, 1950c, **96**, No. 405, 889-907.

289. TIZARD, J., & O'CONNOR, N. Predicting the occupational adequacy of certified mental defectives: an empirical investigation, using a battery of psychological tests and ratings. *Occup. Psychol.*, 1951, **25**, 205–11.

290. TROUP, E. A comparative study by means of the Rorschach method of personality development in twenty pairs of identical twins. *Genet. Psychol. Monogr.*, 1938, **20**, 461–556.

291. ——, & LESTER, O. P. The social competence of identical twins. *J. genet. Psychol.*, 1942, **60**, 167–75.

292. VAN DER HORST, L. Experimentell-psychologische Untervuchungen bei mannlichen und weiblichen Mittelschülern. *Z. angew. Psychol.*, 1916, **11**, 441–86.

293. —— Constitutietypen bij Geesteszieken en Gezonden. Zutphen (Holland), Nauta u. Comp. 1924.

294. VERSCHUER, F. v. Twin research from the time of Francis Galton to the present day. *Proc. Roy. Soc.*, 1939, **B128**, 62–81.

295. WAARDENBURG, P. J. Character traits in twins. *Mensch en Maatschappij.*, 1929, **5**, 17–34.

296. WALLEN, R. Food aversions of normal and neurotic males. *J. abnorm. & Soc. Psychol.*, 1945, **40**, 77–81.

297. WARREN, H. C. *Dictionary of Psychology*. Boston: Houghton Mifflin, 1934.

298. WENGER, M. A. Studies of autonomic balance in army air forces personnel. *Compar. Psychol. Monog.*, 1948, **19**, No. 4, 1–111.

299. WENGER, P. Über weitere Ergebnisse der Psychotherapie im Rahmen einer Medizinischen Poliklinik. *Wien. med. Wchnschr.*, 1934, **84**, 320–5.

300. WESTPHAL, K. Körperbau und Charakter der Epileptiker. *Nervenarzt*, 1931, **4**, 96–9.

301. WEXLER, M. Measures of personal adjustment. In: *Personnel Research and Test Development in the Bureau of Naval Personnel*. Ed. Stuit, D. B. Princeton: Princeton Univ. Press, 1947.

302. WHITEHEAD, A. N. *The Function of Reason*. Princeton: Princeton Univ. Press, 1929.

303. WILDER, J. Facts and figures on psychotherapy. *J. clin. Psychopath.*, 1945, **7**, 311–47.

304. WILSON, P. T. A study of twins with special reference to heredity as a factor in determining differences in environment. *Hum. Biol.*, 1934, **6**, 324–54.

305. WILSON, M. T. Social competence of normal and defective twins. *Amer. J. Orthopsychiat.*, 1941, **11**, 300–4.

306. WINDELBAND, W. *An Introduction to Philosophy*. 1921.

307. WOLFLE, H. A fundamental principle of personality measurement. *Psychol. Rev.*, 1949, **56**, 273–6.

308. WOODWORTH, R. S. Heredity and environment: a critical survey of recently published material on twins and foster children. *Soc. Sci. Res. Co. Bull.*, 1941, **47**, 1–95.

309. WUNDT, W. *Physiological Psychology*. 1910.

310. YASKIN, J. C. The psychoneuroses and neuroses. A review of 100 cases with special reference to treatment and results. *Amer. J. Psychiat.*, 1936, **93**, 107–25.

311. YULE, F. G. The resemblance of twins with regard to perseveration. *J. Ment. Sci.*, 1935, **81**, 389–501.

312. ZERBE, E. Seelische und soziale Befunde bei verschiedenen Körperbautypen. *Arch. Psychiat.*, 1929, **88**, 705–51.

313. ZILIAN, E. Ergebnisse einer psychologischen Untersuchungen an erbgleichen und erbungleichen Zwillingen. *Beih. Z. Angew. Psychol.*, 1938, **79**, 42–50.

314. ZULLIGER, H. *The Behn Rorschach Test.* Bern: Hans Huber, 1941.

INDEX